I0605699

THE PENNINE WAY

THE PENNINE WAY

NATIONAL TRAIL – FROM EDALE TO KIRK YETHOLM

by Paddy Dillon

JUNIPER HOUSE, MURLEY MOSS,
OXENHOLME ROAD, KENDAL, CUMBRIA LA9 7RL
www.cicerone.co.uk

© Paddy Dillon 2025
Fifth edition 2025
ISBN-13: 978 1 78631 131 3
Fourth edition 2017
Third edition 2012
Second edition 2006
First edition 1998

Printed in China on responsibly sourced paper on behalf of Latitude Press Ltd.
A catalogue record for this book is available from the British Library.
All photographs are by the author unless otherwise stated.

1:100K route mapping by Lovell Johns www.lovelljohns.com
Contains Ordnance Survey data © Crown copyright and database rights 2017 OS PU100012932.
NASA relief data courtesy of ESRI.

The 1:25K map booklet contains Ordnance Survey data © Crown copyright and database rights 2025 OS AC0000810376.

Cicerone's EU representative for GPSR compliance is Easy Access System Europe, Mustamäe tee 50, 10621 Tallinn, Estonia. Email gpsr.requests@easproject.com.

Updates to this Guide

While every effort is made by our authors to ensure the accuracy of guidebooks as they go to print, changes can occur during the lifetime of an edition. Any updates that we know of for this guide will be on the Cicerone website (www.cicerone.co.uk/1131/updates), so please check before planning your trip. We also advise that you check information about such things as transport, accommodation and shops locally. Even rights of way can be altered over time. We are always grateful for information about any discrepancies between a guidebook and the facts on the ground, sent by email to updates@cicerone.co.uk.

Register your book: To sign up to receive free updates, special offers and GPX files where available, create a Cicerone account and register your purchase via the 'My Account' tab at www.cicerone.co.uk.

Front cover: Looking back to Kinder Scout from Mill Hill (Day 1)

CONTENTS

The sheer cliff face of Malham Cove (Day 7)

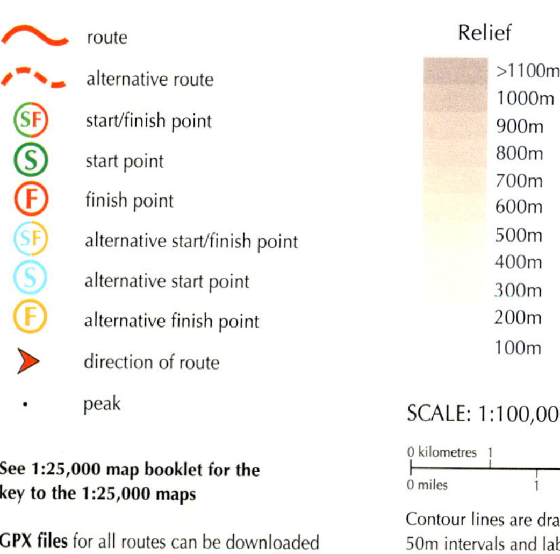
Symbols used on route maps
route
alternative route
start/finish point
start point
finish point
alternative start/finish point
alternative start point
alternative finish point
direction of route
peak
Relief
>1100m
1000m
900m
800m
700m
600m
500m
400m
300m
200m
100m
SCALE: 1:100,000
0 kilometres 1 2
0 miles 1
See 1:25,000 map booklet for the key to the 1:25,000 maps
GPX files for all routes can be downloaded free at www.cicerone.co.uk/1131/GPX.
Contour lines are drawn at 50m intervals and labelled at 100m intervals.

ROUTE SUMMARY TABLE

Day	Start/Finish	Distance	Ascent	Descent	Time	Page
1	Edale to Torside	25km (15.5 miles)	770m (2525ft)	790m (2590ft)	8hr	46
2	Torside to Standedge	20.5km (12.75 miles)	790m (2590ft)	650m (2135ft)	6hr 30min	55
3	Standedge to Callis Bridge	24km (15 miles)	370m (1215ft)	650m (2135ft)	7hr 30min	66
4	Callis Bridge to Ickornshaw	25.5km (16 miles)	930m (3050ft)	830m (2725ft)	8hr	77
5	Ickornshaw to Gargrave	18km (11 miles)	545m (1790ft)	650m (2135ft)	5hr 30min	88
6	Gargrave to Malham	10.5km (6.5 miles)	180m (590ft)	120m (395ft)	3hr	99
7	Malham to Horton in Ribblesdale	23.5km (14.5 miles)	855m (2805ft)	810m (2655ft)	7hr 15min	101
8	Horton in Ribblesdale to Hawes	22km (13.75 miles)	490m (1610ft)	470m (1540ft)	7hr	110
9	Hawes to Keld	20km (12.5 miles)	750m (2460ft)	650m (2200ft)	6hr 15min	117
10	Keld to Baldersdale	23km (14.25 miles)	530m (1740ft)	510m (1675ft)	7hr	124
11	Baldersdale to Middleton-in-Teesdale	10.5km (6.5 miles)	310m (1015ft)	400m (1310ft)	3hr	134
12	Middleton-in-Teesdale to Langdon Beck	14km (8.75 miles)	315m (1035ft)	160m (525ft)	4hr 15min	142
13	Langdon Beck to Dufton	21km (13 miles)	365m (1200ft)	560m (1835ft)	6hr 30min	150
14	Dufton to Alston	31.5km (19.5 miles)	1050m (3445ft)	970m (3180ft)	10hr	158
15	Alston to Greenhead	27.5km (17 miles)	655m (2150ft)	800m (2625ft)	8hr 30min	169

Day	Start/Finish	Distance	Ascent	Descent	Time	Page
16	Greenhead to Housesteads	17km (10.5 miles)	720m (2360ft)	630m (2065ft)	5hr	**181**
17	Housesteads to Bellingham	22.5km (14 miles)	545m (1790ft)	650m (2130ft)	7hr	**191**
18	Bellingham to Byrness	25km (15.5 miles)	585m (1920ft)	480m (15750ft)	8hr	**200**
19	Byrness to Clennell Street	23km (14.25 miles)	865m (2835ft)	550m (1805ft)	7hr	**208**
20	Clennell Street to Kirk Yetholm	22km (13.75 miles)	735m (2410ft)	1160m (3805ft)	7hr	**218**
Total		426km (264.75 miles)	12,355m (40,535ft)	12,485m (40,960ft)		

Warning

Mountain walking can be a dangerous activity carrying a risk of personal injury or death. It should be undertaken only by those with a full understanding of the risks and with the training and experience to evaluate them. While every care and effort has been taken in the preparation of this guide, the user should be aware that conditions can be highly variable and can change quickly, materially affecting the seriousness of a mountain walk. Therefore, except for any liability which cannot be excluded by law, neither Cicerone nor the author accept liability for damage of any nature (including damage to property, personal injury or death) arising directly or indirectly from the information in this book.

To call out the Mountain Rescue, ring 999 or the European emergency number 112: this will connect you via any available network. Once connected to the emergency operator, ask for the police.

The Pennine Way
KELSO
Kirk Yetholm
F
WOOLER
JEDBURGH
The Cheviot
ALNWICK
HAWICK
Clennell Street
SCOTLAND
ENGLAND
Cheviot Hills
Byrness
Rothbury
NORTHUMBERLAND
Kielder
Otterburn
LANGHOLM
MORPETH
KIELDER FOREST
BELLINGHAM
Wark
Hadrian's Wall
Housesteads
HEXHAM
Greenhead
Brampton
NEWCASTLE
HALTWHISTLE
CARLISLE
NORTH PENNINES NATIONAL LANDSCAPE
CONSETT
ALSTON
STANHOPE
DURHAM
Garrigill
Cross Fell
Langdon Beck
PENRITH
Dufton
Teesdale
MIDDLETON
BARNARD CASTLE
LAKE DISTRICT
APPLEBY
DARLINGTON
Bowes

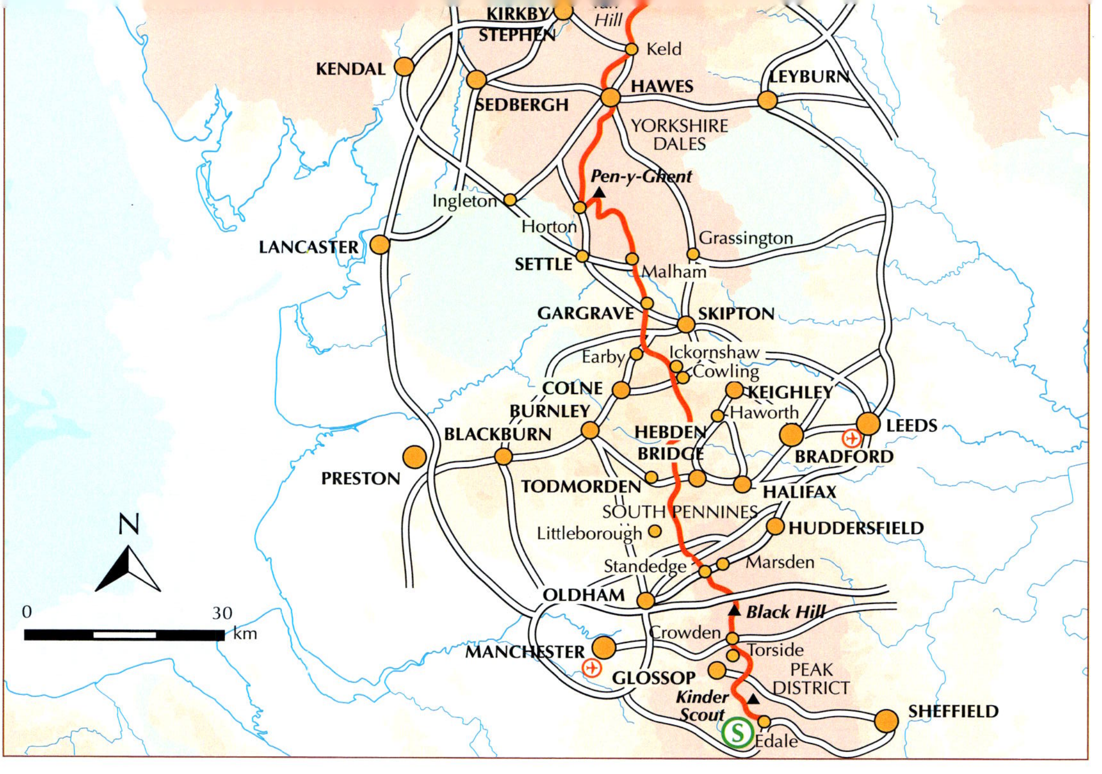
KIRKBY STEPHEN
Hill
Keld
KENDAL
HAWES
LEYBURN
SEDBERGH
YORKSHIRE DALES
Pen-y-Ghent
Ingleton
Horton
Grassington
LANCASTER
SETTLE
Malham
GARGRAVE
SKIPTON
Earby
Ickornshaw
Cowling
COLNE
KEIGHLEY
BURNLEY
Haworth
BLACKBURN
HEBDEN BRIDGE
LEEDS
BRADFORD
PRESTON
TODMORDEN
HALIFAX
SOUTH PENNINES
Littleborough
HUDDERSFIELD
Standedge
Marsden
N
OLDHAM
Black Hill
0
30
km
Crowden
Torside
MANCHESTER
GLOSSOP
PEAK DISTRICT
Kinder Scout
S
SHEFFIELD
Edale

The Pennine Way

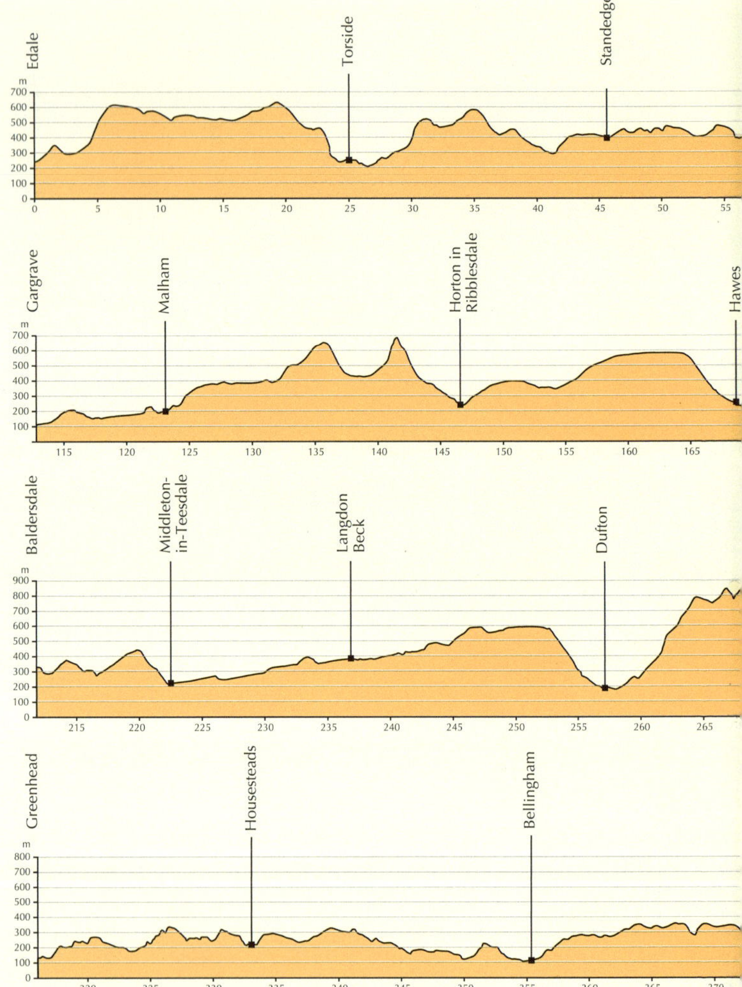

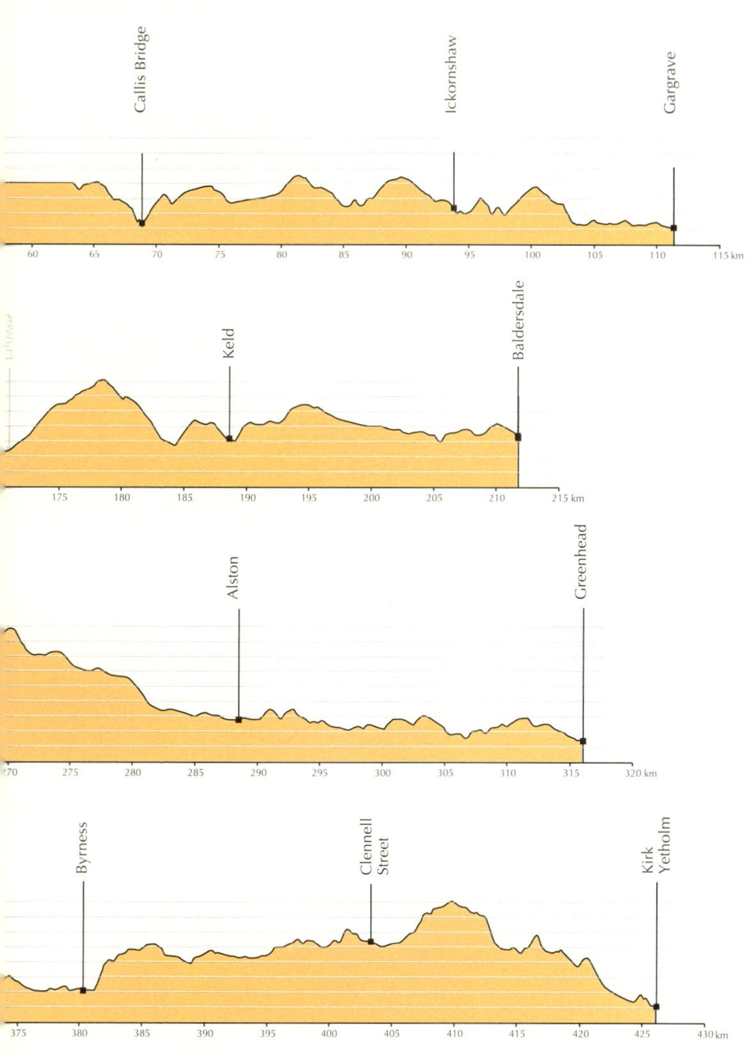

Callis Bridge
Ickornshaw
Gargrave
60 65 70 75 80 85 90 95 100 105 110 115 km
Keld
Baldersdale
175 180 185 190 195 200 205 210 215 km
Alston
Greenhead
270 275 280 285 290 295 300 305 310 315 320 km
Byrness
Clennell Street
Kirk Yetholm
375 380 385 390 395 400 405 410 415 420 425 430 km

STAGE FACILITIES TABLE

Day	Location (ends of stages shown in bold)	Distance from day start	Distance from route start
Day 1	**Edale**	0km (0 miles)	0km (0 miles)
	Upper Booth	3km (2 miles)	3km (2 miles)
	Snake Pass	15.5km (9.75 miles)	15.5km (9.75 miles)
	Torside	25km (15.5 miles)	25km (15.5 miles)
Day 2	Crowden	2.5km (1.75 miles)	27.5km (17.25 miles)
	Wessenden Head	12.5km (7.75 miles)	37.5km (23.25 miles)
	Marsden (off-route)		
	Standedge	20.5km (12.75 miles)	45.5km (28.25 miles)
Day 3	Diggle (off-route)		
	Bleakedgate	6.5km (4 miles)	52km (32.25 miles)
	White House	11.5km (7.25 miles)	57km (35.5 miles)
	Mankinholes (off-route)		
	Hebden Bridge (off-route)		
	Callis Bridge	24km (15 miles)	69.5km (43.25 miles)
Day 4	Colden	3km (2 miles)	72.5km (45.25 miles)
	Ponden	16.5km (10.25 miles)	86km (53.5 miles)
	Stanbury (off-route)		
Day 5	**Ickornshaw**	25.5km (16 miles)	95km (59.25 miles)
	Cowling (off-route)		

Campsite
Hotel/B&B/guesthouse
Hostel/bunkhouse
Refreshments
Shop for provisions
Bus service
Train station
ATM

Campsite	Hotel/B&B/guesthouse	Hostel/bunkhouse	Refreshments	Shop for provisions	Bus service	Train station	ATM
✓	✓	✓ off-route	✓	✓	✓	✓	
✓							
	✓ off-route		✓ off-route				
✓							
			✓ rarely				
	✓		✓	✓	✓	✓	✓
✓ off-route					✓		
	✓		✓	✓	✓		
			✓				
			✓		✓		
	✓	✓	✓				
	✓	✓	✓	✓	✓	✓	✓
					✓		
✓			✓	✓	✓		
✓	✓		✓		✓		
✓	✓		✓		✓		
✓					✓		
			✓	✓	✓		

Day	Location (ends of stages shown in bold)	Distance from day start	Distance from route start
	Lothersdale	4km (2.5 miles)	99km (61.75 miles)
Day 5	Thornton-in-Craven	11km (7 miles)	106km (66.25 miles)
	East Marton	13.5km (8.5 miles)	108.5km (67.75 miles)
	Gargrave	18km (11 miles)	113km (70.25 miles)
Day 6	Airton	6.5km (4 miles)	119.5km (74.25 miles)
	Kirkby Malham (off-route)		
Day 7	**Malham**	10.5km (6.5 miles)	123.5km (76.75 miles)
Day 8	**Horton in Ribblesdale**	23.5km (14.5 miles)	147km (91.25 miles)
	Gayle	21.5km (13.5 miles)	168.5km (104.75 miles)
	Hawes	22km (13.75 miles)	169km (105 miles)
Day 9	Hardraw	2.5km (1.5 miles)	171.5km (106.5 miles)
	Thwaite	15km (9.5 miles)	184km (114.5 miles)
	Keld	20km (12.5 miles)	189km (117.5 miles)
Day 10	Frith Lodge	3km (2 miles)	192km (119.5 miles)
	Tan Hill	7km (4.5 miles)	196km (122 miles)
	Baldersdale	23km (14.25 miles)	212km (131.75 miles)
Day 11	Bowes (alternative route)		
	Cotherstone (well off-route)		
	Grassholme	4km (2.5 miles)	216km (134.25 miles)

Facilities							
off-route			DIY snacks				
			DIY snacks		by arrange-ment		
	off-route						

Day	Location (ends of stages shown in bold)	Distance from day start	Distance from route start
Day 12	**Middleton-in-Teesdale**	10.5km (6.5 miles)	222.5km (138.25 miles)
	Low Way Farm (off-route)		
	Bowlees (off-route)		
	Sayer Hill	13km (8 miles)	235.5km (146.25 miles)
Day 13	**Langdon Beck**	14km (8.75 miles)	236.5km (147 miles)
Day 14	**Dufton**	21km (13 miles)	257.5km (160 miles)
	Greg's Hut	14.5km (9 miles)	272km (169 miles)
	Garrigill	25km (15.5 miles)	282.5km (175.5 miles)
Day 15	**Alston**	31.5km (19.5 miles)	289km (179.5 miles)
	Harbut	1.5km (1 mile)	290.5km (180.5 miles)
	Whitley Castle	4.5km (2.75 miles)	293.5km (182.25 miles)
	Slaggyford	9.5km (5.5 miles)	298km (185 miles)
	Knarsdale (off-route)		
	Greenriggs (off-route)		
	Kellah Farm (off-route)		
Day 16	**Greenhead**	27.5km (17 miles)	316.5km (196.5 miles)
	Holmhead	1km (0.5 mile)	317.5km (197 miles)
	Walltown	2km (1.25 miles)	318.5km (197.75 miles)
	Milecastle Inn (off route)		

Facilities							
					Weds		
basic							
					Weds		
				basic			
bothy							
						South Tyne Rly	
						South Tyne Rly	

Day	Location (ends of stages shown in bold)	Distance from day start	Distance from route start
Day 16	Winshields (off-route)		
	Twice Brewed (off-route)		
	Housesteads	17km (10.5 miles)	333.5km (207 miles)
Day 17	Haughtongreen (off-route)		
	Stonehaugh (off-route)		
	Horneystead	13km (8 miles)	346.5km (215 miles)
	Shitlington	18km (11 miles)	351.5km (218 miles)
	Bellingham	22.5km (14 miles)	356km (221 miles)
Day 18	Cottonshopeburnfoot	22.5km (14 miles)	378.5km (235 miles)
	Byrness	25km (15.5 miles)	381km (236.5 miles)
Day 19	Yearning Saddle	14.5km (9 miles)	395.5km (245.5 miles)
	Windy Gyle	21km (13 miles)	402km (249.5 miles)
	Trows (off-route)		
	Clennell Street	23km (14.25 miles)	404km (250.75 miles)
Day 20	Auchope	10.5km (6.5 miles)	414.5km (257.25 miles)
	Mounthooly (off-route)		
	Kirk Yetholm	22km (13.75 miles)	426km (264.75 miles)

Facilities
off-route
bothy
DIY
snacks
camping
pods
refuge
hut
by
arrange-
ment
refuge
hut
off-route
off-route

Catrake Force is passed on the way out of Keld (Day 10)

PREFACE

The Pennine Way is intricately bound up with my family history. I was born and raised only six miles from the Pennine Way and the route was opened when I was only seven years old. My family included some staunch walkers who used to talk about it from time to time. My Uncle Gerard walked the trail in its early years, returning with tales to inspire others. As young teenagers, a friend and I stumbled across a Pennine Way signpost on the moors and wondered how long it might take us to walk to Scotland. Soon afterwards, a chance copy of Alfred Wainwright's *Pennine Way Companion* laid it all out for me in black and white.

I could have walked the Pennine Way at the age of 16, but I chose to follow it northwards only as far as Cross Fell, then made a beeline for the Lake District, explored for a week and walked home via the Yorkshire Dales. I finally walked the whole route for the first time when I was 21, and it snowed for the first five days!

Throughout the 1970s, if you told anyone you were a keen walker, they would ask, 'And have you walked the Pennine Way?' Anyone actually walking the route might have been asked, 'Are you walking the Pennine Way, or just walking for pleasure?', as if the two were mutually exclusive! The route was regarded, rightly or wrongly, as something that every 'proper' walker should aspire to, generating something of a backlash, with some people vowing never to set foot on it.

One thing became painfully obvious throughout the 1970s: the Pennine Way was being trodden to death. Although I always enjoyed walking parts of the route, it was distinctly unpleasant to wade through the mud, occasionally plumbing waist-deep bogs where the peat had been trodden into the consistency of cold, black porridge. Apart from occasional forays during the 1980s, I left the route well alone while the problems of over-use and erosion were addressed, ultimately by completely rebuilding several stretches of the trail.

Once everything had bedded down and grassed over I renewed my acquaintance. It was worth the wait, and as the years roll by, the stone-paved paths will become as much a part of the Pennine Way as the centuries-old packhorse 'causeys' that preceded it. The scenery remains the same as ever and only the conditions immediately underfoot have changed, and for the better.

Since opening on 24 April 1965 the Pennine Way has remained a firm favourite. This is remarkable, as today's walkers have many other National Trails to choose between, as well as infinite opportunities to walk challenging trails abroad. The Pennine Way remains the toughest of the National Trails; one that every long-distance walker should aspire to. Long may it enjoy a future as part of Britain's rich outdoor heritage.

Paddy Dillon

Looking across a meadow to Low Way Farm near Holwick (Day 12)

INTRODUCTION

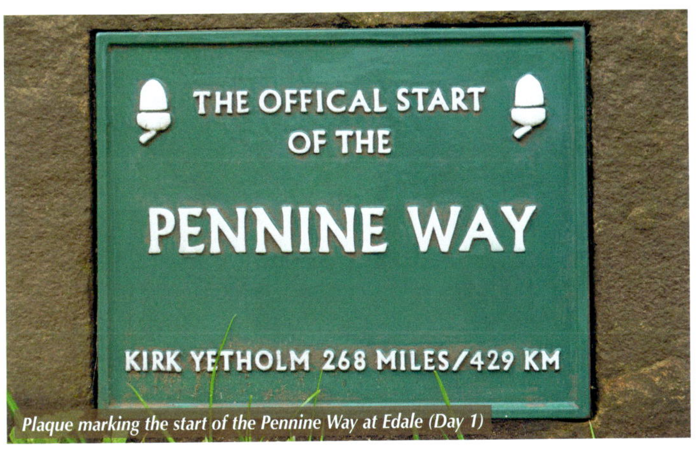

Plaque marking the start of the Pennine Way at Edale (Day 1)

WANTED: A LONG GREEN TRAIL

You could say it all started on 22 June 1935. An article appeared in the *Daily Herald* newspaper entitled 'Wanted: A Long Green Trail', written by the ramblers' champion Tom Stephenson. 'Why should we not press for something akin to the Appalachian Trail?' he asked. 'A Pennine Way from the Peak to the Cheviots.' He imagined that the route would be 'a faint line on the Ordnance Maps which the feet of grateful pilgrims would, with the passing years, engrave on the face of the land.' Well, the engraving went rather deep in places, even to the extent that you could claim the route was carved in stone, but that is only a testimony to its popularity.

It took 30 years of lobbying and hard work to steer the Pennine Way to its official opening in April 1965. As a long-distance walk it is impressive. It traverses three national parks, one National Landscape and a World Heritage Site. In fact, the route could be broken down into five or six unequal stages according to the type of area being traversed.

Only the northern part of the Peak District National Park, the Dark Peak, is on the route. It is characterised by broad, bleak, high-altitude moorland. The Peak District features only for the first two days of walking, from Edale as far as Standedge, where it gives way to the gentler South Pennines. While this isn't a national park, it does

Looking towards Hartleyburn Common (Day 16)

have a distinct identity as far northwards as the Aire Gap, taking two or three days to cover.

The Yorkshire Dales National Park captures the attention of wayfarers for four or five days, from Gargrave to the Tan Hill Inn. Next comes the enormous North Pennines National Landscape, which, although never given National Park status, is one of the wildest and bleakest upland areas of England. It is home to enormous National Nature Reserves and is claimed to be the most scientifically studied upland region in the world. Crossing this area on the Pennine Way takes five or six days.

When the Pennines peter out at the Tyne Gap, the route enters the Northumberland National Park, which is traversed in four or five days. This includes a splendid day's romp along Hadrian's Wall before heading to and through the Cheviot Hills, and finally hopping over the border into Scotland.

It measures over 426km (265 miles), involving a cumulative ascent of 12,355m (40,535ft). Most walkers take between two and three weeks to cover the distance, and there are many ways to create a schedule to suit people's different expectations.

It is well worth reading *The Pennine Way – the Path, the People, the Journey*, by Andrew McCloy, published by Cicerone. The book explains how much hard work, lobbying and political manoeuvring went into the creation of the Pennine Way, and introduces many people and personalities who have been involved in the route over the past half-century.

PLANNING YOUR TRIP

The Pennine Way main route stays high to cross White Law (Day 20)

CHOOSING AN ITINERARY

The Pennine Way is the toughest of the National Trails, so it suits those with previous long-distance walking experience. Those with little or no experience should consider gaining some in advance. Try a weekend walk here and there, staying overnight on your route. Progress to a week-long walk, preferably in upland terrain, carrying everything you would expect to carry on a long trek. Figure out what sort of clothing and footwear suits you best for those conditions. Keep a check on your progress day by day and hour by hour, to gauge how long it takes to cover varying distances and awkward terrain. Timings given in this guidebook are unlikely to be matched by most wayfarers; some will be faster, some slower, but the timings give a consistent standard throughout. Use them as a basic guide. If you complete a couple of stages faster, then it is likely that you will always do so, and you might want to cover extra distances further along the trail. If you fall behind the stated times, then figure out by how much, and apply that to all stages in future. If it is likely that one or two of the longer stages might take too long to cover, consider splitting them into shorter stages.

While some people have run the Pennine Way in as little as two and a half days, most take two or three weeks to walk the distance, and on average it tends to work out at around

18 days. The schedule offered in this guidebook takes 20 days, but there are places where stages can be extended. As with all long-distance walks, take each day at a pace that is neither slow nor stressful, and the trek can be completed comfortably and enjoyably. Fatigue and foul weather can result in alterations to carefully planned schedules, so wise walkers build a day or two into their plans to cover for such eventualities.

The Pennine Way can be adapted to suit walkers of most abilities, and there is no need to follow the schedule outlined in this guidebook rigidly. Long days can be split. Short days can be extended. Pick-ups can be arranged wherever the route crosses a road, with careful planning. Nor is there any need to walk south to north, but this is the direction most people choose. Some do walk north to south. If you do this, you will need to reverse all the route directions, which could be a little confusing at times, but the signposting and waymarking is as good in one direction as it is in the other. The following statistics relate only to the main route and don't include any diversions off-route. Those who walk the Hebden Bridge Loop and Bowes Loop, for example, will cover an extra 8.5km (5.25 miles), while detours off-route and back onto the route in the Cheviot Hills add around 6.5km (4 miles). Given other short detours for accommodation, most Pennine wayfarers will end up walking around 450km (280 miles).

The route summary table at the beginning of this guide is based on a 20-day trek, following the daily stages presented in this guidebook. Below is a suggested itinerary for a 15-day trek, based on combining some of the shorter stages, or breaking the trek at different points to create longer stages. Anything less than two weeks would require considerable stamina and determination.

A dusting of snow in winter near Gorple Lower Reservoir (Day 4)

Day	Start/Finish	Distance	Ascent	Descent	Time	Page
1	Edale to Torside	25km (15.5 miles)	770m (2525ft)	795m (2610ft)	8hr	**46**
2	Torside to Standedge	20.5km (12.75 miles)	790m (2590ft)	620m (2035ft)	6hr 30min	**55**
3	Standedge to Callis Bridge	24km (15 miles)	370m (1215ft)	650m (2135ft)	7hr 30min	**66**
4	Callis Bridge to Ickornshaw	25.5km (16 miles)	930m (3050ft)	830m (2725ft)	8hr	**77**
5	Ickornshaw to Malham	28.5km (17.75 miles)	725m (2380ft)	690m (2525ft)	8hr 30min	**88**
6	Malham to Horton in Ribblesdale	23.5km (14.5 miles)	855m (2805ft)	810m (2655ft)	7hr 15min	**101**
7	Horton in Ribblesdale to Hawes	22km (13.75 miles)	490m (1610ft)	470m (1540ft)	7hr	**110**
8	Hawes to Tan Hill Inn	26km (16 miles)	1010m (3315ft)	735m (2405ft)	8hr	**117**
9	Tan Hill Inn to Middleton-in-Teesdale	27km (16.75 miles)	550m (1805ft)	815m (2670ft)	8hr 30min	**124**
10	Middleton-in-Teesdale to Dufton	33km (20.5 miles)	650m (2130ft)	700m (2295ft)	10hr	**142**
11	Dufton to Alston	31.5km (19.5 miles)	1050m (3445ft)	970m (3180ft)	10hr	**158**
12	Alston to Greenhead	27.5km (17 miles)	655m (2150ft)	800m (2625ft)	8hr 30min	**169**
13	Greenhead to Bellingham	36km (22.5 miles)	880m (2890ft)	890m (2920ft)	11hr	**181**
14	Bellingham to Byrness	25km (15.5 miles)	1090m (3575ft)	480m (1575ft)	8hr	**200**
15	Byrness to Kirk Yetholm	45km (28 miles)	1600m (5245ft)	1710m (5610ft)	14hr	**208**
Total		420km (261 miles)	12,120m (39,760ft)	12,250m (40,190ft)		

WHEN TO WALK

The Pennine Way is naturally busiest in the summer months, when most people take their longest holiday of the year. This is a fine time to walk, as all facilities and services are available, and the weather is generally warm and sunny, with plenty of daylight hours. In early summer, flowers are in bloom, while later in the summer, the heather moors are flushed purple. There is a chance that boggy parts might be drier underfoot, and when the blue sky is flecked with little clouds, the Pennine Way becomes very appealing.

Spring and autumn can feature many fine days, and both seasons have their own particular charms. Spring sees the gradual greening of the landscape and the first flowers of the year, but there might be a late flurry of snow. Hawthorn bushes burst into bloom while new-born lambs bleat plaintively in the lower pastures. Autumn sees the gradual ripening of seeds, hedgerow fruits at their best and many species of fungi pushing strange fruiting bodies into view. The days, however, are notably shorter and there may well be cooler, wetter weather.

Winter can be severe in the Pennines, especially when occasional falls of deep snow blanket the path and make route-finding particularly difficult. While winter traverses of the Pennine Way are rare, those walkers possessing the skills and stamina to complete the trek also have to cope with the fact that many facilities and services are absent. Hardy walkers need to be experienced and self-sufficient to backpack the route in the winter months. The hardiest of all are those who enter the Spine Race, thespinerace.com, whose elite entrants are capable of running the Pennine Way in the deep midwinter in less than 100 hours!

TRAVEL TO AND FROM THE PENNINE WAY

By air

For overseas visitors, the handiest access for the start of the Pennine Way is Manchester Airport, www.manchesterairport.co.uk, served by flights from around the world. Catch a train from the airport to Manchester Piccadilly and change for Edale and the start of the Pennine Way.

Leaving the northern end of the route isn't as simple, requiring careful study of local bus and train timetables, but the airports at Edinburgh, www.edinburghairport.com, and Newcastle, www.newcastleairport.com, can be reached for homeward flights.

By rail

Regular daily Northern trains, www.northernrailway.co.uk, serve Edale from Manchester and Sheffield. Northern train services can be used to reach the Pennine Way via Hebden Bridge, Gargrave and Horton in Ribblesdale. Greenhead, near Hadrian's Wall, no longer has a station, but Northern trains can be caught off-route at Haltwhistle. There are no railways near Kirk Yetholm, so if intending to travel home by rail, it is necessary to catch buses to Galashiels, for ScotRail, www.scotrail.co.uk, trains to Edinburgh, or to Berwick-upon-Tweed for LNER, www.lner.co.uk, and CrossCountry trains, www.crosscountrytrains.co.uk, to Edinburgh or Newcastle.

By bus

There are several local bus routes crossing the Pennine Way. Where useful buses exist, either connecting with other parts of the route, or leading off-route to nearby towns and villages, there is a brief mention of them in the daily route descriptions. To check details of local buses in advance, useful websites include Traveline, www.traveline.info, and Traveline Scotland, www.travelinescotland.com, tel 0871 2002233 for either service. It is also possible to search Google Maps for bus services by using the 'directions' feature. Always obtain up-to-date bus times a day or two before needing them, as some services are sparse. Bear in mind that there are no bus services to or from Kirk Yetholm on Sundays.

TRAVEL ALONG THE PENNINE WAY

Most railway lines and bus routes cross the Pennines from east to west and vice-versa, and only a few routes run parallel to the Pennine Way. Getting to and from the route is reasonably straightforward, but using public transport to get ahead by a stage or two can be quite awkward. Most stages have some form of public transport, but it varies from regular daily services, to one bus per week, and sometimes there is nothing at all. However, there are plenty of services that are worth bearing in mind, and particularly the minibus service offered into the heart of the Cheviot Hills towards the end. Sometimes, it may be necessary to call a local taxi, and it is also worth noting that some accommodation providers offer pick-ups and drop-offs, if given advance notice.

FIRST AND LAST NIGHTS

Most Pennine wayfarers arrive at Edale in the morning and set off walking. Those who arrive the previous evening should bear in mind that Edale is a tiny village and facilities are very limited. At quiet times of the year, food, drink and accommodation are readily available, but at busy times everything is packed to capacity and it would be most unwise to turn up without having made advance bookings.

Most Pennine wayfarers reach Kirk Yetholm in the late afternoon and are more than happy to spend a night in the village. Normally, it wouldn't be a problem to arrive and secure accommodation and a meal, but at busy times, again, it would be well to book in advance. Some finish their trek so early in the day that they aren't inclined to stay overnight, and catch the bus away from the village. Onward travel brings a range of towns and cities within reach and these all offer a greater range of services if a break is needed on the homeward journey.

ACCOMMODATION

When the Pennine Way was opened, it was assumed that the bulk of walkers would carry full packs and camp at intervals along the trail. Many did, but there was also a good selection of youth hostels along the way, and the Youth Hostels Association once offered a service allowing walkers to book all their bed-nights in one fell swoop.

Things have changed over the years, and while many wayfarers still camp, there are far fewer hostels available. Many walkers now choose bed and breakfast (B&B) accommodation, and some are quite happy to pay walking holiday companies to make all their arrangements for them, booking all their overnights and arranging baggage transfers in advance.

The Pennine Way has plenty of accommodation options, but they are unevenly spaced, and in some places may be limited to a single address. Those who wish to guarantee their overnights should book everything in advance, but bear in mind that this means sticking to a rigid schedule. Those who prefer to organise things on a day-to-day basis must accept that at some points they may find all beds taken, and the only way to secure accommodation will be to move off-route. Some people book all their overnights, then sadly have to retire because of injury or illness, and that has the effect of freeing up beds at the last minute, which is useful for those who make bookings at short notice.

A wild camp on the summit of Cross Fell (Day 14)

See the accommodation table in Appendix B for details of hotels, B&Bs, hostels, bunkhouses, campsites and shelters along the Pennine Way. Remember that accommodation comes and goes, contact details change, and the loss of a crucial address in an area with no other options can cause havoc when planning a schedule. If any information on the list needs amending, please send details to Cicerone.

FOOD AND DRINK

Most long-distance walkers start the day with a hearty breakfast, take a break along the way for lunch, and enjoy a good meal in the evenings. Those who like to walk in comfort can book themselves into places offering dinner, B&B, and often with the option of a packed lunch for an additional charge. Youth hostels offer full meals services and packed lunches. If relying on the provision of meals and packed lunches, it is important to find out what is offered as soon as bookings are made, as some providers may be unable to satisfy last-minute requests or special dietary requirements.

Walkers who are backpacking need to know where useful shops are located so that they can buy more food as they travel, rather than carry everything for the duration of their trek. All the towns along the Pennine Way have a range of shops, but some villages have either a limited choice or nothing at all. Be sure to read ahead to discover where re-supply options are sparse, then buy food in advance to cover for those days. Many wayfarers like to take a break at a pub, and there are several along the Pennine Way, but they are unevenly spread and only rarely occur in the middle of a day's walk. Places offering refreshment are duly noted in this guidebook. The most famous pub is surely the Tan Hill Inn, a convivial establishment in the middle of nowhere and the highest pub in Britain.

BAGGAGE TRANSFER

A handful of companies offer accommodation booking and baggage transfer along the Pennine Way. They might appear expensive, but many walkers are willing to pay the price for someone else to make all their arrangements. It's interesting to note that sometimes, when a number of wayfarers have booked through different companies, the same van collects and delivers all their bags. A list of companies offering a baggage transfer service can be found in Appendix A.

WHAT TO TAKE

This depends primarily on your choice of accommodation. From its earliest days, the Pennine Way was intended to be a tough route for tough walkers. In the beginning, many walkers carried heavy packs and planned to camp every night. If

Food fantasy – or an enormous Tunnocks bar? (Day 20)

camping, then full backpacking kit is required but keep everything as light as possible, taking advantage of modern materials and innovative products. There is no need for a full backpack to exceed 10 kilos, and seldom any need to pack more than two days' worth of food.

Youth hostels were originally spartan, but gradually offered more comforts. The provision of B&Bs along the route is pretty good, and these tend to be well-supported by today's Pennine wayfarers. Anyone using hostels or B&Bs need little more than the usual contents of their daysack, plus a lightweight change of clothing for the evenings, allowing the 'walking' clothes to be rinsed and dried every couple of days or so. It really isn't necessary to carry heavy loads along the Pennine Way, and in any case many wayfarers sign up for baggage transfers – sometimes having huge suitcases sent ahead!

MONEY

While an increasing number of shops, pubs and restaurants will accept payment by credit card, many don't, so walkers need to carry plenty of cash to pay for goods and services while on the move, especially on the more remote parts of the Pennine Way. If you are unsure about carrying large amounts of cash, at least try and budget ahead, then be aware of places along the way that have banks and ATMs – these are mentioned in the daily route descriptions. Some supermarkets offer a 'cashback' service or have a cashpoint on their premises.

PLANNING DAY TO DAY

Looking back across Ashop Head towards Kinder Scout from Mill Hill (Day 1)

USING THIS GUIDE

An information box at the beginning of each daily stage provides the essential facts for the day's walk: start and finish points (including grid refs), distance covered, an estimation of time, ascent and descent figures, an overview of the types of terrain you'll encounter, relevant OS Landranger®, OS Explorer® and Harvey sheets, and places en route (as well as slightly off-route) where you can buy refreshments.

Stage maps, extracted from the Ordnance Survey® mapping, are provided at a scale of 1:100,000. In the route description, significant places or features along the way that also appear on the map extracts are highlighted in bold to aid navigation. As well as the route being described in detail, background information about places of interest is provided in brief.

Appendix A provides contact details that may be useful in planning and enjoying a successful walk. Appendix B provides details of further reading, and Appendix C lists accommodation options along the route and, where necessary, options off-route.

GPX tracks

GPX tracks for the routes in this guidebook are available to download free at www.cicerone.co.uk/1131/GPX. If you have not bought the book through the Cicerone website, or have bought the book without opening an account, please register your purchase in your

Cicerone library to access GPX and update information.

In clear weather, providing careful note is taken of route directions, rudimentary map-reading skills will be enough. However, on some bleak and exposed moors, especially in mist, an ability to use a map and a compass is a distinct advantage.

ADDITIONAL MAPPING

This guidebook contains basic 1:100,000 scale maps, which are intended purely to give an overview of each stage of the trail. The Ordnance Survey, www.ordnancesurvey.co.uk, covers the Pennine Way on 10 Landranger maps at a scale of 1:50,000. The sheet numbers are 74, 80, 86, 87, 91, 92, 98, 103, 109 and 110. For greater detail, eight Ordnance Survey Explorer maps cover the route at a scale of 1:25,000, and the sheet numbers are OL1, OL2, OL16, OL21, OL30, OL31, OL42 and OL43. The companion map booklet to this guidebook contains extracts from the Ordnance Survey Explorer maps, at a scale of 1:25,000, with the route highlighted, along with alternatives and off-route spurs.

Harvey, www.harveymaps.co.uk, publishes three maps covering the Pennine Way on water-resistant paper at a scale of 1:40,000. These are Pennine Way South, Pennine Way Central and Pennine Way North. The relevant maps are listed at the start of each stage of the route.

Leaving the route at Windy Gyle allows for a descent to Trows (Day 19)

WAYMARKING AND ACCESS

The Pennine Way is a designated right of way from start to finish; therefore it should be open at all times and always be free of obstructions. The route is made up of public footpaths, public bridleways, public byways and public highways. Signposts usually include the words 'Pennine Way', along with the official National Trail 'acorn' symbol. Marker posts generally feature only the acorn symbol and a directional arrow. Occasionally, the initials 'PW' may be painted or carved onto surfaces to give additional directions.

Yellow arrows denote public footpaths; blue arrows denote public bridleways; and red arrows denote public byways.

Following the 'acorn' symbols is fairly fool-proof, but bear in mind that the Pennine Way intersects with the Pennine Bridleway on a handful of occasions, and also runs concurrent with a considerable stretch of the Hadrian's Wall Path. As all these routes are National Trails, they all bear the 'acorn' symbols, and some walkers do find themselves following the wrong trails!

Note that there are some very long stretches that have no signposts or markers, and this is the policy for what is after all a tough and often remote long-distance trail.

WEATHER FORECASTS

Walking for hours across bleak moorlands on an almost daily basis is fine, so long as the weather is good. There is little anyone can do about the weather, except to be prepared. Get into the habit of checking the forecast as often as possible, and keep an eye on the days ahead, so that if bad weather is predicted on a particularly tricky stretch, at least that can be included in planning. Forecasts on radio or television might be too general, but online forecasts provided by the Met Office, www.metoffice.gov.uk, can be tailored to more specific locations. For example, a detailed forecast is always available for the summit of Great Dun Fell! Numerous weather forecasts are available on smartphone apps.

PHONES AND WI-FI

Mobile phones don't always get a signal along the Pennine Way, and coverage varies depending on your service provider. All of the towns along the Pennine Way have coverage, but some villages don't, and rural telephone kiosks are gradually being removed. For internet access, Wi-Fi is offered by most accommodation providers, but there are a few who don't offer it. If Wi-Fi is important, then be sure to ask about provision when bookings are made. Rural post offices keep disappearing along the route, but the remaining ones are mentioned.

EMERGENCIES

The Pennines and Cheviot Hills are not particularly dangerous, and the biggest problem unwary walkers are likely to face is the prospect of losing their way on a featureless moorland. However, accidents and injuries could occur almost anywhere on the route and the intervention of the emergency services might be required. To contact the police, ambulance, fire service or mountain rescue, telephone 999 (or the European emergency number 112), and state clearly the nature of the emergency. Give them your telephone number and, most importantly, keep in touch while a response is mounted.

ALL ABOUT THE PENNINES

Limestone pavement on top of Malham Cove (Day 6)

PENNINE GEOLOGY

As a teenager and a student of geology, I was not content simply to admire the Pennines. I wielded a hammer and chisel so that I could take great chunks of them home with me!

Pennine geology is relatively easy to understand, although in a few places it becomes very complex. The oldest bedrock is seldom seen on the Pennine Way, revealing itself only around Malham and Dufton. Ancient Silurian slate at Malham Tarn, along with Ordovician mudstone and volcanic rock above Dufton, date back 450 million years. These rocks are revealed only where fault lines bring them to the surface. The Weardale Granite, which underlies the North Pennines, outcrops nowhere and was only 'proved' by a borehole sunk at Rookhope in 1961.

In the Devonian period, around 395 million years ago, violent volcanic activity laid the foundations of the Cheviot Hills, at the northern end of the Pennine Way. All the lower hills are made of andesite lavas, while the central parts are formed of a massive dome of granite, pushed into the Earth's crust some 360 million years ago and only recently exposed to the elements.

During the Carboniferous period, around 350 to 300 million years ago, a warm, shallow tropical sea covered the whole region. Countless billions of hard-shelled, soft-bodied creatures lived and died in this sea. Coral reefs grew, and even microscopic organisms often had hard external or internal structures. Over the aeons, these creatures left their hard parts in heaps on the seabed, and these deposits became the massive grey limestones seen to best effect today in the Yorkshire Dales.

Even while thick beds of limestone were being laid down, storms were eroding distant mountain ranges. Vast rivers brought mud, sand and gravel down into the sea. These murky deposits reduced the amount of light entering the water, causing delicate coral reefs and other creatures to perish. As more mud and sand was washed into the sea, a vast delta spread across the region.

At times, shoals of sand and gravel stood above the waterline, and these became colonised by strange, fernlike trees. The level of water in the rivers and sea was in a state of flux. Sometimes the delta was completely flooded, so the plants would be buried under more sand and gravel. The compressed plant material within the beds of sand and mud became thin bands of coal, known as the Coal Measures. This alternating series of sandstones and mudstones, with occasional seams of coal, can be seen best in the Dark Peak and the South Pennines. Remnants of the series can also be studied on the higher summits of the Yorkshire Dales and North Pennines.

The Carboniferous rocks were laid down in layers, helping to explain what happened next, around 295 million years ago. An extensive mass of molten dolerite was squeezed, under enormous pressure, between the layers of rock – rather like jam between two slices of bread. This rock is always prominent wherever it outcrops, chiefly in the North Pennines and along Hadrian's Wall, where it is referred to as the Whin Sill.

Almost 300 million years are 'missing' from the Pennine geological record, in which time the range has been broken into enormous blocks by faulting. The Yorkshire Dales and North Pennines display plenty of limestone, as their 'blocks' stand higher than the Peak District and South Pennines. Glaciers scoured the entire range during the Ice Age, and many parts are covered with glacial detritus in the form of boulder clay, sand and gravel. More recent climatic changes resulted in the upland soil becoming so waterlogged that thick deposits of peat have formed on most of the higher moorlands.

PENNINE SCENERY

The underlying geology of the Pennines shapes the scenery along the Pennine Way. The Dark Peak and the South Pennines, whose foundations are sandstones and shales, with gritstone 'edges', give rise to acid clay soils, which encourages the formation of thick blanket bog. This bog has been growing for the past 7000 years, but in many places it is decaying, so that the moorlands are riven by peat channels, or 'groughs', with high banks of peat between them, known as 'hags'. Given that the blanket bogs absorb considerable amounts of carbon dioxide, their rapid decay gives cause for concern and efforts are being made to stabilise the remaining bogs and reverse the trend.

Where limestone dominates, particularly in the Yorkshire Dales but also in parts of the North Pennines, the landscape often looks fresh and green, covered in short, dense, sheep-grazed turf, with bright cliffs and outcrops, or 'scars', of limestone poking through. Limestone country is fascinating, mostly because of the way the rock dissolves slowly over the aeons, giving rise to a distinctive landscape known as 'karst' topography. Limestone doesn't just wear down like other rocks but dissolves inside itself, becoming riddled with caves and passages. When these are close to the surface, they may collapse, forming 'shake holes'.

In the North Pennines, the existence of the igneous Whin Sill, sandwiched between older beds of rock, forms some of the most striking landscapes in the North Pennines and Northumberland. The mighty Teesdale waterfalls, the striking High Cup and the rugged crest bearing Hadrian's Wall are all formed by the Whin Sill, which also outcrops along the Northumberland coast.

Technically, and geologically, the Pennines end just south of Hadrian's Wall, so the continuation northwards through Northumberland results in another shift in the scenery. While Carboniferous rocks lie underfoot at first, by the time the high Cheviot Hills are reached, the bedrock is either lava or granite. The central granite mass of The Cheviot stands broad-shouldered, with all the other Cheviot Hills huddled around it. The poor acid soil supports thick blanket bog. Many walkers, seeing the Cheviot Hills after spending so long in the Pennines, are surprised at how hilly they are, but this is short-lived, as the Pennine Way ends suddenly with a descent into rolling, pastoral countryside.

THE HELM WIND

Most walkers on the Pennine Way hear about the 'Helm Wind' but few understand what it is. The Helm Wind is the only wind in Britain with a name. It only blows from one direction and it gives rise to a peculiar set of conditions. Other winds blow from all points of the compass, but the Helm is very strictly defined, restricted to the East Fellside flank of the North Pennines, and according to local lore, no matter how much it rages, it cannot cross the Eden.

First, there needs to be a north-easterly wind, with a minimum speed of 25kph (15mph), which the Beaufort Scale calls a 'moderate breeze'. This isn't the prevailing wind direction and

The Helm Wind blows down the steep western slopes of the North Pennines

it tends to occur chiefly in the winter and spring. Track the air mass from the North Sea, across low-lying country, as far as the Tyne Gap. The air gets pushed over Hexhamshire Common, crossing moorlands at around 300m (1000ft). It next crosses moorlands at around 600m (2000ft) and then Cross Fell and its neighbours are reached at almost 900m (3000ft). There are no low-lying gaps through the North Pennines, so there is nowhere for the air mass to go but over the top.

As the air is pushed up from sea level, it cools considerably. Any moisture it picked up from the sea condenses to form clouds, and these are most noticeable as they build up above the East Fellside. This feature is known as the 'Helm Cap'. If there is little moisture present it is white, while a greater moisture content makes it much darker, resulting in rainfall. Bear in mind at this point that the air mass is not only cooler, but as a result it is also denser than the air mass sitting in the Vale of Eden.

After crossing the highest parts of the North Pennines, the northeasterly wind is cold, dense, and suddenly runs out of high ground. The air literally 'falls' down the East Fellside slope, and if it could be seen, it would probably look like a tidal wave. This, and only this, is the Helm Wind. The greater the northeasterly wind speed, the greater the force with which it plummets down the East Fellside, and if it is particularly strong, wet and cold, it is capable of great damage. Very few habitations have ever been built on this slope, and the villages below were generally built with their backs to the East Fellside, and most of them originally lacked doors and windows on their windward sides.

The air mass now does some peculiar things, having dropped, cold and dense, to hit a relatively warm air mass sitting in the Vale of Eden. A 'wave' of air literally rises up and curls back on itself. As warm and cold air mix, there is another phase of condensation inside an aerial vortex, resulting in the formation of a thin, twisting band of cloud that seems to hover mid-air, no matter how hard the wind blows at ground level. This cloud is called the 'Helm Bar' and is conclusive proof that the Helm Wind is 'on', as the locals say.

Local folk say that no matter how hard the Helm Wind blows, it can never cross the Eden. All the wind's energy is expended in aerial acrobatics on the East Fellside, where it can roar and rumble, while the Vale of Eden experiences only gentle surface winds. Northeasterly winds are uncommon and short-lived, so after only a few days the system breaks down and the usual blustery southwesterly winds are restored. In the meantime, don't refer to any old wind as the Helm Wind until all its characteristics have been noted, including the northeast wind, the Helm Cap and the Helm Bar.

WILDLIFE

Pennine pastures offer good grazing for sheep and cattle, while the higher moorlands offer passable grazing for sheep in the summer months. Only in the North Pennines are fell ponies likely to be seen, and feral goats are occasionally spotted in the Cheviot

Swaledale sheep are common throughout the Yorkshire Dales

A well-camouflaged adder on a heather moor adopts its strike position when approached too closely

Hills. Other mammals that can be seen include foxes, badgers, hares and rabbits, along with small rodents, or bats in the evenings.

The heather moorlands of the Pennines are managed for grouse-shooting, which involves the control of 'vermin', meaning anything likely to affect the numbers of grouse on the moors. Red grouse are dominant, but there are small areas in the North Pennines with black grouse too. The plaintive piping of the curlew will be heard on the moors, while snipe may be flushed from cover. Lapwings are notable in high pastures, usually when trying to distract walkers from their nesting sites. The reservoirs and bog pools attract all manner of wildfowl and waders, and it is not uncommon to find raucous colonies of gulls breeding on the high moors, far from the sea. Emperor moths are also notable on the high moors.

Reptiles include common lizards, adders and grass snakes, although these are rarely seen. Amphibians include frogs and increasingly rare newts, while the native white-clawed crayfish is under great threat from competition and disease introduced by non-native species.

PLANT LIFE

Woodlands are rare in the Pennines, although densely planted commercial forests occur in some places. For the most part, the high Pennines feature tussocky moor grass with boggy patches of sphagnum moss. In the summer months, vast areas of nodding bog cotton give the impression of snow-covered slopes. There

Cloudberries, arctic remnant plants, only grow on the highest and bleakest parts of the Pennine Way

is rather less heather than most people expect, and much of it has been managed to provide a habitat for red grouse. The dominant species is ling, although there are occasional areas of bell heather. Heather is burnt on a rotational basis, so that there are always young heather shoots for grouse to feed on, as well as dense 'leggy' heather for shelter. Heather seeds are fairly resistant to fire, but in places where heather is over-burnt, invasive bracken is quick to take hold. Some heather moorlands also feature bilberry and crowberry, while the higher, bleaker, boggier moorlands are home to an interesting arctic remnant – cloudberry.

There is very little tillage on Pennine farms, and most fields are managed as pastures for farm stock. Some fields are managed for hay, and in the dale-heads of the North Pennines, haymaking comes so late in the summer that wildflowers have a chance to drop their seeds, making the meadows rich in species and remarkably colourful.

The range of plants thriving in Upper Teesdale owes its existence to several factors. Arctic/alpine species survive because the climate in this bleak region suits them, keeping taller and more competitive plants at bay. The underlying crumbling 'sugar limestone' suits some species, while others grow on sodden, acid peat bogs. Plants that once grew in well-wooded areas now survive by adapting to life in the shade of boulders and cliffs. Many people have heard of the spring gentian, which is strikingly blue on sunny days in early summer, but few know where to find it. Large expanses of juniper are easily spotted, but in recent years a fungal disease has attacked these. Other species of note include the mountain pansy, alpine bistort, bird's eye primrose, globe flower, Teesdale violet and blue moor grass. These grow alongside more commonplace wild thyme, tormentil, thrift and harebells, while wood anemones and woodland ferns have adapted to non-wooded habitats. The 'Teesdale Assemblage' of plants are survivors from bygone ages, reminding visitors how habitats have changed over time.

THE PENNINE WAY

Halfway up the slopes of Knock Fell with the Lake District visible beyond (Day 14)

DAY 1

Edale to Torside

Start	Railway Station, Edale, SK 123 853
Finish	B6105 road, Torside, SK 057 980
Distance	25km (15.5 miles)
Total ascent	770m (2525ft)
Total descent	790m (2590ft)
Time	8hr
Terrain	Elevated, extensive and exposed boggy moorlands, with several stretches of firm flagstone path. Careful navigation is required on some stretches in mist.
Maps	OS Landranger 110, OS Explorer OL1, Harvey's Pennine Way South
Refreshments	Pubs and cafés at Edale

In its earliest days, the Pennine Way left Edale in two directions. The 'main' route made a direct ascent of Kinder Scout, crossing soft peat bogs that proved very confusing in mist, while the 'alternative' route skirted round the edge of the plateau. The top of Kinder Scout became very badly over-trodden, so the Pennine Way now follows only one route out of Edale, staying on firm ground. The moors between Kinder Scout and Bleaklow were once trodden into a filthy quagmire, but now boast fine flagstone paths. Attention to route-finding is necessary on Bleaklow, where some walkers drift off-course. Bear in mind that this is a hard day's walk, and some trekkers realise too late that they are not equal to the task. The final descent of the day is quite awkward and rugged underfoot. Originally, this first stage ended at Crowden, but the closure of its youth hostel leaves only a campsite, and wayfarers looking for accommodation are now obliged to leave the route for Padfield or Glossop.

EDALE

This little village can be overwhelmed by visitors, especially on summer weekends. If arriving by train, simply follow the road a short way into the village. The Moorland Centre (open daily from April to September, free entry, tel 01433 670207), a Peak District National Park Visitor Centre, is worth exploring. The unusual building has a waterfall at its entrance and a lush sedum roof. There are a couple of pubs and cafés, as well as a post office and general store. If planning to stay overnight, there are campsites, bunkhouses, B&Bs and a nearby youth hostel.

The Pennine Way starts in the centre of **Edale** at the Old Nags Head, around 250m (820ft). The first signpost is across the road from the pub, pointing towards a commemorative gate that was erected in 2015 for the 50th

The Old Nags Head at the start of the Pennine Way in Edale

2025 marked the 60th anniversary.

anniversary of the route. ◂ An obvious path climbs gently beside a little streambed flanked by trees. Go through a gate to enter a field, turning left through another gate to follow a flagstone path up through a few fields, passing through more gates; there are fine views across the dale to Mam Tor and Lose Hill. Continue gently up an earth path through a couple more fields, then head down through more fields to pick up an enclosed path and track past **Upper Booth Farm**, which has a campsite.

Turn right along a narrow road, crossing a bridge over a stream and passing fields to reach Lee Farm. The Lee Barn Information Shelter is here, containing interesting notices and offering shelter from inclement weather. Follow a track onwards, passing through gates from field to field to reach a narrow, stone packhorse bridge at the foot of Jacob's Ladder.

Turn left or right – left being a long and stony loop once used by packhorses, right being a shorter, steeper, stone-pitched path. Both routes meet at a huge cairn and a stony path climbs onwards. Towards the top, turn right along a flagstone path. Climb a short, steep slope of grass, with tufts of bilberry. When a sprawling cairn is reached in a slight dip, keep left to follow a clear path, passing big boulders and gritstone outcrops. ◂ Pass a trig point on top of a gritstone outcrop on **Kinder Low**, at 633m (2077ft).

Take care in mist while crossing broad, bare moorland.

Walk across an area denuded of vegetation and peat, where the gritstone bedrock is often seen. Keep right to

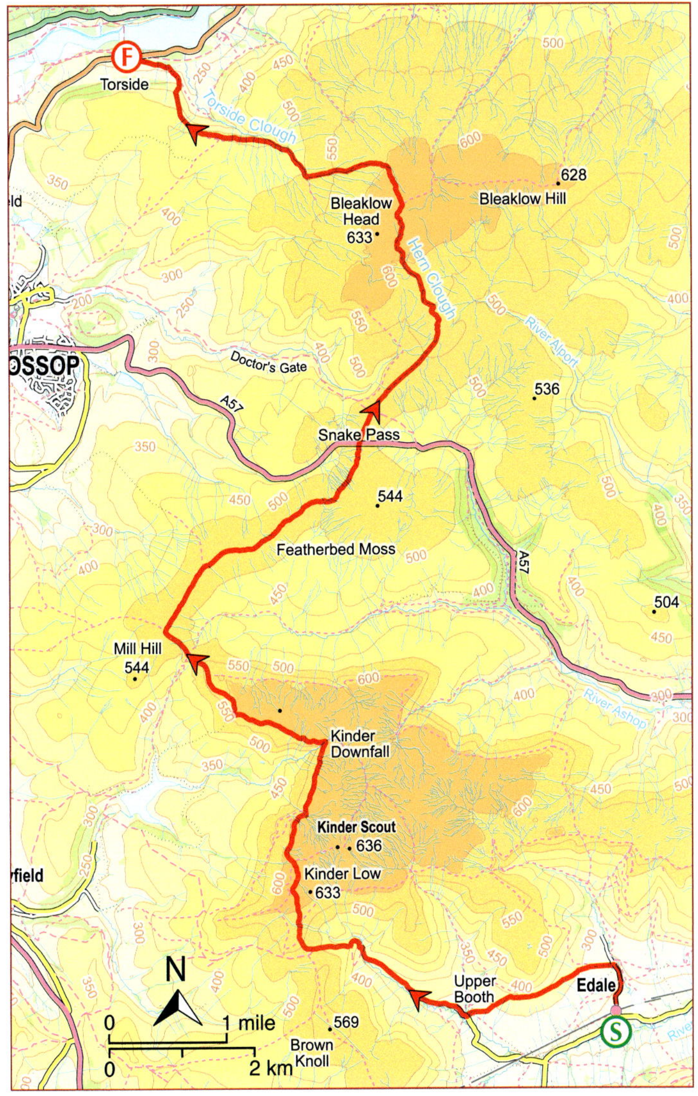
Torside
Torside Clough
Bleaklow Head
633
Bleaklow Hill
628
Hern Clough
River Alport
Doctor's Gate
A57
Snake Pass
536
544
Featherbed Moss
504
Mill Hill
544
River Ashop
Kinder Downfall
Kinder Scout
636
Kinder Low
633
Upper Booth
Edale
569
Brown Knoll
N
0
1 mile
0
2 km

Walkers pass curious gritstone outcrops on Kinder Low

This is a very popular lunch spot, but don't linger too long as the day has barely started.

follow a path round the edge of the broad moorland plateau, heading roughly north above Cluther Rocks. The path is sometimes narrow and occasionally involves hopping from boulder to boulder and slab to slab. Follow the path to reach the waterfall, **Kinder Downfall**. Cross a stream above the waterfall, taking care on blustery days, as the wind can flip all the water back up into the streambed, soaking the unwary! ◂

Keep following the gritstone edge, where a path gradually rises, going through a gate in a fence and reaching rock outcrops on Sandy Heys. This point was gained during the famous 1932 mass trespass, when it was all private property. What a contrast today, when walkers have every right to be here – a right they exercise in great numbers! In mist, don't be tempted to follow a path downhill, but stay on the broadest, clearest path, which turns right and climbs a little to reach a sprawling cairn. Keep left of the cairn to pick up a steep, stone-pitched path leading down to the grassy gap of Ashop Head, around 510m (1675ft).

A flagstone path heads left, but the Pennine Way keeps right along a broad and stony path. Pass a prominent marker post where another path crosses, and climb straight over a grassy hump to reach another gap. A flagstone path climbs straight uphill, giving way to a broad, stony path leading to a cairn at 544m (1785ft) on top of **Mill Hill**. Paths cross on the summit, so turn right to follow another flagstone path onwards.

This used to be one of the worst areas of **bog** on the Pennine Way, but the path now offers a firm, dry footing. The old path can often be seen on the left as a black, boggy line, although it is slowly revegetating. The moorland is predominantly grassy, with areas of bog cotton, sphagnum moss, rushes, bilberry and heather. Look out for cloudberries, a distinctive, broad-leafed arctic remnant plant, that positively thrive on the highest and bleakest boggy moorlands.

The path undulates very gently and writhes to avoid awkward boggy areas on Moss Castle and **Featherbed Moss**. There is a strange sight ahead, where vehicles apparently speed straight across the moor, since the surface of the A57 road on the **Snake Pass** isn't seen until it is reached at a gate. Cross the road with care, as the traffic is sometimes very fast. The roadside bus stops are redundant.

There are no snakes on **Snake Pass**, nor have there ever been. Originally, there was a Snake Inn, whose sign bore a snake emblem that was part of the Cavendish crest, the family being related to the Duke of Devonshire, a major landowner in Derbyshire. Snake Pass took its name from the inn. However, the inn recently changed its name to the Snake Pass Inn, curiously taking its name from the road originally named after itself! The road runs at an altitude of 512m (1680ft) and is one of the first to be blocked by snow each winter. It's a sobering thought, but every so often a walker will abandon their Pennine Way attempt at this point, having seriously under estimated the nature of the route.

A track leaves the road and runs to a gate, where a broad and firm path crosses what was once desperately over-trodden moorland. There is a slight dip where the Pennine Way crosses **Doctor's Gate**. Here, a very worn stone-paved path crosses at right angles, clearly cut across the moorland.

This is thought to be an old **Roman road** linking Glossop with the Hope Valley. Its name comes from an association with the 15th-century Vicar of Glossop, Doctor John Talbot, who had the old road improved.

Some walkers might be noticed turning left. They are going to look at the wreckage of 'Over Exposed', an RB29 Superfortress that crashed in 1948 on Higher Shelf Stones.

Keep straight ahead and follow the path as it rises gently over largely grassy moorland, with heather and bilberry becoming more noticeable after the path changes to flagstones. A few steps lead down into Devil's Dike, a deep cutting in the peat where the stony ground beneath has been exposed. ◂ In wet weather it carries a stream. A gradual ascent through the cutting links with more flagstones, then the path becomes a stony channel flanked by peat. Another stretch of flagstones leads to **Hern Clough**.

Walk upstream, crossing and re-crossing the little stream as necessary. Later, there are more flagstones, as well as a series of helpful marker stones bearing carved directional arrows. These are useful as OS maps mark the route incorrectly. The broad and peaty top of **Bleaklow Head** is worn to sand and grit in places, with a large summit cairn bearing a wooden stake at 633m (2077ft).

Views south are blocked by the plateau of Kinder Scout. Other prominent features include distant Winter Hill and Pendle Hill, with Black Hill closer to hand. In very clear conditions, Pen-y-Ghent can be seen far ahead, maybe as much as a week away via the Pennine Way.

Take care, as many walkers fail to spot this marker.

To leave Bleaklow Head, make a slight left turn, confirming the correct path by looking for 'PW' carved on a rock. ◂ A narrow and gentle path heads roughly north,

The prominent cairn on the sprawling moorland of Bleaklow

then, swinging west down a slope dominated by bilberry with cloudberries dotted around, the path becomes rather awkward, with stones and boulders underfoot on the way down a heathery slope. There are some stretches of flagstones, but the path is quite rugged as it leads down to a confluence of streams. Ford both streams and climb a short, steep slope above **Torside Clough**.

The Pennine Way runs along a heathery edge, passing a few gritstone outcrops overlooking the stream. It can be rugged as it runs downhill, but a good stretch on flagstones passes a fence. At a junction of paths, keep right downhill, later climbing to traverse Clough Edge. There is a view down to Torside Reservoir, with Black Hill beyond. A stone-pitched path descends steeply from the edge, passing through a gate in a fence. Turn left down a broader path, keeping left of a farmhouse at Reaps, following its access track to the B6105 road at 220m (720ft). If carrying a tent, continue along the Pennine Way to Crowden, but if other lodgings are sought, these lie off-route at Padfield and Glossop. Organise pick-ups with accommodation providers or taxis in advance. The

Descending to the Torside Reservoir with Black Hill beyond

road has a Saturday only minibus service linking Glossop and Holmfirth. The bus stop is almost 1.5km (1 mile) off-route at the Torside Visitor Centre, which is of little use to walkers.

DAY 2

Torside to Standedge

Start	B6105 road, Torside, SK 957 980
Finish	A62 road, Standedge, SE 018 095
Alternative finish	Diggle, SE 003 080
Distance	20.5km (12.75 miles); Diggle 22km (14 miles)
Total ascent	790m (2590ft)
Total descent	650m (2135ft); Diggle 820m (2690ft)
Time	6hr 30min; 7hr 15min
Terrain	Mostly moorland walking, with several stretches on flagstone paths, but a couple of wet and boggy areas too. One stretch uses firm tracks and paths through a valley, passing reservoirs.
Maps	OS Landranger 110, OS Explorer OL1, Harvey's Pennine Way South
Refreshments	Snoopy's snack van might be parked at Wessenden Head at weekends. Pubs well off-route at Marsden and Diggle.

Black Hill once had a fearsome reputation among Pennine wayfarers, with its broad top covered in deep black bogs that were desperately over-trodden. The hill now bears a long line of firm flagstones. The 'black' has gone, replaced by 'green' as the whole top has been re-vegetated. The Pennine Way 'main' route originally headed directly to Standedge across truly appalling bogs, with an 'alternative' seeking firmer ground via Wessenden. These days, there is only one designated route, which runs via Wessenden. Standedge is completely lacking facilities, so walkers must detour off-route to find food, drink and lodgings, either on foot or by catching a bus.

Start on the B6105 road near Reaps, following a short tarmac path used as a cycleway, as well as by the Pennine Way. This quickly reaches a track, where a right turn is quickly followed by a sharp left turn down a short track. This gives way to a narrow tarmac road across

Climbing towards Laddow Rocks on the way to Black Hill

There are five reservoirs in Longdendale: Bottoms, Valehouse, Rhodeswood, Torside and Woodhead.

the dam of Torside Reservoir, overlooking Rhodeswood Reservoir. ◂ Climb 30 stone steps from the reservoir dam and go through a gate marked as the Pennine Way. Turn right to follow a path through a belt of pine trees between Torside Reservoir and a busy road. After passing through a gate, turn left up some steps.

Those wishing to visit Crowden should walk straight ahead here down the road.

Cross the busy **A628** road and turn right to go through a gate. A narrow traffic-free tarmac road runs gently uphill. When it runs downhill, the Pennine Way is signposted off to the left. ◂

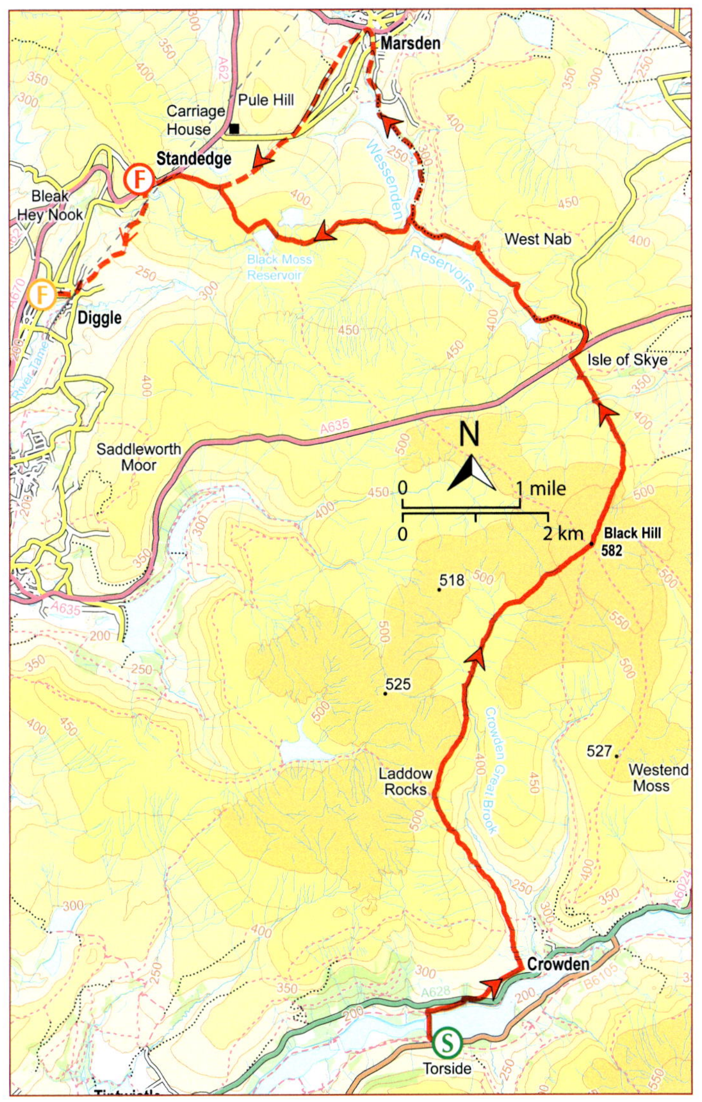

Marsden
Pule Hill
Carriage House
Standedge
Bleak Hey Nook
Wessenden
Black Moss Reservoir
Reservoirs
West Nab
Diggle
River Tame
Isle of Skye
A635
Saddleworth Moor
N
0
1 mile
0
2 km
Black Hill 582
518
525
Crowden Great Brook
527
Laddow Rocks
Westend Moss
Crowden
A628
B6105
Torside

Crowden is barely 500 metres (0.25 mile) off-route; however, facilities are limited to a campsite, following the closure of a long-standing youth hostel. A discount is offered for Pennine Way walkers, but note that there are no food supplies, so you need to carry your own. If starting from Crowden, walk back up the narrow road from the campsite and turn right as signposted for the Pennine Way.

The path rises through gates to reach a small memorial woodland plantation on the hillside. Beyond are slopes of bracken, where the path becomes awkward due to stones protruding from the ground. Heather and bilberry are apparent as the path passes below Black Tor, where a quarried edge bears patchy woodland. The path undulates and crosses a stream, then climbs steeply up a rugged, bracken-clad slope. When the path levels out, there are fine views along the valley. The climb becomes steep and rugged again, crossing Oaken Clough to pick up a stone-pitched path up to the edge of heather moorland.

The crag doesn't look too dramatic, but keep looking back to spot one part that features an overhang.

A narrow path wanders along the top of **Laddow Rocks**, occasionally offering views of gritstone crags that were once popular with rock climbers, but are rarely climbed these days. ◂ The path rises to around 500m (1640ft), then descends gradually across a slope of grass and bilberry, becoming boggy and over-trodden as it runs parallel to **Crowden Great Brook**.

Step across a tributary and walk parallel to the main stream on a firm path. Cross another tributary, then when the main stream bites into a shale bank, cross and re-cross the flow to continue. If there is too much water to ford safely, climb over the shale bank and pick up the path later. The path becomes wet and boggy and walkers sometimes detour too far from the stream, thereby missing the start of a firm, dry flagstone path. This pulls away from the stream, leading to a footbridge and a stile over a fence on Grains Moss.

Simply follow the flagstone path straight up a grassy, rushy slope polka-dotted with bog cotton in early summer. Cross a boggy rise at Dun Hill, then the flagstones end for a while. A firm path passes peat hags that have been stabilised against erosion. Another length of flagstones leads over the broad moorland summit of **Black Hill**, passing through a pool of water at one point, reaching a trig point with a flagstone 'patio' around it at 582m (1908ft).

The summit of **Black Hill** was for many years trodden to death, until not even a blade of grass remained. The bog was so over-trodden that it was often impossible to reach the trig point, which stood on a firm 'island' known as Soldier's Lump. The name derived from a time when Ordnance Survey 'sappers' set up camp on the hill while surveying the land. The trig point they planted on the summit was close to collapse after the wholesale erosion of peat in recent decades, but it has been stoutly buttressed. The 'Moors For The Future' project (www.moorsforthefuture.org.uk) has successfully re-vegetated the summit of Black Hill with grass, bog cotton, heather and bilberry. The Pennine Way originally left the summit in two directions, but has now been confined to a single firm, dry, erosion-proof line across the moors.

Descending from Black Hill over a heather moor to Wessenden Head

Follow the flagstone path onwards, as it gently undulates across the moor. When the flagstones end, a firm path continues downhill with good views eastwards. When another flagstone path is reached, it swings left to pass grouse butts, where heather dominates over grass, bilberry and bog cotton. The path undulates gently, then features a short, steep descent and ascent while crossing Dean Clough. ◂ A lesser stream, rusty red in colour, is crossed before the path climbs to the busy A635, or **Isle of Skye Road**, at Wessenden Head.

There is no bridge, so fording after heavy rain will mean wet feet.

Turn right to follow the road with care. ◂ Turn left up the minor road signposted for Meltham and Huddersfield. Turn left down through a gate to follow a track straight down to Wessenden Head Reservoir. There is a fine view down the valley to another reservoir, and a house among trees, with the distinctive profile of **Pule Hill** beyond. The land from here to White Hill (Day 3) makes up the extensive National Trust Marsden Moor Estate.

If Snoopy's snack van is parked at weekends, you could take a break for food and drink, and lament the fact that a nearby ruin was once a pub called the Isle of Skye.

Ashley Jackson's 'Framing the Landscape' at Wessenden Head

RESERVOIR COUNTRY

The Wessenden reservoirs – Wessenden Head, Wessenden, Blakely and Butterley – drop one after another in a narrow valley. Construction was financed by a consortium of Marsden mill owners, whose mills were located beside the River Colne. The reservoirs were completed in 1800, shortly after the opening of the Huddersfield Narrow Canal. The mill owners jealously guarded their water supply and weren't keen for any of it to be used by the canal company.

Black Moss and Swellands reservoirs, along with four others, were constructed on the high moors to supply the Huddersfield Narrow Canal. A system of drains catches little streams and feeds the water into the reservoirs. Black Moss Reservoir has a dam at either end, being constructed on a broad moorland gap. The dam of Swellands Reservoir broke in November 1810, sending a deluge of peaty water down to Marsden, where it caused great damage in what was called 'The Night of the Black Flood'.

Walk straight down a broad and clear path. This makes a couple of loops round little side valleys to reach the dam of Wessenden Reservoir. Follow a track downhill from the dam, catching a glimpse of Wessenden Lodge behind tall deer fences. The track rises gently to reach a signpost. At this point, turn left for the Pennine Way, down a path on a steep slope of bracken. ▸

Be sure to make this turn if staying on the main route.

Off-route to Marsden

Marsden lies 3km (2 miles) off-route, with a descent of 140m (460ft).

◂ If planning to visit Marsden, at this point you keep straight along the track. After passing Wessenden Lodge, simply follow the clear track down through the valley. Pass Blakeley Reservoir and follow the track onwards past Butterley Reservoir. Turn left when a road is reached, and while this could be followed into town, turn left down a flight of 211 stone steps instead. Turn right to follow a track through a wood before passing between tall mills on the outskirts of **Marsden**. Turn left down a road and pass a small roundabout. Follow Fall Lane and fork left to pass through a tunnel. Turn right along Towngate to follow a river into the town centre.

In the past Pennine wayfarers frequently visited **Marsden**; however, numbers reduced after its youth hostel closed. There are a few other accommodation options, however, and this is a 'Walkers are Welcome' town, marsdenwalkersarewelcome.org. Facilities include a post office, shops, pubs, cafés, an information point (tel 01484 222555) and a Co-op with a cashpoint. Regular daily buses link Marsden with Huddersfield, Standedge, Diggle and Manchester. Regular daily trains link Marsden with Manchester and Huddersfield.

The detour to Marsden leaves Pennine wayfarers in a quandary. Should they walk back to Wessenden to pick up the route? Catch a bus or short-cut to Standedge? The following route is a direct short-cut, measuring 3.5km (2.25 miles) back to the Pennine Way, with an ascent of 210m (690ft).

Leave Marsden by walking along Towngate, climbing beside the churchyard to reach the main **A62** road. Cross the road and climb a short way up Old Mount Road. Turn right where a signpost indicates a 'public footpath' and follow a track towards an isolated house. Turn left before the house as indicated by a marker post. The way is overgrown for a bit until a stile is crossed. A deep-cut, rushy groove climbs up a grassy slope, with fine views of

Marsden and its mills. Keep to the left of the groove to follow a track up to a farmhouse.

Go through gates to pass the farmhouse and climb straight up another grassy slope. Pick up and follow another path in a groove, passing through a gate and climbing to join a broad, clear, stony track. Follow this straight ahead, gently uphill, with fine views back to Marsden, as well as to Black Hill and the moors above Wessenden. The track levels out and rejoins Old Mount Road, which itself drops down to another road.

Cross the road to reach a public footpath sign, and drop down a little to cross a stream. Climb a little and keep right, watching for a grassy path and a marker post. Simply walk straight ahead, gently up the moorland slope, always following the grassy path. After crossing a crest, Redbrook Reservoir comes into view. The path runs along an embankment, and there is a prominent notch where a stream crosses. Beyond this is a clear track, which is the Pennine Way, leading directly to **Standedge** at 387m (1270ft).

Main route to Standege

Cross a footbridge and climb steeply up a rugged path on a slope of heather. The gradient eases at a stone-built structure, where there is a view down the valley to Blakeley Reservoir. The path is almost level as it reaches a stream. Cross it and climb 73 stone steps, then continue along a flagstone path through bracken. A length of stony path is followed by more flagstones, and Black Moss is surely misnamed when masses of white bog cotton nod in the breeze. Pule Hill is seen across Swellands Reservoir, while the Pennine Way crosses a dam on **Black Moss Reservoir**, where there are a couple of small sandy beaches.

Overshoot the end of the dam and cross a substantial wooden road, then soon afterwards the path turns left and it follows a fence to a corner. Keep straight ahead before turning right up a flagstone path, going through a kissing gate in a fence from grassy moorland to heather moorland. Walk downhill and go through another gate, back onto grassy moorland. The flagstones end at a small stream, where a left turn leads up a track on a stout embankment overlooking Redbrook Reservoir, another feeder for the Huddersfield Narrow Canal. The track leads up through a gate, crossing a crest parallel to the busy A62 road, which runs through a deep cutting. Descend to the roadside beside Brunclough Reservoir at **Standedge**, at 387m (1270ft). The Peak District National Park ends beside the main road.

The **Carriage House Campsite** is off-route at Standedge, down the main road in the direction of Marsden. Bear in mind that the Carriage House itself is sometimes booked by stag and hen parties.

STANDEDGE

There are no facilities where the Pennine Way crosses the road at Standedge, so extra distance must be covered in search of accommodation, food and drink. Following the main road is not recommended, as it is too busy. However, there are regular buses. Anyone heading for Marsden or Diggle can either catch a bus, or, if they insist on walking, use the route description offered here.

There are actually four tunnels under Standedge, all measuring a little over 5km (3 miles) in length. A narrow canal tunnel was constructed first, between 1794 and 1811. It was the highest canal in Britain at 147m (645ft) above sea level, but also the deepest underground, lying 145m (638ft) below Standedge. A single-track rail tunnel was cut between 1846 and 1849, followed by another one between 1868 and 1870. A twin-track rail tunnel was built last, between 1890 and 1894. Dozens of transverse tunnels link all four tunnels together, primarily between the rail tunnels and the canal tunnel, for the purpose of extracting waste. The Standedge Tunnel Visitor Centre (open throughout the year, free entry, tel 01484 844298, canalrivertrust.org.uk/places-to-visit/standedge-tunnel-and-visitor-centre) is only a short stroll from Marsden.

Diggle lies 2.5km (1.5 miles) off-route, with a descent of 190m (625ft).

Alternative finish at Diggle

◂ To continue to Diggle, don't cross the main road at Standedge but walk between the road and Brunclough Reservoir. Walk down from the reservoir to a clear track

Entrance to the Huddersfield Canal tunnel at Diggle

to find a Pennine Bridleway signpost. Turn left down a track marked for Diggle, passing a house. Turn right at a marker post and stay on the clearest path downhill, passing a spoil heap and reaching a house on the hillside. Continue down a walled and fenced track past fields, reaching a tarmac road at the Diggle Hotel. Turn right at a road junction to cross a bridge over a railway, then turn left to walk into **Diggle**.

> **Diggle** has two pubs, a fish and chip shop, a small post office shop and a couple of places offering accommodation. Buses run regularly through the village, linking Manchester, Standedge, Marsden and Huddersfield. The entrances to the railway and canal tunnels are fairly close together.

DAY 3

Standedge to Callis Bridge or Hebden Bridge

Start	A62 road, Standedge, SE 018 095
Alternative start	Diggle, SE 003 080
Finish	Callis Bridge, SD 971 264
Alternative finish	Hebden Bridge, SD 991 272
Distance	24km (15 miles); Hebden Bridge 24.5km (15.25 miles)
Total ascent	370m (1215ft)
Total descent	650m (2135ft)
Time	7hr 30min; Hebden Bridge 7hr 45min
Terrain	Gentle moorland walking on good paths gives way to rugged paths on Blackstone Edge. Broad, firm, level reservoir tracks allow speedy progress. Moorland paths and farm tracks later, with an option to follow the Hebden Bridge Loop.
Maps	OS Landranger 103, 109 and 110, OS Explorer OL1 and OL 21, Harvey's Pennine Way South
Refreshments	Café at Bleakedgate. The White House pub near Blackstone Edge. Plenty of choice off-route at Hebden Bridge.

This is a relatively easy stretch of the Pennine Way. Low, gently rolling moorlands give way to the rough and rocky crest of Blackstone Edge. A series of firm, level tracks follow reservoir drains and cross reservoir dams, where it is possible to stride out with confidence and pick up speed. The stout stone monument of Stoodley Pike is seen from time to time. Pennine wayfarers tend to agree that it never seems to draw nearer! At the end of the day there is a descent into post-industrial Calderdale via Callis Bridge. Alternatively, the bustling little town of Hebden Bridge and all its facilities can be reached by using the signposted and waymarked Hebden Bridge Loop.

▸ Start where the Pennine Way crosses the busy **A62** road on **Standedge**, following a clear track uphill. Keep straight ahead at a junction, and keep straight ahead when the Pennine Way and Pennine Bridleway run concurrent for a short distance. At the top of this track, the Pennine Way turns right as signposted, while the Pennine Bridleway continues straight ahead.

If you have stayed in Diggle, either catch a bus or retrace your steps to return to the starting point at Standedge.

The **Pennine Bridleway** and Pennine Way are both National Trails. For the most part, they remain separate while pursuing parallel courses. On a few occasions, they run concurrent for short distances. While the Pennine Way has half a century of history behind it, the Pennine Bridleway is still evolving. It has been opened piecemeal since 2002, and at the time of writing currently starts near Matlock and finishes near Kirkby Stephen. It appears to have ground to a halt at that point, although it was originally planned to extend into Northumberland.

The well-worn path leads away from the track, up a shelf of bare rock. Follow the path up a moorland slope and go through a gap in a wall and fence. A low, rocky edge develops and the path goes through a kissing gate along Standedge. A trig point is passed at 448m (1470ft). The path continues gently, becoming broad and stony, with a low rocky edge to the left and moorland to the

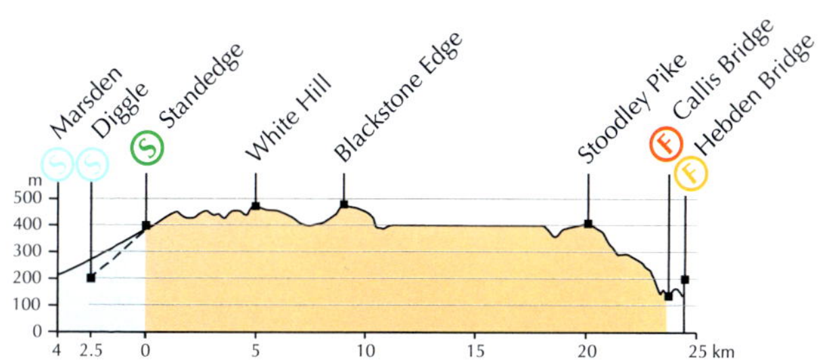

right. A dip is reached where a stone marks the Oldham Way down to the left and the Pennine Way up to the right. A firm gravel path follows a fence and undulates over tussocky moorland with bog cotton and rushes. Cross a footbridge and go through a gate to reach the **A640** road at a small car park.

Cross the road and pick up a path just to the left, climbing up the grassy, rushy slopes of Denshaw Moor. Follow a tumbled wall and a fence over a moorland crest with a pool on top. Bog cotton is abundant on the moors. Walk downhill and cross a stream, with a brief glimpse left down to Readycon Dean Reservoir. Walk uphill and cross a fence to leave the extensive National Trust Marsden Moor Estate. ◂ The grassy top of **White Hill** bears a trig point at 466m (1529ft), with a view of Rochdale below the moors. The path swings right along a high crest passing through a gate, then descends gently to the **A672** road on **Bleakedgate Moor**. ◂

A stone marks the easternmost point in Lancashire.

A curious shipping container café is available here.

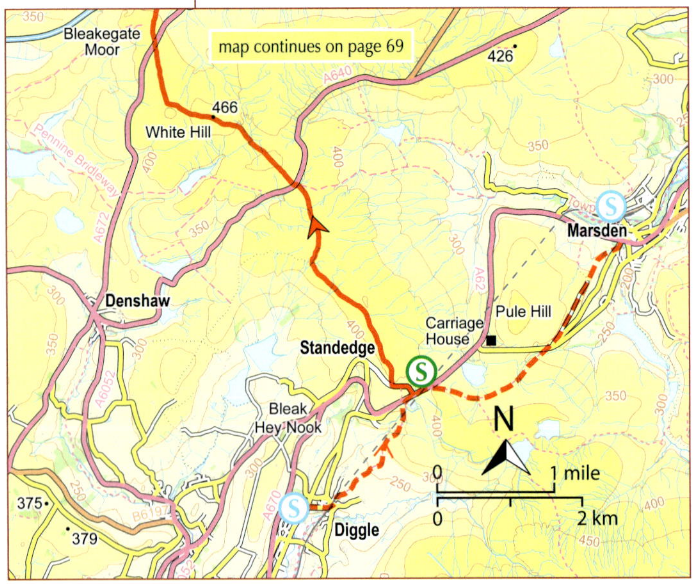

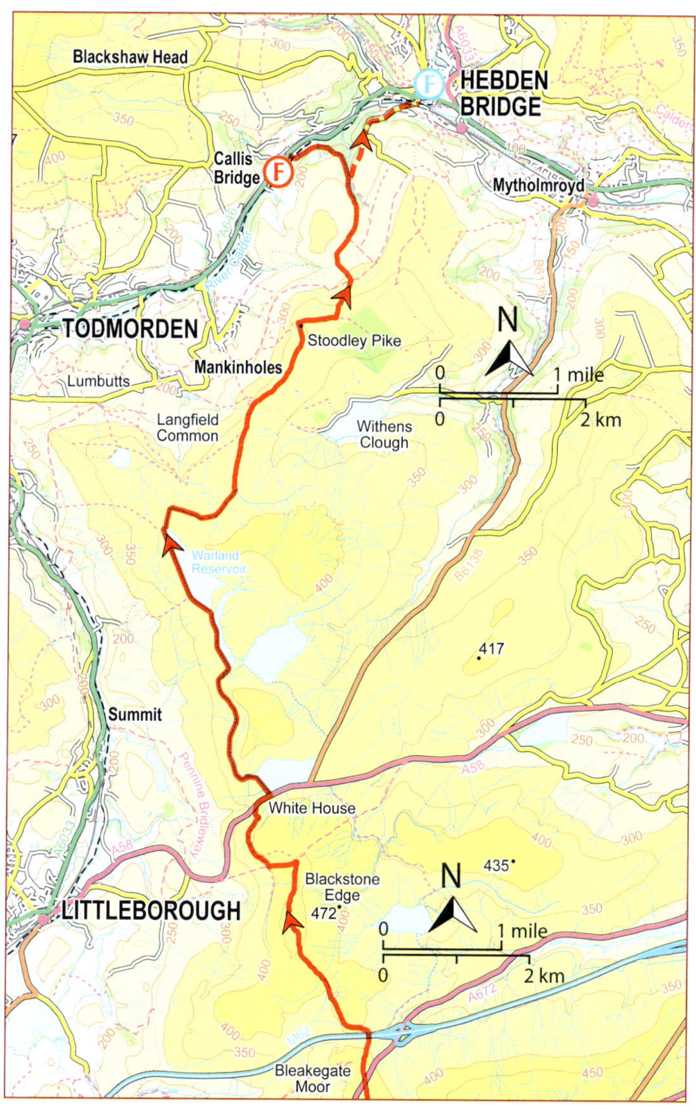

Blackshaw Head
HEBDEN BRIDGE
Callis Bridge
Mytholmroyd
TODMORDEN
Stoodley Pike
Mankinholes
Lumbutts
Langfield Common
Withens Clough
Warland Reservoir
417
Summit
Pennine Bridleway
White House
Blackstone Edge
472
435
LITTLEBOROUGH
Bleakegate Moor
River Calder
A646
A6033
B6138
A58
A672
M62
N
0
1 mile
0
2 km

Cross the road and follow a path over a grassy moor. Cross the access road serving a prominent communication mast on Windy Hill. A flagstone path descends as it approaches the exceptionally busy **M62** motorway.

The **M62 motorway** was opened in 1971, six years after the Pennine Way. A footbridge was installed for Pennine wayfarers, who look down on the endless flow of traffic and wonder 'What's the rush?'

Once across the footbridge, turn left up a stony path, pass through a gate, then head gently downhill on a grassy, rushy moor, following another flagstone path. This bridges a little stream and climbs gently across slopes of bog cotton, with Green Withens Reservoir seen down to the right. There are lots of exposed gritstone boulders towards the top of **Blackstone Edge**. Pass a trig point perched on a rocky outcrop at 472m (1549ft).

BLACKSTONE EDGE

Blackstone Edge in winter

Although the gritstone edge is low, it is remarkably rugged and attractive, and views stretch from the wild moors to urban lowlands, taking in the West Pennines, Whittle Hill, Pendle Hill, Black Hameldon, Boulsworth Hill and Stoodley Pike.

In fact Blackstone Edge, more than any other hill on the Pennine Way, seems to have excited the imaginations of past travellers. Celia Fiennes crossed it in 1698 and wrote: 'Then I Came to Blackstone Edge noted all over England for a dismal high precipice... very troublesome as its a moist ground soe as is usual on these high hills; they stagnate the aire and hold mist and raines almost perpetually... This hill took me up Much tyme to gaine the top and alsoe to descend it and put me in mind of the Description of ye Alpes in Italy.'

Daniel Defoe crossed Blackstone Edge in 1724, in a blizzard in August! He wrote: 'the narrowness of the way, look'd horrible to us... we knew nothing where we were, or whether we were right or wrong... the main hill which we came down from... is properly called Blackstone Edge, or, by the country people, the Edge...' Elsewhere in the same letter he described it as 'the Andes of England'.

The path descends at a slight gradient, but is rugged and stony, winding between boulders. It rises a little and goes through a gate to reach the medieval moorland marker of the Aiggin Stone. Turn left and walk down an old grooved track on the moorland slope. This becomes a splendid stone-paved track, often referred to as a 'Roman road'. The small town of Littleborough is seen far below.

While it is likely that the Romans crossed the Pennines near Blackstone Edge, it is certain that they were not responsible for the fine stone paving on the route. The splendid **causeway**, with its two cobbled lanes and central gutter, was probably constructed after the passing of the first Blackstone Edge Turnpike Act of 1734. A second act authorised the construction of another road further north in 1765. A later variation in 1795 is now the route followed by the modern A58 road.

Go through a gate and turn right along a prominent concrete-walled reservoir drain, the Broad Head Drain, following a level path beside it. ▸ Later, before reaching a house, a path drops down from the drain to go through a gate and join the **A58** road. Turn right to walk up to **The**

This is reminiscent of the 'levadas' that carry water around Madeira.

A trig point on the sprawling moorland summit of White Hill

White House, a pub at around 370m (1215ft), which offers food and drink. Regular daily bus services along the road link Rochdale, Littleborough, Ripponden and Halifax.

Pass the pub and turn left through a gate to follow a track across the grassy dam of Blackstone Edge Reservoir. Go through a gate at the end of the dam and continue along a broad, firm track beside a boggy ditch, the Head Drain. This is all easy, level walking, but some Pennine wayfarers manage to get blisters while hurrying along the hard gravel surfaces. The track features broad curves, passing a gritstone outcrop beside a small quarry, where lines of verse have been carved. Keep straight ahead at track junctions to pass beneath a prominent pylon line on Chelburn Moor. The track runs along the dam of Light Hazzles Reservoir.

> **Light Hazzles Reservoir** is a rather forlorn, narrow and shallow reservoir that never holds enough water to reach its own draw-off tower, which is marooned on dry land. Further along, note how the dam was lowered.

The track continues along the dam of **Warland Reservoir**. Around the middle of this long dam a draw-off tower is passed. At the end of the dam, the track follows the prominent stone-built Warland Drain, turning right at a settling tank. The track gives way to a path as the drain is followed upstream across Langfield Common. When the drain turns sharp right, turn left instead, as signposted for the Pennine Way.

The **reservoirs** of Blackstone Edge, Chelburn, Light Hazzles and Warland were constructed to feed the Rochdale Canal far below. In *A Treatise on Canals and Reservoirs*, published in 1816, John Sutcliffe wrote: 'The reservoirs will be filled twice in the year, and will give 8,871,720 tons of water in that period. If 8,871,720 be divided by 84,000, the amount of supposed tonnage, the product will be nearly 106 tons of water for every ton of goods supposed to be navigated on the line in one year.'

A flagstone path leads across grassy, rushy moorland with areas of bog cotton. Pass a couple of prominent old boundary stones and follow a firm trodden path past gritstone boulders. Looking down to the right, **Withens Clough Reservoir** can be seen. When a dip in the moorland edge is reached, there are views along Calderdale, with Pendle Hill seen beyond. The little mill town of **Todmorden** is also visible, with the village of **Mankinholes** closer to hand, while Stoodley Pike lies ahead. Follow the well-trodden path across the dip and up to a well-marked junction with an old paved 'causey'.

Many walkers used to detour here to the little village of **Mankinholes**, easily reached by walking down this old paved 'causey', linking with the course of the Pennine Bridleway. It is just 1km (0.5 mile) off-route, with a descent of 150m (490ft). However, that was when a youth hostel was available, which was put up for sale in 2023. The Top Brink Inn offers food and drink down near the village of Lumbutts, while a B&B is available on Lee Bottom Road.

Rocky Standedge overlooks the two Castleshaw Reservoirs

Continue straight ahead along the Pennine Way with the path climbing past a prominent upright stone, then rising more gently and winding along a boulder-strewn edge. It is dry and firm underfoot and runs almost level as it reaches **Stoodley Pike**.

> The rather grim monument of **Stoodley Pike**, splattered with graffiti, was built following the exile of Napoleon to Elba in 1814. When he escaped, building work ceased. After the Battle of Waterloo in 1815 work recommenced and the monument was completed. In 1855 the whole thing collapsed; it was rebuilt in 1856. Spiral steps climb to a parapet for wide-ranging views. The monument is a landmark throughout this part of the South Pennines.

Follow a stone-paved path onwards down a grassy slope, away from the monument, to reach a junction of drystone walls. Continue straight ahead a short way, then turn left as signposted over a stone step-stile. A firm path leads across and down a grassy, rushy moorland slope, reaching a track carrying the Pennine Bridleway. Cross over the track to follow the Pennine Way alongside a wall. Go through a stone gateway and follow the wall until it turns right. Cross a stile on the right and head diagonally across a rushy field. Go through a gate at the corner of a wall, then follow the wall straight to a farm at Lower Rough Head.

The farm stands on a corner of a track which runs gently downhill, flanked by walls, passing big fields. Go through a gate and walk down through a wood. This is predominantly oak and birch, but contains other trees. Keep to the main track as it heads downhill.

Alternative finish at Hebden Bridge

Using the 'Loop' adds an extra 2km (1.25 miles) to the Pennine Way: 0.5km (0.25 mile) onto this stage and 1.5km (1 mile) onto Day 4.

▸ Along this main track a right turn is marked for the Hebden Bridge Loop. The path runs down into a wooded valley and swings left to cross a stone-arched bridge over a stream. Go up through a gate and keep left as signposted. The path later goes through another gate and runs alongside the wood, eventually reaching

Hebden Bridge

a wonderful stone-sett road at Horsehold. Turn left and walk down the road, which later gives way to tarmac. Continue and turn left to cross the Rochdale Canal. Turn right to follow the towpath, passing the Hebble End Coffee Lounge. When a canal bridge is reached, turn sharp left to leave the canal and join Holme Street. This runs past a post office to reach the busy **A646** road in the middle of **Hebden Bridge**. Use a pedestrian crossing to reach the pedestrianised Bridge Gate.

HEBDEN BRIDGE

Hebden Bridge was voted by British Airways to be the 'fourth funkiest town on the planet', as well as being the first 'Walkers are Welcome' town. The centre was flooded on Boxing Day 2015, but has recovered. Facilities include banks with ATMs, two post offices, shops, pubs, cafés and restaurants. Accommodation includes B&Bs and an independent hostel. Regular daily buses run to Halifax, Todmorden and Burnley. There are daily buses to Blackshaw Head, with summer weekend buses to Widdop, further along the Pennine Way. Regular daily trains run to Halifax, York, Burnley and Preston. See https://hbwalkersaction.org.uk/pennine-way-loop.

Main route to Callis Bridge

Continue down the track and turn right when a house comes into view. A path short-cuts a bend on a slope of birch. The track continues down into the valley, crossing the Rochdale Canal and River Calder in tandem with the Pennine Bridleway to reach the busy **A646** road at **Callis Bridge**.

Callis Bridge has nothing to offer but regular daily buses to and from Hebden Bridge and Todmorden, linking with Halifax and Burnley. Some walkers continue along the Pennine Way, as described in Day 4, to reach a B&B or campsite above Calderdale. Alternatively, a detour into Hebden Bridge could be made along the Rochdale Canal towpath for 1.5km (1 mile). Attractive houseboats, bridges, locks and the Hebble End Coffee Lounge are passed on the way to the town centre.

DAY 4

Callis Bridge or Hebden Bridge to Ickornshaw

Start	Callis Bridge, SD 971 264
Alternative start	Hebden Bridge, SD 991 272
Finish	A6068, Ickornshaw, Cowling, SD 965 428
Distance	25.5km (16 miles); from Hebden Bridge 27km (17 miles)
Total ascent	930m (3050ft)
Total descent	830m (2725ft)
Time	8hr; 8hr 30min
Terrain	Fiddly paths and tracks need to be linked to climb towards the moors. There are several ascents and descents during the day. Most moorland paths are firm and most boggy stretches have been surfaced with flagstones.
Maps	OS Landranger 103, OS Explorer OL21, Harvey's Pennine Way South
Refreshments	Pubs or cafés off-route at Jack Bridge, Colden, Pack Horse Inn, Ponden and Cowling.

Throughout the climb from Calderdale, maps and route descriptions need to be read carefully, while watching for signposts and waymarks. The area has an incredibly dense network of rights of way, and it is easy to be drawn off course. The Pennine Way and Pennine Bridleway join and part company, so even the National Trail 'acorn' markers could cause confusion. During the day, there are virtually no facilities actually on the Pennine Way, but there are a few pubs, cafés and a shop lying very close to the route. The higher moors are quite easily crossed and the fringes of 'Brontë Country' are visited. Some walkers break this day's walk at Ponden, or head off-route to Haworth, either on foot or by bus.

Alternative route from Hebden Bridge

Leave Bridge Gate in the centre of **Hebden Bridge** to cross a stout stone packhorse bridge that dates from

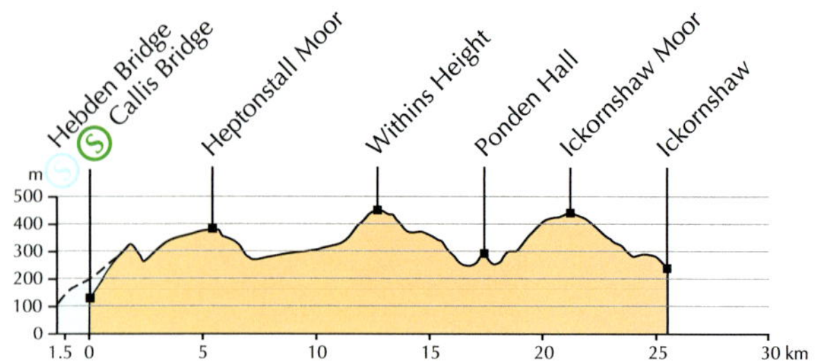

The town was named after this bridge.

1510. ◂ Turn left to follow Old Gate back to the busy **A646** road, or Market Street. Turn right and follow the road past the Co-op, then keep a look out on the right

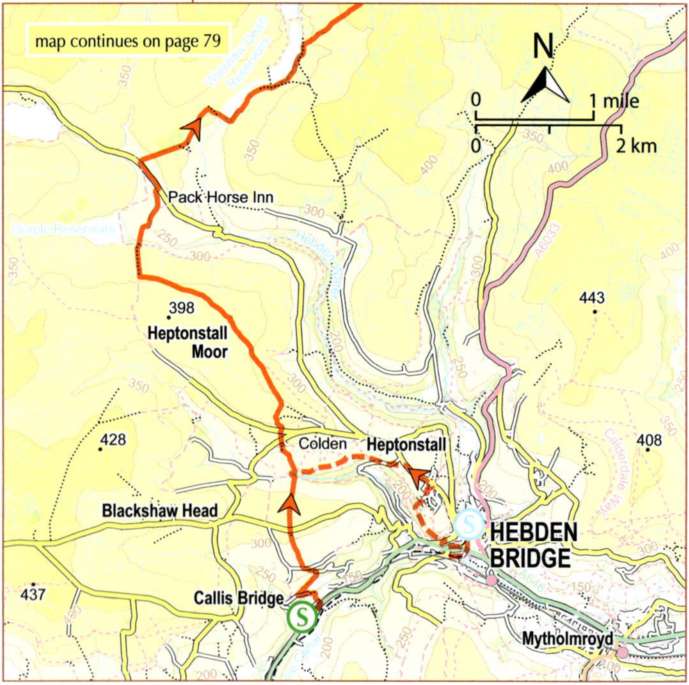

map continues on page 79

for Stoney Lane, which is no more than a gap between houses. Climb the cobbled lane and a steep flight of 95 stone steps and eventually join a road at Lee Royd. Turn right up the road then turn left up a signposted footpath.

The path rises across a wooded slope and the trees give way to heather and bracken for a while, with good views through Calderdale. Pass a striking outcrop of rock that has been left standing at an old quarry, and follow the path up 60 stone steps as marked. A level path runs straight into the village of **Heptonstall**, crossing a couple of roads and heading straight towards the parish church. Keep to the right of the church, following a back street until a junction is reached at Towngate with a stone-sett road.

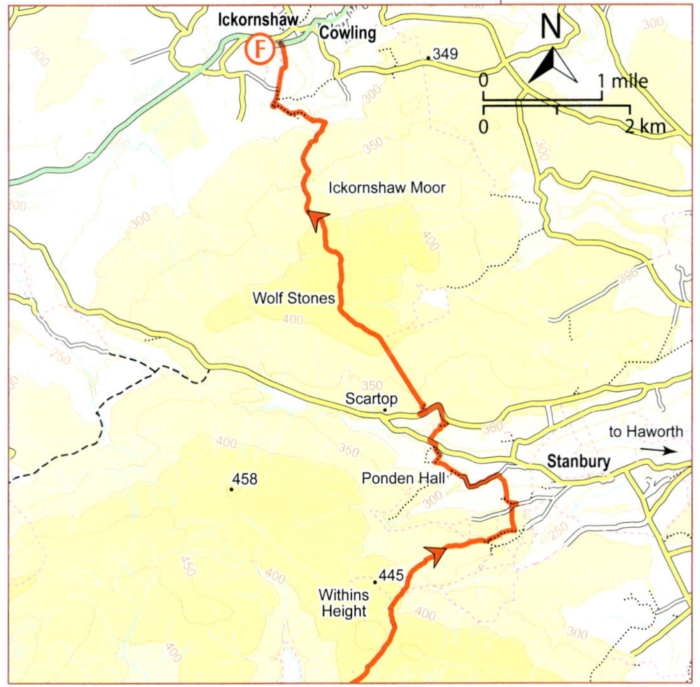

> The splendid little village of **Heptonstall** is well worth exploring. The ruins of the old church of St Thomas à Becket share the same crowded churchyard as the parish church of St Thomas the Apostle. An interesting museum can be visited nearby (tel 01422 843738). Facilities include a tearoom, post office shop and two pubs. Daily bus services link the village with Hebden Bridge and Blackshaw Head.

Follow the stone-sett road up past two pubs towards the top end of the village, admiring old stone houses with mullioned windows along the way. A tarmac road continues rising from the village school, then after leaving the village watch for a footpath signpost on the left, indicating a narrow flagstone path running down through a field. Continue alongside another field to reach a road.

Turn left down the road, then keep right to follow another path to a junction. Keep straight ahead across a stone stile and follow a flagstone path towards a house and a road below the hamlet of Slack. Walk straight along the road, then turn left as signposted down a path. Keep right at a junction and follow another flagstone path through gates and fields. A gap stile is followed by a stone stile as the path enters a wooded valley drained by Colden Water. The path is roughly stone-paved and soon reaches a junction with the main route of the Pennine Way. Turn right up stone steps to follow it.

Main route from Callis Bridge

Use the pedestrian/equestrian crossing on the busy **A646** road at **Callis Bridge**. The Pennine Bridleway turns left and the Pennine Way turns right. Both trails run roughly parallel for half a day until they meet again. The Pennine Way quickly leaves the main road by turning left up Underbank Avenue, going under the stone arch of a railway bridge to reach Lacy Houses.

Climb straight up a steep, cobbled path flanked by walls and, in summer, foxgloves. Swing left to join a track past a few houses, and a narrow road runs up to

Old roadside pump at Heptonstall

a ruined chapel and its overgrown graveyard. Turn right here, where a sign offers a choice of 'Official Route' or 'Wainwright Route', which are at odds with each other for a while. The 'Wainwright Route' quickly links with the Pennine Bridleway. The official route crosses a stile beside a gate and follows a well-vegetated path on a rising traverse across a slope. ▸ A steeper climb features stone steps, passing a curious little building spanning a rusty-coloured stream. Climb past this, and a house, to reach a track.

There are good views of Calderdale, with Stoodley Pike beyond.

Turn left up the track, which becomes a narrow road rising gently past a house at Long Hey. Turn right as signposted through a gap in a wall, following a path straight up through fields. Keep right of one farm and left of another, walking up a track to a road near **Blackshaw Head**. ▸ Cross the road and climb through a field to the left of Badger Fields Farm.

B&B off-route.

Walk down through fields. The path becomes rather awkward underfoot where it is constricted between narrow stone walls. ▸ Continue further down the narrow path and cross another track. Sixty-five uneven stone steps lead down to Colden Water. Cross the river using

A track on the left can be used to reach the New Delight Inn and a campsite at Jack Bridge.

The Hebden Bridge Loop rejoins here.

a stout 'clapper' bridge made of four long stone blocks. Climb 105 stone steps, first at a gentle gradient, then more steeply after a left turn at a junction. ◂

Continue up through fields towards houses at **Colden**, but turn left as marked towards another house. Follow its cobbled access road up to a road close to a bus shelter. Buses run daily to and from Hebden Bridge. Cross the road and walk up a path to reach another road.

There is a view back to Stoodley Pike, as well as a sign inviting a **detour** to the left. The road leads to May's remarkable farm shop at High Gate, claiming to offer 'owt tha wants'. It is well supported locally, but also offers food, drink and a basic camping pitch to wayfarers.

Pick up the Pennine Way across the road and climb a narrow path in a deep groove, reaching a little gate. Swing left up through fields and go through another little gate onto heather moorland. Follow a wall over a crest until level with a farm. Turn left as signposted, walking gradually down a path across the moor. When a wall is reached, don't cross it, but start climbing gently over a broad crest of grass and heather on **Heptonstall Moor**, around 370m (1215ft).

A boggy patch on the moor may feature bog cotton. The path is generally firm, but soft areas have been paved with flagstones. The whitewashed **Pack Horse Inn** appears suddenly in view, followed by Gorple Lower Reservoir and its keeper's house. Follow the path gently downhill and walk beside a tumbled wall and fence across a grassy, rushy moor to reach a track and signpost.

The Pennine Bridleway rejoins the Pennine Way at this point. Turn right down through a gate and follow the track down to a stout iron gate leading onto a reservoir access track near the keeper's house. The Pennine Bridleway turns left here, towards Hurstwood. The Pennine Way runs straight ahead, down an old flagstone 'causey' on a grassy, rushy slope to reach a confluence of streams at Graining Water.

Cross both streams using footbridges and admire the bracken-clad valleys with their gritstone edges. Follow the Pennine Way upstream, up another flagstone 'causey'. ▸ Stay on the path through fields and later turn right up to a walled path and a road.

A stile on the right can be used to reach the Pack Horse Inn for food and drink if desired.

Turn left along the road to pass Well Hole Cottage, walking down to a small car park where the Pennine Bridleway joins from the left. Walk a little further along the road to find the Pennine Way signposted up to the right. Quickly join a narrow road and turn right to follow it uphill. Pass a small forestry plantation and continue down to a junction. Keep left to follow the road uphill again, passing large rushy fields. As the road levels out, a Pennine Way signpost points down to the right.

Go through a gap in a stout stone wall and cross the dam of **Walshaw Dean Lower Reservoir**. Turn left, following a firm gravel path and a flagstone path along the grassy, rushy moorland between the shore and a tall

A flagstone path climbs above the Walshaw Dean reservoirs

Note the big house at the head of the reservoir, originally built for the reservoir keeper, extended in recent years.

stone wall. ◂ Pass the dam of Walshaw Dean Middle Reservoir and pick up a path crossing a metal footbridge.

Follow an embankment between the reservoir and a stone-built drain. Rhododendron bushes have been cut back from the path and reservoir shore. When a stone bridge spans the drain, turn left up a track and cross a stile beside a gate onto open moorland. Turn left after crossing the stile, then quickly turn right as signposted for the Pennine Way, walking up a slope of grass, heather and rushes. The path is mostly firm, but some softer parts are paved with flagstones. Follow the flagstone path over the higher parts of **Withins Height**, around 450m (1475ft). The moor is predominantly grassy and the path runs down beside tumbled drystone walls to the ruined farmstead of Top Withins.

TOP WITHINS

Top Withins has long been associated with Emily Brontë's only novel, *Wuthering Heights*. Despite a disclaimer to the contrary, carved in stone and fixed to the wall of the farm by the Brontë Society, literary-minded romantics and tourists continue to trek up from Haworth, following signposts in English and Japanese (*Arashi Ga Oka*). The ruins have been consolidated and a simple one-roomed shelter has been built alongside.

It is possible to leave the Pennine Way and follow a popular, well-trodden, signposted path from Top Withins to Haworth, home to the Brontë Parsonage Museum (entry charge, open throughout the year, tel 01535 642323, www.bronte.org.uk). The village is quaint and attractive and its cobbled main street runs down to the Worth Valley Railway, beloved of steam train buffs (runs daily throughout the summer, limited winter timetable, tel 01535 645214, kwvr.co.uk). A full range of facilities are available in the village.

Leave Top Withins by following a well-worn path and a flagstone path to a signposted junction beside a tumbled ruin. Turning right downhill leads to Haworth, while the Pennine Way keeps straight ahead along a flagstone path. In fact, there are twin lines of flagstones across the moor, allowing access for farm vehicles. Follow these down a rushy slope to cross a stream, then climb past a tree. The track undulates as it traverses moorland criss-crossed by stone walls. Cross a heathery crest and follow the track past Upper Heights Farm to reach a signposted junction. ▸

Turning right here offers another chance to visit Haworth.

The Pennine Way turns left to pass another house at Lower Heights. Watch for a gate and a kissing gate on the left, signposted for the Pennine Way. The path runs along a broad, grassy swathe flanked by walls, then drops down a moorland slope to reach a track. Turn right to pass houses at Buckley and turn sharp left down another track, almost to a house. Turn right before reaching the house, through a gate down to a path that swings left to reach a road at the dam of Ponden Reservoir. ▸

Walking off-route here leads to a campsite and B&B at Ponden Mill, the Old Silent Inn and the Wuthering Heights pub at Stanbury, and there are daily buses to Haworth and Keighley.

Turn left to follow the road alongside the reservoir, climbing steeply to reach **Ponden Hall**. The hall provided the inspiration for Thrushcross Grange in Emily Brontë's novel Wuthering Heights. Climb along a track, then head down a tarmac road towards a house. Before reaching it, veer left along a grassy path, and later turn right towards the head of Ponden Reservoir to cross a stone-arched bridge.

Thrushcross Grange at Ponden is associated with 'Wuthering Heights'

Turn left along a road, then right over a stone step-stile. Climb straight uphill through fields, watching for marker posts and another step-stile. Climb between farm buildings then walk up their access track. Watch for the Pennine Way signposted left, along a grassy path. Follow it through a couple of gates to reach a road. Turn left to cross a stream at Dean Clough and follow the road past a little terrace of houses to reach Crag Nook Farm.

Turn sharp right at Crag Nook Farm to follow a winding, grassy, stony track uphill. A gate on the left gives access to a gentle, grassy, rushy moorland slope where a path climbs straight ahead alongside a wall. One stretch has a wall on both sides, then a wooden step-stile is crossed. The wall eventually ends abruptly on Bare Hill, but the path continues across a gently rolling moor of grass, bilberry and heather.

A trig point and a small gritstone edge are seen ahead at **Wolf Stones**, but these are not on the route. Pendle Hill and Boulsworth Hill are in view to the left, while the path begins to swing to the right. Cross a heather moor, following a flagstone path over a crest at 438m (1437ft), where wooden posts have been driven into the ground. Descend gently on the other side, passing a stone shelter before the flagstone path finishes. The path is rough and stony for a while, with views of Pendle Hill, the southern Yorkshire Dales and a couple of curious monuments perched above Cowling. Another length of flagstones leads to a stone cottage in a dip on the slopes of **Ickornshaw Moor**. Climb to pass behind the cottage and walk down past four black huts, following a wall on a slope of bilberry and crowberry.

Swing right at the bottom to follow the wall past another hut, then yet another hut is hidden behind a few trees. After passing one final hut, the path drops and goes through a gate. Turn left and follow a path between two farmhouses, then cross a footbridge over a stream. Climb across a slope and go through a gate, then walk up a grassy track. Keep right to pass near a farmhouse at Lumb and turn right above a small waterfall.

Follow the track up through a gate, then, when it turns left, keep straight ahead instead, passing a modern barn. A grassy swathe is flanked by walls and this leads down to a farm. Keep right of the farm buildings and another modern barn, passing through little gates. Walk straight down through a field to reach a gate onto the **A6068** road at **Ickornshaw**. The Pennine Way crosses the road and turns left. Anyone wishing to find food and drink should turn right and follow the road into nearby **Cowling**.

Facilities are limited between **Ickornshaw** and **Cowling**. The main road passes Winterhouse Barn, with its basic campsite and summer house. As the road continues through Cowling it passes the Hop and Vine Micro Pub, Village Local shop, Sam's Pizzas, Bay Horse pub and the Cowling Chippy. Regular daily buses link with Keighley, Colne, Nelson and Burnley, which are useful for walkers looking for hotels or B&Bs off-route.

Stone huts and wooden cabins are passed on the way to Ickornshaw

DAY 5

Ickornshaw to Gargrave

Start	A6068, Ickornshaw, Cowling, SD 965 428
Finish	Dalesman Café, Gargrave, SD 931 541
Distance	18km (11 miles)
Total ascent	545m (1790ft)
Total descent	650m (2135ft)
Time	5hr 30min
Terrain	Mostly low-lying, but hilly fields are threaded by paths and tracks, with one area of heather moorland. Careful attention to route-finding is required.
Maps	OS Landranger 103, OS Explorer OL2 and OL21, Harvey's Pennine Way South
Refreshments	Pub at Lothersdale. Pub and café at East Marton. Pubs and cafés at Gargrave.

There is a distinct broad gap between the end of the South Pennines and the start of the Yorkshire Dales National Park. Generally referred to as the Aire Gap, this low-lying tract is anything but flat. In fact, it is a roller-coaster of low, grassy drumlin hills, criss-crossed by walls, fences and hedgerows. Careful navigation is required on the way through fields where there may be little evidence of a path. There is a stretch of high moorland on Pinhaw Beacon, which is a fine place to look backwards and forwards along the Pennine Way. Strong walkers could reach Gargrave reasonably early and have enough time to be able to continue to Malham.

Starting where the Pennine Way crosses the busy **A6068** road at **Ickornshaw**, walk towards a furniture showroom called Dovetail, which was formerly the Black Bull pub. Before reaching the building, turn right down a path and steps onto a lower minor road. Turn right along the road, passing terraced cottages, then turn left up a road and follow it until the tarmac ends. A Pennine Way signpost points along a field path that passes the end of a row of houses at Middleton. Shortly afterwards, turn right towards a small huddle of buildings and follow an access track to a minor road.

Turn left along the road to reach houses at **Gill**, and turn right down a narrow road to cross a bridge. Turn left along an access road, heading upstream towards a house. Before reaching it, turn right to see the Pennine Way sign-posted up through fields. While climbing uphill, look ahead to spot little stiles and gates in the walls. Watch for a quick left and right turn before climbing straight towards a restored 'longhouse' in the middle of the fields. Keep to the left of the building and climb through a couple more large fields to reach a road on **Cowling Hill**, around 310m (1015ft).

Turn right down the road, then quickly left down another road. This swings left further downhill, but when it later swings right, leave it by crossing a stone step-stile. Walk down through a field, veering right to avoid a steep slope. Go through a gate and continue down to Surgill Beck. Go through a gate and climb beside a line of trees that mark the course of an old hedgerow. Walk past Woodhead Farm and continue up its access road.

Lothersdale is a pleasant little mill village with a pub

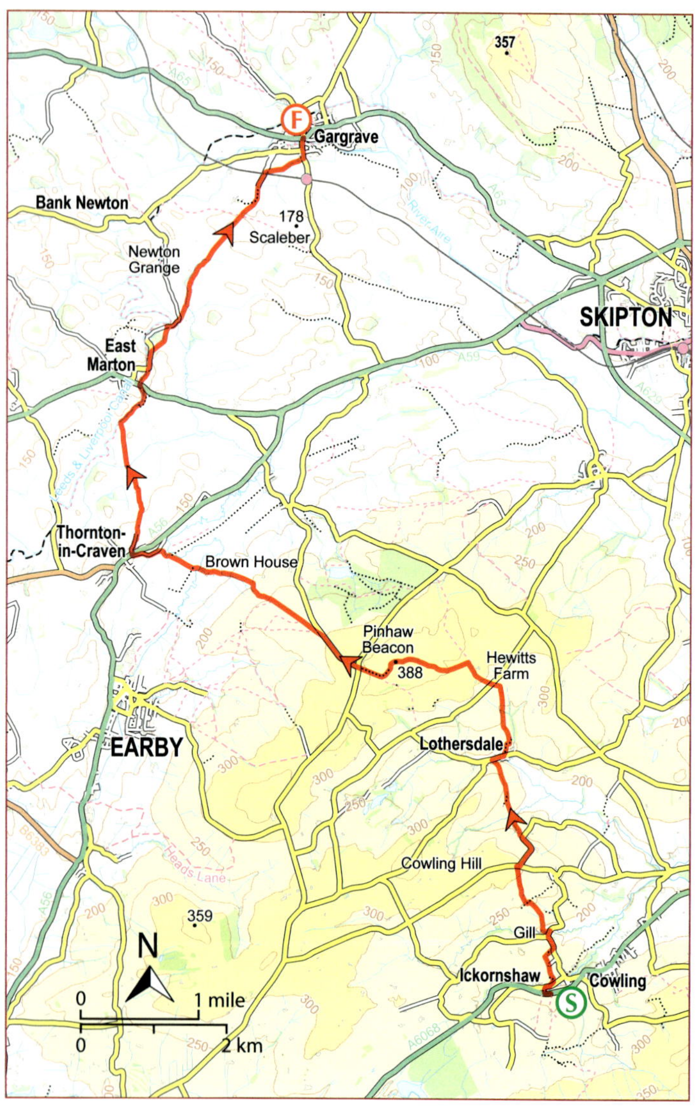
Gargrave
Bank Newton
178
Scaleber
Newton
Grange
SKIPTON
East
Marton
Thornton-
in-Craven
Brown House
Pinhaw
Beacon
388
Hewitts
Farm
EARBY
Lothersdale
Cowling Hill
359
Gill
Ickornshaw
Cowling
357
N
0
1 mile
0
2 km
River Aire
Leeds & Liverpool Canal
Heads Lane
A65
A59
A56
A629
A6068
B6383

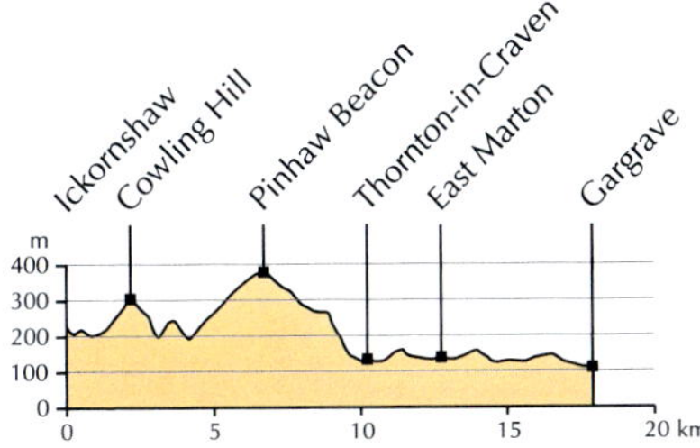

When the road begins to head downhill, veer right as signposted to leave it. A path runs down beside a wall, with a charming view of houses and an old mill nestling in a fold in the hills. Go through a little gate and down a flight of steps to reach a road in **Lothersdale**, and turn right to walk past a pub.

> The charming little village of **Lothersdale** is seen only briefly in passing. Facilities are limited to the Hare and Hounds pub, which offers food and drink. Hidden from view inside Dale End Mill is the largest waterwheel in England, although it is currently in a poor state of repair. It dates from 1861 and has a diameter of 13.5m (44ft). Hopefully it can be saved.

After passing the pub, turn left up a track and follow it up through a gate. Turn left to climb gently beside a field, then head down into a dip to pass into another field. Climb gently beside the field, turning left at the top to head for a minor road. Cross the road and follow a concrete track gently uphill. When this turns left for **Hewitts Farm**, keep straight ahead through a gate and walk uphill beside a field. Cross a stone step-stile onto heather moorland, following a wall uphill and turning left. When the wall and a paved path ends, a firm path climbs open heathery slopes, passing areas of grass, bilberry and bog cotton. A trig point and a view indicator stand on a grassy hump at 388m (1273ft) on **Pinhaw Beacon**. ▸

In clear weather this is a fine viewpoint, looking back to the bleak South Pennines and ahead to the verdant Yorkshire Dales, with Pendle Hill rising prominently between both areas.

Two paths appear to leave the summit: the one to the right is the Pennine Way; however, both join together again later. The path broadens and becomes a fine track as it follows a wall down to a gate and a road junction. Keep straight ahead and follow Clogger Lane down Elslack Moor. There is a wall on the left, and when this veers left away from the road, follow it to continue through a gate.

Ahead is a broad moorland where two paths diverge. One path heads left across a grassy moor, and can be used to reach the village of Earby and its hostel. The other path runs through rushes beside a wall, and this is the Pennine Way. The path is stone-paved as it crosses boggy areas. Walk down beside another field, then wooden steps and duckboards continue down a slope of soft ground. Cross a narrow footbridge within sight of Wood House and head down through a field, swinging right to reach a far corner to go through a gate.

Walk down through a long field, keeping to the left, where the route follows a groove. At the bottom, turn left through a kissing gate and cross another field, walking towards farm buildings. This stretch can be very muddy when wet. Go through the farmyard at **Brown House** as signposted, leaving along its access road. The road rises and falls, passes the stone abutment of a long-gone railway bridge and then turns left to pass beneath a stone arch. Tall trees line the road as it climbs into the village of **Thornton-in-Craven**. Before the road reaches the busy **A56** road, a path on the right climbs up a grassy bank, so that the main road can be crossed to reach Cam Lane. Use a nearby pedestrian crossing if the road is particularly busy. ◂

There are no facilities beyond a café and campsite off-route at Thornton Hall Country Park, and buses to Skipton, Earby, Burnley, Clitheroe and Preston.

Walk up the lane to leave the village, then downhill, then uphill to reach farm buildings. ◂ Just after these, turn right and climb diagonally across a field. Walk down through gates and cross a single-stone 'clam' bridge over a little stream near a house at Langber. Walk up through a field and cross a step-stile at the top. Walk downhill, through a gate, and beware of a wet and muddy patch on the way up to another gate. Turn right to follow the level towpath of the **Leeds and Liverpool Canal**.

DIY snacks in the little Tuck Shop shed.

A double-arched canal bridge at East Marton

Go under bridge number 160 and pass moorings. Go under the curious double-arched bridge number 161, which carries the busy A59 road over the canal. A milepost near the bridge states 'Leeds 38¼ miles Liverpool 89 miles'. Pass moorings, but don't go under bridge 162, or Williamson Bridge. The Pennine Way turns right, away from this bridge, although anyone crossing over it can visit the village of **East Marton**.

> **East Marton** is a charming little village, despite having the busy A59 road running through it. The area near the canal is quiet, and the Abbot's Harbour restaurant is available. Regular daily buses link East Marton with Skipton, Clitheroe and Preston.

Leaving bridge number 162, the Pennine Way runs gently up and down a road, with garlic-scented ramsons growing in woods to the left. Watch for a gate and signpost on the right, where the route is indicated heading left, diagonally across a field. Watch carefully as the route nips in and out of a patch of woodland, then cross another field to reach a broad track. Turn right to follow the track, passing the access road for Trenet Laithe. Just after the access road, cross a stile on the right and turn left as signposted for the Pennine Way. Walk over a rise and downhill to cross a footbridge, then turn left to walk straight through gently rolling fields, looking ahead and lining up stiles and gates. Cross a track near **Newton Grange** and keep straight ahead.

The rolling drumlin hills are criss-crossed by fences, while occasional lines of tall trees mark the courses of old hedgerows. A gradual climb onto a hill near **Scaleber** reveals a sudden view of Gargrave ahead, with Cracoe Fell beyond. Head towards the village, following a track only a short way then linking with another track. This heads downhill, then climbs over a railway bridge spanning a deep cutting. As the track heads downhill again, watch for a gate on the right and pick up a field path to the village of **Gargrave**. Turn left to follow a road past the church and cross the River Aire.

GARGRAVE

This is a large village with a fine range of services. It stands near the site of a Roman fort, and the church contains fragments of 9th and 10th-century Anglo-Danish crosses. A couple of pubs offer lodgings and there are also a couple more B&Bs, as well as a nearby campsite. The famous Dalesman Café has a sign outside reading 'Edale 70 miles Kirk Yetholm 186 miles', but your own distance count may differ. There is also a restaurant and a fish and chip shop, a post office and a few shops, and the Co-op has a cashpoint. There are trains to Lancaster, Leeds, Skipton, Horton-in-Ribblesdale and Carlisle, as well as buses to Skipton, Settle and Malham.

LEEDS AND LIVERPOOL CANAL

The canal measures 127.25 miles (204.75km), with 93 locks and two tunnels carrying it through the Pennines via the low-lying Aire Gap. The Canal Act was passed in 1770, but construction took 46 years and it cost five times the original estimate.

DAY 6

Gargrave to Malham

Start	Dalesman Café, Gargrave, SD 931 541
Finish	The Green, Malham, SD 901 628
Distance	10.5km (6.5 miles)
Total ascent	180m (590ft)
Total descent	120m (395ft)
Time	3hr
Terrain	Gently rolling grassy hills and easy riverside walks, but keep an eye on the map and look out for signposts and waymarks.
Maps	OS Landranger 98 and 103, OS Explorer OL2, Harvey's Pennine Way South
Refreshments	Café off-route at Airton. Pub off-route at Kirkby Malham. Plenty of choice at Malham.

This is a simple and easy half-day walk. Anyone with limited long-distance walking experience might prefer an easy half-day at this stage, after walking for several days over rather bleak and exposed moorlands. There is very little climbing on this stage, just a couple of low, grassy hills and gentle riverside walks. The whole distance could be added to the previous day's walk, but that would leave little time to explore the countryside around Malham. With the afternoon free, a detour can be made from the Pennine Way to follow the signposted Malham Landscape Trail. This visits the awesome gorge of Gordale Scar and the cliff face of Malham Cove. The circuit measures 7km (4.5 miles).

Start at the Dalesman Café in **Gargrave** and walk beside it along West Street. Pass the Village Hall and keep straight ahead to cross bridge number 170 on the Leeds and Liverpool Canal at Higherland Lock. The road is signposted from the canal as the Pennine Way to Malham, but the 5¼-mile distance quoted is too short. The signpost also states 'Leeds 33¾ Liverpool 93½'. Walk straight

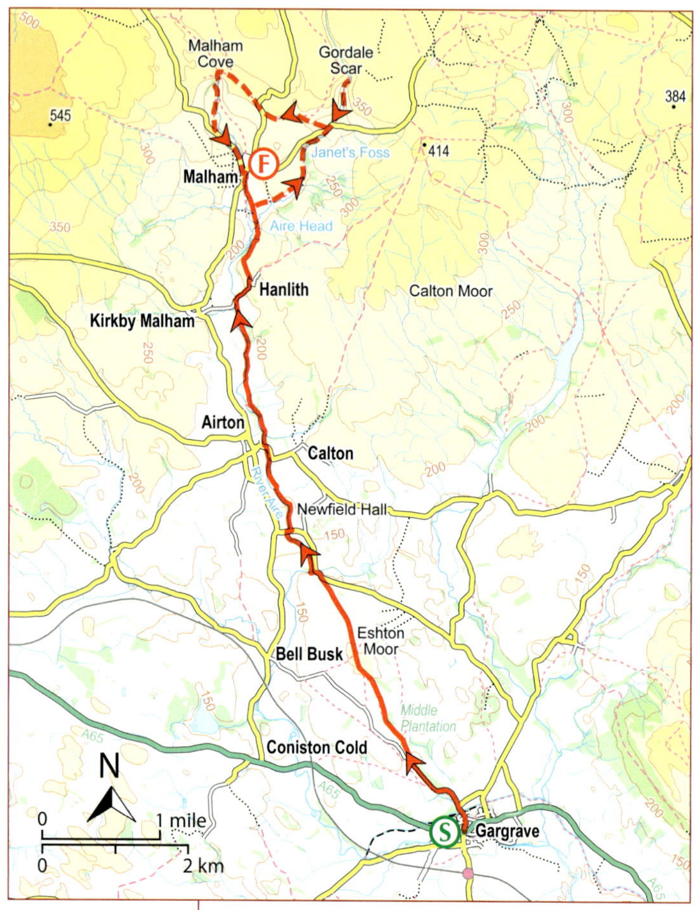

ahead at a junction, along Mark House Lane, passing Gargrave House and its Home Farm, surrounded by a tall stone wall.

As the road runs gently uphill watch for a signpost and stone step-stile on the right. Enter a field and turn left to stay low. Do not go into a field ahead containing a barn,

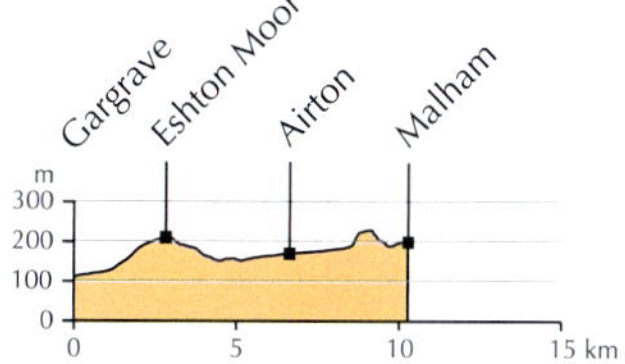

but go into the one to the right of it. Follow a fence, then turn left and climb through another field. Pass the corner of a small wood, **Middle Plantation**, at a higher level. Turn right and walk towards a gateway in a drystone wall, but don't go through it. Instead, keep left to find a kissing gate further along the wall and go through it.

Cross the next two fields diagonally, then bear left to follow a drystone wall to a place where four fields meet. Go through a gate at this point and head diagonally through another field, now walking inside the Yorkshire Dales National Park. From a grassy crest over 200m (655ft), views stretch ahead through Airedale. Walk downhill and eventually go through a gate. Walk down through another field and pass a signpost on **Eshton Moor**. Don't step onto the road below, but keep left of it to walk downstream a little beside the **River Aire**, then cross a footbridge.

Walk upstream beside the river until the stone-arched Newfield Bridge is reached. Nearby **Newfield Hall**, built in 1865, is a country house used by HF Holidays. Cross the bridge and turn left to continue upstream. Another stone-arched bridge is reached, but only cross this if heading a short way off-route into the village of **Airton**.

Airton is seen from the bridge spanning the River Aire. Large mill buildings have been converted into apartments. The Linden Guest House is available and the Friends Meeting House, which dates from the 1650s, offers bunkhouse accommodation and limited camping spaces. Town Head Farm, on the

A rare peaceful moment in the often busy little village of Malham

road towards Malham, has a farm shop, post office and tearoom. Daily buses link Airton with Malham, Gargrave and Skipton.

Cross the road and continue further upstream. The path moves away from the River Aire for a while, and a Pennine Way signpost later confirms the move. When the path runs beside the river again, the scenery near **Hanlith** becomes reminiscent of fine parkland, with tall trees dotted around cattle-grazed pastures. Yet another stone-arched bridge is reached. This can be crossed to reach a pub with lodgings just off-route at **Kirkby Malham**, but the Pennine Way turns right to climb a steep road, passing Hanlith Hall and other former estate buildings.

The road bends left, then just as it bends sharp right, step up through a small gate on the left, then cross a field to go through a larger gate. As a path begins to drift downhill, there are brief glimpses of Malham, Malham Cove and Gordale Scar ahead. The path drops through fields to return to the riverside near **Aire Head**. A grassy path climbs gently up to a signposted junction with two hard-surfaced gravel paths. Keep straight ahead to reach the village of **Malham**. Alternatively, consider turning right, off-route along the other path, to visit **Janet's Foss** and Gordale Scar, which are highly recommended.

MALHAM

As far as possible try to avoid Malham at busy weekends and holidays. The village has a fine range of facilities but they come under considerable pressure. Accommodation includes hotels, B&Bs, a youth hostel, bunkhouse and campsites. There are a couple of pubs, cafés and a shop. The National Park Visitor Centre, just outside the village, is well worth a visit. (Open daily through the summer, weekends in winter, but closed in January, tel 01729 833200.) Daily buses link Malham, Gargrave and Skipton, while summer weekend buses continue onwards to Malham Tarn and Settle.

Detour along the Malham Landscape Trail

The easiest way to visit to Gordale Scar is to make the detour shortly before reaching Malham, from **Aire Head**, following signposts for the Malham Landscape Trail. Alternatively, go into the village and leave your pack at your lodgings, then return to pick up the path.

The path leaving the Pennine Way is signposted for **Janet's Foss** and passes a barn. The surface is compacted gravel, but after heading through fields towards another barn, a flagstone path continues. This leads through fields to a third barn, where a stony path runs into splendid woodland. There are tall trees, lush undergrowth, and masses of garlic-scented ramsons.

A little waterfall enters a large rock pool at **Janet's Foss**. Geography and geology students arrive en masse to learn how the river dissolves limestone on one part of its journey, depositing it elsewhere, notably where the water is agitated. The waterfall at Janet's Foss has deposited a thick mass of tufa, where it pours into the rock pool.

A snack van might be parked at Gordale Bridge.

Leave the waterfall by walking up a rocky path, taking care on slippery boulders polished like marble, and turn right along a road. ◂ Take the next left turn through a gate to follow a broad white path entering **Gordale**. The field near the road is a campsite, while rock walls rear up beyond. Turning a corner, the scenery becomes truly awesome.

Gordale Scar is a great cleft with overhanging sides and a boulder-strewn floor. A waterfall pours from a hole in a rock face, cascading into the gorge, leaving thick masses of tufa that have cemented rocks into a chaotic mass.

Return to Gordale Bridge and follow the Malham Landscape Trail uphill, later crossing a road. Another path leads to a limestone pavement on top of Malham Cove. Descend over 400 stone steps, then follow a path to Town Head Barn and a road back to Malham.

The short detour off-route to Gordale Scar is highly recommended

DAY 7

Malham to Horton in Ribblesdale

Start	The Green, Malham, SD 901 628
Finish	Horton in Ribblesdale, SD 808 724
Distance	23.5km (14.5 miles)
Total ascent	855m (2805ft)
Total descent	810m (2655ft)
Time	7hr 15min
Terrain	Short green grass and limestone pavement around Malham gives way to high moorland on Fountains Fell. Steep rock-steps are climbed on Pen-y-Ghent, followed by a descent on a firm path and a rough and stony track.
Maps	OS Landranger 98, OS Explorer OL2, Harvey's Pennine Way South
Refreshments	Two pubs at Horton in Ribblesdale and a café outside the village.

After a gentle couple of days, allowing walkers to build up their stamina, the Pennine Way heads back into the hills. Malham Cove is a remarkable cliff seen to good effect at the start of the day, while Malham Tarn is seen later. Fountains Fell is climbed and is the highest point gained so far along the trail, but it is quickly followed by Pen-y-Ghent, which is even higher. The climb to the summit is one of the steepest and rockiest parts of the trail, and some wayfarers find its appearance so unnerving that they avoid the ascent altogether. A long descent leads to the straggly village of Horton in Ribblesdale.

▸ Follow the road from **Malham** towards Malham Cove, maybe taking a look inside the National Trust's Town Head Barn, beside a campsite. Follow a path uphill parallel to the road, then head down through fields, noting the rumpled lines of ancient field boundaries along the way. The curved cliff face of **Malham Cove** looms ahead. Either walk to its base then double back, or turn left

A short 'unofficial' wooded riverside path avoids part of the road-walk.

beforehand to climb over 400 stone steps. At the top, go through a gate and turn right to walk across the uneven limestone pavement close to the cliff edge. Turn left only when the grassy green velvet floor of a valley is reached.

MALHAM COVE

The peculiar limestone pavement on top of Malham Cove

Malham Cove, rising sheer for 70m (230ft) and even overhanging in places, attracts rock climbers, walkers and birdwatchers. The RSPB sometimes establish a peregrine falcon watching station for visitors. The rock is limestone, riddled with fissures and caves through which water flows. A stream issues from the base of the cliff, but at the end of the Ice Age, when the fissures in the limestone were partly waterlogged and partly blocked by clay, a river poured over the rim of the cliff. This was 'taller than Niagara Falls', as teachers often say to impress their students. On 6 December 2015, following Storm Desmond, the waterfall re-appeared for the first time in living memory and was briefly the tallest unbroken fall in England.

Leave the top of Malham Cove by walking along the grassy floor of a valley, with a line of little cliffs rising on either side. A drystone wall runs all the way, leading to a rugged flight of stone steps at the head of the valley.

The route passes between Malham Tarn and Great Close Scar

Turn sharp right at the top to follow a path across a rocky slope, then walk beside a little gorge, noting a cave in the cliff opposite. Further up the valley a river is reached. In wet weather it flows further down the valley than in dry weather, but it ultimately vanishes into its own bed at the **Water Sinks**.

> It seems fair to assume that the water flowing from Malham Tarn, draining into the **Water Sinks**, is the same water that flows from the base of Malham Cove. This is not the case. Fluorescent dye was poured down the Water Sinks in the 1960s, and it later surfaced at Aire Head, south of Malham village. The water at the base of Malham Cove actually has its source further west.

A road is reached after the Water Sinks. Turn right and follow it across the river and through a gate. ▶ Turn

Summer weekend buses operate along this road, linking Malham and Settle.

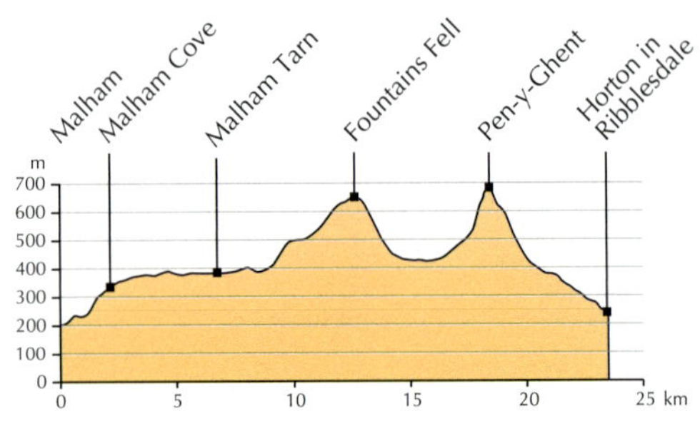

left through a car park and follow a path over a grassy rise to see the outflow of **Malham Tarn**. Keep well to the right of the tarn, and later keep to the right of a wall enclosing woodland, to reach a track. Turn left and

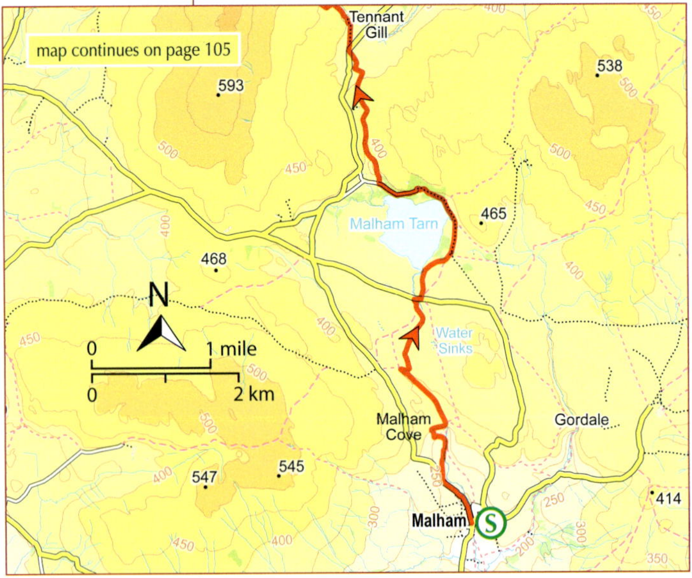

map continues on page 105

follow the track through a gate. The track runs close to Malham Tarn, then it climbs through a wood to reach Malham Tarn House.

All the rock in view around **Malham Tarn** is permeable limestone, so the presence of so much water is curious. In fact, the bed of the tarn is ancient Silurian slate, impermeable to water. The tarn had its level raised by a small dam and Malham Tarn House was built as a shooting lodge. The whole area is a National Nature Reserve, featuring uncommon plants in a lime-rich fen, and woodlands rich in willow and ash, with a rampant understorey. The tarn itself attracts a variety of birds. The area is owned by the National Trust, and the house was leased to the Field Studies Council for several decades, which ran a variety of courses in the area. Pop into the information shelter behind the house.

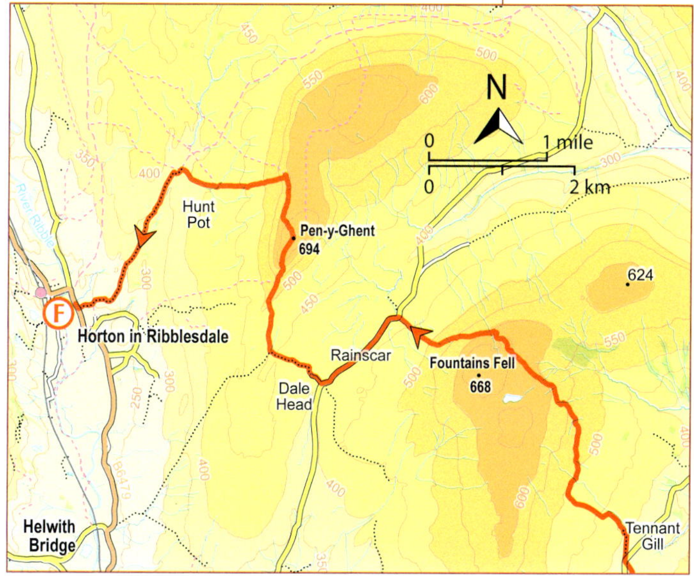

Follow the track round the back of Malham Tarn House, then head down through a rock cutting, passing a viewpoint overlooking Malham Tarn. Emerge from the woods at Water Houses and turn right through a gate. A broad green path follows a drystone wall, rising and falling through a gentle fold in the hills, passing from field to field. Keep to the right of a barn, then keep well to the right of two more barns close together. Cross a ladder stile beside a tree, then walk downhill and turn left down to a gate and stone step-stile. Turn right as signposted up to a junction of a minor road and a track.

Follow the track towards **Tennant Gill**, but keep left of the farm buildings. Climb straight up a broad, grassy path and go through a gate. Turn left across a moorland slope, then turn right to follow a tumbled drystone wall up a slope of grass, sedge and rushes. The gradient eases in an area of sink holes, where the path swings right, away from the tumbled wall, crossing a gentle dip to ford the little stream of Tennant Gill.

Go through a gate in a wall and follow the path onwards, which has been resurfaced across a boggy slope. The path climbs, but it also drops a little later, crossing a stone-slab footbridge flanked by steps. It then climbs more consistently over grass and bilberry moors, with heather and bog cotton at a higher level. Gradients are gentle on top of **Fountains Fell**. The highest point isn't visited and a sign warns against leaving the path, as there are open mineshafts dotted around. Look around to see how the eroding blanket bog is being stabilised. Most walkers are content to step to the right to reach two tall cairns, over 650m (2135ft), and enjoy the views from there.

The name **Fountains Fell** derives from its former owners, the distant Fountains Abbey. Huge areas of the Yorkshire Dales were divided between monasteries and used for sheep-grazing. The broad moorland top was mined for coal and is dotted with bell pits. Flagstones were also quarried, leaving hummocky spoil heaps; ample building material for a wall snaking across the summit, with enough left over for a variety of cairns. The view takes in the famous Three Peaks of Yorkshire – Ingleborough, Pen-y-Ghent and Whernside. Buckden Pike and Great Whernside are also prominent.

The Pennine Way crosses a stone step-stile to leave Fountains Fell. It drops down a steep slope, passing a fine rocky outcrop at one point. The path surface is rough and stony at first, but some lower parts are pleasant and grassy, slicing down across a steep and rushy slope. A prominent groove runs down to a wall and the wall leads down through a gate to a minor road. Turn left to cross a cattle grid, and follow the road gently uphill past a farm at **Rainscar**, hidden among trees. Follow the road across another cattle grid then turn right along a track leading to a farm at **Dale Head**.

Keep right of the farm to follow the track through a field and over rolling, grassy, rushy moorland. When a junction is reached at the prominent deep pit of Churn Milk Hole, turn right and keep climbing. There is some heather on the moor, then a firm path crosses a stretch of boggy ground. The firm path leads up to a junction of walls. Follow the path straight ahead alongside a wall, along a rushy crest, heading towards the rugged southern end of Pen-y-Ghent. ▸

Anyone daunted by the appearance of the slope can short-cut left, signposted for Brackenbottom, down to Horton in Ribblesdale.

Climb a stone-pitched path with rugged steps, which gives way to an intriguing flight of polished natural limestone steps. The path levels out on a shelf dividing the limestone from gritstone bedrock. Climb another stone-pitched path past a chaotic jumble of broken rock, which gives way to natural, chunky gritstone steps. Hands will be needed to get up these. A broad and obvious stone-paved path leads to the trig point on the summit of **Pen-y-Ghent** at 694m (2277ft).

Pen-y-Ghent is the lowest of the famous Three Peaks of Yorkshire, yet it offers an extensive view. Distant Pendle Hill and the Bowland Fells are followed by close neighbours Ingleborough and Whernside.

Descending from Fountains Fell while looking ahead to Pen-y-Ghent

The Howgill Fells, Baugh Fell and Wild Boar Fell are followed by High Seat and Great Shunner Fell. Rogan's Seat is followed by a rather vague skyline of moorlands, leading the eye to the shapely Buckden Pike, Great Whernside and Fountains Fell, with Pikedaw Hill completing the panorama.

Cross one of two stiles over the wall, noting how stone seats have been built to mirror each other on either side of the wall. Walk away from the wall, down an impressive flight of 208 chunky stone steps. When a steep edge is reached, swing right to follow it, and note the transition from gritstone back onto limestone. Looking ahead, spot a pinnacle of rock standing out from a limestone cliff face. The path swings left and is firm underfoot as it drops down a boggy, rushy slope. Cross a dip where there is heather on the moor, then go through a gate to continue downhill. Cross a gentle, rushy rise, but note that **Hunt Pot** could be visited just off-route. Go through another gate, cross a dip and turn left through yet another gate. Alternatively, turn right to detour to Hull Pot.

The limestone slopes of Pen-y-Ghent are riddled with caves. Many have been explored in great detail, but many more are too narrow to enter. **Hunt Pot and Hull Pot** lie close to the Pennine Way, and both of them swallow streams. The waterfall pouring into Hunt Pot later emerges at Douk Gill Scar, while the water seeping into the bouldery bed of Hull Pot emerges at Brants Gill Head. Both resurgences are near Horton in Ribblesdale.

A broad and stony walled track leads off the moors, undulating but generally descending, and it is rather awkward underfoot in places. There is an attractive rugged valley down to the left at first, then there are fields on both sides, and a patch of woodland is passed later. When a junction is reached, turn right to descend to a road in the middle of **Horton in Ribblesdale**. The Pennine Way turns right along the road.

HORTON IN RIBBLESDALE

It takes time to walk from one end of this straggly village to the other, and anyone wishing to head straight for their lodgings should ensure they are heading in the right direction! Horton's accommodation includes B&Bs, bunkhouse and a campsite. There are a couple of pubs as well as a café lying outside the village, past the railway station. Occasional buses run between Horton and Settle, while daily trains run along the celebrated Settle to Carlisle Railway, straight through the heart of the Yorkshire Dales.

SETTLE TO CARLISLE RAILWAY

Opened in 1876, the Settle to Carlisle Railway was constructed by the Midland Railway company as an alternative route northwards through England. It was an expensive undertaking and winter weather often brought trains to a complete halt. The line was threatened with closure in the 1960s and 1980s, but remains as a testimony to the people who planned and built the line. Horton-in-Ribblesdale is on the line, while Hawes, further along the Pennine Way, has a bus link with Garsdale Station. Appleby Station is within walking distance of the Pennine Way at Dufton.

DAY 8

Horton in Ribblesdale to Hawes

Start	Horton in Ribblesdale, SD 808 724
Finish	Market Place, Hawes, SD 872 898
Distance	22km (13.75 miles)
Total ascent	490m (1610ft)
Total descent	470m (1540ft)
Time	7hr
Terrain	Mostly long tracks, running at gentle gradients among rolling hills or across moorland slopes. The highest part is a narrow tarmac road. Keep an eye on signposts and marker posts when following paths linking these tracks.
Maps	OS Landranger 98, OS Explorer OL2, Harvey's Pennine Way Central
Refreshments	None during the day, then plenty of choice around Hawes.

This looks like a long day on maps, as most of the distance is made up of direct old packhorse ways. While there are plenty of ups and downs along these tracks, the overall gradient is uphill for the first half of the day, then downhill for the second half. The countryside is remarkably interesting, honeycombed with caves, and the entrances to some of these can be studied. There is a National Nature Reserve at Ling Gill, where a rocky gorge is full of trees and plants. Cam High Road, followed in the middle of the day, is one of the highest Roman roads in Britain. During the final descent, care is needed to follow an intricate route between the village of Gayle and the bustling little market town of Hawes.

Start in **Horton in Ribblesdale** and follow the road north to the Crown. Turn right and then left through the pub car park to pick up and follow a track uphill, flanked by drystone walls. Go through a gate. The wall on the right later peters out, and the track undulates across grassy hills while climbing to another gate.

Just before this gate, note the **Sell Gill Holes** on the right. This is an entertaining little cave, having 'wet' and 'dry' entrances. Access requires rigging up a rope or a ladder. After descending three pitches there is a final large chamber.

The track undulates up across grassy, rushy moor, and becomes pleasantly grassy underfoot. Go through a gate and enjoy views of Ingleborough and Whernside. A clump of trees on the left hides another cave, called Jackdaw Hole. Simply keep following the track straight ahead through gateways. The track becomes stony,

map continues on page 113

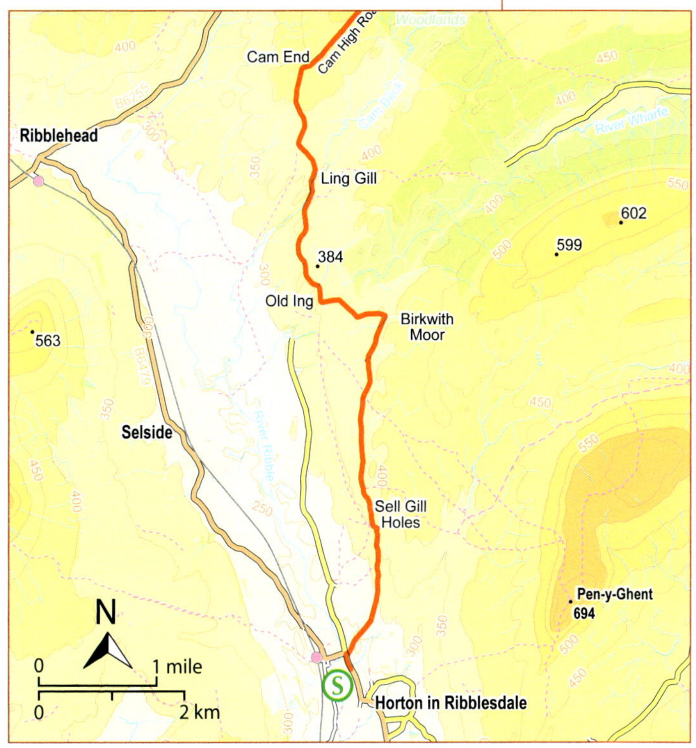

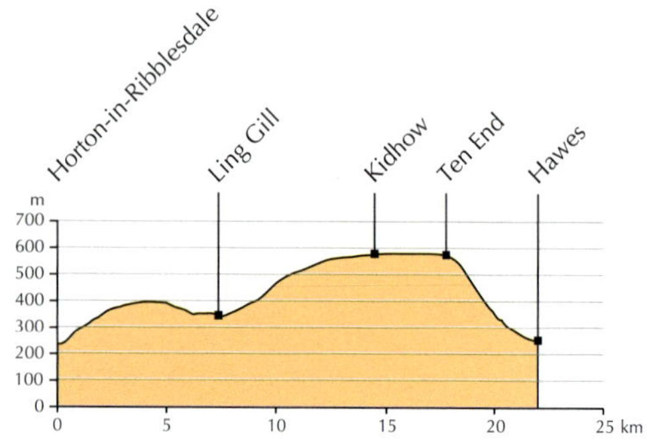

passes between two gentle hills, then becomes grassy again. Cross a stream and go through yet another gate, then walk up an open, grassy, rushy slope. Walk down into a dip to cross a stream, then go up through one final gate on **Birkwith Moor**. Overshooting this point leads to a forest, in which case turn back.

Turn left uphill, as signposted for the Pennine Way, following a gravel path while looking towards distant Ingleborough. Swing right on the descent, now facing towards Whernside, and pass through a gate beside a small ruined hut. Soon afterwards, turn left down a track near a farm at **Old Ing**. Turn right as signposted for both the Pennine Way and Pennine Bridleway. Both trails now run concurrent for the next 7km (4.5 miles). Go through a gate and follow a track flanked by drystone walls, uphill and downhill, reaching another gate where Calf Holes can be inspected on the right.

> **Calf Holes** is a cave often visited by novices, but the initial descent into the cave requires a rope or a ladder. After wading through a flooded passage, there is a flat-out crawl to endure. A walkable passage leads to an exit at the nearby Browgill Cave.

Follow the track onwards, passing a barn and noting little groups of mature trees dotted around the fields. The

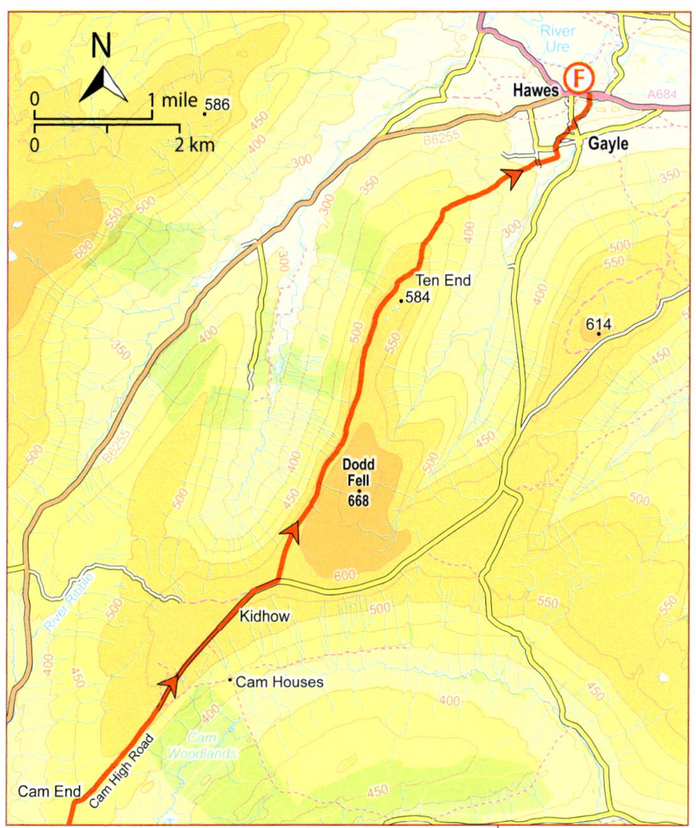

track runs alongside the National Nature Reserve of **Ling Gill**, a rock-walled gorge full of dense woodland. The stream feeding into it, Cam Beck, is equipped with weirs, which are part of a project to conserve native crayfish. Cross an old stone packhorse bridge bearing a tablet with barely decipherable lettering. When light falls across the tablet at the right angle it is possible to read: 'ANNO 1765 THIS BRIDGE WAS REPAIRED AT THE CHARGE OF THE WHOLE WEST RIDING'.

A clear and obvious track is followed towards Ling Gill

Follow the track onwards up a grassy, rushy moor. At a higher level, when views are more extensive, there is a feeling of being embraced by the Three Peaks of Yorkshire. Turn right at a junction of tracks at 438m (1437ft) on **Cam End**, and keep climbing gradually. ◂ The track is called **Cam High Road** and is based on an old Roman road, later restored as a packhorse way, used as part of the Dales Way, and resurfaced in recent years to accommodate heavy forestry trucks. The Pennine Way, Pennine Bridleway and Dales Way run concurrent for over 1.5km (1 mile).

Turning left leads towards Shepherd's Cottage B&B, 2km (1.25 miles) off-route.

Go through a gate in a wall, looking down on the extensive clear-felled forest of **Cam Woodlands**. Keep climbing gradually, passing a cairn and a signpost where the Dales Way descends across a moorland slope to reach Cam Houses. The track, however, keeps rising and passes through a gate. Further along, the track joins the access road rising from Cam Houses, and the Pennine Way continues straight ahead along a narrow tarmac road. There is a dip in the road where a gate is passed, then the road rolls gently across a high limestone pasture at 572m (1877ft). The Pennine Bridleway turns sharp left towards Gayle Wold. Before the road reaches another gate at **Kidhow**, turn left along a track. ▸

Pause to take in the view back to Pen-y-Ghent, Ingleborough, Whernside, along with other Yorkshire Dales giants such as Baugh Fell, Wild Boar Fell, High Seat and Rogan's Seat.

The track crosses a crumbling pavement made of crinoidal limestone, featuring fossils that look like nuts, bolts and washers from nature's toolbox! Follow the track alongside a drystone wall, and note how the stones in the wall change from limestone to sandstone, and later back to limestone, reflecting the rock types underfoot. The track traverses at around 580m (1900ft) across the slopes of **Dodd Fell**. Limestone pavement again shows through before the track heads downhill.

Watch for a signpost on the right, where the Pennine Way leaves the track and instead heads up a green grassy path at **Ten End**. ▸ The path levels out, passing a quarried rock-step and a few sink holes, following a tumbled wall onwards. Go through a gate and wind downhill on a grassy path. Walk along a moorland shelf strewn with gritstone boulders, then head down to a corner formed by drystone walls to go through a gate. Walk downhill beside a wall on a moorland slope of grass, sedge and rushes. It can be squelchy underfoot at Backsides, and the path heads from gate to gate, down past Gaudy House. Join a minor road and walk downhill past fields.

The track can be used to make a direct descent to Hawes.

When a road junction is reached, first turn right, then left as signposted for the Pennine Way, and go through a tiny gate and gap stile. A path leads onwards, down through two fields, then turn left to walk down through two more fields to reach another minor road. Turn right along this road, but quickly turn left down into the little village of **Gayle**. The Pennine Way is signposted on left, following a flagstone path through two fields. Walk along a narrow path through a housing estate, crossing over one road to reach another road. ▸

Nearby entrance to Wensleydale Creamery, with restaurant, cheese-tasting and visitor centre.

Turn left along the road, then right as signposted along a path. A fine flagstone path leads over to a church. The waymarking at a junction beside the church is ambiguous and suggests turning right, but turn left instead. Walk down a flagstone path and pass beneath a house to reach the town centre in **Hawes**.

Walkers descend gently through fields towards Gayle and Hawes

HAWES

This popular and busy little market town has many points of interest and is well worth exploring. Attractions include the Dales Countryside Museum, in the old railway station (open daily, but closed for Christmas and in January, entry charge, tel 01969 666210, www.dalescountrysidemuseum.org.uk). The National Park Visitor Centre is on the same site. The Wensleydale Creamery reminds visitors that Cistercian monks made the first Wensleydale cheese in the dale in 1150. The creamery operates a visitor centre and restaurant (open daily throughout the year, entry charge for tours and cheese-making demonstrations, tel 01969 667664, www.wensleydale.co.uk).

Hawes has the greatest range of services so far along the Pennine Way, including ATM, a post office, shops, pubs, restaurants, cafés and a fish and chip shop. A range of accommodation includes hotels, B&Bs, a youth hostel and nearby campsites. Regular daily buses run through Wensleydale, linking Hawes and Gayle with Leyburn and Northallerton. The Little White Bus links Gayle, Hawes and Hardraw with Garsdale Station on the Settle to Carlisle Railway, except Sunday.

DAY 9

Hawes to Keld

Start	Market Place, Hawes, SD 872 898
Finish	Park Lodge, Keld, NY 893 011
Distance	20km (12.5 miles)
Total ascent	650m (2460ft)
Total descent	670m (2200ft)
Time	6hr 15min
Terrain	The bulk of the day's walk involves a long and gradual ascent and descent over a broad moorland crest. Boggy parts feature flagstone paths, but this is an exposed place in bad weather. The latter part of the route involves contouring round a steep hillside on a rugged path.
Maps	OS Landranger 91 and 98, OS Explorer OL19 and 30, Harvey's Pennine Way Central
Refreshments	Pub and café at Hardraw, Thwaite and Keld.

The Pennine Way runs through fields between Hawes and Hardraw and, before going any further, a highly recommended detour allows Hardraw Force to be visited. Don't be put off if there is heavy rain, since the waterfall will be at its most powerful. A long and gradual climb leads up a broad moorland crest over Great Shunner Fell. In mist, the climb is a treadmill and there is a succession of 'false' summits, but on a clear day the walk is delightful and the views are exceptionally wide-ranging. The descent to Thwaite offers fine views of Swaledale, as does the continuation round the steep slopes of Kisdon, on the way to the charming little village of Keld.

Leave the centre of **Hawes** by following the road signposted for the Dales Countryside Museum. The Pennine Way is signposted left before the turning for the museum and National Park Visitor Centre. The road crosses an old railway bridge and a steam train can be seen alongside the old station building. Walk down the road a little, then, when another road leads off to the left, the Pennine

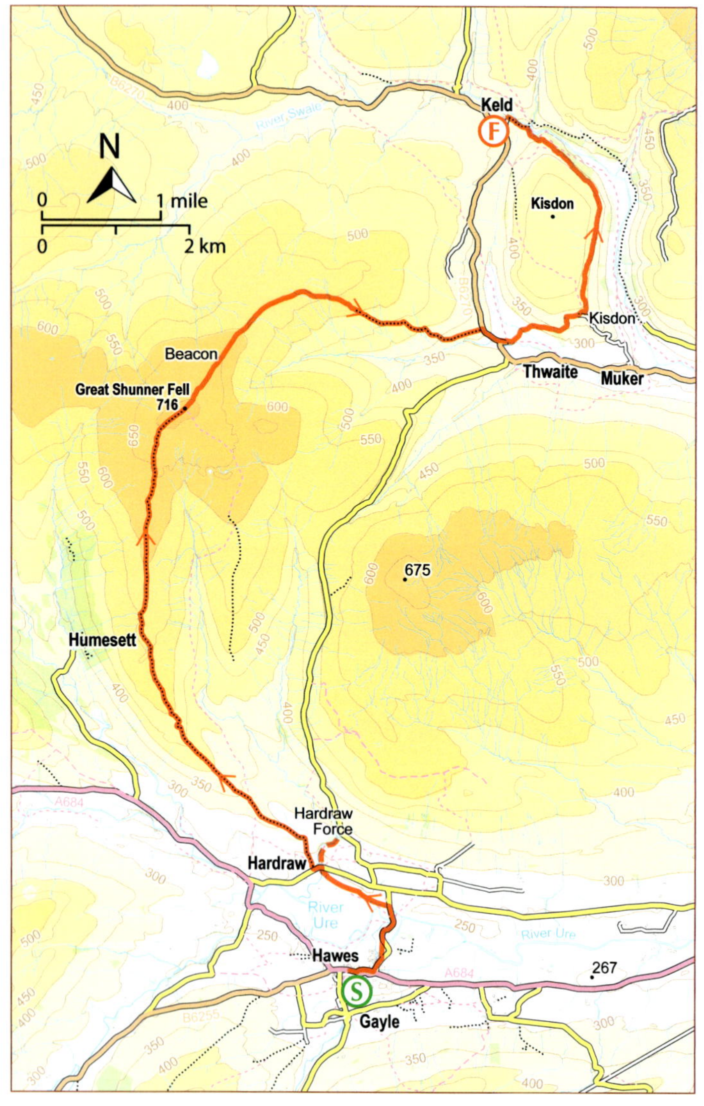
N
0 1 mile
0 2 km
Keld
F
Kisdon
Kisdon
Thwaite
Muker
Beacon
Great Shunner Fell
716
675
Humesett
Hardraw Force
Hardraw
River Ure
Hawes
S
Gayle
267
River Swale
River Ure
B6270
A684
B6255

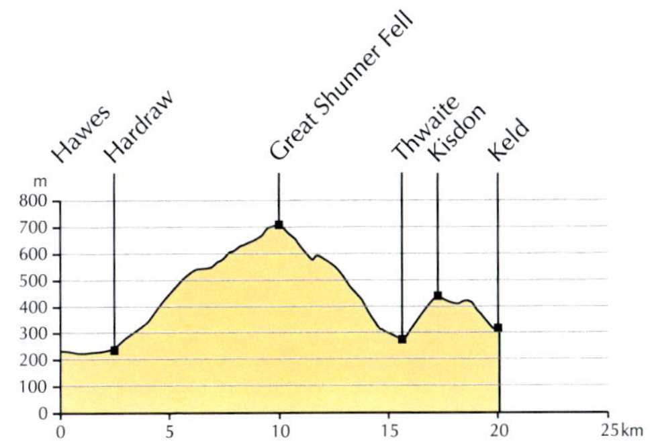

Way is signposted straight along a flagstone path through a field. When the road is joined again, either follow it or take advantage of a short path between the road and the **River Ure**.

Cross a bridge and follow the road until it leaves the riverside and climbs through a belt of woodland. The Pennine Way is signposted to the left, where it runs beside the wood and through a couple of fields. The rest of the path is paved with narrow flagstones, leading to the hamlet of **Hardraw**.

HARDRAW FORCE AND HARDRAW

Hardraw Force can be visited by making a short detour

Hardraw Force is well worth a short detour, especially after heavy rain. It is the highest single-drop waterfall above ground in England, at 30m (98ft), although there are longer drops underground. Access is through a café behind the Green Dragon Inn, where there is an entry charge. An easy path leads into a wooded valley, where the waterfall is revealed quite suddenly, pouring from a rocky lip. Hard layers of sandstone and limestone are underlain by crumbling shale. Charles Blondin, the 19th-century tightrope walker, crossed the gorge and stopped halfway to cook an omelette! The lip of the waterfall collapsed in 1899, but the rock was pinned with iron bars to restore the waterfall to its former glory.

Facilities at Hardraw include the Green Dragon Inn, which offers accommodation, food and drink. The Old Hall Cottage Campsite is behind the Cart House Tea Room. The Hardraw Old School Bunkhouse offers accommodation for groups.

The Pennine Way runs along the road from the pub, past the tearoom and old school, to reach the edge of Hardraw. Turn right as signposted along a walled track, passing a house, climbing past fields and a woodland, crossing a gentle hump to reach a gate onto the open moors. Fork left at a track junction and climb a grassy, rushy crest with increasingly wide-ranging views. Climb further and pass a wall, and notice how the bedrock varies from sandstone to limestone. Go through a gate in a wall, where the track is worn down to the limestone bedrock.

Walk a short way up the track, then turn right as signposted for the Pennine Way. A broad and grassy path rises gently along a broad moorland crest. ◂ Some parts may be squelchy underfoot after rain. A series of cairns mark the way ahead, which are useful guides in mist. Gritstone boulders are dotted around on the way to and from a low gritstone edge bearing a prominent cairn at **Humesett**. Other tall, columnar cairns standing on the moorland slopes are referred to as 'beacons'.

A black grouse recovery project is underway in this area.

The path is worn down to gritstone bedrock, which forms a natural paved surface. The path stays on the high crest, generally following a firm, sandy path. A broad and gentle dip in the crest at Black Hill Moss features peat hags, and a flagstone path provides a firm footing.

Watch while crossing a rocky streambed to see marks that look remarkably like **tyre tracks**. These are the imprints of ancient fossil trees, such as lepidodendron or sigillaria, which grew as tall as 40m (130ft).

Longer stretches of flagstones follow the grassy crest and a bog pool stands on the left. Climb a stony, grassy path, which levels out, then follow flagstones to cross another slight dip on the crest. A stony path climbs to a prominent cairn, or beacon. Follow a level path along a broad crest, then use a flagstone path to cross a slight depression where the boggy ground features grass and bilberry. Climb gently up a firm path, which alternates between a stony surface and flagstones; another slight depression features a longer stretch of flagstones, with bog cotton alongside. A steeper slope is equipped with stone steps, then the path undulates up and down stone-slab steps among peat hags and boggy patches. The path is firm and dry along a high crest, crossing a fence to reach a stone cross-shelter that incorporates a trig point on top of the highest point gained so far on the Pennine Way, **Great Shunner Fell**, at 716m (2349ft).

In the past the broad whaleback crest of **Great Shunner Fell** featured appalling bogs, and in wet and misty weather the climb seemed endless. When available, the view is remarkably extensive.

Climbing from Hardraw onto the lower slopes of Great Shunner Fell

> Look along the Vale of Eden, with Cross Fell, the Dun Fells, Mickle Fell and the North Pennines rising above it. Closer to hand are Rogan's Seat and Swaledale, along with the eastern parts of the Yorkshire Dales. Great Whernside and Buckden Pike lead the eye to Fountains Fell and Pen-y-Ghent, with the Bowland Fells more distant. Ingleborough, Whernside and Gragareth are followed by Baugh Fell. The distant skyline of the Lake District includes the Coniston Fells, Scafells, Helvellyn and High Street ranges, followed by Skiddaw and Blencathra. Closer at hand are Wild Boar Fell, High Seat and Nine Standards Rigg.

Follow a paved path away from the shelter and cross another fence. The path descends and undulates, passing a stout cairn, or **beacon**, later crossing a footbridge at one point. There is a break in the flagstone path while crossing a grassy hump, then another paved path continues. A stony path and a flagstone path lead down to a prominent little spoil heap where coal was once mined. Walk down another stony path and another flagstone path.

In a word, Kearton's supplies everything here, offering accommodation, a tea shop and provisions to take away.

Turn left to follow a stony track to a gate, enjoying fine views along the length of Swaledale, taking note of all its field barns. These are so numerous that almost every field has its own barn. The track is uncomfortably stony underfoot, flanked by drystone walls, and leads to the **B6270** road. Turn right to follow the road down into the little village of **Thwaite**. ◂

Walk through the village by road, but watch for a Pennine Way signpost on the left. Walk through a couple of little fields, then turn left and go through a gate. Cross a field and a stream, then go through another gate and turn right. The path climbs, then a level, grassy track which leads to a farm at **Kisdon**. Go through a gate at the farm and immediately turn left as signposted up through another gate, to follow a broad path flanked by drystone walls. When a building is reached, keep left above it, then follow a path running more or less level, with fine views along Swaledale.

The path drifts downhill and when a junction is reached, fork right downhill. Traverse boulder-scree on the slopes of **Kisdon** and be thankful that a path has been made through it, although some parts are still uneven underfoot. Cross a steep slope of bracken above a wood predominantly planted with birch trees. In summer there may be masses of primroses on the slope. There is a tumbled wall alongside the wood, and after following it for a while, step down through a gap in the wall, and later keep left to maintain a falling traverse.

A signpost is reached, where the Pennine Way makes a sharp right turn downhill in tandem with the popular Coast to Coast Walk. If continuing directly towards Tan Hill, then turn right. Visiting **Keld** requires a short detour off the Pennine Way, straight ahead along a clear path. The village is reached at its lowest point, near Park Lodge.

KELD

Keld is a delightful little village, full of stout stone houses and of no great size. Anyone breaking here will probably have time to wander around and explore, and if so, then take a stroll beside the River Swale. Kisdon Force lies downstream while Catrake Force and Wain Wath Force lie upstream. The former United Reformed Church buildings have been transformed into the Keld Resource Centre (keld.org.uk), which is worth visiting.

Facilities include the hotel of Keld Lodge, based in a former youth hostel, Butt House B&B, and campsites at Park Lodge and Hoggarths – with the Keld Bunkbarn and Yurts in-between. There is a small shop and café at Park Lodge. Greenlands B&B is outside the village. Bear in mind that the Pennine Way and the Coast to Coast Walk pass through Keld, which puts a lot of pressure on accommodation. If lodgings cannot be secured, then press onwards to Frith Lodge or Tan Hill Inn. Buses run from Keld, through several Swaledale villages to Richmond, but study timetables carefully if planning to leave the route in search of other accommodation, and return the following day.

DAY 10

Keld to Baldersdale or Bowes

Start	Park Lodge, Keld, NY 893 011
Finish	Lay-by, Clove Lodge, Baldersdale, NY 935 176
Alternative finish	St Giles' Church, Bowes, NY 992 135
Distance	23km (14.25 miles); Bowes Loop 20.5km (12.75 miles)
Total ascent	530m (1740ft); Bowes Loop 330m (1080ft)
Total descent	510m (1675ft); Bowes Loop 370m (1215ft)
Time	7hr; Bowes Loop 6hr 30min
Terrain	Broad and open moorland slopes, which might be wet on the way to Tan Hill, and are often wet and boggy beyond Tan Hill, towards Baldersdale. On the alternative route, fiddly field paths lead to Bowes.
Maps	OS Landranger 91, OS Explorer OL30 and OL31, Harvey's Pennine Way Central
Refreshments	Tan Hill Inn, the highest pub in Britain. The Ancient Unicorn is available on the 'Bowes Loop'. DIY snacks at Clove Lodge.

After leaving Keld, the Pennine Way climbs to Tan Hill and its celebrated inn – the highest in Britain. Many walkers structure their schedules so that they can stay at the inn, or camp alongside. Beyond Tan Hill lies the bleak and boggy Stainmore, where the Pennine Way splits into 'main' and 'alternative' routes, which later join again in Baldersdale. There was once a youth hostel in Baldersdale, and, when that closed, Clove Lodge offered B&B, bunkhouse and camping, before it too closed. The Fox and Hounds pub, well off-route in Cotherstone, offers pick-ups and drop-offs. Alternatively, keep walking to stay at Hunter House Farm near Grassholme Reservoir. Those who take the 'Bowes Loop' can stay at the Ancient Unicorn. Both routes have their pros and cons, so read both descriptions carefully before making a choice.

Leave **Keld** by following a path downhill from Park Lodge. When a fork is reached, this is where the Pennine Way comes in on the right from Thwaite, and continues down on the left to reach a footbridge over the River Swale. Cross over and follow a path uphill. ▸ The path climbs steeply to a track and a left turn leads up to some farm buildings at East Stonesdale.

Take the time here to look down on the lovely waterfall of East Gill Force.

Pass between the buildings and climb straight through a gate to follow a grassy path flanked by drystone walls. This leads up to a gate, then the route passes to the right of a barn at Shot Lathe, onto a grassy, rushy open space beyond. Keep climbing and look back to Keld one last time. Go through a gate and note that the rushy moor can be squelchy, but drier heather moorland lies further ahead. Go through another gate and follow the path as it undulates across a moorland slope of grass, sedge and rushes. Pass well below a farmhouse at **Frith Lodge**, which offers accommodation, and go through a little gate.

Join and follow a track straight ahead, keeping right of a barn. Go through a gate and follow a firm gravel track towards two more barns. Go through gates to pass these and cross a little stream. Walk straight along a broad path on the wet, rushy, grassy moorland slopes of Low Brown Hill. The path appears to drift down towards a minor road and a couple of bridges over Stonesdale Beck, so swing right and cross a stone-slab footbridge over Lad Gill.

The path climbs onto **Stonesdale Moor** and becomes a stony track, levelling out among grass, sedge and

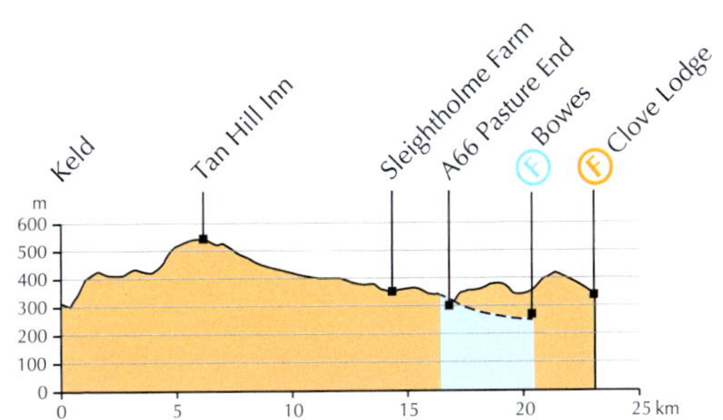

The inn majrks the end of the Yorkshire Dales National Park and the start of the extensive North Pennines National Landscape.

rushes. Keep right at a fork, as signposted for the Pennine Way. There is a gentle rise along another old track, passing the spoil heap of an old coal mine. The Tan Hill Inn suddenly comes into view at this point. The track swings right, but two signposts send it left and left again along a broad, clear, stony track. Join a road literally at the front door of the **Tan Hill Inn**. ◂

THE TAN HILL INN

The Tan Hill Inn, the highest pub in Britain, stands at a lonely moorland road junction at 530m (1732ft). William Camden mentioned an inn at this remote spot in 1586, but the current structure dates from the 17th century. The inn stood at a focal point on packhorse ways and caught the passing trade. Bell pits and open mine shafts dot the bleak moors and coal mining provided a more regular clientele. There is good local support for the inn but it relies heavily on tourist traffic, and Pennine wayfarers seldom pass if the doors are open.

Tan Hill Inn was 'transferred' to County Durham during the local government reorganisation of April 1974, and this was a sore point with many locals. It was brought back into Yorkshire following a boundary change in April 1991. The pub has featured in television advertising to promote double-glazing, and in foul weather a blazing fire should be burning, but there may be competition for a fireside seat! Live music events take place regularly, with no neighbours to complain about the noise. A variety of accommodation is available, from B&B to bunkhouse, domes and camping (tel 01833 533007, www.tanhillinn.com).

The Tan Hill Inn is the highest pub in Britain

A fine track runs parallel to Sleightholme Beck, becoming a road as it reaches Sleightholme Farm

Leaving the Tan Hill Inn, follow the road towards a nearby cattle grid. Turn left just beforehand as signposted, and follow a firm, grassy path downhill. The bedrock is limestone, then the bleak and boggy **Sleightholme Moor** begins. Grass, sedge and rushes give way to heather. Follow widely-spaced white-tipped marker posts gently downhill. ▸ The gradient is almost level and the path runs well to the left of a drystone sheepfold. The course of Frumming Beck is followed downstream. The route runs along the northern bank, where it was transferred after the southern bank was trodden into a miserable morass.

The moor can be wet, especially where bare, black peat or bright green sphagnum moss is seen.

Simply keep the beck in view while following it downstream, generally walking on a brow some distance from the flow. There are a couple of little footbridges over inflowing streams, then a stout pepperpot cairn is passed. Another little footbridge is followed by a few lengths of duckboard, and two more sheepfolds stand away to the right. The path gets better and better along a brow of grass and sedge, eventually drifting down to a track.

Turn right to cross a bridge and walk up the track, passing a barrier gate to reach a junction. Turn left

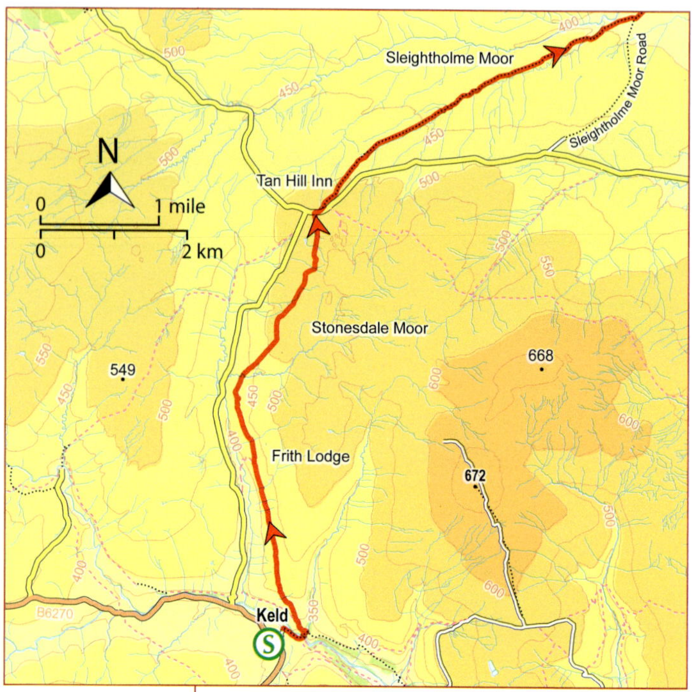

map continues on page 129

along a broad, stony track over moorland of rushes and sedge, now running parallel to Sleightholme Beck, although high above the flow. The track undulates and is part gravel and part patchy tarmac, eventually running down through a gate to pass **Sleightholme Farm**. Follow the farm road past fields to pass a converted barn at Kingdom Lodge.

Turn left through a gate, as signposted for the Pennine Way, and aim straight for another gate to pass from field to field. A layered, crumbling cliff is seen ahead, so aim to the right of it to go through another gate and cross a footbridge over Sleightholme Beck. Turn right, but almost immediately fork left up a grassy path. Walk roughly parallel to a wall along a brow covered

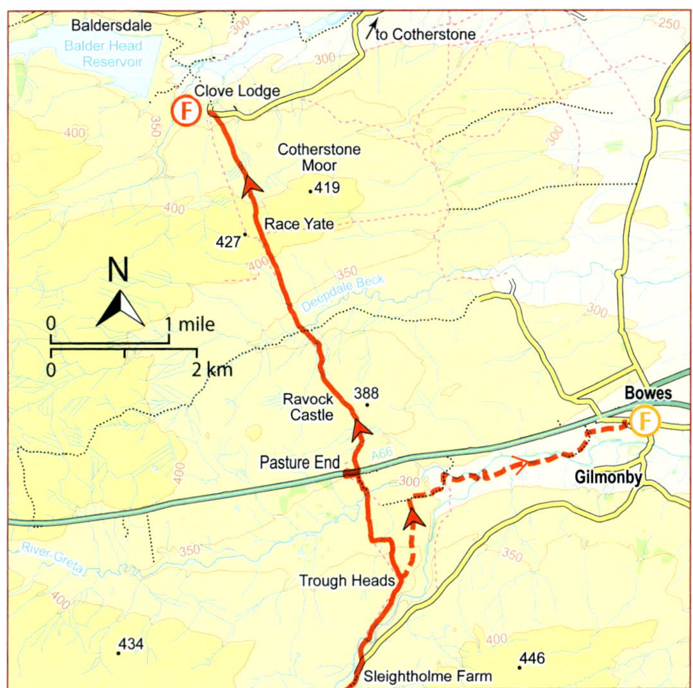

in rushes and bracken, eventually going through a gate on the left. Turn right to continue following the wall towards a farmhouse at **Trough Heads** and a three-way Pennine Way signpost.

Alternative 'Bowes Loop'

At this signpost, keep straight ahead alongside a drystone wall, as signposted 'Bowes Loop', along the edge of a rushy, mossy moor. When the wall turns left, turn with it and walk down to a corner. Go through a gate, through a field, through another gate and follow a gritty path to a farm road. Turn right to follow the road across a cattle grid and through fields, then keep left of the farm buildings at East Mellwaters to reach an access road.

Some 5500 years of farming history have been excavated around **East Mellwaters**. Iron Age dwellings were unearthed beside the farm road, as well as a rectangular settlement in a field. A Romano-British house lies across Sleightholme Beck, while the modern farmhouse stands on the site of a medieval dwelling. The farm provides specialist accommodation for people with disabilities. A noticeboard explains about a network of trails around nearby fields, which includes the Pennine Way.

Walk towards the farmhouse, but turn left through a gate beside a barn, where the wall bears a signpost for the Pennine Way. Walk through a field, following the wall straight ahead, then turn left and go through the third gate in the wall. Follow a gritty path downstream and cross a footbridge. Keep left of the buildings ahead to reach an access track. Turn right through a gate and keep left of West Charity Farm, then turn left to follow the track through a couple of fields to the next farm, Lady Myres.

The 12th-century Bowes Castle was built of stone taken from an earlier Roman fort

Follow the farm access road onwards and watch for a signpost pointing down through a gate in a wall below

the road. Walk through a field and cross a footbridge above a weir on the River Greta. Walk downstream, but veer left, uphill and away from the river. Pass a farmhouse and continue along its access road. Turn right as indicated by a Pennine Way signpost, crossing a field to reach a step-stile and a little gate in a wall. Line up a series of stiles and little gates to pass through fields, keeping right of Bowes Castle. Turn left to follow Back Lane between the castle and St Giles' Church to enter **Bowes**.

BOWES

Travellers have crossed Stainmore for thousands of years, as this broad gap on the moors allows an obvious east–west link. The Romans regulated traffic by constructing a road equipped with forts, camps and signal stations. The fort at Bowes was called Lavatris, and its square, grassy platform can be discerned, but all its masonry was incorporated into Bowes Castle in 1170. The castle watched over an area that was an unsettled borderland, and can be visited free of charge at any time. The Stainmore wastes were bleak, and monastic hospices were established to serve travellers. A memory of these places lingers in the place-name 'spital'. A turnpike road was constructed in 1743 and literally paved the way for cross-country coaching. The South Durham and Lancashire Union Railway came in 1861, lasting for a century until closure.

Charles Dickens visited Bowes in 1838 and collected material about the notorious Yorkshire Schools, which included the Bowes Academy, now Dotheboys Hall. A boy who ran away from the academy is buried at St Giles, and provided the inspiration for Smike in *Nicholas Nickleby*. Dickens met William Shaw, the headmaster, who was transformed into Wackford Squeers. Some of Dickens' information was gleaned at the bar of the Ancient Unicorn, although descendants of Shaw claim he was a kindly gentleman. Whatever the truth, the furore following the publication of Dickens' work resulted in the ultimate closure of the Yorkshire Schools.

Facilities in Bowes are limited to the Ancient Unicorn, a coaching inn with a cobbled courtyard that once provided stabling for horses and now provides food, drink and accommodation. There is a basic campsite at Ivy Hall Farm. The Bowes Museum, despite its name, is actually 6.5km (4 miles) off-route at Barnard Castle. It is built in the style of a French château set among ornamental gardens and parkland, housing a fine collection of European art.

God's Bridge is a natural limestone slab bridge over the River Greta

Main route to Clove Lodge

Turn left at the three-way Pennine Way post at **Trough Heads**, as signposted for God's Bridge, and walk across the heathery Wytham Moor, which is spiked with patches of rushes. The ground gets wet and boggy and there is a sparse line of marker posts. When a drystone wall is reached, turn left to follow it, still on wet and boggy ground. Go through a gate on the right and walk down a moorland slope of grass, sedge and rushes. Walk roughly parallel to a drystone wall, over a hump and down to God's Bridge. ◂ Walk up a track and go through a gate where there was once a railway bridge. Pass a cottage and climb towards the busy **A66** road. This is too fast and dangerous to cross, so turn left until an underpass is reached, then double back on the other side to reach the house called **Pasture End**.

This is a remarkable natural feature – a huge flat slab of limestone bedrock, with the River Greta flowing beneath it!

Climb a rushy slope, following a drystone wall to a corner. Walk straight ahead then drift to the right, later drifting to the left, while crossing Rove Gill on an undulating moor covered in patchy, varied vegetation. The moorland becomes heathery and the path is worn down to black peat. A series of cairns are passed, but one of them is actually the ruins of a small hut called **Ravock Castle**. Drift right and left on the way down to a track, where one end of a hut is left open as a shelter. Use a nearby footbridge to cross **Deepdale Beck**.

Follow a drystone wall up a slope of grass, sedge and moss. Go over a slight rise and through a gate in a fence. Follow the wall across a boggy depression and climb further uphill, reaching the crest of **Race Yate** at 427m (1401ft). Desolate moorland stretches in all directions, and while this can be a fine place to walk in good weather, it can be a treadmill in foul weather. Walk downhill to pass through a gate where a fence joins a corner on the wall.

Walk straight ahead, gently down the moorland slope as signposted for the Pennine Way. Cross a boggy dip, then walk over a broad crest. The moorland is covered in tussocky grass and the path is rather vague. Watch carefully for a couple of helpful marker posts, as it is easy to be drawn off-course, especially in mist. A minor road is reached at a Pennine Way signpost. Turn left to reach a small lay-by before a dip in the road leads to **Clove Lodge** in Baldersdale.

Baldersdale has always been short on **facilities**, and when the Pennine Way was first established, a youth hostel was provided. When this closed, Clove Lodge offered B&B, bunkhouse and evening meals, before it too closed. However, DIY snacks are offered in an adjacent barn, as well as shelter in nasty weather. The Fox and Hounds pub, which is well off-route in the village of Cotherstone, offers pick-ups and drop-offs by prior arrangement. For the sake of another 4km (2.5 miles) along the Pennine Way, walkers can stay at Hunter House Farm B&B before reaching Grassholme Reservoir.

DAY 11

Baldersdale or Bowes to Middleton-in-Teesdale

Start	Lay-by, Clove Lodge, Baldersdale, NY 935 176
Alternative start	St Giles' Church, Bowes, NY 992 135
Finish	Horsemarket, Middleton-in-Teesdale, NY 947 254
Distance	10.5km (6.5 miles); Bowes Loop 19.5km (12 miles)
Total ascent	310m (1015ft); Bowes Loop 450m (1475ft)
Total descent	400m (1310ft); Bowes Loop 500m (1640ft)
Time	3hr; Bowes Loop 6hr
Terrain	Gently rolling moorland with some wet and boggy patches, as well as fiddly field paths in the dales.
Maps	OS Landranger 91, OS Explorer OL31, Harvey's Pennine Way Central
Refreshments	DIY snacks at Clove Lodge and Wythes Hill. Plenty of choice around Middleton.

Walkers on the alternative Bowes Loop spend all morning heading back to the Pennine Way main route near Clove Lodge in Baldersdale. First, the rolling moorlands of Stainmore are crossed, where the gritstone cap of Goldsborough is a prominent landmark. The Pennine Way through Baldersdale and Lunedale features a succession of reservoirs, and between them are the flowery hayfields of Hannah's Meadow nature reserve. Middleton-in-Teesdale lies a little off-route, but most walkers will visit the town, which is full of charm and interest. Those who start the day with a drop-off near Clove Lodge, however, may wish to continue walking through Teesdale to Langdon Beck.

Alternative 'Bowes Loop'

Start at St Giles' Church in **Bowes** and follow the road west to the aptly named West End of the village, passing Dotheboys Hall. Turn right to cross a bridge over the busy **A66** road and follow the road uphill, keeping left at a junction. The road is fenced and passes fields where signs warn of 'unexploded ordnance and toxic material'.

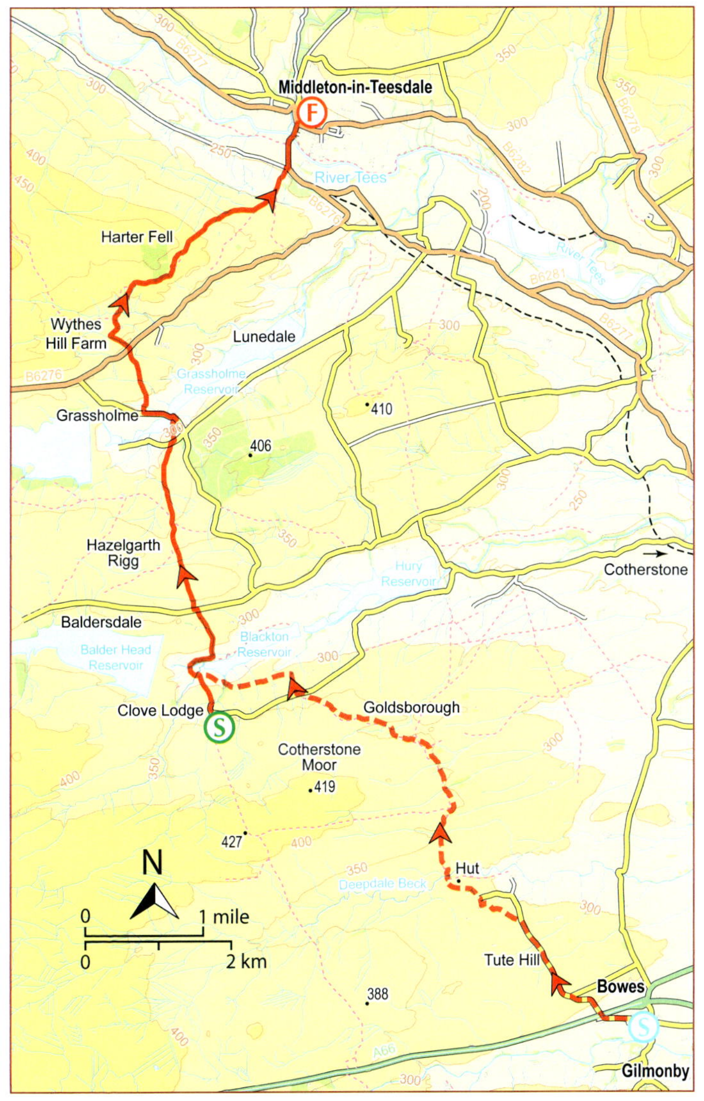
Middleton-in-Teesdale
F
River Tees
B6277
B6276
B6278
B6282
B6281
Harter Fell
Wythes Hill Farm
Lunedale
Grassholme Reservoir
Grassholme
410
406
Hazelgarth Rigg
Hury Reservoir
Cotherstone
Baldersdale
Balder Head Reservoir
Blackton Reservoir
Clove Lodge
S
Goldsborough
Cotherstone Moor
419
427
N
0
1 mile
0
2 km
Hut
Deepdale Beck
Tute Hill
Bowes
388
A66
Gilmonby
300
350
400
450
250
200

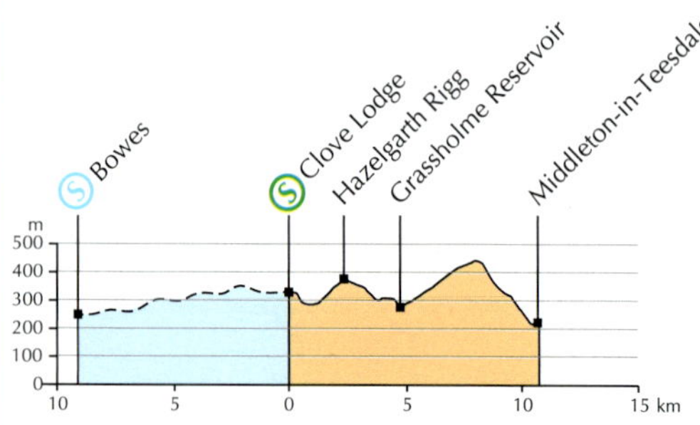

The former **RAF Bowes Moor site** on Tute Hill was used for the storage and disposal of chemical weapons, including mustard gas, phosgene and lewisite. All that remains are a few ruins on a rushy moor, occasionally tested for lingering toxicity.

The road runs downhill and when the fence on the left reaches the corner of a wall, cross a stone step-stile. If the grass is very wet, the field path can be avoided by staying on the tarmac road. Walk diagonally across a field, keeping right of a barn to cross two more step-stiles. Walk towards West Stoney Keld, keeping just to the right of the farm to find a gate onto its access track. Turn right along the track, through another gate, then turn left.

Follow a track straight ahead, over a cattle grid and down towards restored buildings at Levy Pool. Keep just to the left of these to find a footbridge over **Deepdale Beck**. Head downstream a little, then turn left uphill to follow a path indicated by sparse marker posts. These lead over a grassy, rushy moor with some boggy patches. Cross a crest, which offers good views of desolate, rolling Stainmore, then go down to cross a stream. Walk uphill and turn right along a firm path through bracken to reach a fence and a gate around 360m (1180ft). ◂

In very clear weather distant views stretch eastwards to the North York Moors and the smoky industrial Teesmouth.

Turn left to follow the fence, which leads to a wall and a roller-coaster walk over the moors. The wall has been rebuilt, except for one old stretch where a stream flows through a gap. The wall gives way to a fence, which is also the boundary of a military firing range, marked by 'danger' signs. When the fence reaches a wall, there are two gates. Be sure to go through the one on the left, as the one on the right leads onto the firing range.

An extensive grass, rush and sedge moor stretches towards a hill with a distinctive gritstone cap. If the day is misty, then take care while following a vague path towards it, but in clear weather there is no problem. There is a slight dip in the moor, drained by the stream of Yawd Sike, which is spanned by a footbridge. The path keeps to the left of **Goldsborough**, whose gritstone crags form dramatic overhangs.

As a moorland crest is crossed around 370m (1215ft), Mickle Fell rises in the far distance while Baldersdale, closer to hand, is filled with the **reservoirs** of Balder Head, Blackton and Hury. Keep left at path junctions to avoid descending too early to a minor road. The road is eventually reached at a Pennine Way signpost. Turn left, then turn right down the access track to the farm of East Friar.

Squeeze past the building on the left and cross a stone step-stile on the left. A path heads straight across five fields, so line up stone step-stiles to pass from one to another. Drop down through another field to cross a bridge over a stream, then climb to cross another stone step-stile. Head diagonally right, slightly downhill through a field to cross another stone step-stile, then head down to a three-way signpost where the Bowes Loop rejoins the main Pennine Way below **Clove Lodge**. ▸

Detour up to a barn at Clove Lodge for DIY snacks.

Main route from Clove Lodge

Leaving **Clove Lodge**, simply follow a track away from the farm, down through fields. ▸ Cross a wall, as a stout iron gate ahead may be locked, then cross Blackton Bridge at the head of **Blackton Reservoir**. A grassy track runs beside the reservoir, rising to a notice explaining about the Blackton Nature Reserve, which covers the head of the reservoir. Go through another stout iron gate to reach Low Birk Hatt, and turn left to follow the access

A three-way signpost is passed where the Bowes Loop rejoins the main route.

Hannah's Meadow, where a path leads to an information barn

road away from it, up through Hannah's Meadow Nature Reserve.

> The two flowery meadows beside the road, **Hannah's Meadow**, are fine examples of North Pennine hayfields. Hannah Hauxwell, who achieved fame after being 'discovered' by a TV producer who was walking the Pennine Way, once managed these fields in a traditional manner, so that they are species-rich. She lived at Low Birk Hatt. At the top of the fields, near High Birk Hatt, a barn can be visited by making a short detour along a duck-board path. The barn serves as a simple unstaffed visitor centre for the reserve and also offers shelter in nasty weather.

The road up through Hannah's Meadow reaches a gate and a minor road. Turn left and then right over a stone step-stile. Walk up a rushy, grassy slope and cross a little stream in a dip. Follow a wall uphill and cross the crest of **Hazelgarth Rigg** at 375m (1230ft), where there is a view of Lunedale ahead. Walk downhill and cross another little stream, eventually reaching a junction of walls. Cross a stone step-stile and follow a fence to another stone step-stile. Cross over and turn left downhill, but drift away from the wall to aim for a couple of barns built beside each other in a field. Cross two stone step-stiles to reach them, then keep right to pick up a field path. Walk through three fields using gates, reaching a road and farm at How. ▸

Turn left along the road to stay at Hunter House Farm B&B.

Turn right along the road, then left as signposted for the Pennine Way to pass the farm. Walk downhill and cross a step-stile over a fence to continue down through a wooded enclosure. Turn right to cross two stone step-stiles to reach a road, then turn left down the road to cross a five-arched stone bridge over **Grassholme Reservoir**. ▸ There is a picnic site to the right of the road, otherwise walk up the road to the farm of **Grassholme** and turn right through the farmyard.

When the water level in the reservoir is low, an older twin-arched stone bridge is seen, spanning the River Lune and surrounded by mudflats.

Walk down a stony track in a field, then turn left up a path as marked. The path is fairly straight, but if help is needed to find stiles and gateways, then keep well to the left of one barn on a crest, then well to the right of another, before going down into a dip, then keep well to

Grassholme Bridge spans the head of Grassholme Reservoir

the left of a third, on a crest, and finally keep well to the left of a ruined barn beyond a dip. Walk up to the **B6276** road and cross over it to follow a tarmac access road up to **Wythes Hill Farm**, where DIY snacks are available.

Keep left of the farm and left of a nearby house, following a track which later turns right down to a stream. Ford this and go through a gate, then climb towards the top corner of a field. Cross a stone step-stile and head diagonally up the next field, across a dip to cross a little stream, then up to a gap in a wall. Walk up the next field to join a track as it passes through a gate. Turn right to follow the track, and follow it from field to field, either using gates or stone step-stiles. Pass to the left of a ruined barn, and later keep to the right of a small building on the slopes of **Harter Fell**.

Middleton-in-Teesdale can be seen below, with a distinctive clump of trees on the knoll of Kirkcarrion far to the right.

Go through a gate on a crest around 430m (1410ft). ◂ Walk down through a grassy field and go through a gate. A path runs down a broad, grassy slope with large patches of bracken and occasional rashes of boulders. Walk downhill and go through a gate in a fence. Further downhill, don't worry about a fork in the

A clear track descends to Middleton-in-Teesdale

track, or a tangle of loops, since everything leads to a gate in a wall.

Walk straight downhill and cross an old railway trackbed, then go down a short, steep slope to reach a gate and a minor road. Turn right along the road, then left down the **B6276** road. A campsite is signposted to the right, while the Pennine Way is later signposted to the left, beside a cattle mart. Most walkers will want to cross the bridge over the **River Tees** to visit **Middleton-in-Teesdale**.

MIDDLETON-IN-TEESDALE

Middleton has 12th-century origins and was close to the hunting and grazing grounds of distant Rievaulx Abbey. The Horsemarket and Market Place point to the settlement's importance in a farming region, and the old market cross and remains of the village stocks survive. Water from Hudeshope Beck powered two corn mills. St Mary's Church dates from 1857, but an old arch and detached belfry belong to an earlier church dating from 1557. The churchyard holds the grave of Richard Watson, the celebrated miner-poet of Teesdale.

Middleton became an important lead-mining centre and the town was developed by the London Lead Company (otherwise known as the 'Quaker Company' after the religious persuasion of its directors). It dominated mining activities in Teesdale and far beyond. The region was formerly the world's greatest producer of lead, and the company provided a stable continuity of employment and development for two centuries, from the 1700s to the 1900s. The company superintendent lived in grand style at Middleton House, while loyal employees could expect good accommodation and access to education and other services. At one time 90 per cent of Middleton's working population was employed directly by the company.

Middleton has a full range of facilities, including two hotels with bars, B&Bs and a campsite with a pub. There is a post office, cafés, fish and chip shops, a Co-op with a cashpoint and other shops. Regular daily buses run to Barnard Castle and Darlington, while a Wednesday-only bus runs to Langdon Beck.

DAY 12

Middleton-in-Teesdale to Langdon Beck

Start	Horsemarket, Middleton-in-Teesdale, NY 947 254
Finish	Langdon Beck Hotel, NY 853 312
Alternative finish	Langdon Beck Youth Hostel, NY 860 304
Distance	14km (8.75 miles)
Total ascent	315m (1035ft)
Total descent	160m (525ft)
Time	4hr 15min
Terrain	Easy field paths and riverside paths, passing stunning waterfalls. The route drifts onto more rugged ground later then returns to the riverside.
Maps	OS Landranger 91, OS Explorer OL31, Harvey's Pennine Way Central
Refreshments	Cafés off-route at Low Way Farm and Bowlees. Pubs off-route at High Force and Langdon Beck.

This is a gentle and easy day's walk, and of course the temptation would be to extend it. It could be tagged onto the previous day's walk, or the following day's walk. However, this should be resisted, partly in order to conserve energy for a couple of hard days ahead, but also because there is a lot to see and admire in Teesdale, and it is worth allowing plenty of time. Enjoy the gentle paths beside the River Tees and maybe detour to the Bowlees Visitor Centre to find out more about the natural wonders of Upper Teesdale. Spend time admiring spectacular waterfalls and look out for a range of wildflowers. Detours off-route are necessary to find accommodation around Langdon Beck.

Start from **Middleton-in-Teesdale** and walk down Bridge Street to cross the County Bridge over the **River Tees**. Pass a cattle mart and turn right along a track signposted as the Pennine Way. The track runs from field to field, and from barn to barn, dwindling to a path by the time it reaches a stone step-stile. Cross over and walk along

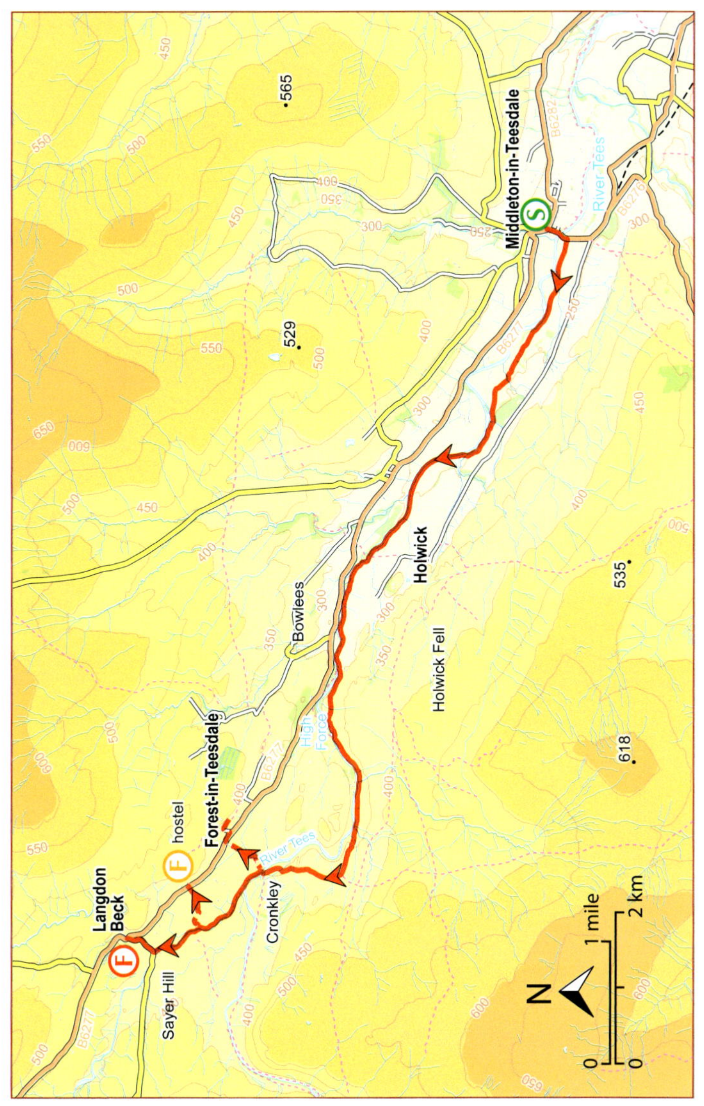

Middleton-in-Teesdale
River Tees
B6282
B6276
B6277
Holwick
Holwick Fell
Bowlees
High Force
Forest-in-Teesdale
hostel
River Tees
Cronkley
Langdon Beck
Sayer Hill
565
529
535
618
N
0
1 mile
0
2 km

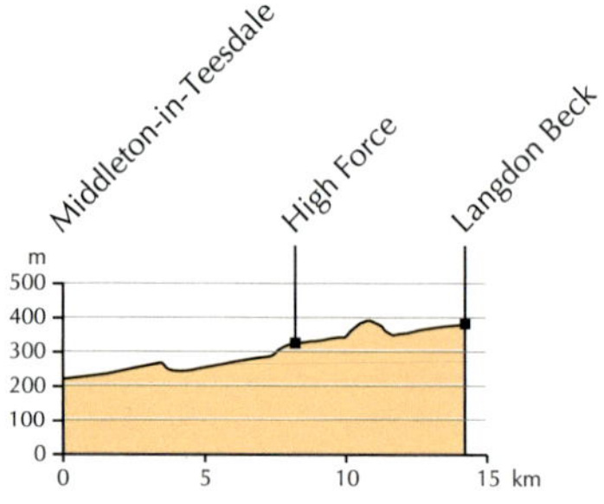

a wooded brow above the Tees, where stout ash and dense alder grow.

The path soon pulls away from the river, avoiding sweeping meanders to take a direct line through flowery fields and grassy pastures, passing more trees and small woods. Cross stone step-stiles over drystone walls, as well as an iron ladder stile. Continue through fields with no views of the river. Climb a little and cross a stream at Park End Wood before catching sight of the Tees. Don't go up to a barn, but watch for a stone step-stile to continue parallel to the river. Notice how many farms and houses are painted white.

Flower-filled meadows are a feature of Teesdale in the summer months

Dozens of **whitewashed farmsteads** are dotted throughout Teesdale, standing in stark contrast to the green fields. There are many tales to explain the colour scheme. One relates that the Duke of Cleveland was wandering lost on the moors in foul weather. He approached a house for shelter, believing it was occupied by his tenants, and was embarrassed to discover that it wasn't. He ordered all the buildings on his estate to be whitewashed, so that he wouldn't make the same mistake again! To this day, Raby Estate properties continue to be whitewashed, with their doorposts and lintels painted black. This doesn't apply south of the Tees, which is part of the Strathmore Estate.

Walk along a wooded brow then head down to cross a footbridge over a stream. Follow a path beside the bouldery, cobbly, swift and noisy River Tees. Pass within sight of Low Way Farm, which offers the Farmhouse Kitchen café and a bunkhouse, and later reach a footbridge called Scoberry Bridge. Don't cross it, but notice how a path leaves the footbridge and heads through fields on the left, leading up to the nearby village of **Holwick**.

Holwick was once the most northerly village in Yorkshire, before being annexed to County Durham. From the River Tees, there is a glimpse of Holwick Lodge, which was built in the late 19th century. It looks palatial and is said to have been used by the late Queen Mother on her honeymoon. Other buildings in the village lie along a road at the foot of rugged cliffs on the Whin Sill.

Further along the riverside path, pass a small waterfall where the Tees is constricted in a rocky channel. Lush greenery flanks a paved stretch of path as the Pennine Way enters the Upper Teesdale National Nature Reserve. When the Tees is seen beyond, it sports low falls and rapids, followed by a stretch where the river slides through a rocky channel with barely a ripple. Wynch Bridge and Low Force are soon reached among mixed woodland.

WYNCH BRIDGE TO BOWLEES

In 1741 the first chain suspension bridge in the country, Wynch Bridge, was strung across the Tees. It collapsed in 1802 and was subsequently repaired and strengthened. The present bridge dates from 1830 and spans the rocky gorge close to the original site. It too has been strengthened and is only designed to allow one person to cross at a time. Crossing the bridge allows a detour off the Pennine Way to visit the nearby village of Bowlees.

Pride of place in Bowlees is an old Methodist chapel converted into a fine visitor centre (free entry, tel 01833 622145). The centre, which is operated by the Durham Wildlife Trust, offers background information and displays relating to the geology, history and natural history of Teesdale. There are plenty of notes about wildflowers, and some species grow outside the building. There is helpful literature on sale, including plant guides specifically about the flowers of Upper Teesdale. There is also a small café on site.

Beyond Wynch Bridge, pass a stone sculpture of a couple of sheep, then pause to admire Low Force, where the Tees pours over a rock-step, then splits into two separate falls over another rock-step. A gravel path continues through a gate, passing riverside trees such as alder, birch and rowan. The path becomes rockier and the Tees alongside seems short of water. In fact, the river splits around a large island and only a little water is seen below. An easy grass or gravel path leads onwards beside the main flow, reaching a footbridge, Holwick Head Bridge. ◂

Don't cross this bridge unless intending to visit the High Force Hotel on the other side of the river.

Crazy paving and steps lead up a slope of flowery turf where delightful little mountain pansies grow. Walk through a gate to follow a gravel path, with birch to the right and juniper to the left. Soon, the land either side of the path is covered in juniper and bracken – this is the most extensive juniper wood in the country. Notices point out that the juniper is suffering from a fungal disease. There is no sight of the Tees, but a rumbling sound gives away the location of **High Force**.

Low Force is one of many splendid waterfalls passed in Teesdale

High Force is England's most powerful waterfall. The best view is from a spur path on the right, before reaching the fall, leading to a cliff-top perch. Don't miss it, or the only other view is from the top of the fall. Enjoy the spectacle of water pouring furiously from a rocky channel, over a rock-step, boiling in a turbulent pool, before rushing through a deep and rocky gorge. This is all seen for free, while people in the gorge have paid for access from the High Force Hotel.

Go through a kissing gate at the top of the waterfall and continue upstream along a gravel path. ▸ This becomes rough and bouldery among bracken and heather later. Cross a footbridge below the little waterfall of Bleabeck Force. Walk along an easy path where rapid progress can be made at Pasture Foot, which is welcome, since there is a noisy, dusty quarry cutting into the Whin Sill on the opposite side of the river.

There might be a disinfectant wash for footwear, to prevent spreading the fungal disease, *Phytophthora austrocedri*, that is killing nearby juniper.

Cross two footbridges close together at Skyer Beck, then the path weaves between clumps of juniper bushes. Walk up stone-slab and duckboard steps on a wet slope.

THE WHIN SILL

Many dramatic landforms in Upper Teesdale, around the North Pennines and into Northumberland, owe their existence to the Whin Sill. This enormous sheet of dolerite was forced into the limestone bedrock under immense pressure in a molten state around 295 million years ago. As the heat dissipated, the limestone in contact with the dolerite baked until its structure altered, forming peculiar 'sugar limestone', which breaks down into a soil preferred by many of Teesdale's wildflowers.

While weathering, the Whin Sill proves more resistant than the rocks above and below it, so it forms dramatic landforms such as Holwick Scars, Cronkley Scar and Falcon Clints. Where the Whin Sill occurs in the bed of the Tees, its abrupt step creates splendid waterfalls such as Low Force, High Force, Bleabeck Force and Cauldron Snout. Later on the Pennine Way, it is responsible for the cliffs of High Cup and the rugged crest bearing Hadrian's Wall. The Whin Sill has been quarried throughout Teesdale, generally being crushed and used as a durable road-stone.

Continue up a firm slope of close-cropped green turf studded with boulders. On top of a grassy crest, a stone bears two arrows. Left is 'GT', for the Green Trod over Cronkley Fell. Right is 'PW' for the Pennine Way. The path is paved with flagstones, heading down into a dip and crossing a stile over a fence.

Follow a wall uphill and go through a gate in a fence. The flagstone path crosses a wet and rushy area, then walk downhill beside the wall. Go through a little gated stile on the right, then continue down through a breach in the Whin Sill, where the path is rugged underfoot and juniper covers nearby slopes. Walk up a path to reach the farm of **Cronkley**. Go through the farmyard and walk down the access track, passing flowery meadows before crossing a bridge over the River Tees.

Turn left to follow the Pennine Way upstream. A narrow path beside the river passes through a kissing gate and crosses a slope of boulder clay subject to slow landslip. Rather than curse the uneven cobbles and mud, spend a while admiring the impressive array of wildflowers. Many species thrive here simply because the ground is unstable, preventing other species from colonising the slope and crowding out the rarities. The path passes the confluence of the River Tees and Langdon Beck, and the latter is followed upstream.

The lonely looking farm of Wheysike House is seen across the broad and bouldery river. The riverside path is rather narrow as it runs beside a wall, and is prone to collapsing into the river at intervals. When Saur Hill Bridge is reached, the Pennine Way turns left to cross it. However, anyone stopping for the night at **Langdon Beck** will need to head off-route.

The aptly named High Force waterfall

Facilities are limited around **Langdon Beck**, and it is not obvious where to find everything. Sayer Hill Farm offers basic riverside camping with no facilities. The access road climbing from the river leads to the B6272 road, where a left turn leads to Langdon Beck Youth Hostel, while a farm road climbs directly to East Underhurth B&B. Walking upstream from Saur Hill Bridge leads to a minor road, where a right turn quickly leads to the Langdon Beck Hotel at a junction with the B6272 road. Steps will need to be retraced the following morning to return to Saur Hill Bridge.

DAY 13

Langdon Beck to Dufton

Start	Langdon Beck Hotel, NY 853 312
Alternative start	Langdon Beck Youth Hostel, NY 860 304
Finish	Dufton Hall, Dufton, NY 690 250
Distance	21km (13 miles)
Total ascent	365m (1200ft)
Total descent	560m (1835ft)
Time	6hr 30min
Terrain	Riverside paths give way to moorland paths. The ascent is gradual, while the descent is rugged at first, with a steep track and road at the end.
Maps	OS Landranger 91, OS Explorer OL19, Harvey's Pennine Way Central
Refreshments	Pub and café at Dufton.

This is a wonderfully varied day, starting in the flowery meadows and hayfields of Upper Teesdale, over 350m (1150ft). The Pennine Way follows the River Tees upstream to the powerful Cauldron Snout. There are fine little falls on Maize Beck during a moorland traverse in the middle of the day. A footbridge installed in recent years avoids the need to use a former 'flood route' further upstream. High Cup appears suddenly and boasts a stunning symmetry, where the Whin Sill forms cliffs on either side of the valley, framing a distant view of the Lake District. A long descent leads to the charming village of Dufton, built of red sandstone on the fringe of the Vale of Eden.

Returning to the Pennine Way

If returning from the Langdon Beck Hotel, follow the riverside path and don't cross Saur Hill Bridge. From Langdon Beck Youth Hostel, turn left along the road, then right down a farm access road to cross Saur Hill Bridge over Langdon Beck.

The Pennine Way turns left just before the farm at **Sayer Hill**. Cross a grassy rise to find the first of a few white-painted stone step-stiles. Walk from one to another through fields that have occasional short duckboards over wet patches. The path runs along a brow overlooking the River Tees then gradually drops to run alongside it. Stay close to the river, keeping away from **Widdybank Farm**.

> Haymaking comes late around **Widdybank Farm** compared to farms further down Teesdale, owing to the altitude and resulting lower temperatures. Flowers growing in this area have a chance to ripen and drop their seeds before mowing takes place, resulting in self-regenerating, species-rich meadows. The farm is a base for Natural England staff working on the Upper Teesdale and Moor House National Nature Reserves.

Join and follow a track away from the farm, through a gate and further upstream at Holmwath. The track becomes a broad carpet of short green grass. After passing through a kissing gate, the riverside path crosses small boulders, a duckboard, then big, awkward boulders. Alternating duckboard and paved stretches pass a juniper-covered island in the Tees. The path becomes rough and bouldery again, with crumbling, baked rock revealed

Walkers cross awkward boulder slopes at Falcon Clints

beneath the whinstone cliffs of **Falcon Clints**, with an impressive amount of wild thyme.

Cross some big, awkward boulders, then follow easy stretches of flagstone path and duckboards, keeping walkers off a boulder-scree and bog. More wild thyme grows on the dry parts, while bog asphodel grows on the wet parts. After one last stretch of boulder-hopping, the path reaches the confluence of the River Tees and Maize Beck, for a sudden view of **Cauldron Snout**.

The Tees is confined to a steep and narrow rock gorge, where the water boils furiously as it beats against the walls and tumbles over rock-steps. Hands must be used to scramble up big, chunky rock-steps alongside. The rock can be slippery when wet, and has been polished by the boots of previous visitors. At the top of the falls, a flagstone path leads to a narrow road beneath the concrete dam of **Cow Green Reservoir**.

> **Cow Green Reservoir** was constructed to slake the thirst of Teesmouth and its burgeoning industries. Sadly, an area rich in rare plants was drowned, despite vociferous protests, although some

last-minute transplantation took place. The dam was built between 1967 and 1970 and holds 41 million cubic metres of water (9000 million gallons). The surface of the water covers 310 hectares (770 acres) and is 489m (1603ft) above sea level. Water is not piped away, but simply impounded and released as required, regulating the flow of the River Tees, allowing water to be abstracted much further downstream at Broken Scar, for domestic use, and at Blackwell and Yarm, for industrial use.

Turn left to follow the road over a bridge, then keep left to follow a track over a cattle grid to cross a rushy

The River Tees in a constricted channel at Cauldron Snout

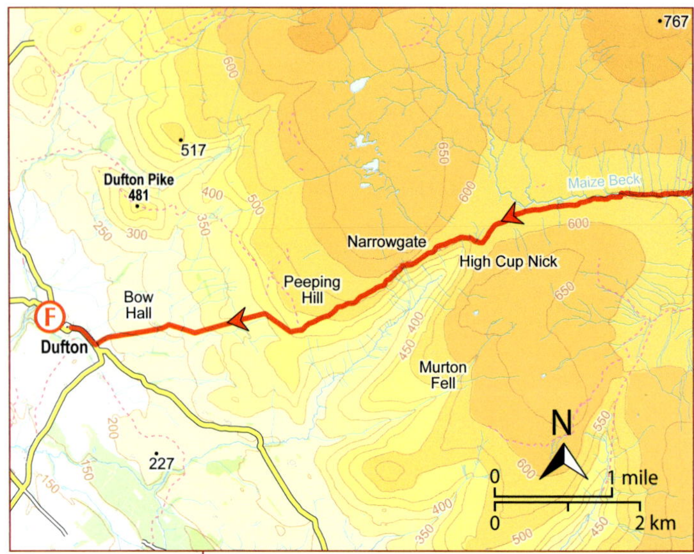

rise near a barn. The track undulates onwards, crossing another cattle grid and passing a couple more barns, before reaching a remote farm at **Birkdale**. Pass in front of the farmhouse and follow the track through a couple of fields to reach Grain Beck, crossing a footbridge. Ahead stretch extensive, open and exposed moorlands.

A flagstone path climbs easily on a grassy, rushy moorland and a stony track winds further uphill, eventually climbing onto an old mine spoil at **Moss Shop**. Nearby is a flagpole that will usually be flying a red flag. This marks the boundary of a military firing range, the Warcop Training Area. At no point does the Pennine Way enter it, but 'danger' notices are seen at regular intervals. A firm, stony track continues beyond the mine spoil. The moorland is heather and grass, mossy in places, with sedge, rushes and a little bog cotton. The track was recently constructed to replace a path across the moors, and while it offers easy walking and route-finding, it also reduces the feeling of being in a wild area. The ground

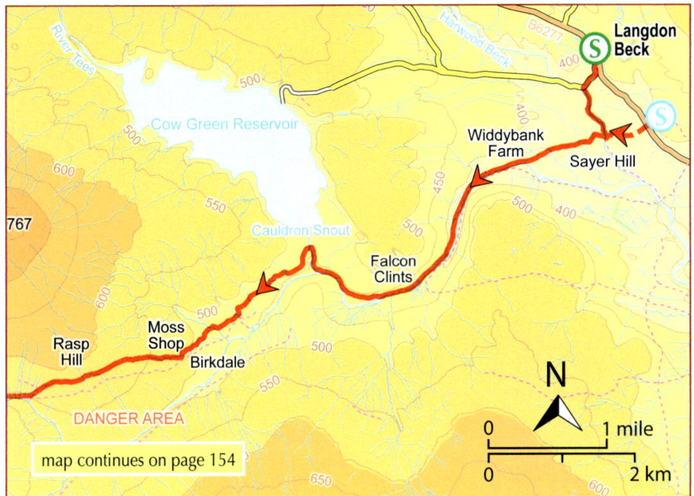

map continues on page 154

rises to around 590m (1935ft) on **Rasp Hill**, speckled with flowers and abundant thistles. ▸

A signpost points left down a path, where blanket bog features grass, sedge and rushes, with little bridges across drainage ditches, and several wet patches. Further downhill there is a stretch of flagstone path, then firmer ground is reached as the path drops towards **Maize Beck**. Head upstream along a pleasant strip of limestone grassland, passing a spring near an attractive little waterfall over a rock-step. Head upstream to find a footbridge, and cross to the other side. ▸

Walk along a short flagstone path and turn right to continue upstream, gradually climbing above the beck. The path is covered in uneven stones and crosses a grassy, rushy slope. The path becomes easier once it is routed along another band of limestone, where the path is smooth and covered in short, green turf. The path climbs gently uphill, pulls away from the beck and crosses the broad and level gap of High Cup Plain.

Watch for occasional upright stone slabs beside the path, especially in mist, as one of them bears a carved

Rising on the skyline are some of the bleakest, boggiest and most forbidding moorlands in England, such as Mickle Fell, Little Fell, Murton Fell and Meldon Hill.

The Pennine Way used to ford the river, or if it was in flood, an alternative route continued upstream to another footbridge.

Dolerite is sandwiched between layers of limestone at High Cup

According to a local story, Nichol was a Dufton cobbler who scaled the column, then soled and heeled a pair of shoes on top.

arrow indicating a right turn downhill. The path quickly reaches a little stream that passes through a rocky cleft at **High Cup Nick**. Cross the stream and walk on the level rocky top of the Whin Sill, and be sure to seek out great viewpoints to appreciate the striking lines of columnar cliffs on either side of High Cup. In the distance, the eastern parts of the Lake District can be seen across the Vale of Eden. Climb uphill a little and follow a path along a limestone terrace along the northern rim of the valley. Walk on pleasant short turf, with the whinstone cliffs below and boulder-scree above. Watch carefully for a brief glimpse of Nichol's Chair – a whinstone pinnacle. ◂

The Pennine Way originally stayed close to the edge along a natural paved path called **Narrowgate**, but has been diverted a little further uphill onto a roller-coaster path crossing boulder-scree and flagstones. Either way, the route crosses a couple of gushing streams, then there is a single path marked later. Leaving High Cup, the path rises and falls across slopes of grass, sedge and rushes, almost touching 590m (1935ft). Views encompass the Lake District and the northern parts of the Yorkshire Dales. It can be rough and stony where the bedrock is sandstone, or smooth where the bedrock is limestone. One stretch runs down a slope of sandstone boulders, while later the track winds down a limestone edge at **Peeping Hill** to reach a drystone wall and gates.

Pass through a sheepfold to pick up a stony track leading down a steep and grassy slope. The track swings right and aims directly towards the conical form of **Dufton Pike**, passing through a gate. It later swings left, more directly downhill, passing through another gate. Now enclosed by drystone walls, the track passes a number of large trees, the first seen since Birkdale, then it continues as a narrow road passing **Bow Hall**.

The road passes large, rough pastures, and there are a lot of gorse bushes along one stretch. When a road junction is reached, turn right uphill to enter the village of **Dufton**, and follow the road past Brow Farm to Dufton Hall. Note that the Pennine Way turns right here, but anyone heading for the central village green should turn left and right by the road, returning to Dufton Hall to pick up the route again.

DUFTON

The village is an Anglo-Saxon settlement, originally formed of simple huts arranged around a broad green. This allowed animals to be corralled, and in later times safeguarded them from border reivers and raiders. In the early 17th century the houses were rebuilt in red sandstone, then further improvements came in the 18th century with the support of the London Lead Company, or 'Quaker Company'. Lead was mined in Great Rundale, ceasing around 1900, but barytes was mined until 1924. More recently the spoil has been worked for fluorspar, which was originally a 'waste' mineral.

Accommodation in Dufton is limited to the Pennine Potting Shed at Dufton Barn, a youth hostel and a campsite with Hobbit Huts. The Post Box Pantry is a café that also sells basic provisions. The Stag Inn offers food and drink, while the youth hostel has a small food store. Everything is arranged around a central green, surrounded by towering lime trees. There is an attractive old water pump, installed by the London Lead Company. The town of Appleby, which has a full range of services, lies 5km (3 miles) off-route.

DAY 14

Dufton to Alston

Start	Dufton Hall, Dufton, NY 690 250
Finish	The Firs, Alston, NY 716 461
Distance	31.5km (19.5 miles)
Total ascent	1050m (3445ft)
Total descent	970m (3180ft)
Time	10hr
Terrain	The highest, most remote and most exposed part of the route. Mostly good paths and tracks, but careful route-finding is required on the initial ascent and over Cross Fell, where paths are vague. Most of the descent is along a clear track.
Maps	OS Landranger 86 or 87 and 91, OS Explorer OL19 and OL31, Harvey's Pennine Way Central
Refreshments	Plenty of choice around Alston.

This is the longest and toughest day on the Pennine Way. It can be shortened by calling a halt at Garrigill, and, in case of real difficulty, the route can be abandoned before Great Dun Fell, where there is a road, or beyond Cross Fell, where Greg's Hut offers basic shelter. In clear weather, this is a splendid stage, climbing high and staying high, enjoying wide-ranging views. However, these hills hold the English records for bad weather. Spare a thought for the miners who once had to live and work high on the moors, enduring cold, damp and the slow poisoning of their health in lead mines.

To leave **Dufton**, pick up the course of the Pennine Way from the corner of the road beside Dufton Hall, where the route is signposted along a track. Follow the track down into a dip, then turn left through a gate to follow a flagstone path enclosed by trees. This gives way to a fenced path between fields, passing through gates. Cross a stream and follow the path up past some trees.

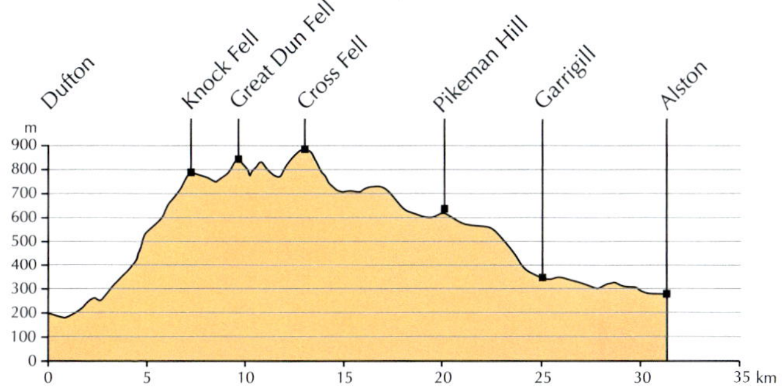

Continue straight along a track to pass a bungalow and Coatsike Farm. A short-cut is available from Dufton. Take the road heading for **Knock** and turn right to follow the access road to Coatsike Farm.

Go straight through the farmyard and follow a grassy track through gates. The way is quickly flanked by ash and hawthorn, and as the rugged track climbs it diminishes to a sunken path, passing a ruined farmhouse at Halsteads. Continue straight ahead, following a track over a grassy rise and down to a gate. Cross a stone 'clapper' footbridge over Great Rundale Beck, then walk up the track and turn right to climb straight uphill, alongside a wall, on a rushy slope. ▶

The highest Pennine summits are ahead, with the foothills of Dufton Pike to the right and Knock Pike to the left. The Lake District is behind, far across the Vale of Eden.

Go through a couple of gates and the track turns sharp left, away from the wall, climbing up a grassy, rushy moorland slope. When a signpost for the Pennine Way is reached, turn left along a narrow, grassy path. Cross a stone step-stile over a wall and walk across a slope of heather and bilberry. Cross another stone step-stile to reach a stout footbridge spanning **Swindale Beck**.

Climb a few stone steps and pass a sign announcing the Moor House and Upper Teesdale National nature reserves. Follow a narrow, grassy path up a steep, grassy slope bearing rashes of boulders. Throughout the climb, steep and gentle slopes alternate on slopes of grass, sedge and moss, where there are a couple of marker posts.

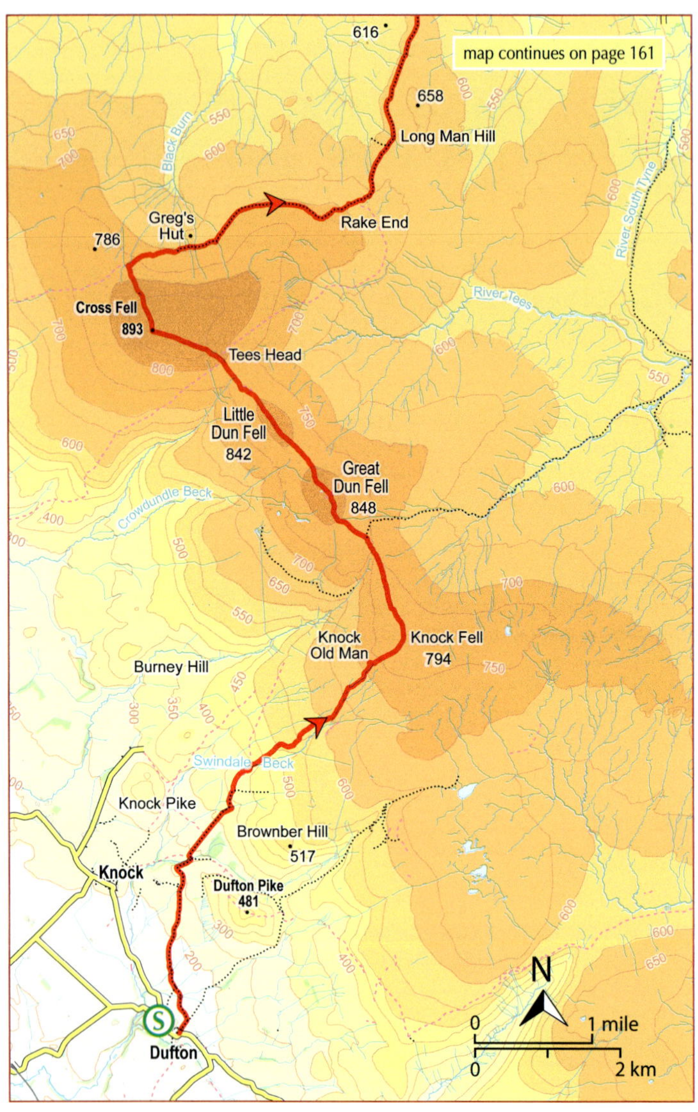

map continues on page 161
616
658
Long Man Hill
Black Burn
Rake End
Greg's Hut
786
Cross Fell
893
River Tees
River South Tyne
Tees Head
Little Dun Fell
842
Great Dun Fell
848
Crowdundle Beck
Knock Old Man
Knock Fell
794
Burney Hill
Swindale Beck
Knock Pike
Brownber Hill
517
Knock
Dufton Pike
481
Dufton
N
0
1 mile
0
2 km

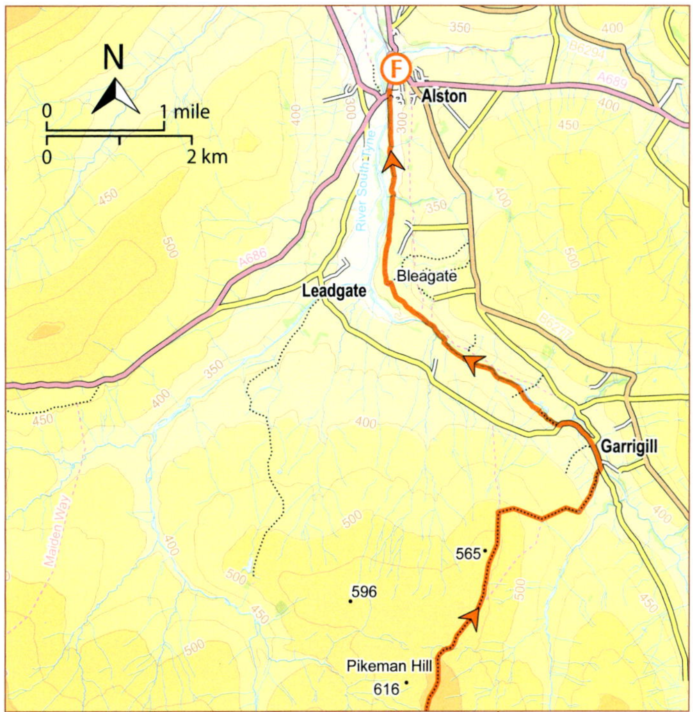

The bouldery parts may bear cairns. In clear weather, a prominent cairn can be seen on the skyline, and this will be reached in due course. In mist, stay on the path at all times and take note of occasional stone slabs bearing directional arrows, especially where the trodden path varies slightly from the route marked on OS maps on Green Fell.

One marker stone occurs where the path swings left and climbs alongside a straight stream, known locally as a 'hush'. ▸ At the top of the hush, a small ruined hut can be seen away to the left. The path crosses a wet, peaty shelf, then more marker stones indicate a path winding up a steep limestone slope, which is firm and dry underfoot.

A hush was formed by miners continually damming and releasing water to scour the hillside, exposing the bedrock in the hope of finding mineral veins.

The cairn of Knock Old Man with Great Dun Fell seen beyond

The path finally reaches a large, square-built cairn on a boulder-strewn moor. This is the cairn that was seen earlier on the skyline, called **Knock Old Man**. In mist, be aware that it does not mark the summit. Climb a little further at a gentle gradient to reach a final hump and a smaller cairn on **Knock Fell**, at 794m (2605ft). This is the highest point so far along the Pennine Way, but its moment of glory is short-lived and soon to be eclipsed!

Veer left to pick up the path leaving the summit, although the line gets lost among black peat and stony patches, grass and sedge. In clear weather, this is no problem since the 'radome' on the top of Great Dun Fell is a prominent feature to aim for, but in mist great care needs to be taken to locate a flagstone path downhill. This winds between bog pools and has a couple of gaps in its course. The flags run out as the path crosses firmer ground on a gap where the bedrock is limestone.

In foul weather, if inclined to abandon the route, turn left to follow the road down to the village of Knock and return to Dufton.

Step up onto a road and turn right to follow it gently uphill. ◀ There is a barrier across the road, as well as a gate across a track on the right. The Pennine Way simply leaves the road, avoids the track, and climbs straight uphill. Another 'hush' is encountered and the path climbs alongside, then turns right to cross it using a few steps. Climb towards the 'radome' on top of **Great Dun Fell**, at 848m (2782ft). Once again, this is the highest point so far along the Pennine Way, and once again it will soon be surpassed!

> The big white 'radome' makes **Great Dun Fell** unmistakeable in distant views. It has operated since 1988, replacing a radar array that operated since 1948. National Air Traffic Services (NATS) monitors aircraft as well as the weather. Among decades of weather archives, some all-England records for weather conditions are found, including the greatest number of foggy days, the highest wind speed and the most prolonged frost. Bear in mind that the annual mean temperature is only 4°C (39°F), while over 200 days may feature mist, and over 100 days feature gale-force winds! The road to the 'radome' is the highest in England. Note how lush the grass and flowers are inside the compound fence, compared to the bleak sheep-grazed moorlands stretching endlessly beyond.

A flagstone path crosses bogs on the way to Great Dun Fell

CROSS FELL

View from Cross Fell to Little and Great Dun Fell, home of English records for extreme weather

Cross Fell is the highest point on the Pennine Way and the highest point in England outside the Lake District. Imagine how high it would be if it rose to a peak, instead of being a flat plateau. It used to be called Fiends Fell, recorded as such in 1340 and 1479. William Camden, writing in *Britannica*, published in 1586, said that a cross had been planted on the summit to banish the 'fiends'. It seems that they weren't banished far, as there is a Fiends Fell rising northwest, near Hartside.

In fine weather there are extensive views, but the broad plateau prevents any sense of depth. The patchwork Vale of Eden stretches to the Yorkshire Dales, Howgill Fells and the serrated skyline of the Lake District. Parts of southern Scotland are in view, and the Cheviot Hills form a conspicuous group. Closer to hand are some of the bleakest and most formidable of the North Pennines. Most walkers crossing the plateau are aware of the dimpled ground underfoot. Look carefully and you will see that slight humps of stones are separated by lower areas of gravel. These are 'stone polygons', formed by repeated freezing and thawing of the ground since the end of the Ice Age.

Leaving the summit is no problem in clear weather, but in mist be sure to pick up the flagstone path that offers a sure guide northwest. The path crosses grass, sedge, moss and bog cotton, but shortly after rising from a gap the flagstones finish. Climb straight up a steep, grassy slope and walk along a broad crest of short turf, passing a cairn. The summit of **Little Dun Fell** is 842m (2762ft) and the crest becomes boulder-strewn, bearing a couple of shelter cairns.

Pass the shelter cairns and follow a vague path down a boulder-studded grassy slope. A long flagstone path leads almost to a broad and boggy gap at **Tees Head**, where there is bog cotton and a National Nature Reserve notice. Follow a flagstone path uphill. The path has steps and climbs a rugged slope to pass a spring among masses of moss. Climb further up a bouldery slope to reach a tall cairn on a gentle, boulder-strewn slope. In mist, proceed with care as there is only a vaguely trodden path leading to another cairn, and it is necessary to walk across a broad plateau to reach the summit cairn, trig point and cross-shelter on **Cross Fell**, at 893m (2930ft).

Leaving the summit of Cross Fell, a vague path is marked by cairns, and there are pieces of flagstones scattered around as the ground begins to fall. Expect lots of wet and boggy ground on the way downhill, where multiple paths try to outflank difficulties. A large cairn is reached where a clear path, known as the Corpse Road, slices across the hillside. Turn right to follow it downhill, passing sink holes, going through a gate and joining a track to **Greg's Hut**.

The remote bothy known as **Greg's Hut** was once a mining 'shop', or a lodging house for miners who

The remote bothy of Greg's Hut offers shelter near Cross Fell

lived and worked in this remote place, only going home at weekends. It stands at 700m (2300ft) and offers basic shelter to considerate users. In foul weather, bear in mind that only half the distance between Dufton and Garrigill has been covered, and the Pennine Way stays remarkably high on exposed moors for most of the way to Garrigill.

There are views across Alston Moor and far beyond to the distant Cheviot Hills.

Leave Greg's Hut by walking along the track, gently downhill, then gradually uphill, passing a couple more ruins associated with old lead mines. ◀ When the track crosses a moorland rise above the Lambgreen Hills, there is a view back to Cross Fell, Little Dun Fell, Great Dun Fell, Knock Fell and the Cow Green Reservoir. The track winds down past old mine spoil, where little chips of purple fluorspar catch the eye. Keep straight ahead where another stony track heads off to the right to **Rake End**.

Walk down the winding track, through a gate, and continue with a fence running parallel on the right, although it later drifts away. Keep straight ahead at another junction, where a track heads off to the left, and again keep straight ahead where another track heads off to the right. A gradual climb leads across a rushy slope on **Long Man Hill**. The track undulates across the high moors on **Pikeman Hill**, at 616m (2021ft), where there is later grass and heather. A fence appears on the right and runs alongside the track. Go through a gate and cross another heather moor, where a drystone wall appears on the right.

Go through a gate and the track climbs gently with walls on both sides, still running across grass and heather moorland. The track is enclosed throughout its descent from the moors, turning a series of corners as it drops down past fields into South Tynedale. **Garrigill** is in view long before it is reached. Turn left along a road to reach the green in the middle of the village.

Accommodation and services come and go at **Garrigill**. The George and Dragon Inn was being restored in 2024, while the Post Office barely

The Pennine Way runs through fields from Garrigill to Alston

survives and East View offers B&B accommodation. The Village Hall operates a bunkroom and the field alongside is used as a basic campsite. If a greater range of services are required, then continue to Alston.

Leave Garrigill along the road signposted for Leadgate. The road passes an old school and runs beside the **River South Tyne**, then, when it climbs above it, turn right through a small gate beside a large gate, and follow a track to some spoil heap and assorted junk. Bear left to pass this and cross a stile, then follow a path up a grassy bank to walk beside a stand of Scots pine. Walk down a grassy slope and follow a wooded riverside path, crossing stiles to emerge in a field and reach a footbridge. ▸

This footbridge was closed for repairs in 2024 and an alternative route was signposted on the opposite side of the river after passing the old school.

Cross the River South Tyne and turn left, soon following the path away from the river, rising gently to reach a farmhouse at Sillyhall. Follow a field path as marked, over a rise to reach the farm of **Bleagate**. Turn left between the buildings and then right to continue through fields. The path stays away from the river, crossing stone step-stiles or passing through gaps in walls. Pass below a couple of houses at Cowgap and head down to cross a footbridge over a stream. The path continues through fields, then up onto a brow, passing between fields and big beech trees. This stretch is known as The Firs, reaching the youth hostel at the bottom end of **Alston**. The Pennine Way is signposted left down a path, where steps lead to a road, but most wayfarers will wish to enter the town, in which case they should keep straight ahead.

ALSTON

Alston claims to be the highest market town in England, It rises from the banks of the River South Tyne at 280m (920ft), reaching 320m (1050ft) at a primary school at the top of the town. The Market Cross in the town centre is essentially a roof supported on stone pillars. It has been demolished by runaway trucks, not once, but twice. It was gifted to the town in 1765 by William Stephenson, an Alston man who became Mayor of London. St Augustine's Church is easily spotted because of its tall spire. Several fine stone buildings have been erected by public subscription. It is well worth wandering around the quaint and poky back alleys, such as The Butts, once used for archery practice, and Gossipgate.

Most of Alston's facilities are arranged beside the steep, cobbled Front Street, where a shopping trip needs careful planning to avoid unnecessary ascents and descents! Alston has one of the best ranges of services on the Pennine Way. There is a post office, pubs, cafés, a fish and chip shop, and the Spar and Co-op have cashpoints. A range of accommodation includes hotels, B&Bs and a youth hostel. Buses run daily, except Sundays, to Haltwhistle, and occasionally to Hexham. The South Tynedale Railway runs from Alston to Slaggyford (tel 01434 338214, www.south-tynedale-railway.org.uk). It is accompanied by the South Tyne Trail, which some walkers prefer to use instead of the Pennine Way. Tourist information is available at the Town Hall (tel 01434 382244).

DAY 15

Alston to Greenhead

Start	The Firs, Alston, NY 716 461
Finish	Greenhead Hotel, Greenhead, NY 659 653
Distance	27.5km (17 miles)
Total ascent	655m (2150ft)
Total descent	800m (2625ft)
Time	8hr 30min
Terrain	The route runs through a valley, but includes several ascents and descents, in and out of fields, using paths and tracks. Paths become vague as the route heads across broad and boggy moorlands.
Maps	OS Landranger 86, OS Explorer 31 and 43, Harvey's Pennine Way Central
Refreshments	Farm shop and café near Whitley Castle. Little Buffet Car at Slaggyford Station when trains are running. Pub off-route at Knarsdale. Pub and tearoom at Greenhead.

On the map, this seems like an easy day's walk, but it can be time-consuming negotiating fiddly field paths. The Pennine Way wanders up and down the slopes of South Tynedale using vague paths, passing houses and farms, crossing stiles and going through gates. The old railway trackbed linking Alston to Haltwhistle now carries both the South Tynedale Railway and South Tyne Trail. Some walkers take a short-cut along the South Tyne Trail from Alston to Knarsdale, but this smacks of cheating and you would miss seeing Whitley Castle Roman fort. The course of the Maiden Way Roman road is used to cross low moorlands. Later, there is awkward route-finding over the moorlands of Hartleyburn Common.

SOUTH TYNEDALE RAILWAY

The Newcastle & Carlisle Railway Company originally planned a railway from Haltwhistle to the lead mines at Nenthead, but later decided to terminate the line at Alston, abandoning what would have been a steep climb towards the end. The line was constructed between 1851 and 1852, featuring nine viaducts spanning the River South Tyne and some of its tributaries. As well as transporting lead ore, the railway carried passengers until closure in 1976.

The South Tynedale Railway Preservation Society (tel 01434 338214, www.south-tynedale-railway.org.uk) operates a narrow-gauge railway along the old trackbed from Alston, which currently terminates at Slaggyford. Beyond Slaggyford the trackbed continues as the South Tyne Trail and is popular with cyclists and walkers all the way to Haltwhistle.

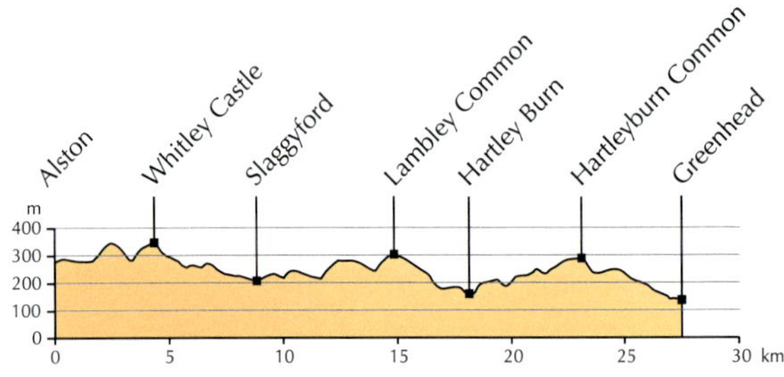

Leave The Firs at **Alston** by walking down a short flight of steps on a wooded slope to reach the main **A686** road. Turn left to cross a bridge over the **River South Tyne**, then turn right at a junction with the **A689** signposted for Brampton. Almost immediately, turn right down a track and turn left to avoid a house. Walk through a wood and up towards another house. Keep left to pass the house using a narrow, enclosed path. Walk straight ahead along a field path, passing an old gateway and crossing a wide, grassy bridge over a stream. Turn left up towards Harbut Lodge.

Keep left of all the buildings, then turn right and follow the edge of a field. Turn left up a track to reach the **A689** road and turn right to pass **Harbut Law B&B**. Turn left as signposted for the Pennine Way to leave the road. Pass through a couple of gates and pass a barn, then follow a narrow, grassy path straight up a rushy slope. Climb alongside a wall, but drift right at the top to cross a stone step-stile over another wall. Walk gently down across two rushy fields, passing gates, then drop steeply down to a footbridge over Gilderdale Burn.

Climb steeply uphill to the right from a little limestone terrace. Continue over a rushy field to pass through a gate in a wall as marked. Head uphill using a fence as a guide on rumpled ground and go through another gate in a wall as marked. Walk up a grassy track and go through a gate in a fence, around 340m (1115ft). A noticeboard explains about **Whitley Castle**, or Epiacum.

All that remains of **Whitley Castle** hillside fort, which the Romans called Epiacum, is the square ground plan and an impressive series of parallel embankments and ditches – up to eight of them at one point. Two corners stand proud, where watchtowers would have stood. The site affords fine views over South Tynedale and the fort was an important point on the Maiden Way Roman road, a stretch of which is followed later. A noticeboard explains about the site and illustrates how it might once have looked. The site can be explored more closely by crossing a ladder stile over a wall, to reach the earthworks. It is also possible to walk down to The Nook Farm Shop and Café using a permitted path.

Follow the track gradually down to a gateway in a wall and pass through. Continue down towards the farm of Castle Nook. Don't enter the farmyard, but duck left into a wood and cross a stream, then follow a path down to the **A689** road. Cross the road and go through a gate, then head left down towards a building. Keep right of this and other houses, passing through gates. A field path runs gently down towards a farm, and the embankment of the South Tynedale Railway is seen to the right. There is access to the tiny Kirkhaugh Station.

Turn left up a narrow farm access road at Kirkhaugh, then right as signposted for the Pennine Way just above the farm. Look ahead to spot stiles to pass through a couple of fields then go through a gate in the next field. Don't

The route passes beneath a fine railway arch at Lintley

head downhill, but contour across a slope to find a ladder stile. Two more ladder stiles need to be crossed before the field path runs along the foot of the old railway embankment, near the tiny Lintley Station. Cross the access track serving the nearby farm of **Lintley**. Don't approach the farm, but cross a footbridge over Thornhope Burn, then turn right to pass under a railway viaduct.

A well-wooded riverside path, often overgrown later, leads to a small field where the broad and brown **River South Tyne** is followed downstream. The path crosses a steep, wooded slope, then runs easily through another field. As the path broadens, it climbs to the **A689** road, where a right turn leads straight to the village of **Slaggyford**. Refreshments are available at the Little Buffet Car when the South Tynedale Railway is running trains. Turn left to follow a road up through the village green, then turn right at the Yew Tree Chapel. A track leads gently uphill among trees, running parallel to the old railway trackbed. Don't join, cross or follow the trackbed, but follow the track uphill, until it diminishes to a path and runs downhill. Stout stone 'PW' markers keep walkers on course.

A farm is passed at Kirkhaugh on the way to Slaggyford

Cross a little footbridge and walk down into a wooded valley to cross a footbridge over Knar Burn below a towering stone viaduct. Turn right to reach a field, then left to find an arch under the old railway. Pass through it and climb straight ahead up a groove beside a field. A grassy track leads up to the farm of **Merry Knowe**. Keep just to the right of the buildings, crossing stone step-stiles over walls between a couple of yards beside buildings. Leave the farm by following a field path, lining up stiles and gates while heading downhill to reach a minor road.

Cross the road and cross a ladder stile, then head up through a field to cross another ladder stile. Walk across a couple of fields, then down stone steps. Go through an arch under a railway viaduct to reach a house and the **A689** road at **Burnstones**. ▶ Turn left to follow the road across a river and back through another arch under the railway viaduct. An access road for Knarsdale Hall is reached, where the Pennine Way is signposted.

The Kirkstyle Inn & Sportsman's Rest pub lies nearby.

Go through a gate, climb through a field and head for its top corner to go through a kissing gate. Turn right to follow a track uphill until the Pennine Way is signposted off to the right, above Side House, and note a

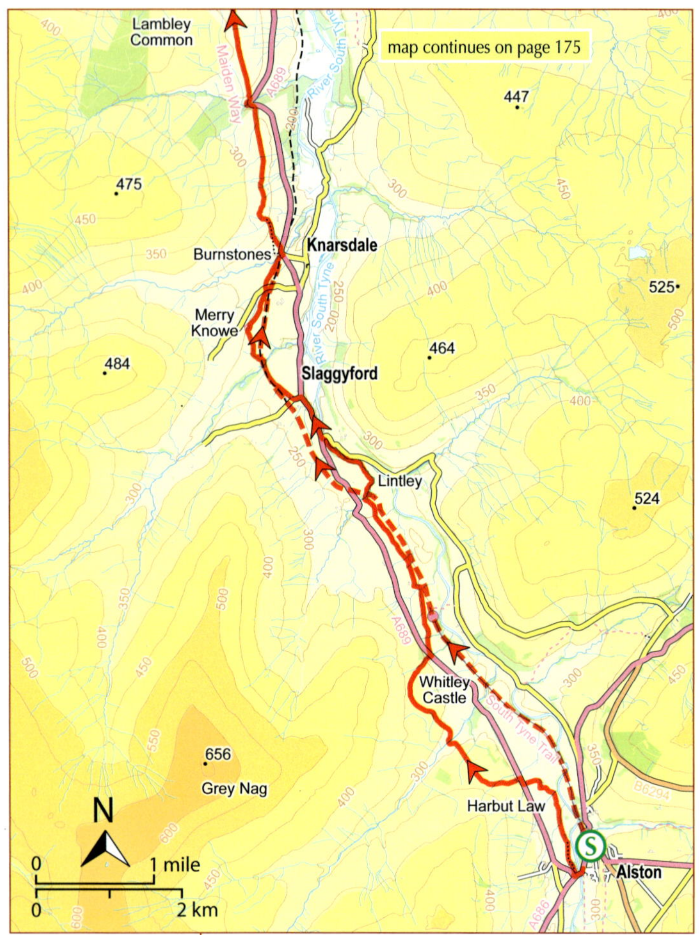

distant view of The Cheviot. A vague path leads down a rushy slope, then turn left along a broad, boggy, rushy old track. This is the Roman road of **Maiden Way** and it becomes drier later, passing through a gate, gaining a stony surface. However, the stony track bends uphill,

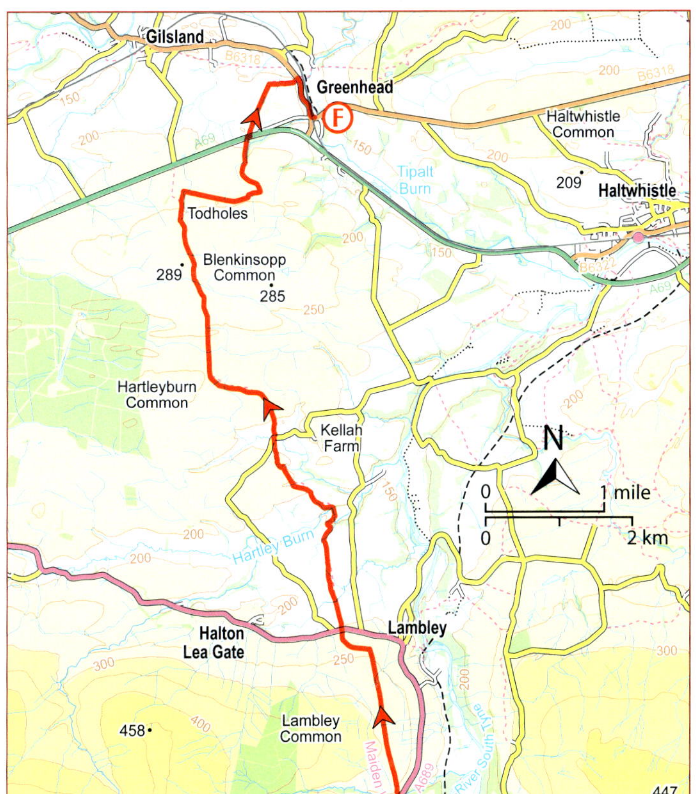

so fork right, straight ahead across a rushy slope to pass through another gate. Further along, cross a ladder stile and a step-stile over two fences close together.

The Romans might have penetrated the North Pennines to search for mineral riches, but no-one knows for sure. Nor does anyone know if they had names for their roads. **Maydengathe** was the name of this route in an abbey record of 1179. William Camden, writing in his book *Britannica*, which was published in 1586, mentioned 'a street called Mayden Way, which is paved with stones throughout the moors, about some forty miles in length'. It is still known as Maiden Way to this day.

A narrow path continues between a drystone wall and a fence along a broad, grassy, rushy strip of moorland. At first the path is beside the wall, heading over a gentle rise and downhill, but the wall and fence both drift away later. Cross a step-stile over a fence, and although a road bend is in view ahead, keep well to the left to miss it and cross a footbridge over Glendue Burn. Cross a step-stile over a fence and climb to the right, following the fence and a drystone wall between a patch of woodland and a heather moor. Cross a stone step-stile and continue to follow the wall uphill. There is grass and bracken on this side of the wall, with plenty of rushes later, while on the other side there is a grass and heather moor mixed with mossy bog.

Cross a step-stile over an adjoining fence and continue over a rushy crest at almost 300m (985ft) on **Lambley Common**. The drystone wall ends suddenly.

The Roman road of Maiden Way is followed across Lambley Common

Cross another step-stile over an adjoining fence and continue walking straight ahead, now using a fence as a guide. The ground is very boggy at first, with rushes and squelchy moss, but it gets firmer and starts to descend gently. Cross yet another step-stile over an adjoining fence.

Follow the fence down a rushy slope and cross a final step-stile over an adjoining fence. Continue down a gentle, grassy, rushy slope where a track forms underfoot. This leads down to a road and a house, but the Pennine Way doesn't go that far. ▸ Instead, turn left across a step-stile over the fence, as indicated by an 'acorn' marker. Walk along a narrow path across a heather and bilberry moor. The path becomes vague, so drift downhill to the right, reaching the **A689** road where there is a step-stile over a fence, and a Pennine Way signpost.

Go that way if staying off-route at the Greenriggs Campsite & Shepherd's Huts.

Cross over the road and cross a ladder stile over a drystone wall, also signposted for the Pennine Way. Follow a wall down and across a grassy, rushy area. Most of what lies to the right was formerly a coal mine and the grassy slope is all colliery spoil. When the wall levels out and turns left, leave it and cross a stone-slab footbridge over Black Burn. Walk straight up a vague path on a gently sloping grass and rushy moor. A few stretches of flagstones cross boggy patches, then a marker stone on a little hump of spoil indicates a drift to the right. Cross a step-stile over a fence and continue across tussocky, rushy moorland, with extensive bog cotton. Look ahead to spot a few marker posts, then cross a muddy dip and climb on firm ground to reach a prominent ruined barn.

Turn right and head down a grassy crest, keeping to the left-hand side of a deepening groove. When alder and birch woods are reached, swing left downhill, then turn right to cross a footbridge over **Hartley Burn**. Turn left to head upstream, cross a step-stile over a fence, and make a short, steep climb up a wooded slope. Turn left to continue as marked across a field, reaching another step-stile over a fence. The stile is inscribed 'NOT Pennine Way', so do not cross it, but turn right to follow the fence uphill, passing a few trees. At the top of the grassy, rushy field, the fence gives way to a drystone wall. Turn left through a gate and aim diagonally across a field to reach a fence. Turn right as marked, in and out of a steep-sided little valley.

Follow the fence towards the farm at Batey Shield, where there are lots of outbuildings. On reaching these, turn right to go through a gate in a wall, then turn left along a track to pass between some of the outbuildings. Go through a gate on the right, marked with an 'acorn', to keep right of the farmhouse. Walk down a field and cross a footbridge over Kellah Burn, then immediately cross a minor road and walk straight up a track. ◄ Go through a gate and pass just to the left of a cottage, then cross a ladder stile.

Kellah Farm B&B lies off-route to the right.

Take care from this point, first climbing straight up through a field, with barely a trace of a path. Watch carefully to spot the top of a ladder stile over a fence, lost among rushes at the top of the field. Once across, continue along a narrow path across the rushy moor of **Hartleyburn Common**. Gradually, this begins to drift left, but be careful not to drift too far left. The correct line follows a sort of broad, high crest, avoiding rushy, boggy

The last house before the boggy moorland of Hartleyburn Common

hollows, to reach a marker post beside a fence, at almost 250m (820ft). If the path is lost, the main thing is to head towards the fence, then use it as a guide.

Turn right to follow the fence, which runs down onto a level, squelchy bog and crosses a little footbridge. Climb uphill beside the fence, over a rise and down into another boggy dip. The fence leads to a drystone wall, which is crossed using a ladder stile flanked by duck-boards. Climb uphill on a grassy, tussocky moor, veering left to reach another fence. Climb further uphill on Wain Rigg, possibly spotting a ruin across the fence. Leave the fence at a corner and follow the path across undulating, boggy moorland. Keep to the path no matter how much it wriggles and writhes, to reach a ladder stile over a drystone wall. ▸ Walk across the boggy moorland of **Blenkinsopp Common**.

There is a trig point to the left, at 289m (948ft), but this isn't visited.

Walk downhill to cross a step-stile over a fence, then head down a pathless slope to reach two ruined brick buildings. Pass to the right of them, going under a power line at the same time. Go down a path on a grassy embankment and cross a stone-slab footbridge to reach a gate. Turn right as signposted to follow a stony track gently up through a big field, passing under the power line again. Continue straight ahead along a grassy track to pass a little stone hut at **Todholes** and cross a ladder stile beside a gate.

Follow the grassy track up a rushy slope and it later drops a bit and runs alongside a fence, reaching a junction with another track. Turn left down through a gate, as signposted for the Pennine Way. The track follows a fence across a rushy moor, passing through another gate and running beneath the power line again. Lines of beech flank the track, then after passing through a gate a birch wood is passed as the track runs down to the busy **A69** road.

Cross the road with care to find the Pennine Way signposted a short way downhill on the right. Climb a flight of steps, cross a step-stile over a fence, go through a gate in another fence, then head diagonally right to reach the far corner of a field. Cross a step-stile over a fence, quickly followed by a ladder stile over a drystone wall. Follow the wall downhill beside a small mixed woodland, continuing down beside a golf course. The route climbs a short way before it is signposted right, over a ladder stile onto the golf course.

Keep to the right of a strip of rumpled rough grassland, where the Roman earthwork known as the Vallum runs across the golf course. Cross a footbridge in a slight dip. A steep and overgrown path drops down to a ladder stile, reaching the **B6318** road at a short terrace of houses. At this point, the Pennine Way and Hadrian's Wall National Trail coincide, and while both routes can be followed straight across the road, this is far enough for the day. Turn right along the road to reach the little village of **Greenhead**. Turn left along the road if staying at the Hadrian's Holiday Lodges at Longbyre.

Facilities are limited in **Greenhead**, and they come under a lot of pressure from people walking along Hadrian's Wall, as well as from cyclists. The Greenhead Hotel, Greenhead Hostel and Greenhead Tea Room are in the village. Holmhead Guest House, just a few more minutes along the Pennine Way, also offers a bunk barn and a space for a few tents. In case of difficulty securing accommodation, the special Hadrian's Wall AD122 bus and other bus services offer links with Haltwhistle, Brampton and Carlisle, which have plenty more facilities.

DAY 16

Greenhead to Housesteads

Start	Greenhead Hotel, Greenhead, NY 659 653
Finish	Housesteads Visitor Centre, NY 794 684
Distance	17km (10.5 miles)
Total ascent	720m (2360ft)
Total descent	630m (2065ft)
Time	5hr
Terrain	A roller-coaster route with several short, steep ascents and descents. Paths are usually obvious and some steep slopes feature steps.
Maps	OS Landranger 86, OS Explorer OL43, Harvey's Pennine Way North
Refreshments	Cafés and snacks available at Walltown. Pubs off-route at Cawfields and Twice Brewed. Café at Housesteads.

This is only a short day's walk, but it proves quite fascinating and there is much to see. There are plenty of Pennine wayfarers who just want to keep moving, and they might set their sights on distant Bellingham. However, those who want to learn about Hadrian's Wall should ensure that they have plenty of time to visit forts and museums. Bear in mind that Hadrian's Wall can get very busy and all the nearby accommodation can be fully booked at peak periods. On the other hand, people do cancel at the last minute, so beds occasionally become available. The route lies within the Northumberland National Park and is something of a roller-coaster, following Hadrian's Wall along the crest of the rugged Whin Sill. Housesteads is off-route at the end of the day, but is too interesting to omit from the route.

HADRIAN'S WALL

In AD122 the Emperor Hadrian ordered the building of this remarkable coast-to-coast fortification, and it took eight years to complete. Large forts

Hadrian's Wall passes Milecastle 39 while following the crest of the Whin Sill towards Crag Lough

were built at intervals, with milecastles every Roman mile, equating to 1481m (4859ft). Between each milecastle were two small turrets. Roman miles are counted from east to west and the turrets are labelled A and B after each milecastle. There are plenty of gaps in the numbering system where fortifications have been destroyed.

The Venerable Bede noted 'it is eight feet in breadth, and twelve in height; and, as can be clearly seen to this day, ran straight from east to west'. Interest in the wall increased from the 16th century, due in part to curiosity generated by William Camden's *Britannica*. General Wade's construction of the 'Military Road' in the 1750s made Hadrian's Wall more accessible, although much of the masonry was destroyed to lay the foundations of the road. In 1801, at the age of 78, William Hutton explored Hadrian's Wall in a remarkable 965km (600-mile) round trip on foot from Birmingham. The Rev John Hodgson published the first detailed description of the wall in 1840. The archaeologist J Collingwood Bruce led the first 'pilgrimage' along the wall in 1849, and such 'pilgrimages' continue to this day. Some 32km (20 miles) of the best stretches of Hadrian's Wall were included in the Northumberland National Park when it was designated in 1956. Hadrian's Wall and its surrounding landscape were designated as a World Heritage Site in 1987. After a lengthy period of consultation, the course of Hadrian's Wall was designated as a National Trail. Walkers are often exhorted to walk in single file along paths, but are requested to spread themselves out while following Hadrian's Wall, to avoid damaging potential archaeology underfoot. Anything that damages the Wall and its surroundings is to be discouraged, and that includes scrawling either 'ROMANES EUNT DOMUS' or 'ROMANI ITE DOMUM' on the masonry!

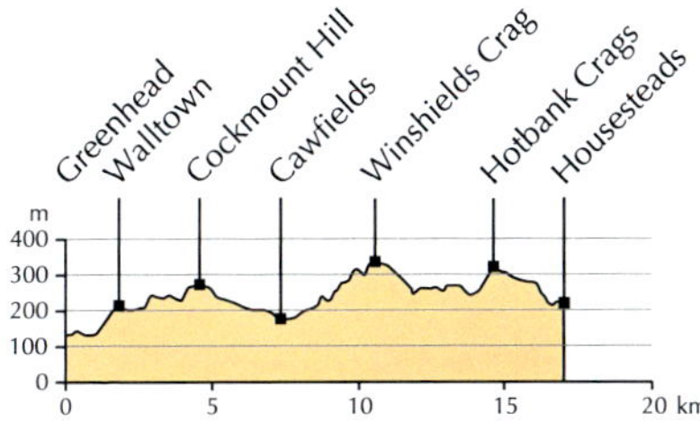

Start by following the road from **Greenhead**, as signposted for Gilsland, back to the little terrace of houses and the junction of the Pennine Way and Hadrian's Wall National Trails. Turn right in front of the terrace, cross a railway line at a level crossing, cross a footbridge over a stream, and cross a cycleway, all close together. Follow a grassy path onwards, bending left, to reach a track below the 14th-century ruins of Thirlwall Castle. Either climb to the castle and explore, or turn right along the track and cross a footbridge over a stream.

Pass Holmhead Farm Guest House. ▸ Follow the track uphill, bending left to go up through a gate. Walk up a grassy slope beside a prominent ditch associated with Hadrian's Wall, although all the stonework was robbed to build Thirlwall Castle. Cross a ladder stile over a drystone wall and the ground levels out, with a view back to Cross Fell. Walk downhill a little to a reach a kissing gate and minor road. Turn right as signposted 'National Trails', then turn left.

The farm offers a bunk barn and space for a few tents, as well as guest house accommodation.

Turning left leads into an old whinstone quarry at **Walltown**, which now serves as a picnic site. There is a small shop offering information and basic refreshments. The Hadrian's Wall bus turns in the car park, serving plenty of sites both on and off the course of the Wall.

However, by walking straight along the road, the **Roman Army Museum** could be visited. Located beside the Roman fort of Magnis, stunning

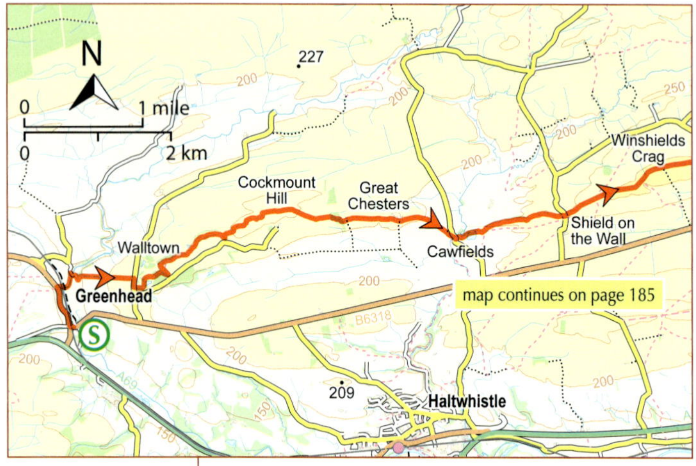

audio-visual displays are featured and there is also a café for paying visitors (tel 01697 747485, www.vindolanda.com).

Leave the quarry by following paths marked with the 'acorn' symbol. Keep well to the left of the flooded quarry bottom, then pass below the tallest quarried rock face. The path leads up to a gate and a left turn leads up to a splendid stretch of Hadrian's Wall. Turn right to follow it above Walltown Crags. There are extensive views back to the Pennines and ahead across the border forests into southern Scotland. The wall is tall and well-built, rising and falling on the crest, leading to the square base of Turret 45A. The wall ends where it was destroyed by another quarry.

Note how the Romans dug a ditch across the gap, creating an extra defence across a vulnerable low area.

Only a hummocky ridge of tumbled masonry represents the next stretch of the wall, and it is easy to pass the site of Milecastle 45 without realising. Walk down to a gap and cross a ladder stile over a drystone wall. ◂ A flagstone path and stone steps lead uphill and Turret 44B is passed. The wall along the crest has completely collapsed.

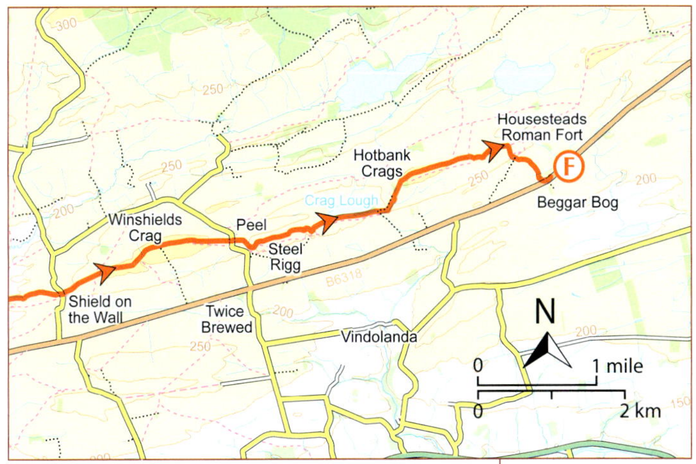

Cross another gap, where there is another stile over a wall. Climb past low rocky outcrops, and note that the path misses the crest, where another tumbled stretch of the old wall can be followed. Cross a ladder stile over another wall and head downhill. Low stretches of

Turret 44B is passed above Walltown on Hadrian's Wall

Hadrian's Wall can be seen. A drystone wall was built on top in 2009 to aid conservation. Walk onwards, crossing a track and later crossing a ladder stile over a wall. Follow a gravel path through mixed woodland, climbing another ladder stile to leave it, passing a house at **Cockmount Hill**.

Walk through a field and cross a ladder stile into another field.

> Ahead is the farm of Great Chesters, where the grassy ramparts of the **Roman fort** of Aesica can be explored. Features include a well beneath a stone arch, and a Roman altar covered with handfuls of assorted coins, which legions of walkers fail to notice.

The Milecastle Inn offers food and drink 1km (0.5 mile) off-route on the B6318 road, while Herding Hill Farm, with its campsite shop and pizzas, is another 1km (0.5 mile) beyond the inn.

Cross a couple more ladder stiles while walking gently downhill through fields, passing a few low stretches of Hadrian's Wall, incorporated into a drystone wall. Pass a gate and ladder stile, then walk down through a field to pass Burnhead. Cross a stone step-stile and turn right along a minor road. Cross a bridge over a stream and turn left along a road, then right into a quarry at **Cawfields**. ◂

A 'National Trails' sign indicates a path keeping left of the flooded quarry bottom, which leads up to a gate in a gap. Turn left to arrive at Milecastle 42, which has chunky stone gateways. A fine stretch of Hadrian's Wall can be followed up and down along a grassy crest. The wall is continuous, except where a farm gate has been installed. Climb stone steps and walk along the crest, then drop into a dip and climb more stone steps back onto the crest. Cross a step-stile over a fence, then pass the low base of Turret 41A. A low wall runs down to a gate onto a minor road at Caw Gap, near **Shield on the Wall**.

Cross the road and go through a gate, climbing stone steps to continue following a drystone wall. Walk along the crest and down to a gap, then climb steeply. There are a couple of lesser ups and downs, then after passing a gate in a drystone wall, climb again.

A stretch of Hadrian's Wall runs along the top, merging almost seamlessly with a drystone wall built from the old Roman masonry. Follow this wall down to a gap and go through a gate in a wall, then climb on rocky ground, which gives way to a gentler crest. ▸ Keep walking ahead to reach a trig point at 345m (1132ft) on **Winshields Crag**, the highest point on Hadrian's Wall. Views are extensive, with the North Pennines dominated by Cross Fell and Cold Fell. Parts of southern Scotland and the Border Forest are seen, and the humps of the Cheviot Hills rise beyond.

A signpost points right, off-route to Winshields campsite, bunkbarn and tearoom.

Follow the crest onwards and the drystone wall gives way to a short stretch of Hadrian's Wall. Further downhill, only the low base of the original wall survives, with a drystone wall on top of it. A grassy path leads down through a small and a large gate, then a stone step-stile leads onto a minor road near **Peel**. ▸

Twice Brewed and The Sill lie less than 1km (0.5 mile) off-route, on the B6318 road.

According to one story, the **Twice Brewed Inn** gained its name in 1464, the night before the Battle of Hexham. Yorkist soldiers complained that the beer was too weak, and demanded that it be brewed again. Whatever the truth, it has long offered accommodation, food and drink. Fast-forward through the centuries to 1934, when a youth hostel opened alongside, which was named Once Brewed. The hostel and an adjacent visitor centre were demolished and a stunning new development called The Sill was opened. This incorporates a much larger hostel, along with the National Landscape Discovery Centre and an intriguing rooftop walk offering fine views. There is also a café on site. Tel 01434 341200, www.thesill.org.uk.

Cross a stone step-stile to leave the road and walk, for a change, along the northern side of Hadrian's Wall. Go through a small gate and walk downhill, using a flagstone path to cross a gap. Unseen on the other side of the wall is the curious Turret 39AB. Lying between the sites of 39A and 39B, Turret 39AB is the exception to the 'rule' for the spacing of turrets. Climb steep stone steps beside the dramatic cliffs of **Steel Rigg**. Cross a ladder stile over a wall and continue along an easy gravel path. A good stretch of Hadrian's Wall runs along the crest and down to a gap.

Cross a ladder stile over a wall and climb again, now following only the tumbled remains of the old wall. However, an iconic stretch of Hadrian's Wall appears later, where the path features steps to drop down to a gap, passing Milecastle 39, then climb up the other side.

Old shielings are passed on the crest, then steep stone steps drop down to Sycamore Gap, a former iconic scene on the wall until the sycamore was felled in 2023. Cross Hadrian's Wall and climb stone steps, then cross a ladder stile at the end of the old wall. An easy gravel path runs beside tumbled masonry, overlooking the attractive **Crag Lough**. Rowans cling to the cliffs, then the path passes through a plantation of Scots pine and sycamore. Cross a ladder stile and note the willow growing at the head of the lake.

A ladder stile leads onto a track on a gentle gap, then a gate takes the path onwards, beside a drystone wall. The path is broad and grassy, rising gently beside tumbled masonry to pass the grassy ramparts of Milecastle 38 opposite a farm at Hotbank. Cross a ladder stile over a fence and climb steeply. Pick up and follow a long

Blocky dolerite cliffs rise proudly above Crag Lough as the route continues towards Hotbank

stretch of Hadrian's Wall along an undulating crest above **Hotbank Crags**. A drystone wall drops down to Rapishaw Gap, where the Pennine Way parts company with Hadrian's Wall. Staying on the Pennine Way, the nearest shelter is a remote bothy, off-route at Haughtongreen. However, it is well worth making a detour further along the wall to Housesteads, even though it means walking a further 1.5km (1 mile), and finishing in a place with little accommodation.

Cross a ladder stile over a wall, then climb a short, rocky slope to pick up another good stretch of Hadrian's Wall. Follow it over a hill, then down and up stone steps to cross yet another iconic gap. Pass Milecastle 37 and follow the wall onwards, through a gate in a wall, along a path through a sycamore wood. Emerge at the corner of **Housesteads Roman Fort**, and go through a gate on the right to reach a nearby museum. The exterior of the fort can be enjoyed for free, but there is an entry charge to explore the interior.

HOUSESTEADS ROMAN FORT

This site has a long and complex history, with notable gaps. Bronze Age farming settlements were cleared during the construction of Hadrian's Wall. Housesteads, known to the Romans as Vercovicium, was probably garrisoned by 500 men. The fort was abandoned at the end of the fourth century. There is no evidence of settlement at Housesteads until 1326, and even then there were only summer shielings (huts used while pasturing animals). Permanent settlement was probably inadvisable due to border strife. William Camden didn't visit Housesteads when researching his book *Britannica*, declaring 'I would not with safetie take the full survey of it for the rankie-robbers thereabouts'.

Some excavation work was done at Housesteads in 1849, but work to restore Hadrian's Wall commenced in earnest from 1908. Housesteads Fort was given to the National Trust by JM Clayton in 1930, after a failed attempt to auction it, and the Trust has since acquired other properties in the area. English Heritage actually takes care of the structure. The visitor centre and museum (tel 01434 344363) have entry charges and there is a café on site.

The communal latrines inside the Roman fort at Housesteads

Follow a broad gravel track away from the fort and museum, rising and falling, then rising a little again to reach a visitor centre, café and car park beside the **B6318**, or 'Military Road'. Accommodation is sparse hereabouts and the nearest is **Beggar Bog B&B**, but the Hadrian's Wall AD122 bus can be used to reach lodgings lying further afield.

DAY 17

Housesteads to Bellingham

Start	Housesteads Visitor Centre, NY 794 684
Finish	Town Hall, Bellingham, NY 838 833
Distance	22.5km (14 miles)
Total ascent	545m (1790ft)
Total descent	650m (2130ft)
Time	7hr
Terrain	Low moorlands, forest tracks and paths, along with field paths and farm tracks. There are some wet, boggy or muddy patches. Careful route-finding is required at times.
Maps	OS Landranger 80 and 86, OS Explorer OL42 and OL43, Harvey's Pennine Way North
Refreshments	Self-service snacks at Horneystead. Plenty of choice around Bellingham.

Once the Pennine Way leaves Hadrian's Wall, it becomes very quiet. It is possible to walk all the way to Bellingham without meeting another walker, and even if some are met, they are mostly likely to be other Pennine wayfarers. There are extensive areas of forest, as well areas of open moorland, farmland and fields. On the latter half of the day's walk, the course of the Pennine Way actually follows the boundary of the Northumberland National Park. The land on the left lies inside the park, while the land on the right lies outside it; however, it all looks the same! At the end of the day, Bellingham is the last little town with a full range of services, so it is well worth having a plan in place for the rest of the route before leaving, and making sure that provisions are bought from the shops.

From the information centre on the **B6318** road, return to the Pennine Way following the clear gravel path as it rises and falls through fields to reach **Housesteads Roman Fort**. Keep just to the left of the fort, climbing past the museum, to find a small gate in a wall. Go through it and

Rapishaw Gap is where the Pennine Way leaves Hadrian's Wall

Look back before leaving the gap, as this is one of the most popular views on Hadrian's Wall.

turn left to follow a path up through a strip of sycamore woodland, walking parallel to Hadrian's Wall. Leave the wood at another gate and follow the wall along a crest, passing Milecastle 37.

Walk down stone steps to a gap, then up the other side. ◂ Continue along the crest then head left as marked, as the wall ends abruptly above a small cliff. Turn right to reach a ladder stile crossing a wall on **Rapishaw Gap**. Almost immediately, another ladder stile crosses a wall on the right, where the Pennine Way is signposted north, away from Hadrian's Wall.

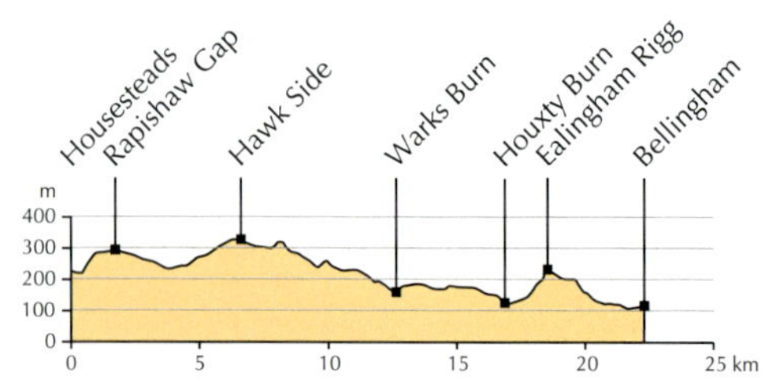

There are two grassy paths, and the Pennine Way is the one crossing a huge field diagonally. Follow it down into a rushy dip where there are flagstones, then walk up to a gate in a wall. On the other side there are two grassy tracks, so keep left and head down into another rushy dip to cross a stream, with a view of **Broomlee Lough** far to the right. Walk up to a gate in another wall, go through and follow a fine grassy track across another broad dip on a rushy, tussocky moorland, crossing Jenkins Burn. Rise gently to cross a heathery crest, then head gently downhill and fork left to reach a gate and signposts beside a track near the ruins of Cragend.

Cross the track and watch for a series of marker posts. These indicate a path bending left downhill, with a view of **Greenlee Lough**. Cross a muddy, rushy area with some firm flagstones underfoot. Head gently uphill and drift right as marked. Drift left downhill to reach a rushy dip and cross a wall. Cross a footbridge, then drift left up a grassy slope to spot a tall, stout wooden post bearing acorn markers. Cross a ladder stile beside a gate in a wall, then walk down to a track near the farm of East Stonefolds.

Turn right to follow the track up through a gate and into a forest. ▸ Climb gently with an open moorland on

A path on the right leads to a remote bothy, offering shelter 1km (0.5 mile) off-route at Haughtongreen.

A long-abandoned sheepfold on the moorland of Haughton Common

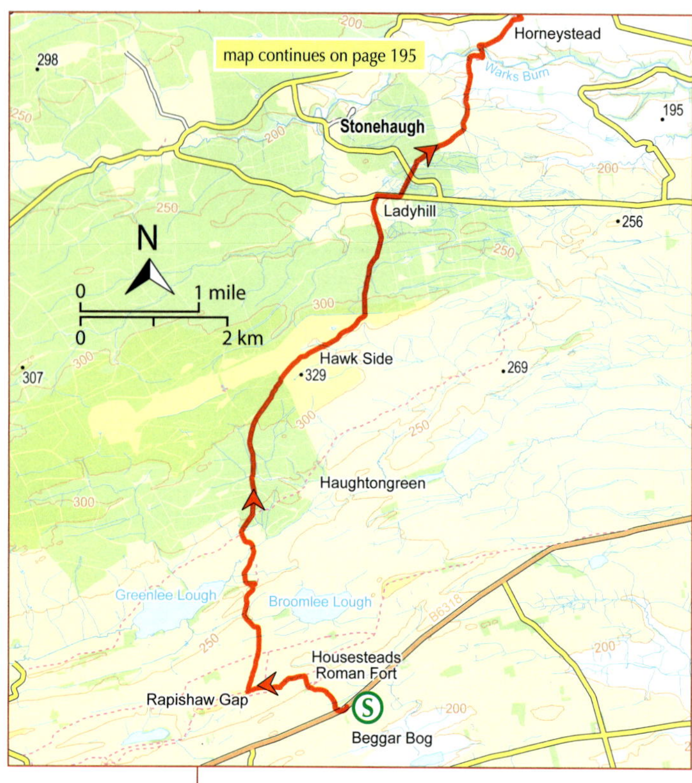

A detour to the left leads to a viewpoint where a noticeboard explains about the bog of Bellcrag Flow.

the right and trees on the left, crossing a crest where there are trees on both sides. The track runs down into a dip where open moorland lies on the left and trees on the right, then climbs a slope where trees on the right have been clear-felled. When signposts appear on the right, the Pennine Way leaves the track and veers right to follow a squelchy forest ride. Pass a little clearing and eventually reach a step-stile and gate in the forest fence. ◂

Wet, boggy, tussocky moorland is crossed near **Hawk Side**. The path is fairly obvious and direct throughout.

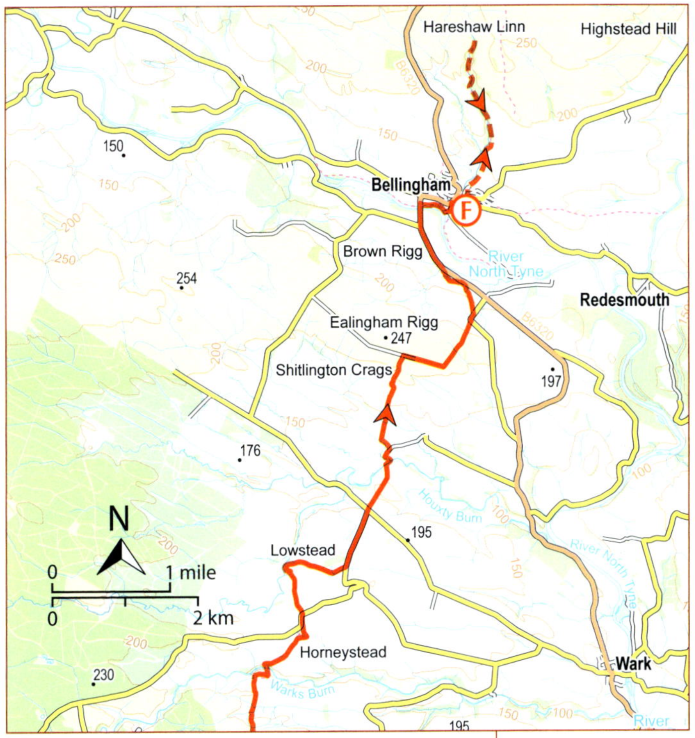

There is a dip in the middle of the moor, where a footbridge spans a stream. Later, keep left of a small, stone-walled enclosure containing a few pines and birch. The path leads to a gate to enter an area of clear-felled forest. Follow a direct path, crossing a track and continuing among trees, then later turn right along a track, then turn left down a path. Tracks are crossed two more times before the path levels out beside a wall at the edge of the forest.

Cross a step-stile and walk straight ahead over a grassy, rushy moor with bog cotton, keeping to the left of a tumbled wall and fence. Turn right to follow a minor road uphill, passing the access road for Willowbog, which cultivates bonsai, to reach the access road for **Ladyhill** and 'Falconry Days'.

> At **Ladyhill** you can experience 'Falconry Days', where you can witness falcons and owls in flight. It is wise to check times and dates in advance (tel 01434 689681 or 07766 752711, www.falconrydays.com), and then be sure to turn up on time. Complimentary tea and coffee are offered to visitors.

Turn left along the road to reach a basic campsite at Stonehaugh.

Turn left off the road down a track between a wall and a forest to reach another road. ◂ Cross the road and follow a level path, then cross a track. The path rises beside a forest, then there are trees on both sides before a gate is used to leave the forest. The path leading onwards down a tussocky moorland slope can be vague, especially in mist. Avoid being drawn along other trodden paths, but the only real landmark is an old white stone sink! Pass this and continue down to the small stream of Fawlee Sike.

Climb to the corner of a drystone wall. Keep right of the wall to cross a crest, then head straight downhill keeping to the left of a fence. When a drystone wall and a gate are reached, turn right as signposted for the Pennine Way, and pass to the right of a ramshackle corrugated barn. Walk through bracken and watch for a path down to the left into a valley. **Warks Burn** cannot be seen, because it is cut deep into the bedrock and flanked by trees. Look carefully to find a footbridge and cross to the other side.

Shelter, food and drink is available in the farmyard 'Pit Stop' on a serve-yourself basis. Feel free to leave a donation for this kindness.

A path climbs from the burn, swinging left up a slope of bracken, then right to reach a grassy brow. A field path leads up to a step-stile over a fence then passes the farm of **Horneystead**. ◂ Line up other stiles and gates to pass the farmhouse called The Ash. Turn left to cross a dip where there is a stone step-stile over a wall. Aim to the right of a house at Leadgate, crossing a minor road to pass it.

Walk down into a field and cross a wall into another field. Cross a dip and climb uphill, keeping right of tall ash trees. Keep right of the attractive house and gardens of **Lowstead** as marked, turning a succession of little corners to reach its access road. Turn right to follow this away from the house, across a cattle grid, and keep straight ahead along a road to cross another cattle grid. When a triangular road junction is reached, turn left uphill. Follow the road downhill to cross yet another cattle grid. The road is enclosed by walls and hawthorns as it descends past fields to reach another road junction.

Walk straight ahead through fields and down towards **Houxty Burn**, but take care on the last part of the descent. A signpost might be spotted in the bottom corner of the field, but this is for a ford. There is a footbridge further upstream, but this can't be seen on the descent. Locate it and cross it, then turn right downstream, and cross another footbridge over an inflowing stream. Turn left through a gate and follow a track that bends right as it climbs up to the farm of Shitlington Hall.

Pass the farm and turn left behind it along a field track. This later turns right through a gate and expires, so walk uphill along the edge of a field. There is a slight dip where a step-stile crosses a fence beside Slade Sike to enter the next field. Climb again and cross a ladder stile over a wall to reach a track. The Pennine Way crosses the track and climbs straight uphill, bending left where a broad path has been hammered out of the low gritstone edge of **Shitlington Crags**.

A marker post shows the Pennine Way heading straight up a gentle, rushy moorland slope, reaching a narrow road. Turn right to follow this towards a prominent tall mast on **Ealingham Rigg**, over 230m (755ft). Continue straight ahead, gently down a grassy track beside a wall. A marker post indicates a left turn across a rushy moor. The path is vague, so look for more marker posts, which reveal a couple of footbridges over boggy patches. Walk down a grassy slope and cross a ladder stile onto a minor road. Turn left along the road, which suddenly turns right downhill.

Watch for a ladder stile on the left and cross a wall into a field. A path appears to head down towards the **B6320** road, but doesn't immediately join it. Instead, keep off the road until later, and even then there is a path running beside it as far as a caravan site at **Brown Rigg**. Follow the road onwards to cross a four-arched bridge over the River North Tyne. Go down steps on the right to follow a short riverside path. Enter **Bellingham** by road and turn left past St Cuthbert's Well, walking up a path to the Town Hall.

Bellingham, pronounced 'Bellinjam', is a surprisingly busy village, serving a large rural area. Facilities include a couple of hotels, B&Bs and a campsite. There is a post office, pubs, café, shops, and the Co-op has a cashpoint. Buses run to and from Hexham, except Sundays. There is a Heritage Centre and tearoom at the former railway station, open from April to October, for which there is an entry fee (tel 01434 220050, www.bellingham-heritage.org.uk).

Off-route to Hareshaw Linn

In its earliest days, the Pennine Way left Bellingham by way of a splendid waterfall called Hareshaw Linn, reached by a popular path through a wonderfully wooded gorge. Unfortunately, there has been no link between the waterfall and the Pennine Way for decades, but anyone with a couple of hours to spare could complete a there-and-back walk measuring 5km (3 miles), taking 1hr 30mins.

Start at the bridge on the Redesmouth road, opposite the garage in Bellingham, where a road is signposted for Hareshaw Linn. The road runs upstream beside Hareshaw Burn, almost reaching the First and Last Brewery and Taproom, but keep left to pass a small car park and the road gives way to a track rising past a caravan site. This in turn gives way to a fine path that works its way through dense woodlands with a rampant understorey, featuring flights of stone steps. Seven footbridges are crossed

The lovely waterfall of Hareshaw Linn is well worth a visit

before **Hareshaw Linn** is finally reached, cascading down a multi-layered rock-face into a deep pool. Retrace steps back to Bellingham.

DAY 18

Bellingham to Byrness

Start	Town Hall, Bellingham, NY 838 833
Finish	Forest View Walkers Inn, Byrness, NT 764 027
Distance	25km (15.5 miles)
Total ascent	585m (1920ft)
Total descent	480m (1575ft)
Time	8hr
Terrain	Farmland quickly gives way to rolling heather moorland, with increasingly boggy patches. A firm track allows rapid progress through extensive forest.
Maps	OS Landranger 80, OS Explorer OL16 and OL42, Harvey's Pennine Way North
Refreshments	Bar and restaurant at Forest View Walkers Inn in Byrness.

This is a bleak and remote day, passing very few habitations. After leaving Bellingham, fields give way to broad and gently rolling grass and heather moorland. There are extensive views in fine weather, but in foul weather it is simply a treadmill. There are areas of soft, wet bogs later, getting progressively worse until a huge forest is reached. At that point, with a firm and dry track underfoot, it is possible to stride out and make rapid progress to Byrness. Be sure to have a plan in place before tackling the last stages of the Pennine Way through the Cheviot Hills. Day 19 outlines some options. Compare and contrast your plan with those of other wayfarers too.

Starting from the Town Hall in **Bellingham**, follow the Main Street as far as the post office. Turn right along the Redesmouth road to cross a bridge over Hareshaw Burn and later keep left as signposted for West Woodburn. The road climbs past the Heritage Centre, which is on the site of a former railway station. Pass a caravan park to leave the village and climb further up the road. Turn left along a narrow, tarmac farm access road, passing through gates to reach **Blakelaw Farm**.

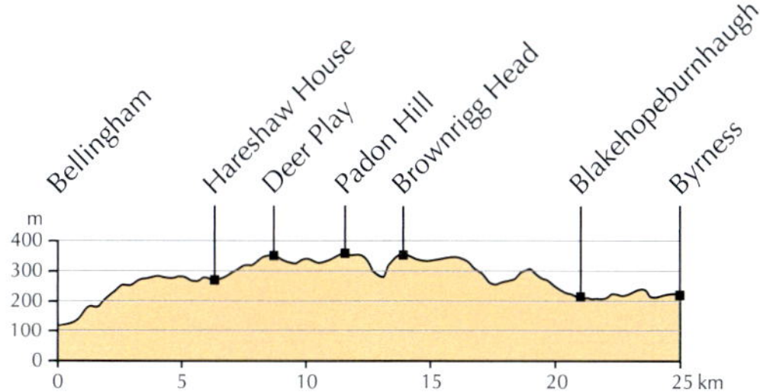

Turn left to walk through the farmyard and go through a gate into an enormous field. There is no trodden path, so look ahead to spot signposts and marker posts. Reach a gate in a wall, well to the right of a plantation of Scots pine. There are wide-ranging views around Northumberland, stretching to the North Pennines, Cross Fell and Cold Fell. Go through the gate and walk straight ahead along a grassy strip flanked by rushes, to reach a signpost on a broad dip in the moorland. The Pennine Way is straight ahead. ▶

An 'alternative' route is signposted to the left: it follows a fence and drystone wall across the moorland slope, crosses a minor road, then follows another drystone wall straight ahead to rejoin the main route.

The path is rather vague ahead climbing gently on a grassy, rushy moor, passing rugs of heather. It

A prominent pepperpot cairn sits on the summit of Padon Hill

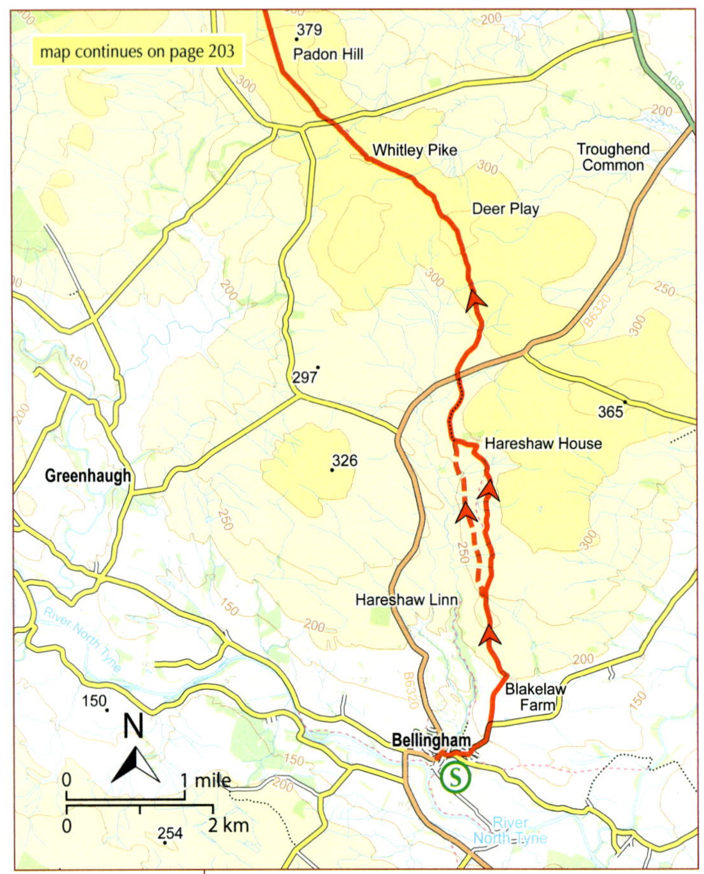

almost reaches the corner of a fence, as if heading up to Callerhues Crag. However, it levels out to aim for Hareshaw House, seen in the distance with a small forest plantation behind it. Keep to the right of a circular drystone sheepfold, which is a handy feature once the distant house is lost to view.

Extensive areas of heather and bracken are passed on the moor, as well as bog cotton. The path becomes more

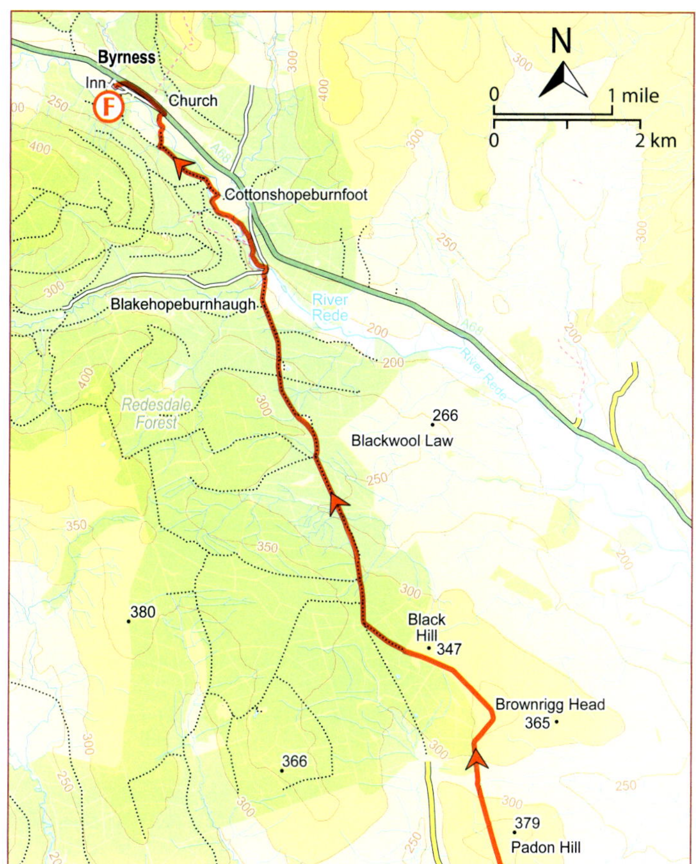

obvious and is unlikely to be lost. It drifts downhill and uphill and can be wet and boggy in places. Pass to the right of a band of tall Scots pine. Go through a gate and cross a footbridge over a small stream, then head straight for a gate onto a minor road. Turn right to pass a derelict house, then turn left behind it at a stile and gate.

Walk across a small field below **Hareshaw House** and cross a ladder stile beside a gate. A grassy track runs down a field towards a solitary sycamore tree, reaching another ladder stile beside a gate. Follow a grassy track across a rushy moorland slope. Walk straight ahead down a clearer track, noticing old colliery spoil on both sides of a road. Go through gates to cross the **B6320** road, then of all the vague paths in view, follow the one that keeps just to the left of a small hump of colliery spoil.

The path is vague across a grassy, rushy moor, but a series of little footbridges are crossed on the way towards a gentle slope where it becomes more obvious through heather. The route misses the summit of Lough Shaw then crosses a broad dip. Marker posts show the way up to the summit of **Deer Play**, where a cairn and signpost stand at 361m (1184ft). A gentle descent leads across a broad and boggy dip, then the path becomes firm and grassy as it climbs to the heathery summit of **Whitley Pike**, where a cairn stands at 356m (1168ft). Cross a step-stile over a fence, then head right to pick up a worn, peaty path down a heathery slope. A level flagstone path is slowly sinking into bog on the way to a minor road crossing a gap.

Cross the road and follow a firm path uphill, following a fence and passing a prominent little outcrop of rock. A steeper climb is followed by a walk along a gently undulating crest. Cross a level boggy patch using a flagstone path. A conspicuous 'pepperpot' cairn stands just off-route, at 379m (1243ft) on **Padon Hill**.

Padon Hill, which can be approached by a short detour from a gate in a fence, is named after Alexander Peden, a 17th-century Scottish Covenanter who preached in remote locations to avoid persecution. A story tells how every worshipper who gathered on the hill was required to bring one stone with them to make a cairn. Much of the old cairn was subsequently re-used to make the stout 'pepperpot' cairn, which dates from the 1920s.

The path beside the fence heads down a heathery slope to reach a wall. Cross a ladder stile and follow a flagstone path across a flat bog where bog asphodel grows. Cross a step-stile over a fence and climb uphill beside a forest, following a tumbled wall and a fence. The climb is steep and muddy at times and may rank as one of the worst stretches of the Pennine Way. Cross a step-stile over a fence at the top and follow a wall away from the forest, climbing gently along a stony path across heather moorland. The wall meets a fence on **Brownrigg Head** at 365m (1198ft).

Turn left to follow the path gently downhill parallel to a fence, which separates heather moorland from grassy moorland. A line of boundary stones bearing the letters 'GH' occur at intervals. These were planted to mark the estate of Gabriel Hall, High Sheriff of Northumberland, in 1705. Cross a broad and boggy dip, then rise very gently over **Black Hill**. The fence runs back towards the forest, then later there is forest on both sides. The path reaches a firm track at a gate beside a Forestry Commission sign, at 347m (1138ft).

The Pennine Way descends gently from Brownrigg Head to a forest

Turn right to pass through the gate and follow the track downhill. Two tracks join from the left, then the Pennine Way is signposted off to the left. Think twice before following it, since it merely runs parallel to the track, but on a rather rough vegetated slope where the path dwindles away completely. In fact, many who take this path quickly head back to the track. There is another sign at the bottom, but little evidence of a trodden path. Follow the track uphill from a dip, passing another track that joins from the left. Climb straight uphill to a crest at 296m (971ft), where there is a grassy short-cut on the left.

Follow the track onwards, passing a track joining from the left. After a gentle ascent and descent, pass a track joining from the right, then pass another one joining from the left. The track simply runs straight ahead and downhill, leaving the forest briefly to pass a house at **Blakehopeburnhaugh**. ◂ Pass a toilet block and turn right along a road, crossing a bridge over the **River Rede**. Turn left as signposted for the Pennine Way, along a forest track. There are tall trees here and the track gives way to a pleasant, grassy riverside path.

Just before the house, note a path on the left leading to the waterfall of Hindhope Linn.

Simply follow the river upstream until it can be crossed by a bridge at **Cottonshopeburnfoot**. ◂ Follow the track past fields and back into the forest. Turn right at a track junction, heading down and out of the forest to a ford and footbridge. Walk up the track and turn right at a junction, reaching the **A68** road beside a small **church** at **Byrness**. Turn left and walk alongside the main road, leaving the Pennine Way to reach the **Forest View Walkers Inn**.

There is a caravan site and camping pods here, and it also happens to be the longest placename on the Pennine Way!

BYRNESS

Byrness is a tiny place, made up of a few buildings near a little church, and a nearby huddle of buildings originally housing workers employed in the construction of Catcleugh Reservoir. The houses were then acquired by the Forestry Commission, and two of them were later converted into a youth hostel, which closed in recent years.

Facilities are sparse at Byrness and almost entirely revolve around the Forest View Walkers Inn. This was formerly a youth hostel, but now offers

B&B accommodation with evening meals, a small bar and small foodstore. Camping is available for a few tents in the garden, and is 'free' for those who order evening meals. They also offer a vehicle shuttle from April to September, allowing walkers to leave Byrness via the Pennine Way, descend from Windy Gyle, to be collected at Trows and brought back to Byrness. The following morning, they can be taken back to Trows to continue through the Cheviots.

Peter Hogg's bus links Byrness with Jedburgh and Newcastle, daily except Sundays.

The little waterfall of Hindhope Linn can be seen from a short detour

DAY 19

Byrness to Clennell Street

Start	Forest View Walkers Inn, Byrness, NT 764 027
Finish	Clennell Street, NT 871 160
Alternative finish	Trows, NT 855 125; Cocklawfoot, NT 853 185
Distance	23km (14.25 miles); Trows 24.5km (15.25 miles); Cocklawfoot 26.5km (16.5 miles)
Total ascent	865m (2835ft)
Total descent	550m (1805ft)
Time	7hr; Trows 7hr 30min; Cocklawfoot 8hr
Terrain	Broad, high and exposed boggy moorlands, with some stretches of duckboard and flagstone paths. Careful navigation is required in mist.
Maps	OS Landranger 80, OS Explorer OL16, Harvey's Pennine Way North
Refreshments	None.

Before leaving Byrness, ensure that you have a good weather forecast and enough food to get you through the Cheviot Hills, and, if planning to move off-route in search of accommodation, it is essential to book in advance. After a steep, forested climb from Byrness, the moorland crest beyond has some bad boggy patches, although paths become firmer later. The Pennine Way passes the enormous Otterburn Ranges, which are surrounded by 'danger' notices. While some walkers leave Byrness very early to complete the whole distance to Kirk Yetholm in a day, others camp overnight at Clennell Street, head off-route to Trows or Cocklawfoot, having arranged pick-ups with accommodation providers, or stay in a remote and basic shelter hut.

OPTIONS FOR THE CHEVIOT HILLS

Have a plan in place for the final stages of the Pennine Way, through the bleak and remote Cheviot Hills. There is no accommodation on the route, so unless you are prepared to camp in the middle of the hills, a detour off-route will be necessary. Options can be summarised as follows:

Walking along an easy path before climbing steeply onto Windy Gyle

1 Leave Byrness, having arranged to be collected off-route at Trows, after 24.5km (15.25 miles). Return to Byrness for a second night, and be taken back to Trows to continue to Kirk Yetholm the next day in 27km (16.75 miles). Transport is only available April to September.
2 Leave Byrness, having arranged a pick-up in advance at Cocklawfoot leaving the route at Clennell Street to descend, finishing after 26.5km (16.5 miles). After a lift back to Cocklawfoot the next day, walk 3.5km (2.25 miles) back to Clennell Street, then 22km (13.75 miles) to Kirk Yetholm.
3 Leave Byrness, with a view to establishing a wild camp somewhere along the route, covering any distance. If planning to stay in the very basic mountain refuge hut at Auchope, it is 33.5km (20.75 miles) from Byrness. It is also possible to descend from there to a bunkhouse at Mounthooly, but it is another 3km (2 miles) off-route.
4 Leave Byrness early, with the intention of walking all the way to Kirk Yetholm in one go, bearing in mind that this will be the longest and toughest stage on the Pennine Way, at 45km (28 miles).
5 Most Pennine wayfarers omit the spur to The Cheviot, which is a great shame, but omitting it does cut 4km (2.5 miles) off the distances above, and saves just over an hour. It would make option 4 a more bearable 41km (25.5 miles).

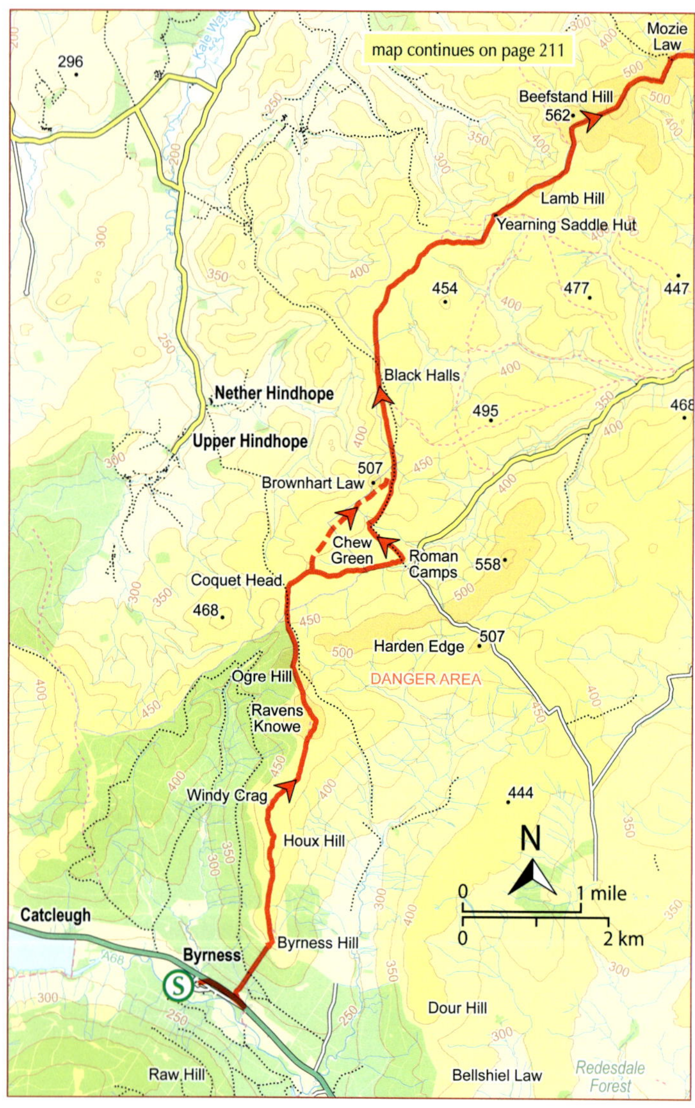
map continues on page 211
Mozie Law
Beefstand Hill
562
Lamb Hill
Yearning Saddle Hut
454
477
447
Black Halls
495
468
Nether Hindhope
Upper Hindhope
507
Brownhart Law
Chew Green
Roman Camps
558
Coquet Head
468
Harden Edge
507
DANGER AREA
Ogre Hill
Ravens Knowe
Windy Crag
444
Houx Hill
N
0
1 mile
0
2 km
Catcleugh
Byrness
Byrness Hill
A68
S
Dour Hill
Raw Hill
Bellshiel Law
Redesdale Forest
296
Kale Water

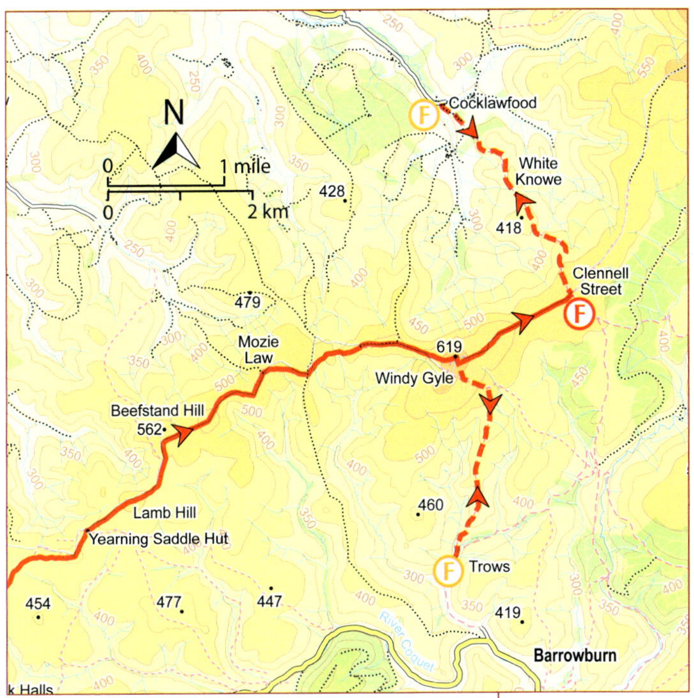

Start from the Forest View Walkers Inn and walk back along the main road towards the church in **Byrness**. Before reaching the church, cross over the **A68** and walk up a path signposted from the road. This narrow tarmac path links with a tarmac drive. Walk down the drive, but quickly turn right as signposted for the Pennine Way, through a gap in a beech hedge. Keep to the right of a small field, going in and out of it using small gates. Climb straight up a path as marked, through bracken among tall conifers. Climb over a rise and drop down to a forest track. Cross over and climb up a bracken-clad forest ride and keep climbing to cross two more forest tracks.

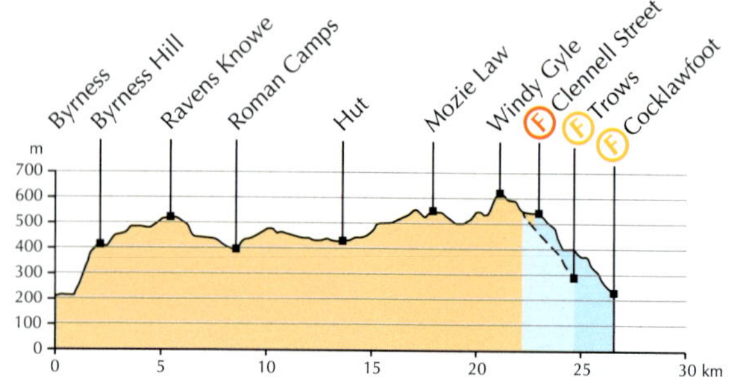

Rest assured that at no point does the Pennine Way enter the military firing range.

The path is steep and is studded with boulders as it leaves the forest; scramble up a slope of bracken and bilberry, using hands to climb a low gritstone edge. Go through a gate where there may be a note about the Otterburn Ranges. ◂ Climb to the grassy moorland crest of **Byrness Hill**. There is a large cairn to the right, at 414m (1358ft), but the Pennine Way turns left along the grassy crest.

There are some squelchy spots along the crest, and bilberry grows among the grass in places. Climb a couple of short, steep slopes that have bouldery collars, on **Houx Hill** and **Windy Crag**, then follow a fence. A formerly horrible bog is now equipped with a fine flagstone path, and later a firm grassy path follows a fence onwards and downhill, on a slope bearing heather and bilberry. Cross a gap and climb, reaching a cairn at 527m (1729ft) on **Ravens Knowe**. The path passes briefly behind a 'danger' sign, although there is nothing to worry about.

Walk down to a broad and boggy gap and pick up a long stretch of duckboard, avoiding black peat, tussocky grass, sphagnum moss and bog cotton. The duckboard ends and the fence crosses the grassy **Ogre Hill**, with forest to the left. Follow the fence and forest downhill, reaching a boggy valley at **Coquet Head**, where there is a junction of fences, a gate, a 'danger' sign and a signpost. Go through the gate, from England to Scotland, and follow the fence gently uphill, as signposted for the

Pennine Way. The fence later turns left, while the path drifts slightly right up a tussocky, squelchy moor. A lone Pennine Way signpost is reached, so fork right to follow a path down the moorland slope, reaching a stream, fence, gate and step-stile beside the River Coquet.

Climb as marked, from Scotland back into England. A three-way Pennine Way signpost is reached, where the main route turns right and heads down below the **Roman Camps**, where Roman soldiers set up a temporary marching camp. ▶ Cross a grassy slope to reach a signpost and turn left uphill. A path climbs parallel to the grassy embankments of the camp. Pass a prominent archaeological sign and later turn right to cross a footbridge flanked by short flagstone paths.

The alternative route rises left, passing well above the Roman Camps, and is 1km (0.5 mile) shorter.

Follow a grassy path uphill, later passing a signpost. Keep straight ahead and go through a gate in a fence. Pass another signpost and follow the path straight ahead, beside a fence, known as the 'border fence'. This only roughly marks the border between England and Scotland. Keen map-readers will spot a tiny bit of Scotland lies on what appears to be the 'English' side of the fence. Follow the fence across tussocky moorland, although looking over onto the Scottish side of the fence it is largely heather moorland. Reach a signpost at a gate on a kink in the fence at **Black Halls**, where the Roman road of Dere Street crosses.

Keep to the right-hand side of the fence, and in fact, drift right away from it up a gentle slope of tussocky grass. The ground is boggy on the way up, but dry and grassy on top, where there is a marker post at 456m (1496ft). Walk gently downhill, crossing a dip and noticing more and more patches of heather on the moor. Flagstones appear on a broad and boggy dip, but more are needed. Pass a cairn on a firm patch of ground, then undulate across firm and boggy areas at Broad Flow, before following a short line of flagstones sinking into the bog. Cross another dip later and climb more steeply, becoming gentler on a hill at a fence corner. Follow the path directly to the **Yearning Saddle** mountain refuge hut.

The Yearning Saddle mountain refuge hut offers basic shelter

Yearning Saddle mountain refuge hut is a purpose-built shelter located at 440m (1445ft), 14.5km (9 miles) from Byrness, at NT 804 128. It serves more as a place to shelter for lunch than an emergency shelter for the night. On the other hand, anyone walking the Pennine Way north to south who has seriously underestimated their abilities after leaving Kirk Yetholm might well find themselves spending the night here. The next shelter on the Pennine Way is 19km (11.75 miles) ahead, or 15km (9.25 miles) if omitting The Cheviot.

Leave the hut and cross a dip, then follow the path uphill beside the fence. The tussocky grass gives way to heather towards the top. Pick up a flagstone path, passing close to a trig point at 511m (1677ft) on **Lamb Hill**. Walk down a heather slope to reach a broad gap. Follow the flagstone path across to the other side, then climb a peaty path on a heather slope. Another flagstone path continues onwards, bending right over a gentle rise and later climbing onto the top of **Beefstand Hill** at 562m (1844ft).

Following a flagstone path beside the border fence on Mozie Law

The flagstone path expires on the way downhill. Pass a gate and ladder stile where another fence joins the border fence. Continue along another flagstone path, down across a broad gap, then up onto a hill to turn round a sharp left corner. Walk gently down onto a gap, then follow a short, steep, peaty path to the top of **Mozie Law** at 552m (1811ft). Yet another flagstone path runs downhill, pulling away from the fence to cross a broad dip, returning to the fence later. A firm, grassy path runs downhill, although there is heather over the fence on the Scottish side. A gate and signpost are reached where a track is known simply as The Street, around 500m (1640ft).

Step over the track and head straight over a grassy moor. Cross a stream and cross a grassy hill, then walk down to a boggy dip. A short, steep climb leads back to the border fence and over a grassy rise. Either walk alongside the fence, or stay well to the right for a short-cut across the hillside. Walk down onto a grassy gap, then follow the path and the fence up to a gate and step-stile. Cross to the Scottish side of the fence and climb up a slope of grass and bilberry. A huge burial cairn and a trig point stand on the summit of **Windy Gyle** at 619m (2031ft). ▶

From Windy Gyle extensive views stretch well beyond the Cheviot Hills, into southern Scotland and back towards the North Pennines. On a calm night, camping near the summit is possible.

Distance one-way is 3km (2 miles), with 330m (1080ft) of descent, taking 1hr.

Alternative finish at Trows

◂ From the summit of Windy Gyle, walk straight for the border fence, as signposted for the Coquet Valley. Go through the gate and walk straight down a path, keeping left at a marker post at a junction, and right at a marker post at another junction. Grassy wheelmarks lead down a rounded ridge. Keep right at a junction, cutting across a slope to descend through a gate. Continue downhill, through another gate, towards a huddle of farm buildings. Cross a footbridge beside a ford and walk to the farm of **Trows**, at 280m (920ft), to reach the start of a narrow tarmac road. This is the pick-up point for those returning by minibus to Byrness for another night. Pick-ups are at 5pm, April to September, but be sure to double-check.

The Pennine Way is signposted straight ahead from Windy Gyle, but recent path-work makes it preferable to head through the gate in the border fence, back into England, then turn left and walk downhill. Pick up a flagstone path over boggy moorland, passing grass, heather, bilberry and bog cotton. The slabs end near the large Russell's Cairn, but once an adjoining fence has been crossed at a step-stile, more flagstones continue along a boggy, hummocky crest. The stone slabs alternate with a couple of stony stretches of path, then a gate and signpost are reached where the track known as **Clennell Street** crosses the broad moorland crest at 542m (1778ft).

There is nothing at **Clennell Street** except a gate in a fence where a track crosses the high moor. Self-contained backpackers could camp just off the track, or if a really good weather forecast has been issued, camping on top of Windy Gyle might also be considered. Those who have arranged a pick-up in advance could follow the track down to a farmhouse at Cocklawfoot (see below). Walkers who intend to continue to Kirk Yetholm, or at least to the next mountain refuge hut, should keep straight ahead along the Pennine Way.

The vehicle track of Clennell Street can be followed to Cocklawfoot

Alternative finish in Cocklawfoot

Distance one-way is 3.5km (2.25 miles), with a descent of 300m (985ft), taking 1hr.

▶ Go through the gate in the border fence to enter Scotland. Follow a track down a grass and heather moor, with a fence on the left-hand side. The track winds downhill and goes through a gate, then there is a gentle ascent. The stony surface gives way to grass and as the track descends it runs through a small forest, passing through a gate. Continue beside another small forest and drop down to a gate. The farm of **Cocklawfoot** is on the right, but follow the access road to a metal bridge. Accommodation providers from Kirk Yetholm might pick up here if given advance notice, and return walkers the following day.

DAY 20

Clennell Street to Kirk Yetholm

Start	Clennell Street, NT 871 160
Alternative start	Trows, NT 855 125; Cocklawfoot, NT 853 185
Finish	The Green, Kirk Yetholm, NT 827 282
Distance	22km (13.75 miles); from Trows 27km (16.75 miles); from Cocklawfoot 25.5km (16 miles)
Total ascent	735m (2410ft)
Total descent	1160m (3805ft)
Time	7hr; Trows 8hr 30min; Cocklawfoot 8hr
Terrain	Broad, high and exposed boggy moorlands, with some stretches of flagstone path and duckboard. Careful navigation is required in mist.
Maps	OS Landranger 74 and 80, OS Explorer OL16, Harvey's Pennine Way North
Refreshments	Pubs at Kirk Yetholm and nearby Town Yetholm.

The final day's walk on the Pennine Way is far from straightforward. Some walkers may have to return from Byrness by minibus to Trows, then climb Windy Gyle. Anyone dropped off at Cocklawfoot has to walk back up to Clennell Street. Other wayfarers might start from a high-level wild camp in the middle of the Cheviot Hills. Once the walk is underway, those who find themselves running out of time or energy omit the spur route to The Cheviot. After passing The Schil, the final stage is wholly in Scotland, but there is still one more decision to be made. Originally, the Pennine Way headed straight down to Halterburn, but this quickly became an 'alternative' route. A new 'main' route was marked over an attractive range of hills. Either way, the route reaches its conclusion at Kirk Yetholm.

The first task, for those who moved off-route to Trows or Cocklawfoot, is to return to Windy Gyle and/or Clennell Street.

◂ The trail continues northwest alongside the border fence, following a flagstone path along a crest of heather and bog cotton. Cross a ladder stile over an adjoining fence on a broad gap at **Butt Roads**, then climb a little until the flagstones finish. The path can be squelchy underfoot, then more flagstones pass a trig point at 531m (1742ft) on the way to **King's Seat**.

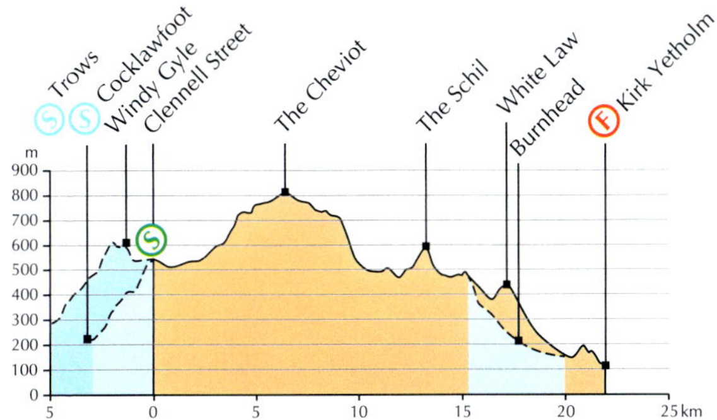

Continue onwards and upwards past Score Head until the flagstones finish again. ▸

There is a steep climb on a peaty path, where the slope sprouts masses of cloudberry. A stony path runs through a grassy channel cut into the blanket bog, then another flagstone path completes the climb. A long flagstone path runs along a broad and boggy crest to reach a junction of fences at 743m (2438ft).

It is at this point that even the most ardent Pennine wayfarer struggles to decide whether to take a spur path to The Cheviot, 2km (1.25 miles) distant, returning an hour or so later, or whether to turn left through a gate and head straight for Kirk Yetholm.

Those who keep a close eye on their maps may be surprised to notice how the so-called border fence rarely runs along the actual border.

Whether or not to include **The Cheviot** depends on the weather, and how much time and stamina is available. Officially, this spur is part of the Pennine Way, and not an optional detour! In the past, the route to the summit was a horribly boggy morass, but now there are firm flagstone paths most of the way there.

Cross a step-stile over the fence, as signposted for the Cheviot Summit. Follow a flagstone path down among peat hags on a broad and boggy gap. Rise to

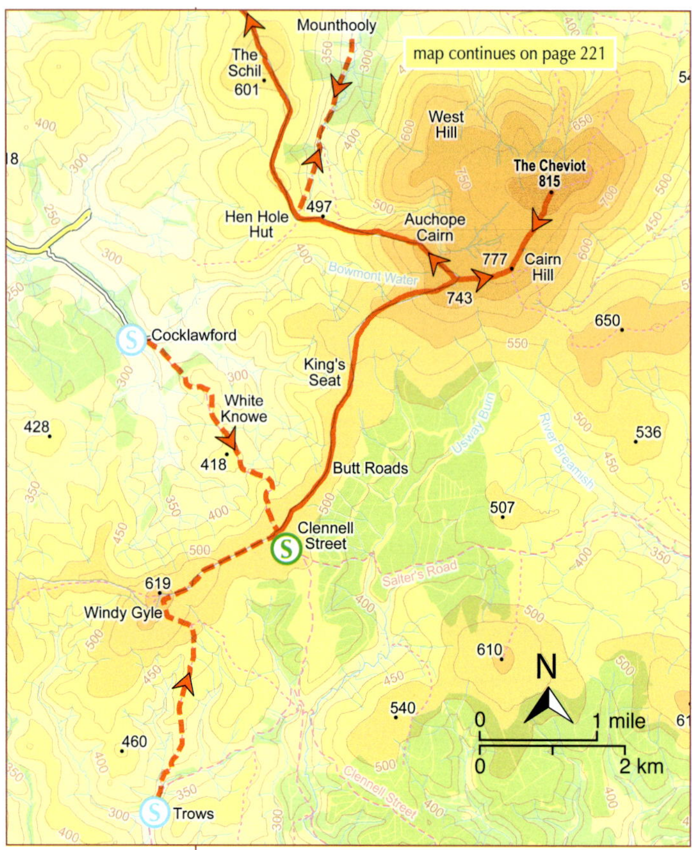

the corner of a fence, where the flagstones finish. Walk up a grassy slope that can be wet and boggy, passing bog cotton and cloudberry. Either follow the fence or keep away from it, depending on conditions underfoot. Pass a signpost on the summit of **Cairn Hill** at 777m (2549ft), then walk down a firm, grassy slope beside the fence.

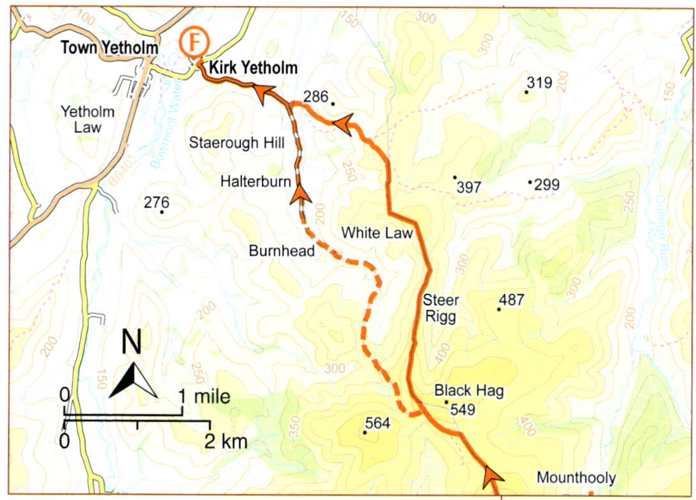

A flagstone path leads down to a broad and boggy gap, then climbs gently uphill. ▸ The path climbs and passes through a triangular fenced enclosure. Masses of cloudberry grow as the path levels out and reaches the summit of **The Cheviot** at 815m (2674ft). A stoutly buttressed trig point stands on a flagstone 'patio', where there was once a filthy, over-trodden peat bog. Unfortunately, this is not a good viewpoint because of the broadness of the summit plateau. Retrace your steps back to the junction of fences at 743m (2438ft).

The boggy heather moorland supports an amazing range of plants, including swathes of cloudberry, as well as bilberry, crowberry, bog cotton and tiny dwarf willows.

Daniel Defoe travelled extensively around Britain and was a little too enthusiastic when he compared British scenes with landscapes he had seen elsewhere in the world. The Cheviot was not immune from this 'over-interpretation' in 1726, when he compared it to El Teide on Tenerife, or imagined during the ascent that the summit would turn out to be a pinnacle! He wrote:

We were the more uneasy about, mounting highery because we all had a Notion, that when

> we came to the Top, we should be just as upon a Pinnacle, that the Hill narrowed to a Point, and we should have only Room enough to stand, with a Precipice every way round us; and with these Apprehensions, we all sat down upon the Ground, and said we would go no farther. Our Guide did not at first understand what we were apprehensive of; but at last by our Discourse he perceived the Mistake, and then not mocking our Fears, he told us, that indeed if it had been so, we had been in the Right, but he assur'd us, there was Room enough on the Top of the Hill to run a Race, if we thought fit, and we need not fear any thing of being blown off the Precipice, as we had suggested; so he Encouraging us we went on, and reach't the Top of the Hill in about half an Hour more.

Auchope Cairn is followed by a steep descent

Cross a step-stile and turn right to go through a gate. Follow a flagstone path across a gentle boggy gap, climbing slightly onto the firm, grassy hump of **Auchope Cairn**, which bears two square-built cairns at 725m (2379ft). Drop down a steep and stony slope and follow a fence

downhill on a grassy slope. Cross a gap and climb to a mountain refuge **hut** perched high above Hen Hole.

> The purpose-built **Auchope** mountain refuge hut (NT 879 201) is located at almost 480m (1575ft), 13km (8 miles) from Kirk Yetholm. Most Pennine wayfarers will poke their heads round the door, or use it briefly for shelter. A few, having overestimated their ability to walk all the way from Byrness to Kirk Yetholm in a day, may end up spending the night there. If a night at the hut doesn't appeal, it may be worth dropping northwards into the College Valley, heading for a bunkhouse at Mounthooly, 3km (2 miles) away, with a descent of 230m (755ft).

Follow the path onwards to cross a gentle rise and a broad gap beyond, passing heather, bilberry and crowberry. There is a fine view along the College Valley. Walk over another broad and boggy hump bearing heather, bilberry and crowberry. A flagstone path crosses a boggy gap, but there are none leading uphill beside the border fence. Walk over a boggy hump and follow a flagstone path across a broad and boggy gap. Cross a step-stile over a fence beside a gate, then climb a heathery slope, which becomes steep and grassy with patches of boulder-scree. ▸

Towards the top, if a slight detour appeals, cross the fence to inspect the rocky peak and summit cairn on The Schil, at 601m (1972ft).

Follow the fence downhill onto a heathery slope. Join a tumbled drystone wall at a corner and follow it straight ahead across a squelchy bog. Cross a step-stile over a fence, beside a gate, then walk alongside the fence and wall onwards. Turn left to cross a ladder stile, passing from England to Scotland for the last time. Follow a grassy path on a gently rising traverse to a three-way signpost on a cairn below **Black Hag**. Turn right here as signposted to take the Pennine Way high-level option. ▸

This route is slightly longer than the alternative route and includes 150m (490ft) more ascent and descent.

Alternative route

This used to be the main route, but it suffered severe erosion in the early years of the Pennine Way and its use was discouraged. It is in good shape these days, and anyone

If the weather is poor then follow a low-level route via Halter Burn

suffering appalling weather on the Cheviot Hills will welcome the opportunity to use it. The path simply cuts across a grass and heather slope to reach a grassy gap. Go through a gate in a fence and follow a grassy track down across a grass and bracken slope. A zigzag stretch leads down to a wall and fence. Go through a gate and follow the path across a grassy slope, followed by extensive bracken, to reach some fields. Keep to the right of these to reach the ruins of Old Halterburnhead among ash and sycamore trees.

Pass the ruin using a grassy track and turn left as signposted. Cross a little stream and follow the track gently up and down towards the farm at **Burnhead**. However, turn right long before the farm to cross a footbridge. Turn left and go through a gate to walk beside a drystone wall and a fence. Turn left through another gate to join the farm access track, turning right to follow it to a cattle grid. Continue straight along a minor road and later pass buildings at **Halterburn**. Shortly afterwards, the main Pennine Way joins from the right.

Main route to Kirk Yetholm

The path leaves the three-way signpost and rises gently. Go through a gate at a junction of fences on a grass and heather hump, enjoying views across a patchwork landscape of fields to the prominent three peaks of the Eildon Hills. Walk straight ahead, keeping to the left side of the border fence. The grassy crest runs downhill and passes a curious little outcrop of rock on **Steer Rigg**. When a junction of fences is reached, go through a gate and follow the fence down to reach a grassy gap. Cross a little hump and pass a small outcrop, then walk further downhill to reach another grassy gap.

Climb straight up a steep and grassy slope, swinging left at the top and just missing the summit of **White Law**, at almost 430m (1410ft). Walk downhill beside the fence to reach a Pennine Way signpost beside gates and a ladder stile where the fence joins a drystone wall. Follow the wall downhill, then uphill a little, then veer left through bracken to pass a marker post. Walk up to another Pennine Way signpost and turn left to pick up a grassy track and follow it downhill. The next signpost is a combined one for the Pennine Way and St Cuthbert's Way. Keep walking downhill and keep right of a tin hut, following a narrow path across a slope of bracken. Walk down to a ford and footbridge over Halter Burn and cross to a road on the other side. ▸

The alternative route joins at this point.

Turn right to climb steeply up the minor road, over a gap between low hills. There are benches beside the road for weary walkers, and journey's end can be seen ahead. The road leads straight down past a row of houses to reach a spacious green in the centre of **Kirk Yetholm**. The Border Hotel stands to the right, declaring itself 'The end of the Pennine Way'. Some walkers will check to see if the bar is open for a celebratory drink, while others will sit by the green and quietly reflect on the long journey that brought them here. All must consider, at some stage, how on earth they are going to get back home!

KIRK YETHOLM

This little village is very proud of its Gypsy heritage, and on the way down the High Street, walkers pass the 'Gypsy Palace', although it is only a little cottage. The two most notable Gypsy families were the Faas and the Marshalls.

Kirk Yetholm offers a small range of services, including the Border Hotel, a couple of B&Bs and a hostel. If any further services are required, a short walk leads to neighbouring Town Yetholm, where there is the Plough Hotel, a B&B and a campsite, as well as a post office shop. When the time comes to leave either village, there are occasional daily buses, except Sunday, heading for Kelso for onward bus connections. Buses from Kelso lead direct to Berwick upon Tweed and Edinburgh, which have railway stations. On Sundays, when there are no buses from Kirk Yetholm, local taxis can be used to reach Kelso.

The Border Hotel in the village of Kirk Yetholm

APPENDIX A

Useful contacts

Pennine Way National Trail

The Pennine Way has a trail manager who ensures that the route remains free of obstructions, and that any damage occurring is repaired. The Pennine Way National Trail website is an excellent source of information about the route, and if any problems are encountered, use the link in the National Trail website to contact the Trail Manager.

www.nationaltrail.co.uk/en_GB/trails/pennine-way

To understand more about how the Pennine Way came into being, after decades of lobbying, and to learn about some of the people who have been associated with the route through the years, be sure to read: *The Pennine Way – the Path, the People, the Journey*, by Andrew McCloy, published by Cicerone.

National Parks and National Landscapes

The Pennine Way passes through three national parks: the Peak District, Yorkshire Dales and Northumberland. It also passes through the South Pennines Park and the North Pennines National Landscape.

Peak District National Park Authority
Aldern House
Baslow Road
Bakewell
Derbyshire
DE45 1AE
tel 01629 816200
www.peakdistrict.gov.uk

South Pennines Park Organisation is now closed. Website active for information only
southpenninespark.org

Yorkshire Dales National Park Authority
Yoredale
Bainbridge
Leyburn
North Yorkshire
DL8 3EL
tel 0300 4560030
www.yorkshiredales.org.uk

North Pennines National Landscape
Weardale Business Centre
1 Martin Street
Stanhope
County Durham
DL13 2UY
tel 01388 528801
northpennines.org.uk

Northumberland National Park Authority
Eastburn
South Park
Hexham
Northumberland
NE46 1BS
tel 01434 605555
www.northumberlandnationalpark.org.uk

Pennine transport

Traveline, www.traveline.info, and Traveline Scotland, www.travelinescotland.com, tel 0871 2002233, can be used to search for any type of public transport. Google Maps can also be used to check public transport. Simply use the 'directions' facility, then choose your start and finish points, and have a look at the transport options that are returned, selecting one that suits your needs. Alternatively, click on bus stops and railway station symbols for information.

Tourist information

A few towns and villages along the Pennine Way have tourist information centres or visitor centres, and these are mentioned throughout the route description. Use these places as the best source of local accommodation information. They also hold details of local attractions and events, as well as timetables for local bus and rail services. Some have detailed town or village plans, maps, guidebooks, local crafts and souvenirs for sale. Some lie on or close to the Pennine Way.

Edale
tel 01433 670207
www.peakdistrict.gov.uk

Uppermill
tel 01457 870336
www.visitoldham.com

Malham
tel 01729 833200
www.yorkshire.com

Hawes
tel 01969 666210
www.yorkshire.com

Appleby
tel 017683 51177
www.visiteden.co.uk

Alston
tel 01434 382244
www.visiteden.co.uk

Haltwhistle
tel 01434 321863
www.visitnorthumberland.com

Accommodation and baggage transfer

Brigantes Walking Holidays
Bob's Laithe
Halton Gill
Nr Skipton
North Yorkshire
BD23 5QN
tel 01756 770402
www.brigantesenglishwalks.com

Discovery Travel
Hamilton House
24 Place Rd
Cowes
Isle of Wight
PO31 7UA
tel 01983 301133
www.discoverytravel.co.uk

Sherpa Van
Unit 8 Mowbray House
Olympic Way
Richmond
North Yorkshire
DL10 4FB
tel 01748 826917
www.sherpavan.com

Wandering Aengus
Fellside End
Fellside
Cumbria
CA7 8HA
tel 016974 78443
www.wanderingaengustreks.com

Alpine Exploratory
63A George Street
Edinburgh
EH2 2JG
tel 0131 2141144
www.alpineexploratory.com

APPENDIX B

Further reading

The Pennine Way – the Path, the People, the Journey, by Andrew McCloy, published by Cicerone. An entertaining read about how the Pennine Way came into being.

Pennine Way, by Damian Hall, published by Aurum Press. Written by one of the few people capable of completing the Spine Race along the Pennine Way.

Pennine Way Companion, by Alfred Wainwright, published by Francis Lincoln. A hand-scribed classic from the early years, written by someone who detested the route!

One Man and His Bog, by Barry Pilton, published by Corgi. Originally written for Radio 4, a bleak-humoured account of a walk along the Pennine Way.

Pennine Walkies, by Mark Wallington, published by Arrow. An account of a trek along the Pennine Way in the company of a very odd dog indeed!

Pennine Way South, Central and North, published by Harvey. A set of three waterproof maps made especially for trekking along the Pennine Way.

The Pennine Way, by Tom Stephenson, published by HMSO. This is the only guidebook to the Pennine Way written by its creator, but it is long out of print.

Walking Home – Travels with a Troubadour on the Pennine Way, by Simon Armitage, published by Faber & Faber. The author read poetry in return for lodgings.

Pennine Way, by Edward de la Billiere and Keith Carter and Chris Scott, published by Trailblazer. Trekkers tend to have this if they don't have the Cicerone guide.

The Pennine Way, by Kenneth Oldham, published by Dalesman. Long out of print – the author used to march teenagers along the route regardless of the weather.

Rambles of a Pennine Way-ster, by Richard Pulk, published by Touchline. Honesty in the face of adversity and torrents of foul language and abuse!

Laughs along the Pennine Way, by Pete Bogg, published by Cicerone. Long out of print, but a commendable book of cartoons featuring peat-black humour along the Pennine Way.

Dozens of guidebooks have been published about the Pennine Way over several decades, and most of them have long been out of print. The one you are reading right now is as good as it gets!

APPENDIX C
Accommodation

This table includes everything from hotels, guest houses and B&Bs, through hostels and bunkhouses, to shelter huts and campsites, including some very basic places with no facilities. While some Pennine wayfarers set out to camp every night along the trail, they may find long stretches without campsites. Wild camping, while requiring permission to be legal, is generally tolerated so long as you pitch well away from habitations, pitch late, leave early, and leave absolutely no trace at all.

There were once plenty of youth hostels, so that almost every night on the trail could be spent at one, but many have closed, although a few have continued as private enterprises. Staying in a hostel or bunkhouse every night isn't possible, but it would work most nights. Most trekkers currently seem to favour B&B accommodation, guesthouses and hotels. These are available every night, but in some places there may only be a single address. Breaking for the night in the middle of the Cheviot Hills requires advance planning, and options are very limited.

If accommodation can't be found where you intend breaking for the night, then it

Name	Type	Tel number
Day 1		
Edale		
The Rambler Inn		01433 670268
The Old Nags Head		01433 670291
Ollerbrook Farm Bunkhouses		01433 670235 or 07971 865944
Newfold Farm Campsite		01433 670401
Fieldhead Campsite		01433 670386
Nether Booth		
YHA Edale Activity Centre		0345 3719514
Edale Camping Barn		01433 670273 or 07507 405161
Upper Booth		
Upper Booth Farm Campsite		

may be necessary to move off-route. Sometimes, there will be a bus service offering a link with a nearby village or town with a greater range of facilities, or it may be possible to call a taxi. Some accommodation providers are willing to provide pick-ups and drop-offs, but if relying on such assistance, it is wise to check in advance.

Most on this list are on the Pennine Way, or a very short distance off-route. Anywhere more than 1km (0.5 mile) off-route carries a note of the distance, and the further off-route an address is, the more likely that transport will be required. Bear in mind that while some accommodation options are as old as the Pennine Way, some lodgings appear and disappear with very little notice. Readers are invited to contact Cicerone if they notice any changes on the following list.

Where an accommodation provider does not have a dedicated website, details of host websites are given. Use the search facility on these sites to access the details of the accommodation provider.

Many places can be booked through www.booking.com, and it is also worth checking www.airbnb.com for places that don't usually feature on accommodation lists, which can only be booked through the Airbnb website.

Campsite
Hotel
Hostel
Self-catering
Unmanned hostel/bothy
B&B

Website	Comments
www.theramblerinn.co.uk	
www.the-old-nags-head.co.uk	
www.ollerbrookfarm.co.uk	
www.newfoldfarmedale.com	
www.fieldheadcampsite.co.uk	
www.yha.org.uk/hostel/yha-edale-activity-centre	
independenthostels.co.uk/members/edalecampingbarncotefieldfarm	At Cotefield Farm
www.nationaltrust.org.uk/holdays/peak-district-derbyshireupper-booth-farm-campsite	

Name	Type	Tel number
Padfield (4km off-route)		
White House Farm		01457 854695
Windy Harbour		01457 843107
Day 2		
Crowden		
Crowden Camping & Caravanning Club		01457 866057
Standedge (1km off-route)		
Carriage House Campsite		07914 852762
Marsden (3km off-route)		
The New Inn		01484 841917
The Olive Branch Inn		01484 844487
Diggle (2.5km off-route)		
The Diggle Hotel		01457 872741
The Gate Inn		01457 321707
The Saddleworth Hotel		01457 871888
Sunfield Accommodation		01457 874030
Day 3		
Stoodley (1km off-route)		
Two Hoots Cottage		07792 447356
Hebden Bridge (on Hebden Bridge Loop) Also options on www.airbnb.com		
Garnett B&B		07912 966944
The White Lion Hotel		01422 842197
Hebble End View		07990 616181
The Smithery B&B		07957 256154
IOU Hebden Bridge Hostel		01422 553578

Website	Comments
windyharbour.co.uk	
www.campingandcaravanningclub.co.uk/campsites/uk/glossop/crowden/crowden-camping-and-caravanning-club-site	
newinnmarsden.co.uk	
olivebranch.uk.com	
thedigglehotel.com	
www.saddleworthhotel.co.uk	
www.sunfieldaccom.co.uk	
twohootsguesthouse.co.uk	Pre-booked lunch and evening meals available
www.whitelionhotel.net	
www.smithery.co.uk	
hebdenbridgehostel.org	

Name	Type	Tel number
Blackshaw Head/Colden		
Hebden Bridge Campsite		07763 574060
Highgate Farm Campsite		01422 842897
Rambles B&B		07921 500090
Day 4		
Top Withins		
Top Withins (basic shelter)		
Stanbury (1km off-route)		
Old Silent Inn		01535 647437
The Wuthering Heights Campsite		01535 643332
Ponden		
The Mill at Ponden B&B and Campsite		01535 643923
Ickornshaw		
Winterhouse Barn Campsite and Summerhouse		01535 632234
Day 5		
Earby (3km off-route)		
Earby Holiday Hostel		01282 842349 or 07791 903454
Thornton-in-Craven (1km off-route)		
Thornton Hall Camping		01282 841148
Gargrave		
The Mason's Arms		01756 749304
The Old Swan		01756 630679
Old Hall Croft Barn B&B		07890 632113
Eshton Road Caravan and Campsite		01756 749229

Website	Comments
www.hebdenbridge-camping.co.uk	At New Delight Inn
theoldsilent.co.uk	
www.thewutheringheights.co.uk	
www.themillatponden.com	
www.nationaltrail.co.uk/en_GB/accommodation/ winterhouse-barn	Camping field and summerhouse with two fold-up beds in it. Breakfast available.
earbyhostel.co.uk	
thorntonhallcamping.co.uk	
masonsarmsgargrave.co.uk	
www.pubanddining.co.uk/ old-swan-hotel-gargrave	
www.campingandcaravanningclub.co.uk	

Name	Type	Tel number
Premier Inn		0333 3218798
Day 6		
Airton		
Airton Friends' Meeting House and Barn		01729 900018
Lindon Guest House		01729 830418
Kirkby Malham		
The Victoria		01729 830499
Malham		
River House B&B		01729 830315
Miresfield Farm B&B and Campsite		01756 541197
Beck Hall		01729 830729
The Buck Inn		01729 830317
Lister Arms		01729 830444
Malham Youth Hostel		0345 3719529
Hill Top Farm Bunkbarn		01729 830320
Riverside Campsite		01729 830287
Gordale Scar Campsite		01729 830333
Day 7		
Horton in Ribblesdale		
Broad Croft House & Lodges		07715 678918
Golden Lion Hotel		01729 860206
3 Peaks Bunkroom		07870 849419
Holme Farm Campsite		01729 860281
Crown Hotel		01729 860209

Website	Comments
www.premierinn.com	1km off-route
airtonbarn.org.uk	
www.lindonguesthouse.co.uk	Evening meals available
www.victoriakirkbymalham.co.uk	
www.riverhousemalham.co.uk	
miresfieldfarm.co.uk	
www.beckhallmalham.com	
www.vixen-pubs.co.uk/buck-inn-pub-malham	
listerarms.co.uk	
www.yha.org.uk/hostel/yha-malham	
hilltopmalham.co.uk	
www.malhamdale.com/camping	
gordalescarcampsite.co.uk	1.5km off-route
broadcrofthouse.co.uk	
goldenlionhotel.co.uk	
www.3peaksbunkroom.co.uk	
www.facebook.com/HolmeFarmCampsite	
www.crown-hotel.co.uk	

Name	Type	Tel number
The Rowe House		01729 860070
Day 8		
Gearstones (2km off-route)		
Shepherd's Cottage		01524 242377 or 07807 018463
Gayle		
Blackburn Farm Campsite		01969 667524
Hawes		
The House at Hawes B&B		01969 667348
Woodlands B&B		01969 667497
Ebor House B&B		01969 667337
Wensleydale House B&B		01969 666020
Chapel Gallery Bunkhouse		07474 138536
Herriots in Hawes B&B		01969 667536
White Hart Inn		01969 667214
Laburnum House B&B		01969 667970 or 07437 079770
Fountain Hotel		01969 667206
The Crown Hotel		01969 667017
The Board Inn		01969 667223
Cocketts Hotel		01969 667162
Dales House B&B		01969 667437
Hawes Youth Hostel Cabins and Camping		0345 3719120
Day 9		
Hardraw		
Old Hall Cottage Campsite		01969 667691

Website	Comments
therowehousehorton.co.uk	
shepherdscottage.co.uk	
www.blackburnfarmcampsite.co.uk	
thehouseathawes.co.uk	
www.eborhouse.co.uk	
www.wensleydalehouse.co.uk	
chapelgalleryhawes.com	
www.herriotsinhawes.co.uk	
www.whiteharthawes.co.uk	
laburnumhousehawes.co.uk	
www.fountainhawes.co.uk	
www.theboardinnhawes.com	
www.daleshousehawes.co.uk	
www.yha.org.uk/hostel/yha-hawes	
www.oldhallcottagecampsite.co.uk	

Name	Type	Tel number
Muker (1km off-route)		
Stoneleigh B&B		01748 886375
Usha Gap Campsite		01784 886110
Keld		
Butt House B&B		01748 886374
Keld Lodge Hotel		01748 886259
Greenlands B&B		01748 886532 or 07917 391236
Keld Bunkbarn		01748 886549
Swaledale Yurts		01748 886159
Park Lodge and Rukins Campsite		01748 886274
Hoggarths Campsite		01748 886335
Frith Lodge B&B		01748 886489
Day 10		
Tan Hill		
Tan Hill Inn, Bunk Room, Domes and Camping		01833 533007
Deep Dale (main route)		
Shelter		
Bowes (on Bowes Loop)		
The Ancient Unicorn		01833 628576
Ivy Hall Farm Campsite		07776 491253
Day 11		
Cotherstone (9km off-route)		
Fox & Hounds		01833 650241
Grassholme		
Hunter House Farm B&B		01833 640245

Website	Comments
www.stoneleighcottage.co.uk	
ushagap.co.uk	
www.butthousekeld.co.uk	Evening meals are available
www.keldlodge.com	
www.greenlandskeld.co.uk	Evening meals are available
keldbunkbarn.com	Meals are available
swaledaleyurts.com	
rukins-keld.co.uk	
www.swaledalecamping.co.uk	
www.frithlodgekeld.co.uk	Evening meals are available
tanhillinn.com	
www.ancientunicorn.co.uk	
www.nationaltrail.co.uk/en_GB/accommodation/ivy-hall-farm-bowes	
www.cotherstonefox.co.uk	Pick-up near Clove Lodge
www.hunterhousefarm.com	Evening meals are available

Name	Type	Tel number
Middleton-in-Teesdale		
Daleview Caravan and Campsite		01833 640233
The Hill B&B		07881 812607
Gentian House		01833 640832
The Teesdale Hotel		01833 640264
Forresters Hotel		01833 641435
Belvedere House B&B		01833 641277
Brunswick House B&B		01833 640393
Grove Lodge B&B		01833 640798
Day 12		
Holwick		
Low Way Farm Camping Barn		01833 640506
High Force		
High Force Hotel		01833 622336
Langdon Beck		
Sayer Hill		
Langdon Beck Youth Hostel		0345 371 9027
East Underhurth Farm B&B		01833 622062
Langdon Beck Hotel		01833 622267
Day 13		
Dufton		
Pennine Potting Shed B&B		01768 352167 or 07990 582422
Dufton Youth Hostel		0345 3719734
Dufton Caravan Park, Campsite and Hobbit Huts		017683 53582 or 07825 148885 or 07736 394509

Website	Comments
daleviewcaravanpark.com	
www.thehillbandb.co.uk	
www.teesdalehotel.co.uk	
www.forrestersmiddleton.co.uk	
www.belvederehouse.co.uk	
www.brunswickhouse.net	
grovelodgemiddletoninteesdale.co.uk	Evening meals are available
www.lowwayfarm.co.uk	
www.raby.co.uk/high-force/hotel	
	Basic camping beside river
www.yha.org.uk/hostel/yha-langdon-beck	1km off-route
www.nationaltrail.co.uk/en_GB/accommodation/ east-underhurth-farm-bed-and-breakfast	1km off-route
www.facebook.com/LangdonBeckHotel	1km off-route
duftonbarnholidays.co.uk/holiday-barns/ pennine-potting-shed	
www.yha.org.uk/hostel/yha-dufton	
duftoncaravanpark.co.uk	

Name	Type	Tel number
Day 14		
Cross Fell		
Greg's Hut		
Garrigill		
East View B&B		01434 381561
Garrigill Village Hall Bunkhouse and Campsite		01434 647516
Alston		
Alston Youth Hostel		01434 381509
Cumberland Inn		01434 381875
Gilderdale B&B		07460 177683
Alston House Hotel		01434 382200
The Angel Inn		01434 381363
Victoria Inn		01434 381194
Town View B&B		07903 923300
Lowbyer Manor Country House		01434 381230
Temple Croft B&B and Bunkhouse		01434 382660
Day 15		
Harbut		
Harbut Law B&B		01434 381950
Knarsdale		
Kirkstyle Inn & Sportsman's Rest		01434 671526

Website	Comments
	Basic mountain bothy
garrigillbedandbreakfast.co.uk	
www.garrigillvh.org.uk	
alstonyouthhostel.co.uk	Breakfast available
www.cumberlandalston.co.uk	
www.alstonhousehotel.co.uk	
www.booking.com/hotcl/gb/victoria-inn.en-gb.html	
www.booking.com/hotel/gb/town-view-alston.en-gb.html	
www.lowbyer.com/wp	
temple-croft.co.uk	Evening meals available
harbutlawcottages.co.uk	
theksi.co.uk	

Name	Type	Tel number
Lambley		
Greenriggs Campsite & Shepherd's Huts		07866 639960
Kellah		
Kellah Farm B&B		01434 320816 or 07751 882122
Longbyre		
Chapel House Farm Campsite		07717 700049
Hadrian's Holiday Lodges		01697 747972
Greenhead (1km off-route Hadrian's Wall Bus links with all points from Hexham to Greenhead		
Greenhead Hotel and Hostel		01697 747411
Day 16		
Holmhead		
Holmhead Guest House, Bunk Barn and Campsite		01697 747402
Cawfields		
Bridge House B&B and Camping Cabins		01434 307742
Twice Brewed (1km off-route)		
Winshields Campsite and Bunkbarn		07968 102780
Vallum Lodge Guest House		01434 344248
Twice Brewed Inn		01343 344534
YHA The Sill at Hadrian's Wall		0345 2602702

Website	Comments
greenriggsshepherdshutandcampsite.co.uk	
kellah.co.uk	
chapelhousefarmgilsland.com	
www.hadriansholidays.com	
www.greenheadbrampton.co.uk	
bandb-hadrianswall.co.uk	
bridgehousehadrianswall.co.uk	
www.winshieldscampsite.co.uk	
www.vallum-lodge.co.uk	
www.twicebrewedinn.co.uk	
www.yha.org.uk/hostel/ yha-the-sill-at-hadrians-wall	

Name	Type	Tel number
Housesteads		
Beggar Bog B&B		01434 344652
Day 17		
Haughtongreen (1km off-route)		
Haughtongreen Bothy		
Stonehaugh (2km off-route)		
Stonehaugh Campsite		07415 759268
Bellingham		
Bellingham Camping & Caravanning Club		01434 220175
Brown Rigg Lodges Guest Rooms		01434 220390
The Barn B&B		07850 795762
Fountain Cottage Café and B&B		01434 239224
Riverdale Hall Hotel		01434 220254
Lyndale Guest House		01434 220361 or 07718 308870
Black Bull Hotel		07535 291117
The Cheviot Hotel		01434 211130
Demesne Farm Campsite		01434 220258 or 07967 396345
Day 18		
Cottonshopeburnfoot		
Border Forest Holiday Park and Camping Pods		01830 520259
Byrness		
Forest View Walkers Inn and Campsite		07928 376677

Website	Comments
stonehaughcampsite.com	
www.campingandcaravanningclub.co.uk	
www.brownrigglodges.com	Breakfast available
www.thebarnbandbbellingham.co.uk	
fountain-cottage.com	Café on site
www.riverdalehallhotel.co.uk	
sites.google.com/view/lyndaleguesthouse	
www.blackbull-bellingham.com	
www.booking.com/hotel/gb/the-cheviot-bellingham.en-gb.html	
www.demesnefarmcampsite.co.uk	
www.borderforest.com	
www.forestviewbyrness.co.uk	Camping is available if you dine there in the evening

Name	Type	Tel number
Day 19		
Yearning Saddle		
Mountain Refuge Hut		
Trows (2.5km off-route) Pick-up point for return to Byrness		
Cocklawfoot (3.5km off-route) Pick-up point for transfer to Kirk Yetholm		
Day 20		
Auchope		
Mountain Refuge Hut		
Mounthooly (3km off-route)		
Mounthooly Bunkhouse		01668 216358
Kirk Yetholm		
Border Hotel		01573 420237
Mill House B&B		01573 420604 or 07721 463547
Blunty's Mill B&B		07428 527865
Kirk Yetholm Friends of Nature Hostel		01573 420639
Town Yetholm		
Plough Hotel		01573 420215
Rutherford House B&B		07434 632445
Kirkfield Caravan and Campsite		01573 420346 or 07791 291956

Website	Comments
www.college-valley.co.uk/accommodation/bunk-house	
www.borderhotel.co.uk	
https://millhouseyetholm.co.uk	
https://friendsofnature.org.uk/houses/kirk-yetholm	Evening meals and breakfast are available in the adjacent Border Hotel
www.theploughhotelyetholm.co.uk	
rutherfordhouseyetholm.co.uk	
www.kirkfieldcaravanpark.co.uk	

The descent from Pen-y-Ghent (Day 7)

DOWNLOAD THE GPX FILES

All the routes in this guide are available for download from:

www.cicerone.co.uk/1131/GPX

as standard format GPX files. You should be able to load them into most online GPX systems and mobile devices, whether GPS or smartphone. You may need to convert the file into your preferred format using a conversion programme such as gpsvisualizer.com or one of the many other such websites and programmes.

When you follow this link, you will be asked for your email address and where you purchased the guidebook, and have the option to subscribe to the Cicerone e-newsletter.

www.cicerone.co.uk

LISTING OF CICERONE GUIDES

BRITISH ISLES CHALLENGES, COLLECTIONS AND ACTIVITIES

Great Walks on the England Coast Path
Map and Compass
The Big Rounds
The Book of the Bivvy
The Book of the Bothy
The Mountains of England and Wales:
Vol 1 Wales
Vol 2 England
The National Trails
Walking the End to End Trail

SHORT WALKS SERIES

Short Walks Hadrian's Wall
Short Walks Lake District — Keswick, Borrowdale and Buttermere
Short Walks Lake District — Windermere Ambleside and Grasmere
Short Walks Lake District — Coniston and Langdale
Short Walks in Arnside and Silverdale
Short Walks in Nidderdale
Short Walks in Northumberland: Wooler, Rothbury, Alnwick and the coast
Short Walks on the Malvern Hills
Short Walks in Cornwall: Falmouth and the Lizard
Short Walks in Cornwall: Land's End and Penzance
Short Walks in the South Downs: Brighton, Eastbourne and Arundel
Short Walks in the Surrey Hills
Short Walks on Dartmoor — South: Ivybridge and Princetown
Short Walks on Exmoor
Short Walks Winchester
Short Walks in Pembrokeshire: Tenby and the south
Short Walks in Dumfries and Galloway
Short Walks on the Isle of Mull
Short Walks on the Orkney Islands
Short Walks on the Shetland Islands

SCOTLAND

Ben Nevis and Glen Coe
Cycling in the Hebrides
Cycling the North Coast 500
Great Mountain Days in Scotland
Mountain Biking in Southern and Central Scotland
Mountain Biking in West and North West Scotland
Not the West Highland Way Scotland
Scotland's Best Small Mountains
Scotland's Mountain Ridges
Scottish Wild Country Backpacking
Skye's Cuillin Ridge Traverse
The Borders Abbeys Way
The Great Glen Way
The Great Glen Way Map Booklet
The Hebridean Way
The Hebrides
The Isle of Mull
The Isle of Skye
The Skye Trail
The Southern Upland Way
The West Highland Way
Walking Ben Lawers, Rannoch and Atholl
Walking in the Cairngorms
Walking in the Pentland Hills
Walking in the Scottish Borders
Walking in the Southern Uplands
Walking in Torridon, Fisherfield, Fannichs and An Teallach
Walking Loch Lomond and the Trossachs
Walking on Arran
Walking on Harris and Lewis
Walking on Jura, Islay and Colonsay
Walking on Rum and the Small Isles
Walking on the Orkney and Shetland Isles
Walking on Uist and Barra
Walking the Cape Wrath Trail
Walking the Corbetts Vol 1 South of the Great Glen
Walking the Corbetts Vol 2 North of the Great Glen
Walking the Fife Pilgrim Way
Walking the Galloway Hills
Walking the John o' Groats Trail
Walking the Munros
Vol 1 — Southern, Central and Western Highlands
Vol 2 — Northern Highlands and the Cairngorms
Walking the West Highland Way
West Highland Way Map Booklet
Winter Climbs in the Cairngorms
Winter Climbs: Ben Nevis and Glen Coe

NORTHERN ENGLAND ROUTES

Cycling the Reivers Route
Cycling the Way of the Roses
Hadrian's Cycleway
Hadrian's Wall Path
Hadrian's Wall Path Map Booklet
The Coast to Coast Cycle Route
The Coast to Coast Map Booklet
The Coast to Coast Walk
The Pennine Way
Pennine Way Map Booklet
Walking the Dales Way
The Dales Way Map Booklet

LAKE DISTRICT

Bikepacking in the Lake District
Cycling in the Lake District
Great Mountain Days in the Lake District
Joss Naylor's Lakes, Meres and Waters of the Lake District
Lake District Winter Climbs
Lake District: High Level and Fell Walks
Lake District: Low Level and Lake Walks
Mountain Biking in the Lake District
Outdoor Adventures with Children — Lake District
Scrambles in the Lake District —
North
South
Trail and Fell Running in the Lake District
Walking The Cumbria Way
Walking the Lake District Fells —
Borrowdale
Buttermere
Coniston
Keswick
Langdale
Mardale and the Far East
Patterdale
Wasdale
Walking the Tour of the Lake District

NORTH-WEST ENGLAND AND THE ISLE OF MAN

Cycling the Pennine Bridleway
Isle of Man Coastal Path
The Lancashire Cycleway
The Lune Valley and Howgills
Walking in Cumbria's Eden Valley
Walking in Lancashire
Walking in the Forest of Bowland and Pendle
Walking on the Isle of Man
Walking on the West Pennine Moors
Walking the Ribble Way
Walks in Silverdale and Arnside

NORTH-EAST ENGLAND, YORKSHIRE DALES AND PENNINES

Cycling in the Yorkshire Dales
Great Mountain Days in the Pennines
Mountain Biking in the Yorkshire Dales
The Cleveland Way and the Yorkshire Wolds Way
The Cleveland Way Map Booklet
The North York Moors
Trail and Fell Running in the Yorkshire Dales
Walking in County Durham

Walking in Northumberland
Walking in the North Pennines
Walking in the Yorkshire Dales:
North and East
South and West
Walking St Cuthbert's Way
Walking St Oswald's Way and Northumberland Coast Path

DERBYSHIRE, PEAK DISTRICT AND MIDLANDS

Cycling in the Peak District
Dark Peak Walks
Scrambles in the Dark Peak
Walking in Derbyshire
Walking in the Peak District —
White Peak East
White Peak West

WALES AND WELSH BORDERS

Cycle Touring in Wales
Cycling Lon Las Cymru
Great Mountain Days in Snowdonia
Hillwalking in Shropshire
Mountain Walking in Snowdonia
Offa's Dyke Path
Offa's Dyke Map Booklet
The Pembrokeshire Coast Path
Pembrokeshire Coast Path Map Booklet
Scrambles in Snowdonia
Snowdonia: 30 Low-level and Easy Walks — North, South
The Cambrian Way
The Snowdonia Way
The Wye Valley Walk
Walking Glyndwr's Way
Walking in Carmarthenshire
Walking in Pembrokeshire
Walking in the Brecon Beacons
Walking in the Wye Valley
Walking on Gower
Walking the Severn Way
Walking the Shropshire Way
Walking the Wales Coast Path

SOUTHERN ENGLAND

20 Classic Sportive Rides in South East England
20 Classic Sportive Rides in South West England
Cycling in the Cotswolds
Mountain Biking on the North Downs
Mountain Biking on the South Downs
The North Downs Way
North Downs Way Map Booklet
Walking the South West Coast Path
South West Coast Path Map Booklet
— Vol 1: Minehead to St Ives
— Vol 2: St Ives to Plymouth
— Vol 3: Plymouth to Poole
Suffolk Coast and Heath Walks
The Cotswold Way
The Cotswold Way Map Booklet
The Kennet and Avon Canal
The Lea Valley Walk
The Peddars Way and Norfolk Coast Path
The Pilgrims' Way
The Ridgeway National Trail
The Ridgeway Map Booklet
The South Downs Way
The South Downs Way Map Booklet
The Thames Path
The Thames Path Map Booklet
The Two Moors Way
Two Moors Way Map Booklet
Walking Hampshire's Test Way
Walking in Cornwall
Walking in Essex
Walking in Kent
Walking in London
Walking in Norfolk
Walking in the Chilterns
Walking in the Cotswolds
Walking in the Isles of Scilly
Walking in the New Forest
Walking in the North Wessex Downs
Walking on Dartmoor
Walking on Guernsey
Walking on Jersey
Walking on the Isle of Wight
Walking the Dartmoor Way
Walking the Jurassic Coast
Walking the Sarsen Way
Walks in the South Downs National Park
Cycling Land's End to John o' Groats

ALPS CROSS-BORDER ROUTES

100 Hut Walks in the Alps
Alpine Ski Mountaineering Vol 1 — Western Alps
The Karnischer Hohenweg
The Tour of the Bernina
Trekking the Tour du Mont Blanc
Tour du Mont Blanc Map Booklet
Trail Running — Chamonix and the Mont Blanc region
Trekking Chamonix to Zermatt
Trekking in the Alps
Trekking in the Silvretta and Ratikon Alps
Trekking Munich to Venice
Walking in the Alps

FRANCE, BELGIUM, AND LUXEMBOURG

Camino de Santiago — Via Podiensis
Chamonix Mountain Adventures
Cycling London to Paris
Cycling the Canal de la Garonne
Cycling the Canal du Midi
Mont Blanc Walks
Mountain Adventures in the Maurienne
Short Treks on Corsica
The Grand Traverse of the Massif Central
The Moselle Cycle Route
Trekking in the Vanoise
Trekking the Cathar Way
Trekking the GR10
Trekking the GR20 Corsica
Trekking the Robert Louis Stevenson Trail
The GR5 Trail
The GR5 Trail —
Vosges and Jura
Benelux and Lorraine
Via Ferratas of the French Alps
Walking in Provence — East
Walking in Provence — West
Walking in the Auvergne
Walking in the Brianconnais
Walking in the Dordogne
Walking in the Haute Savoie: North
Walking in the Haute Savoie: South
Walking on Corsica
Walking the Brittany Coast Path
Walking in the Ardennes

PYRENEES AND FRANCE/SPAIN CROSS-BORDER ROUTES

Shorter Treks in the Pyrenees
The Pyrenean Haute Route
The Pyrenees
Trekking the Cami dels Bons Homes
Trekking the GR11 Trail
Walks and Climbs in the Pyrenees

SPAIN AND PORTUGAL

Camino de Santiago: Camino Frances
Costa Blanca Mountain Adventures
Cycling the Camino de Santiago
Mountain Walking in Mallorca
Mountain Walking in Southern Catalunya
Spain's Sendero Historico: The GR1
The Andalucian Coast to Coast Walk
The Camino del Norte and Camino Primitivo
The Camino Ingles and Ruta do Mar
The Mountains Around Nerja
The Mountains of Ronda and Grazalema
The Sierras of Extremadura
Trekking in Mallorca
Trekking in the Canary Islands
Trekking the GR7 in Andalucia
Walking and Trekking in the Sierra Nevada
Walking in Andalucia
Walking in Catalunya —
Barcelona
Girona Pyrenees
Walking in the Picos de Europa
Walking La Via de la Plata and Camino Sanabres
Walking on Gran Canaria
Walking on La Gomera and El Hierro
Walking on La Palma
Walking on Lanzarote and Fuerteventura
Walking on Tenerife
Walking on the Costa Blanca
Walking the Camino dos Faros
Portugal's Rota Vicentina

The Camino Portugues
Walking in Portugal
Walking in the Algarve
Walking on Madeira
Walking on the Azores

SWITZERLAND

Switzerland's Jura Crest Trail
The Swiss Alps
Tour of the Jungfrau Region
Trekking the Swiss Via Alpina
Walking in Arolla and Zinal
Walking in the Bernese Oberland — Jungfrau region
Walking in the Engadine — Switzerland
Walking in the Valais
Walking in Ticino
Walking in Zermatt and Saas-Fee

GERMANY

Hiking and Cycling in the Black Forest
The Danube Cycleway Vol 1
The Rhine Cycle Route
The Westweg
Walking in the Bavarian Alps

POLAND, SLOVAKIA, ROMANIA, HUNGARY AND BULGARIA

The Danube Cycleway Vol 2
The High Tatras
The Mountains of Romania

SCANDINAVIA, ICELAND AND GREENLAND

Hiking in Norway — North
Hiking in Norway — South
Trekking the Kungsleden
Trekking in Greenland — The Arctic Circle Trail
Walking and Trekking in Iceland

SLOVENIA, CROATIA, SERBIA, MONTENEGRO AND ALBANIA

Hiking Slovenia's Juliana Trail
Mountain Biking in Slovenia
The Islands of Croatia
The Julian Alps of Slovenia
The Mountains of Montenegro
The Peaks of the Balkans Trail
The Slovene Mountain Trail
Walking in Slovenia: The Karavanke
Walks and Treks in Croatia

ITALY

Alta Via 1 — Trekking in the Dolomites
Alta Via 2 — Trekking in the Dolomites
Day Walks in the Dolomites
Italy's Grande Traversata delle Alpi
Italy's Sibillini National Park
Ski Touring and Snowshoeing in the Dolomites
The Way of St Francis
Trekking Gran Paradiso: Alta Via 2
Trekking in the Apennines
Trekking the Giants' Trail: Alta Via 1 through the Italian Pennine Alps
Via Ferratas of the Italian Dolomites:
Vol 1
Vol 2
Walking in Abruzzo
Walking in Italy's Cinque Terre
Walking in Italy's Stelvio National Park
Walking in Sicily
Walking in the Aosta Valley
Walking in the Dolomites
Walking in Tuscany
Walking in Umbria
Walking Lake Como and Maggiore
Walking Lake Garda and Iseo
Walking on the Amalfi Coast
Walking the Via Francigena Pilgrim Route — Part 2
Walking the Via Francigena Pilgrim Route — Part 3
Walks and Treks in the Maritime Alps

IRELAND

The Wild Atlantic Way and Western Ireland
Walking the Kerry Way
Walking the Wicklow Way

EUROPEAN CYCLING

Cycling the Route des Grandes Alpes
Cycling the Ruta Via de la Plata
The Elbe Cycle Route
The River Loire Cycle Route
The River Rhone Cycle Route

INTERNATIONAL CHALLENGES, COLLECTIONS AND ACTIVITIES

Europe's High Points
Walking the Via Francigena Pilgrim Route — Part 1

AUSTRIA

Innsbruck Mountain Adventures
Trekking Austria's Adlerweg
Trekking in Austria's Hohe Tauern
Trekking in Austria's Stubai Alps
Trekking in Austria's Zillertal Alps
Walking in Austria
Walking in the Salzkammergut: the Austrian Lake District

MEDITERRANEAN

The High Mountains of Crete
Trekking in Greece
Walking and Trekking in Zagori
Walking and Trekking on Corfu
Walking on the Greek Islands — the Cyclades
Walking in Cyprus
Walking on Malta

HIMALAYA

8000 metres
Everest: A Trekker's Guide
Trekking in the Karakoram

NORTH AMERICA

Hiking and Cycling the California Missions Trail
The John Muir Trail
The Pacific Crest Trail

SOUTH AMERICA

Aconcagua and the Southern Andes
Hiking and Biking Peru's Inca Trails
Trekking in Torres del Paine

AFRICA

Kilimanjaro
Walking in the Drakensberg
Walks and Scrambles in the Moroccan Anti-Atlas

NEW ZEALAND AND AUSTRALIA

Hiking the Overland Track

CHINA, JAPAN, AND ASIA

Annapurna
Hiking and Trekking in the Japan Alps and Mount Fuji
Hiking in Hong Kong
Japan's Kumano Kodo Pilgrimage
Japan's Kumano Kodo Pilgrimage
Trekking in Bhutan
Trekking in Ladakh
Trekking in Tajikistan
Trekking in the Himalaya

TECHNIQUES

Fastpacking
The Mountain Hut Book

MINI GUIDES

Alpine Flowers
Navigation
Pocket First Aid and Wilderness Medicine

MOUNTAIN LITERATURE

A Walk in the Clouds
Abode of the Gods
Fifty Years of Adventure
The Pennine Way — the Path, the People, the Journey
Unjustifiable Risk?

For full information on all our guides, books and eBooks, visit our website:
www.cicerone.co.uk

CICERONE

Trust Cicerone to guide your next adventure, wherever it may be around the world...

Discover guides for hiking, mountain walking, backpacking, trekking, trail running, cycling and mountain biking, ski touring, climbing and scrambling in Britain, Europe and worldwide.

Connect with Cicerone online and find inspiration.

- buy books and ebooks
- articles, advice and trip reports
- GPX files and updates
- regular newsletter

cicerone.co.uk

A clear and obvious track is followed towards Ling Gill (Day 8)

THE PENNINE WAY

This map booklet shows the 426km (265 mile) Pennine Way. This National Trail is Britain's oldest, toughest and best-known long-distance footpath. It stretches from Edale in the Derbyshire Peak District to Kirk Yetholm in the Scottish Borders and can be completed in 2–3 weeks.

Contents and using this guide

This booklet of Ordnance Survey® 1:25,000 Explorer maps has been designed for convenient use on the trail and includes:

- a key to map pages (pages 4–5) showing where to find the maps for each stage
- the full and up-to-date line of the National Trail
- an extract from the OS Explorer map legend (pages 129–131).

In addition, the *Pennine Way* guidebook describes the full route from south to north alongside all you need to know to plan a successful trip and lots of incidental information about local history, geography and wildlife.

Note that the route described in this map booklet is the actual route walked by the author. The route marked 'Pennine Way' on the Ordnance Survey maps differs slightly from the on-the-ground reality.

© Cicerone Press 2025
Second edition 2025
ISBN-13: 978 1 78631 141 2
First edition 2017
Photos © Paddy Dillon 2017

© Crown copyright and
database rights 2025
OS AC0000810376

Cicerone's EU representative for GPSR compliance is Easy Access System Europe, Mustamäe tee 50, 10621 Tallinn, Estonia. Email gpsr.requests@easproject.com.

PENNINE WAY

Route symbols on OS map extracts
route
alternative route
S
start point
F
finish point
SF
start/finish point
SF
alternative start/finish
N
0
½ mile
0
1km
Scale 1:25,000
For OS legend see pages 129–131

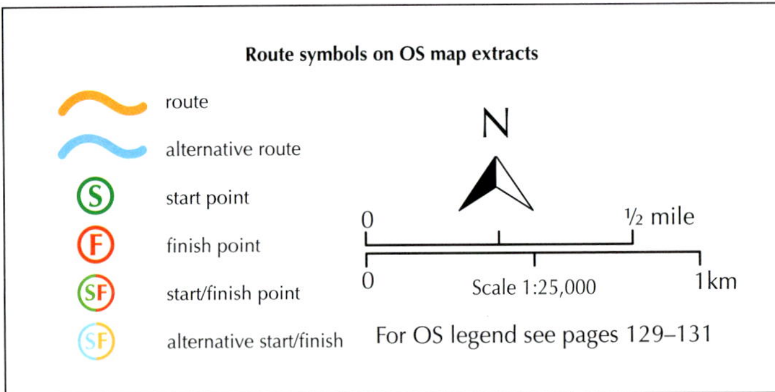

Looking across a meadow to Low Way Farm near Holwick (Stage 12)

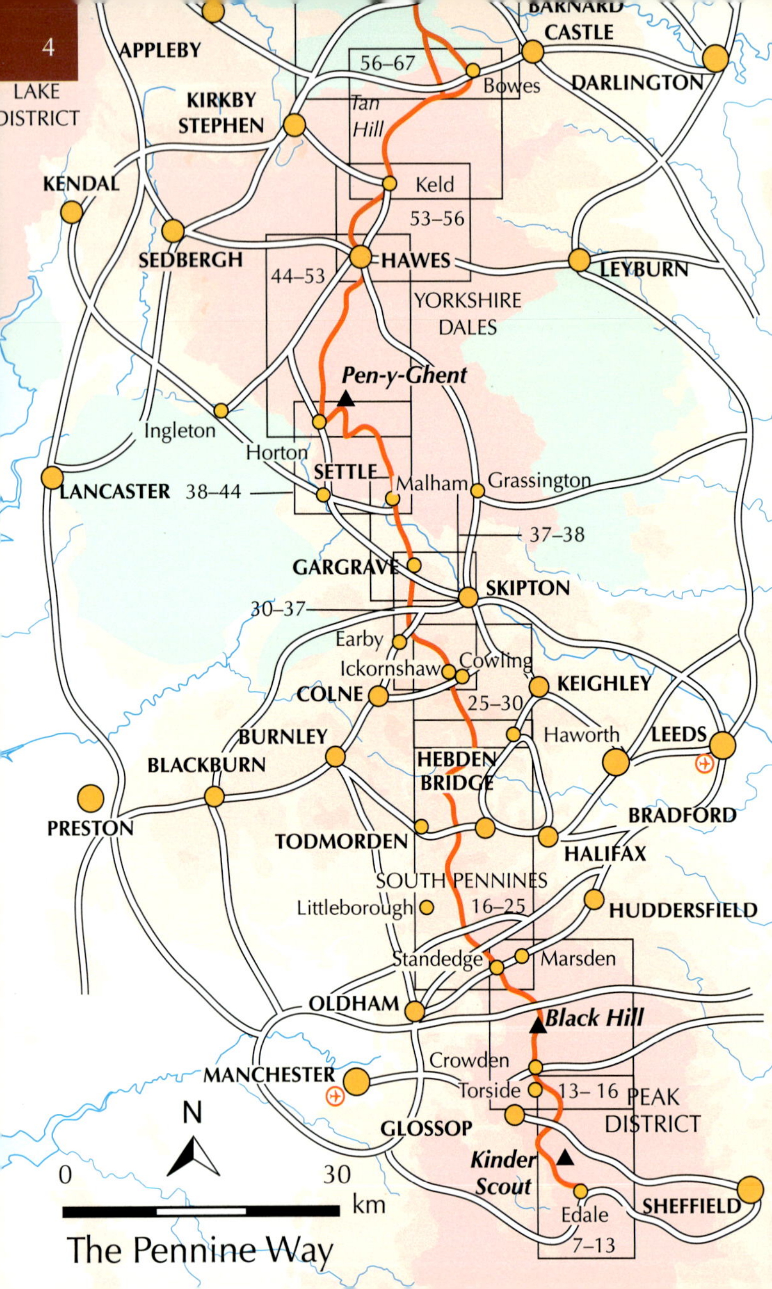
4
LAKE DISTRICT
APPLEBY
BARNARD CASTLE
DARLINGTON
56–67
Bowes
Tan Hill
KIRKBY STEPHEN
KENDAL
Keld
53–56
SEDBERGH
HAWES
LEYBURN
44–53
YORKSHIRE DALES
Pen-y-Ghent
Ingleton
Horton
SETTLE
Malham
Grassington
LANCASTER
38–44
37–38
GARGRAVE
SKIPTON
30–37
Earby
Ickornshaw
Cowling
KEIGHLEY
COLNE
25–30
Haworth
BURNLEY
LEEDS
BLACKBURN
HEBDEN BRIDGE
PRESTON
BRADFORD
TODMORDEN
HALIFAX
SOUTH PENNINES
Littleborough
16–25
HUDDERSFIELD
Standedge
Marsden
OLDHAM
Black Hill
Crowden
MANCHESTER
Torside
13–16
PEAK DISTRICT
GLOSSOP
N
Kinder Scout
0
30
km
Edale
SHEFFIELD
7–13
The Pennine Way

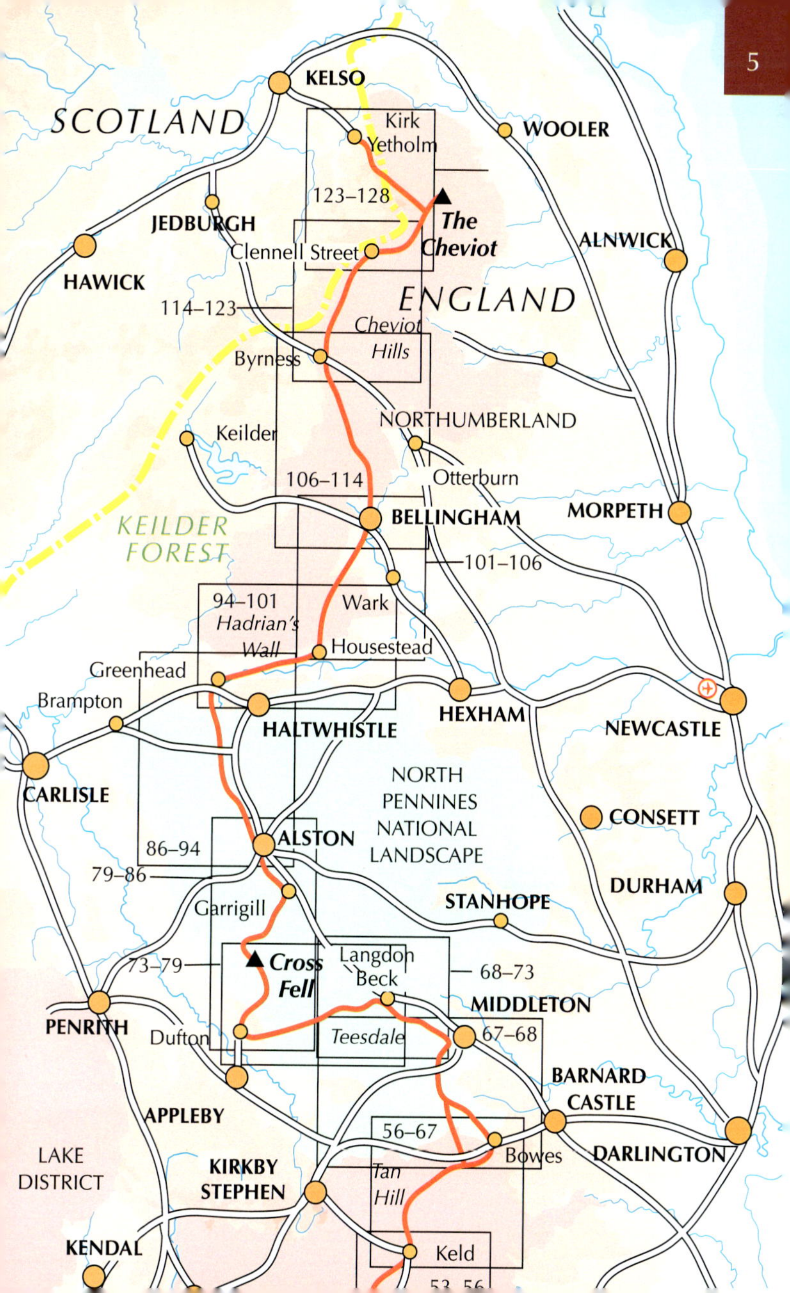

KELSO
SCOTLAND
Kirk Yetholm
WOOLER
123–128
JEDBURGH
The Cheviot
HAWICK
Clennell Street
ALNWICK
114–123
ENGLAND
Cheviot Hills
Byrness
NORTHUMBERLAND
Keilder
Otterburn
106–114
BELLINGHAM
MORPETH
KEILDER FOREST
101–106
94–101
Hadrian's Wall
Wark
Housestead
Greenhead
Brampton
HALTWHISTLE
HEXHAM
NEWCASTLE
CARLISLE
NORTH PENNINES NATIONAL LANDSCAPE
CONSETT
86–94
ALSTON
79–86
Garrigill
STANHOPE
DURHAM
73–79
Cross Fell
Langdon Beck
68–73
MIDDLETON
PENRITH
Dufton
Teesdale
67–68
BARNARD CASTLE
APPLEBY
56–67
Bowes
DARLINGTON
LAKE DISTRICT
KIRKBY STEPHEN
Tan Hill
KENDAL
Keld
53–56

6

Fords
Fall
Kinder Downfall
River Kinder
Fords
Kinder Gates
Crowden Head
Kinder Scout National Nature Reserve
Kinder Scout
Red Brook
Ford
Fords
Edale Moor
629
632
623
Pennine Way
636
Fords
Fords
Fords
Falls
Kinder Low
Edale Head
Fords
Pym Chair
619
Crowden Tower
633
Cairn
Noe Stool
Wool Packs
Fords
Fords
Ford
Edale Rocks
The Cloughs
564
Crowden Brook
Fords
Swine's Back
Jacob's Ladder (Path)
Crowden Clough
Ford
Ford
Sheepfold
Sheepfold
FB
541
533
Cross
FB
Fall
AK DISTRICT
559
Lee Farm
Sheepfold
FB
Gauge
Shelter
Sheepfold
Rain Gauge
Grain Clough
FB
Fords
Brown Knoll
569
High

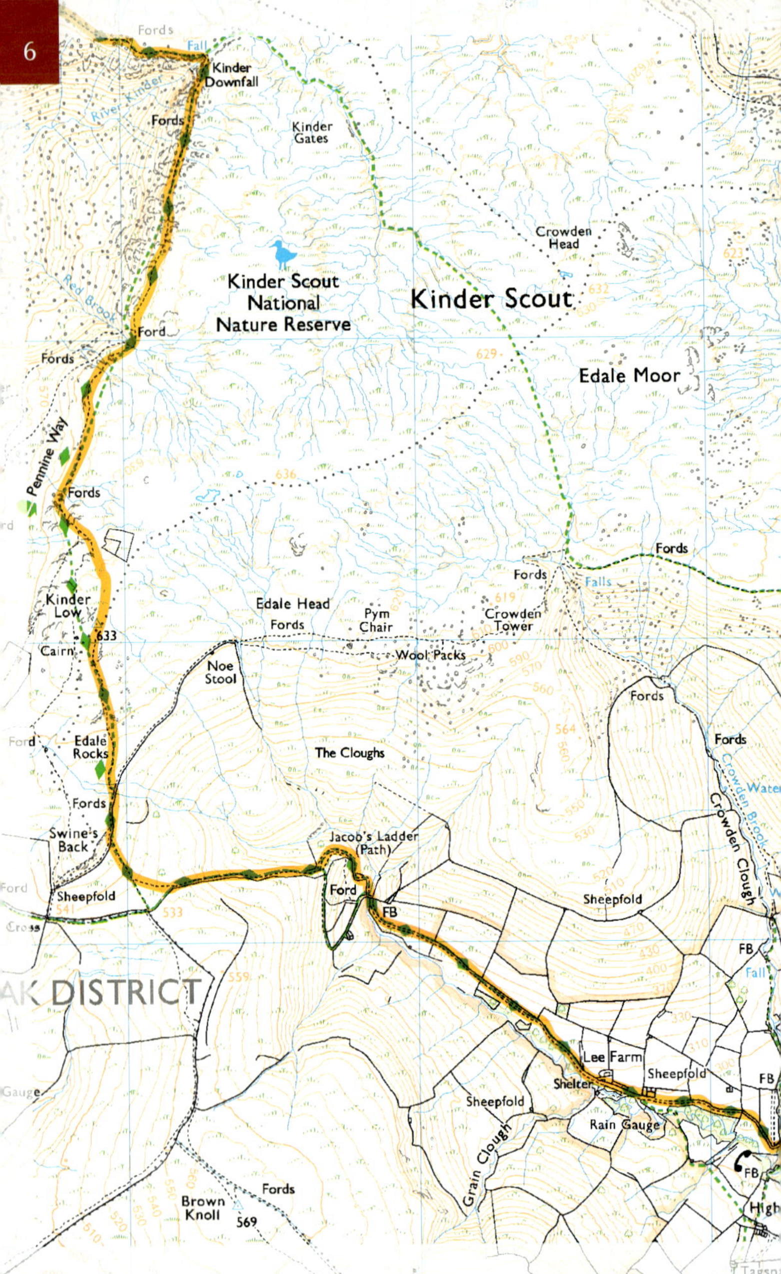

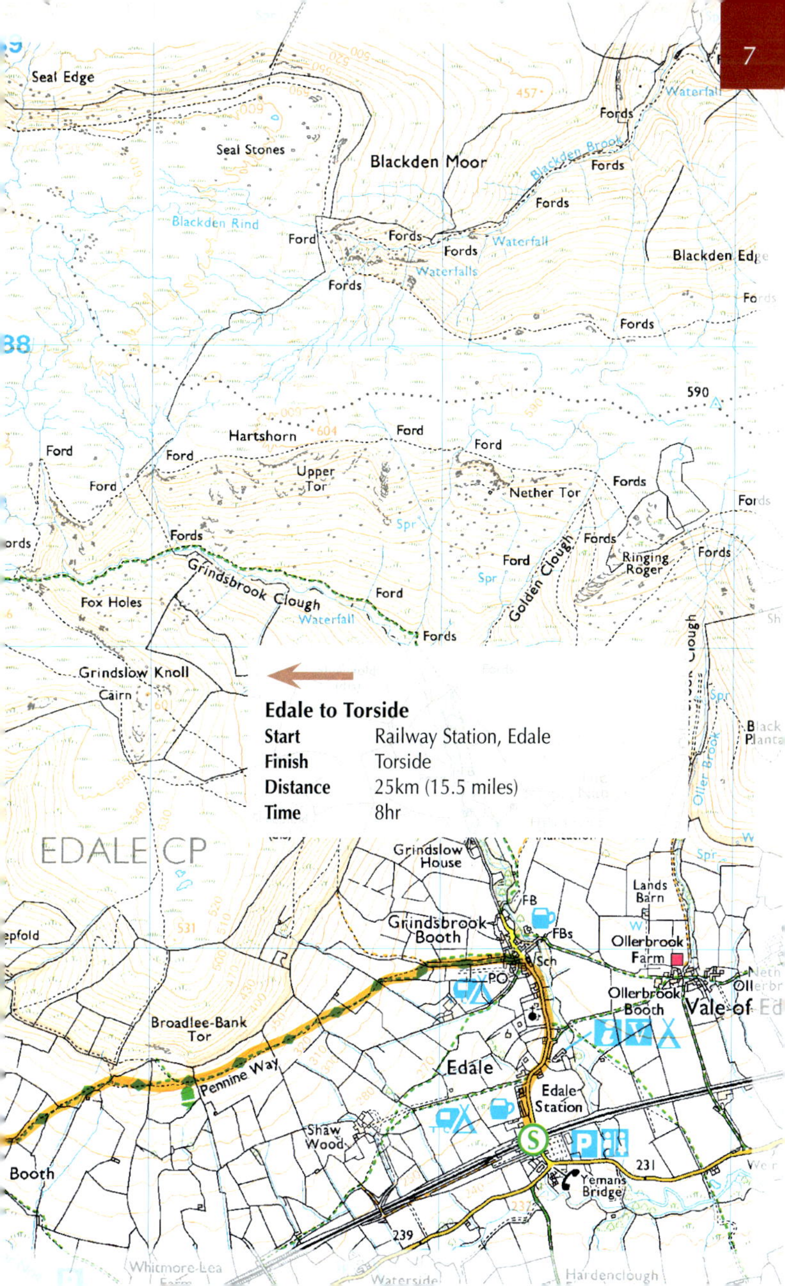

Edale to Torside

Start	Railway Station, Edale
Finish	Torside
Distance	25km (15.5 miles)
Time	8hr

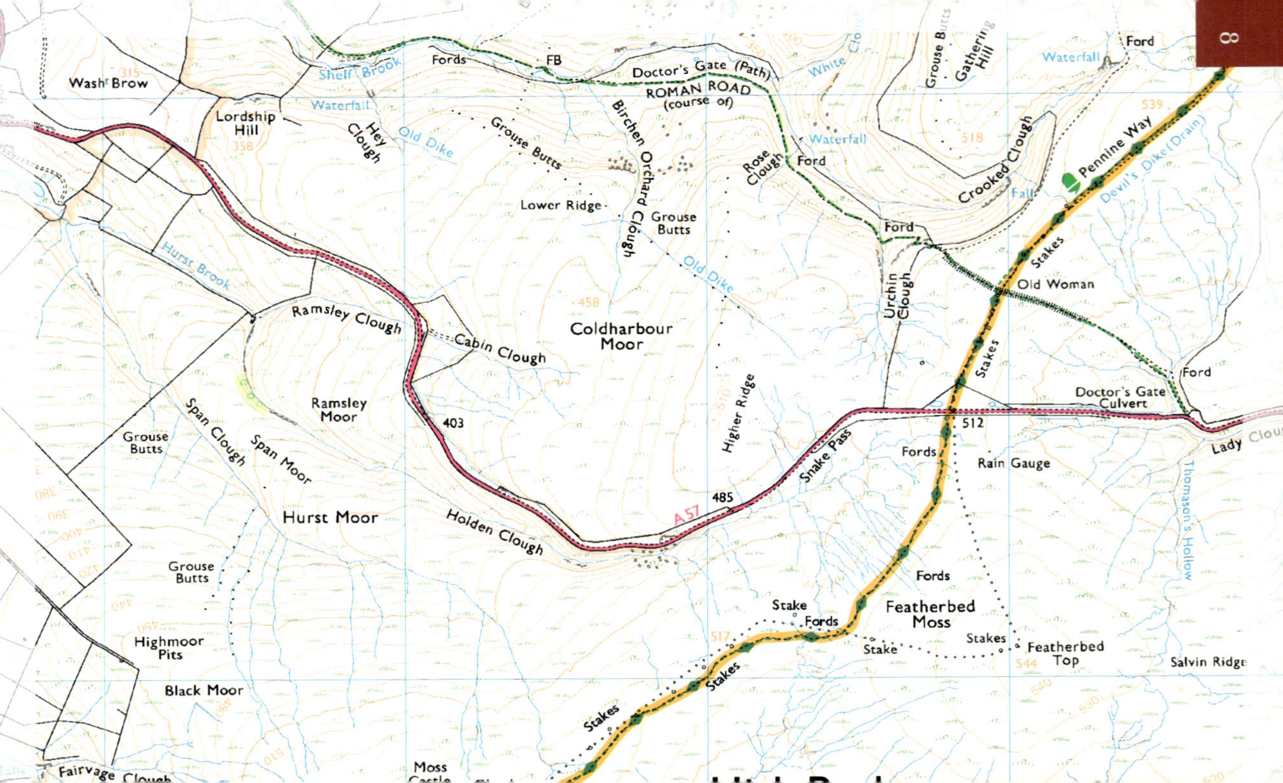
Wash Brow
315
Lordship Hill
358
Shelf Brook
Waterfall
Hey Clough
Fords
FB
Doctor's Gate (Path)
ROMAN ROAD (course of)
Old Dike
Grouse Butts
Birchen Orchard Clough
White Clough
Grouse Butts
Gathering Hill
Ford
Waterfall
Waterfall
Rose Clough
Ford
518
Crooked Clough
Fall
539
Pennine Way
Devil's Dike (Drain)
Lower Ridge
Grouse Butts
Ford
Hurst Brook
Old Dike
458
Coldharbour Moor
Urchin Clough
Stakes
Old Woman
Ramsley Clough
Cabin Clough
Stakes
Ford
Doctor's Gate Culvert
Ramsley Moor
403
Higher Ridge
510
512
Lady Clough
Grouse Butts
Span Clough
Span Moor
Snake Pass
Fords
Rain Gauge
Thomason's Hollow
485
A57
Hurst Moor
Holden Clough
Fords
Grouse Butts
Stake
Fords
Featherbed Moss
517
Stake
Stakes
Featherbed Top
544
Salvin Ridge
Highmoor Pits
Stakes
Black Moor
Stakes
Fairvage Clough
Moss Castle

Pennine Way
Stakes
Stakes
Within Clough
Red Clough
Grouse Butts
Grouse Butts
Upper Gate Cl
Nether Gate
Mill Hill
06
Stake
Ashop Head
07
08
09
Snake Path Ford
Ashop Clough
River Ashop
Black Ashop Moor
Grouse Butts
FB
Upper Red Brook
Nether Red Brook
The Edge
Fairbrook Naze
Falls
Fall
624
Sandy Heys
Kinder Downfall
William Clough
Moor
Fords
Ford
447
527
544
575
619
620
625

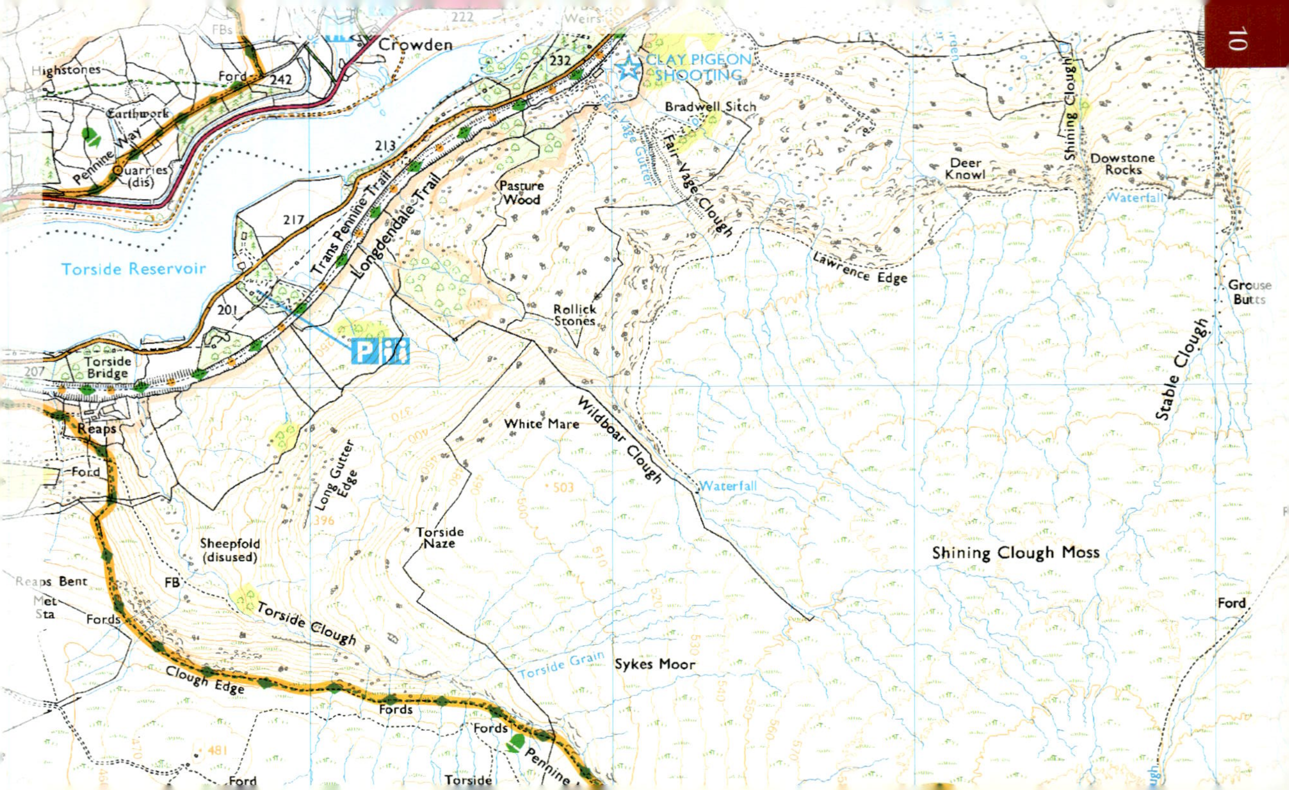
Crowden
Highstones
Ford
242
Earthwork
Pennine Way
Quarries (dis)
222
FBs
Weirs
232
CLAY PIGEON SHOOTING
Bradwell Sitch
Fair Vage Gutter
Fair Vage Clough
Shining Clough
Deer Knowl
Dowstone Rocks
Waterfall
213
Torside Reservoir
217
Trans Pennine Trail
Longdendale Trail
Pasture Wood
Lawrence Edge
Grouse Butts
201
Rollick Stones
Stable Clough
Torside Bridge
207
Reaps
White Mare
Wildboar Clough
Ford
Long Gutter Edge
396
Waterfall
503
Torside Naze
Sheepfold (disused)
Shining Clough Moss
Reaps Bent
FB
Met Sta
Fords
Torside Clough
Ford
Torside Grain
Sykes Moor
Clough Edge
Fords
Fords
481
Pennine
Ford
Torside

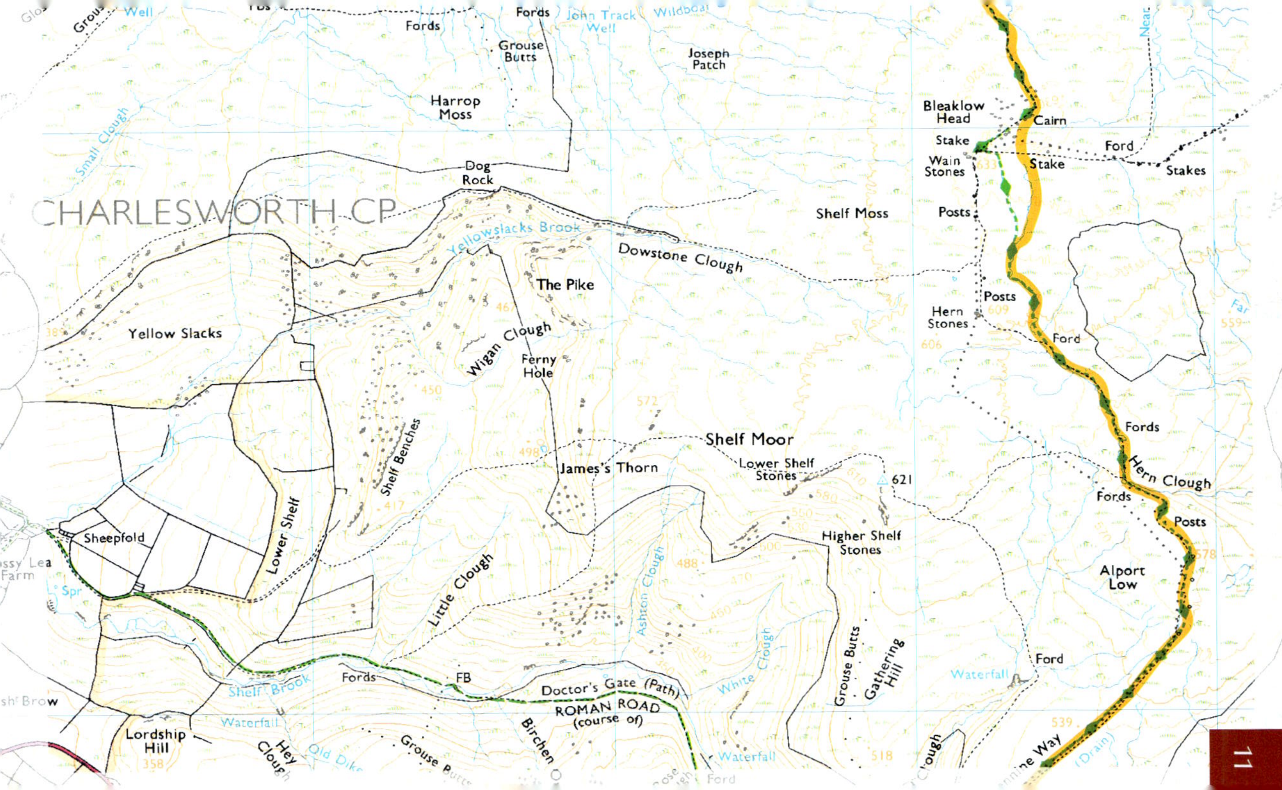

Fords
Fords
John Track Well
Grouse Butts
Joseph Patch
Harrop Moss
Small Clough
Dog Rock
CHARLESWORTH CP
Yellowslacks Brook
Dowstone Clough
The Pike
Yellow Slacks
Wigan Clough
Ferny Hole
Shelf Benches
James's Thorn
Shelf Moor
Lower Shelf Stones
621
Higher Shelf Stones
Sheepfold
Lower Shelf
Spr
Little Clough
Ashton Clough
White Clough
Grouse Butts
Gathering Hill
Shelf Brook
Fords
FB
Doctor's Gate (Path)
ROMAN ROAD (course of)
Birchen
Waterfall
Lordship Hill
Hey Clough
Old Dike
Ford
Bleaklow Head
Cairn
Stake
Wain Stones
Stake
Ford
Stakes
Posts
Shelf Moss
Posts
Hern Stones
Ford
Fords
Hern Clough
Fords
Posts
Alport Low
Ford
Waterfall
(Drain)

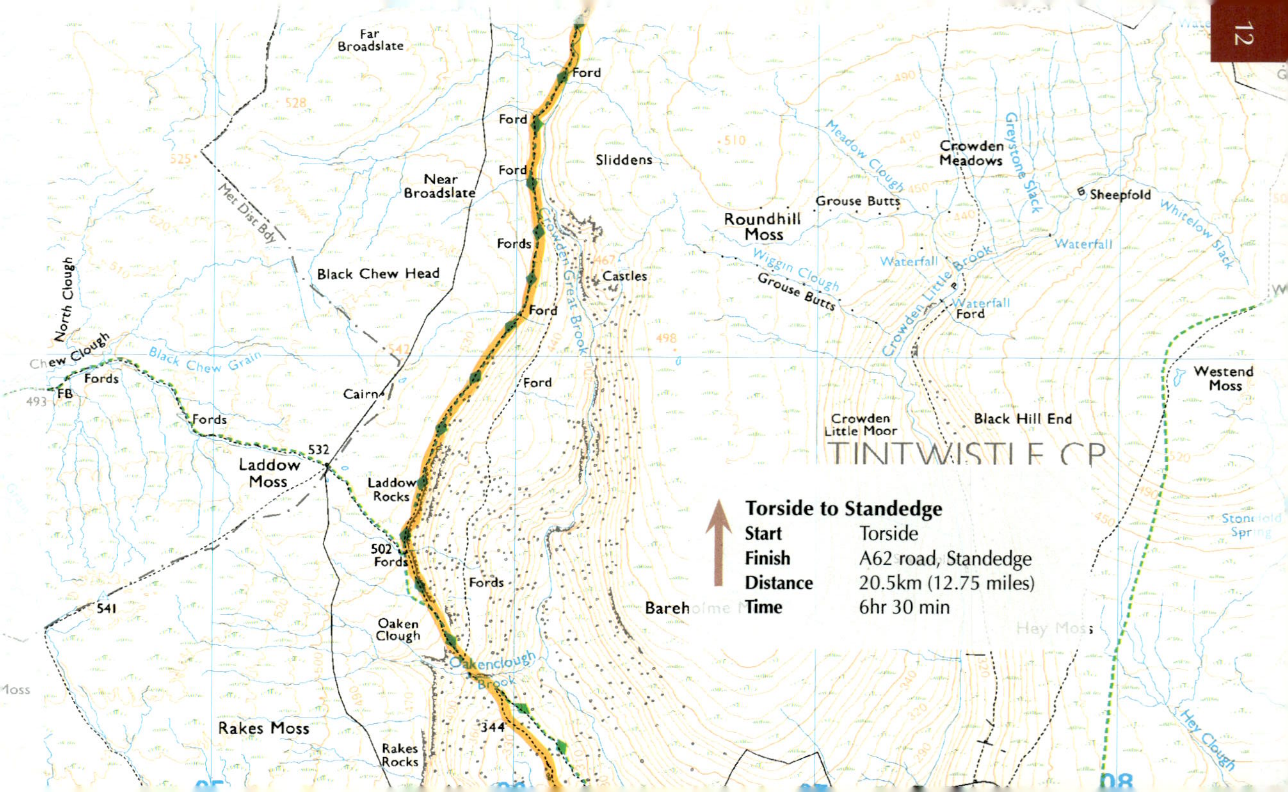
Torside to Standedge
Start Torside
Finish A62 road, Standedge
Distance 20.5km (12.75 miles)
Time 6hr 30 min
Far Broadslate
Near Broadslate
Black Chew Head
Met Dist Bdy
Ford
Fords
Sliddens
Castles
Crowden Great Brook
Roundhill Moss
Grouse Butts
Wiggin Clough
Meadow Clough
Crowden Meadows
Greystone Slack
Sheepfold
Whitelow Slack
Waterfall
Crowden Little Brook
Westend Moss
Crowden Little Moor
Black Hill End
TINTWISTLE CP
Stonefold Spring
Hey Moss
Hey Clough
Bareholme Moss
North Clough
Chew Clough
Black Chew Grain
FB
Cairn
Laddow Moss
Laddow Rocks
Oaken Clough
Oakenclough Brook
Rakes Moss
Rakes Rocks

Torside to Edale

Start	Torside
Finish	Railway Station, Edale
Distance	25km (15.5 miles)
Time	8hr

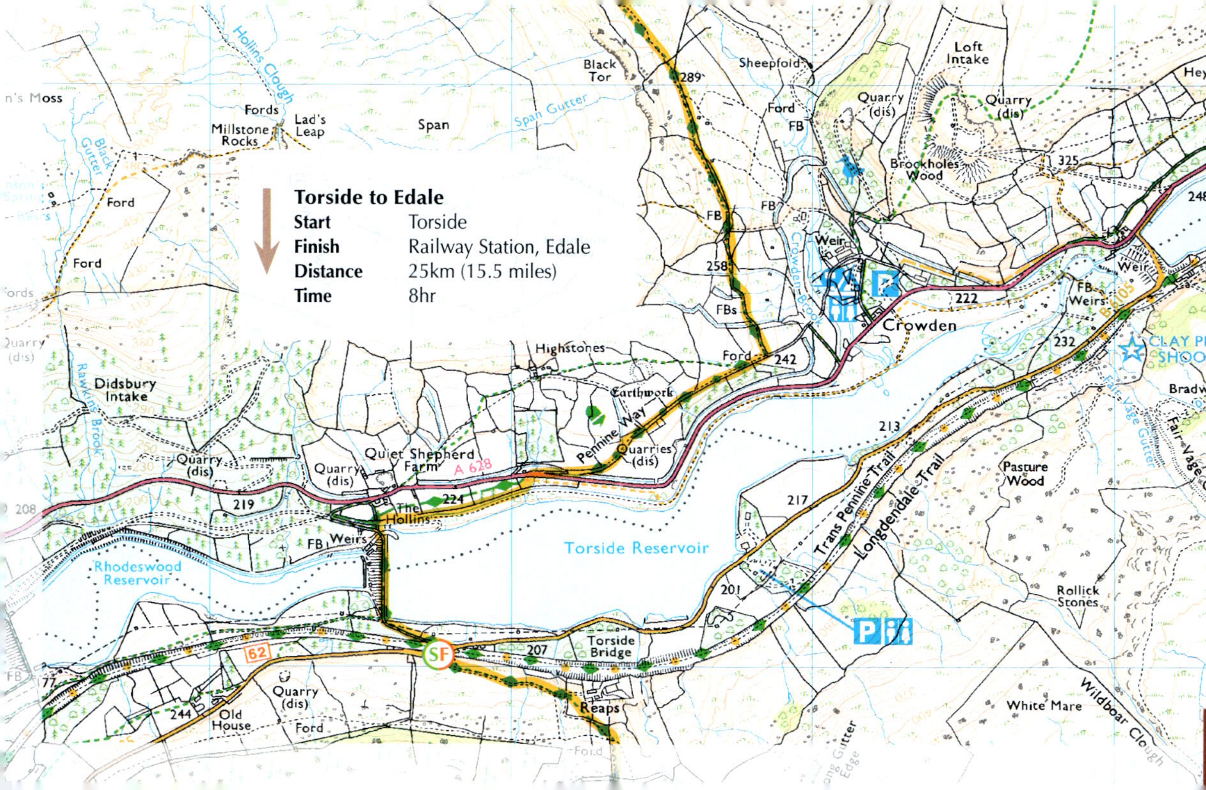

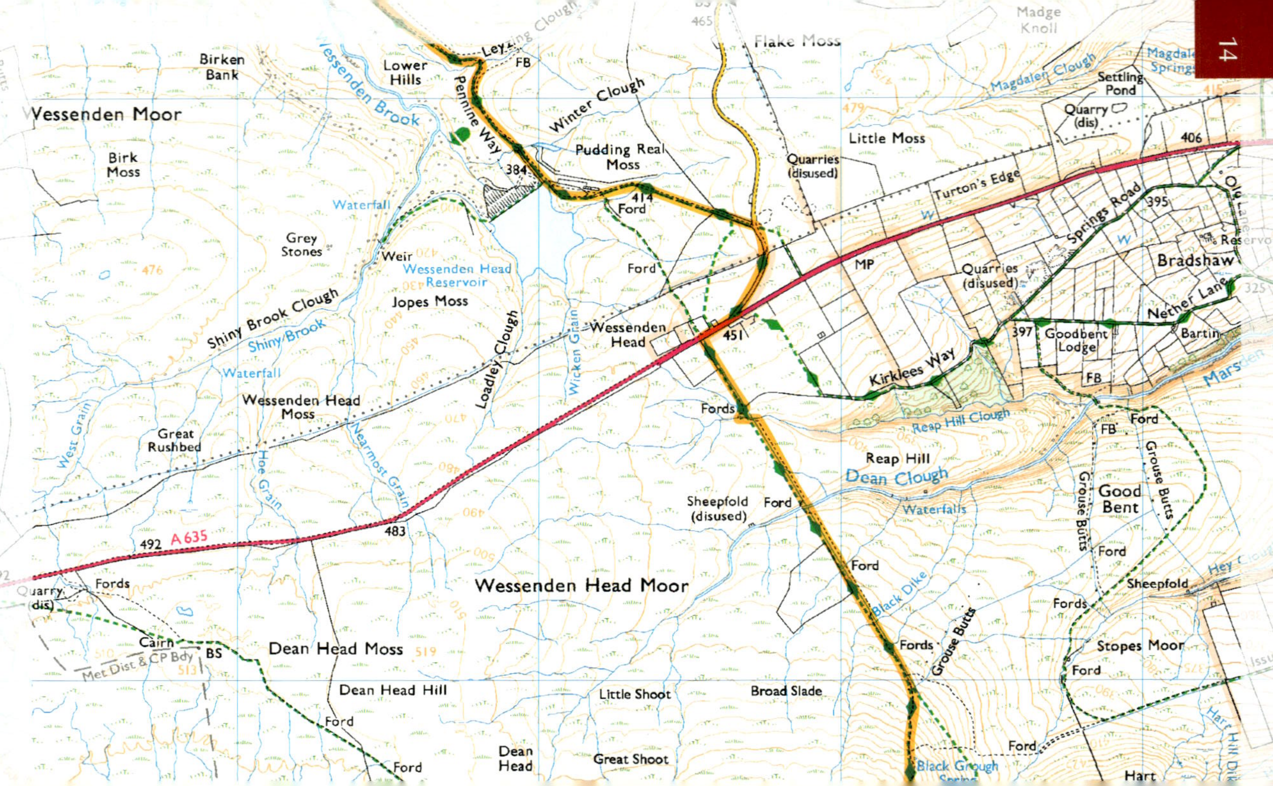

Wessenden Moor
Birken Bank
Birk Moss
Lower Hills
Wessenden Brook
Pennine Way
Winter Clough
Pudding Real Moss
Flake Moss
Madge Knoll
Magdalen Clough
Settling Pond
Quarry (dis)
Little Moss
Quarries (disused)
Turton's Edge
Springs Road
Bradshaw
Nether Lane
Goodbent Lodge
Bartin
Kirklees Way
Reap Hill Clough
Reap Hill
Dean Clough
Waterfalls
Good Bent
Grouse Butts
Sheepfold
Stopes Moor
Wessenden Head
Wessenden Head Reservoir
Weir
Waterfall
Grey Stones
Jopes Moss
Loadley Clough
Wicken Grain
Shiny Brook Clough
Shiny Brook
Wessenden Head Moss
Great Rushbed
West Grain
Hoe Grain
Nearmost Grain
A 635
Sheepfold (disused)
Black Dike
Wessenden Head Moor
Dean Head Moss
Dean Head Hill
Dean Head
Little Shoot
Great Shoot
Broad Slade
Cairn
BS
Met Dist & CP Bdy
Black Grough
Hart
Fords
Ford
FB
MP
451
414
384
406
395
397
483
492
519

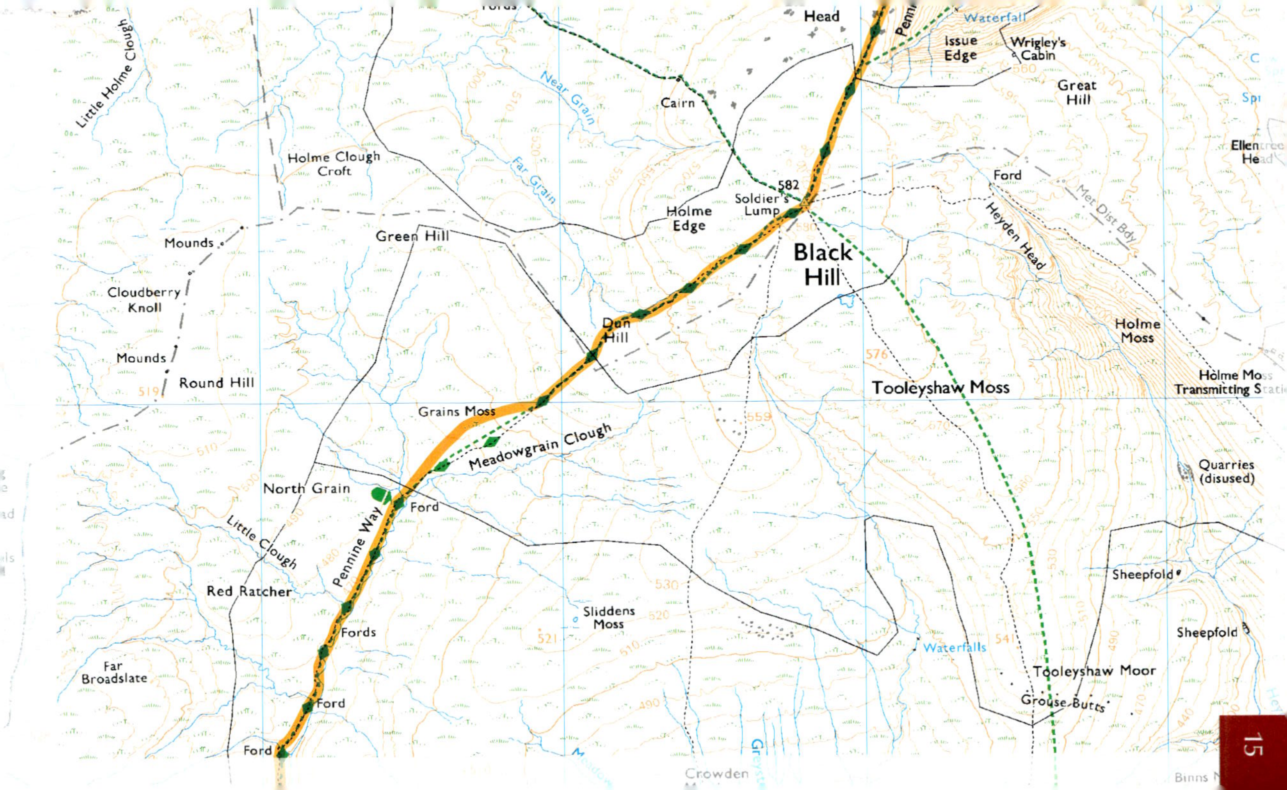
Head
Waterfall
Issue Edge
Wrigley's Cabin
Great Hill
Little Holme Clough
Cairn
Near Grain
Far Grain
Holme Clough Croft
Ford
Met Dist Bdy
582
Soldier's Lump
Holme Edge
Heyden Head
Mounds
Green Hill
Black Hill
Cloudberry Knoll
Dun Hill
Holme Moss
Mounds
Round Hill
Holme Moss Transmitting Station
Tooleyshaw Moss
Grains Moss
Meadowgrain Clough
Quarries (disused)
North Grain
Ford
Little Clough
Pennine Way
Sheepfold
Red Ratcher
Sliddens Moss
Fords
Sheepfold
Waterfalls
Far Broadslate
Tooleyshaw Moor
Ford
Grouse Butts
Ford
Crowden
15

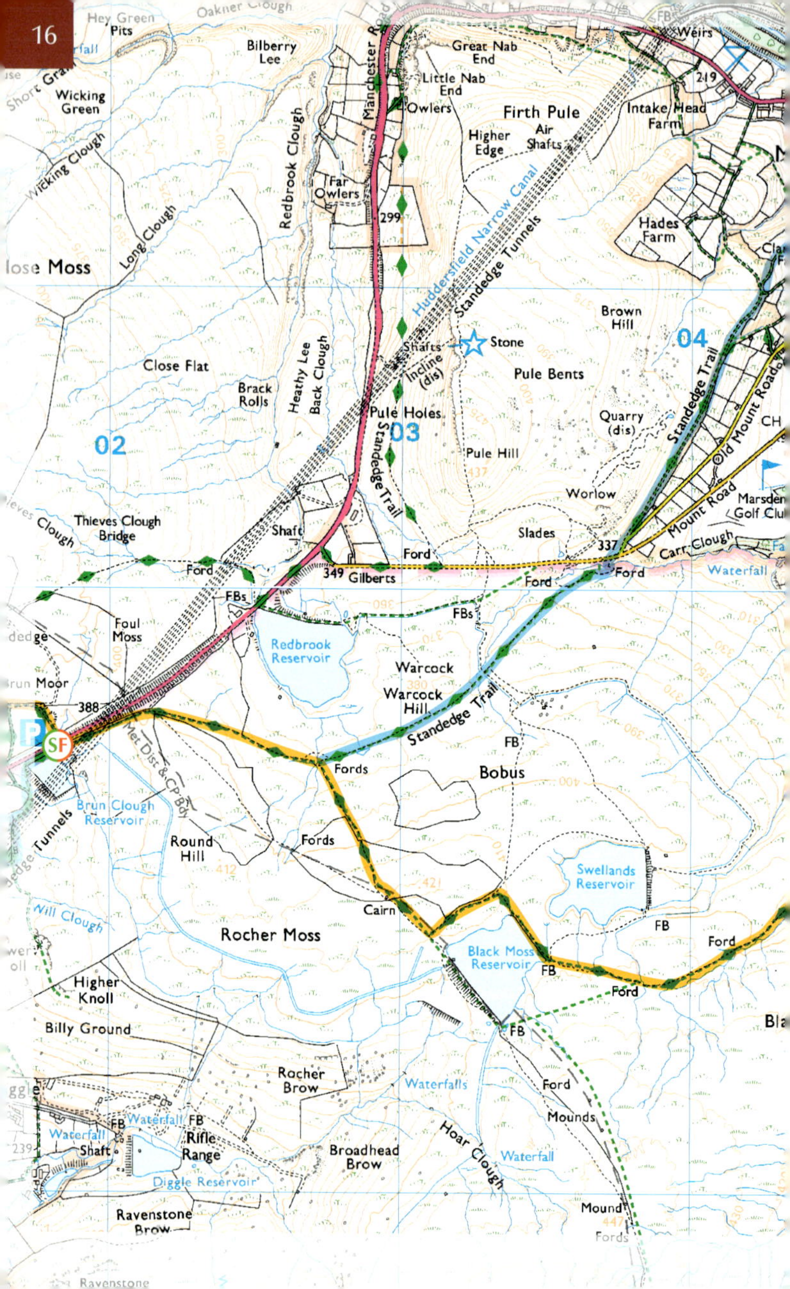

Great Nab End
Little Nab End
Owlers
Firth Pule
Air Shafts
Higher Edge
Intake Head Farm
Hades Farm
Bilberry Lee
Wicking Green
Wicking Clough
Long Clough
Redbrook Clough
Manchester Road
Far Owlers
Huddersfield Narrow Canal
Standedge Tunnels
Close Moss
Close Flat
Brack Rolls
Heathy Lee Back Clough
Shafts
Stone
Incline (dis)
Pule Bents
Brown Hill
Pule Holes
Standedge Trail
Pule Hill
Quarry (dis)
Old Mount Road
Mount Road
Marsden Golf Club
Worlow
Slades
Carr Clough
Thieves Clough Bridge
Shaft
Ford
Gilberts
Waterfall
FBs
Foul Moss
Redbrook Reservoir
Warcock
Warcock Hill
Met Dist & CP Bdy
Brun Clough Reservoir
Fords
Bobus
FB
Round Hill
Swellands Reservoir
Cairn
Rocher Moss
Black Moss Reservoir
Higher Knoll
Billy Ground
Rocher Brow
Waterfalls
Mounds
Hoar Clough
Rifle Range
Diggle Reservoir
Broadhead Brow
Ravenstone Brow
Mound
Fords
Ravenstone

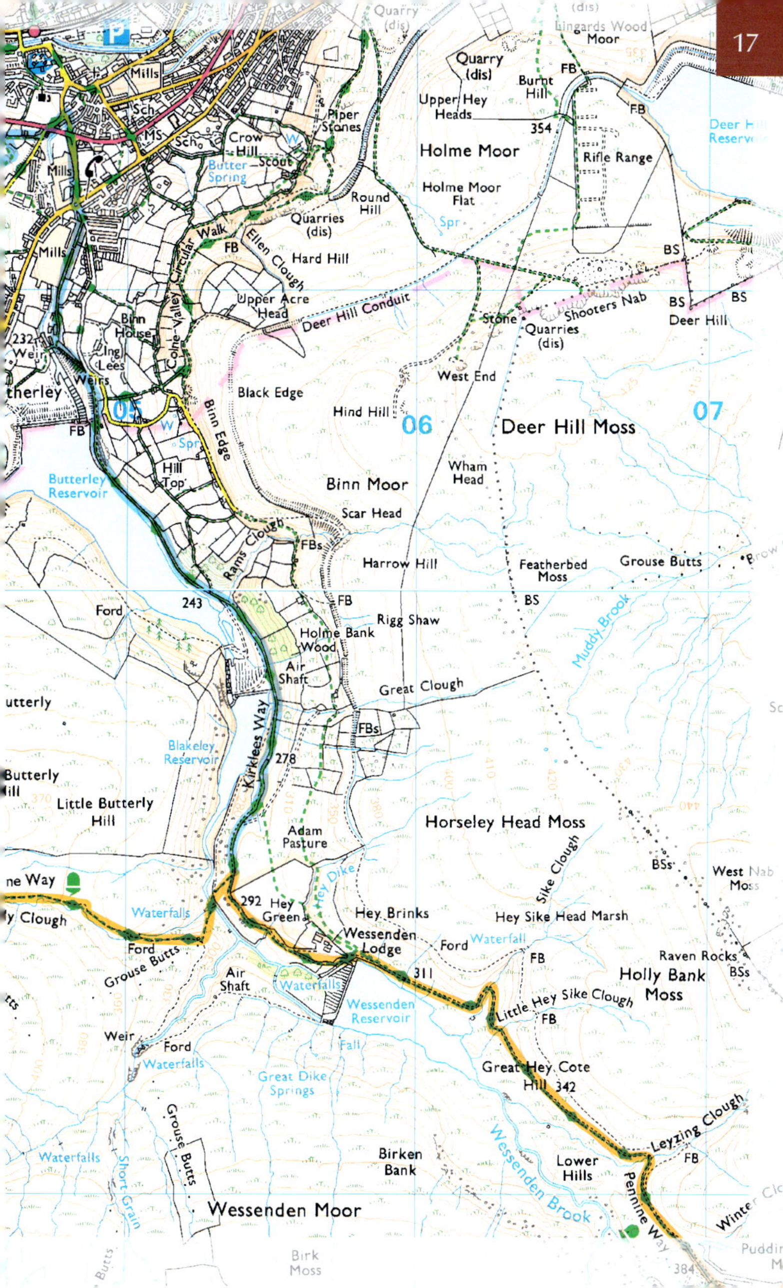

Quarry (dis)
Lingards Wood Moor
Quarry (dis)
Burnt Hill
FB
Mills
Sch
MS
Sch
Crow Hill
Piper Stones
Upper Hey Heads
354
Holme Moor
Rifle Range
Deer Hill Reservoir
Butter Spring
Scout
Mills
Round Hill
Holme Moor Flat
Spr
Quarries (dis)
Colne Valley Circular Walk
Ellen Clough
Hard Hill
Mills
BS
Upper Acre Head
Deer Hill Conduit
Stone
Shooters Nab
BS
Deer Hill
Binn House
Quarries (dis)
232
Weir
Ing Lees
Weirs
West End
therley
05
Black Edge
Hind Hill
06
Deer Hill Moss
07
FB
Binn Edge
Spr
Hill Top
Wham Head
Butterley Reservoir
Binn Moor
Scar Head
Rams Clough
FBs
Harrow Hill
Featherbed Moss
Grouse Butts
Ford
243
FB
BS
Rigg Shaw
Holme Bank Wood
Muddy Brook
Air Shaft
Great Clough
utterly
FBs
Blakeley Reservoir
Kirklees Way
278
Butterly Hill
Little Butterly Hill
Adam Pasture
Horseley Head Moss
Sike Clough
BSs
West Nab Moss
ne Way
292
Hey Green
Hey Dike
Waterfalls
y Clough
Hey Brinks
Hey Sike Head Marsh
Wessenden Lodge
Ford
Grouse Butts
Ford
Waterfall
FB
Raven Rocks
BSs
311
Air Shaft
Waterfalls
Holly Bank Moss
Wessenden Reservoir
Little Hey Sike Clough
FB
Weir
Ford
Waterfalls
Fall
Great Dike Springs
Great Hey Cote Hill 342
Grouse Butts
Leyzing Clough
FB
Waterfalls
Short Grain
Birken Bank
Wessenden Brook
Lower Hills
Pennine Way
Wessenden Moor
Winter Cl
Birk Moss
Puddin M
384

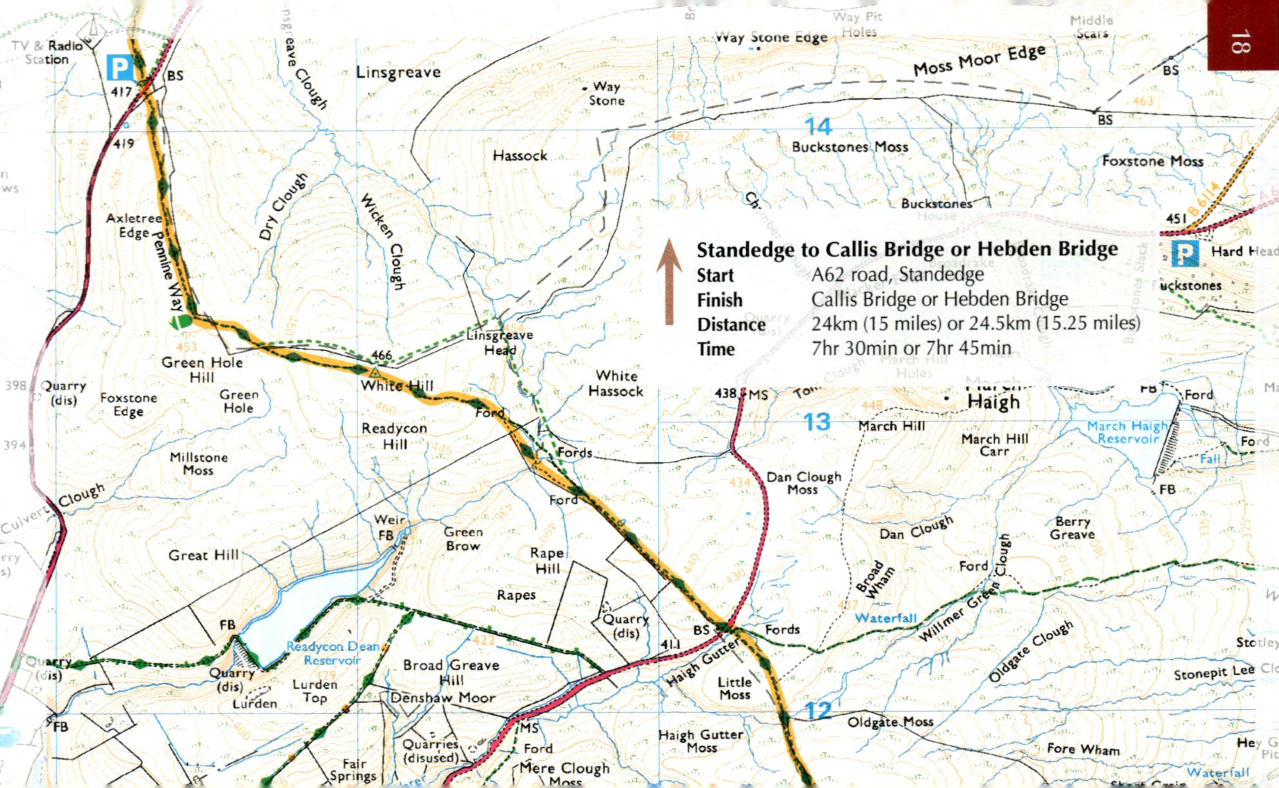
Standedge to Callis Bridge or Hebden Bridge
Start A62 road, Standedge
Finish Callis Bridge or Hebden Bridge
Distance 24km (15 miles) or 24.5km (15.25 miles)
Time 7hr 30min or 7hr 45min
TV & Radio Station
Linsgreave
Way Stone Edge
Moss Moor Edge
Way Stone
Hassock
Buckstones Moss
Foxstone Moss
Buckstones
Hard Head
Axletree Edge
Pennine Way
Dry Clough
Wicken Clough
Linsgreave Head
Green Hole Hill
Green Hole
White Hill
White Hassock
Foxstone Edge
Readycon Hill
Millstone Moss
March Hill
Haigh
March Hill Carr
March Haigh Reservoir
Dan Clough Moss
Dan Clough
Berry Greave
Great Hill
Green Brow
Rape Hill
Rapes
Broad Wham
Willmer Green Clough
Oldgate Clough
Readycon Dean Reservoir
Lurden Top
Lurden
Broad Greave Hill
Denshaw Moor
Haigh Gutter
Little Moss
Oldgate Moss
Haigh Gutter Moss
Fore Wham
Stonepit Lee
Stotley
Mere Clough
Fair Springs
Quarries (disused)

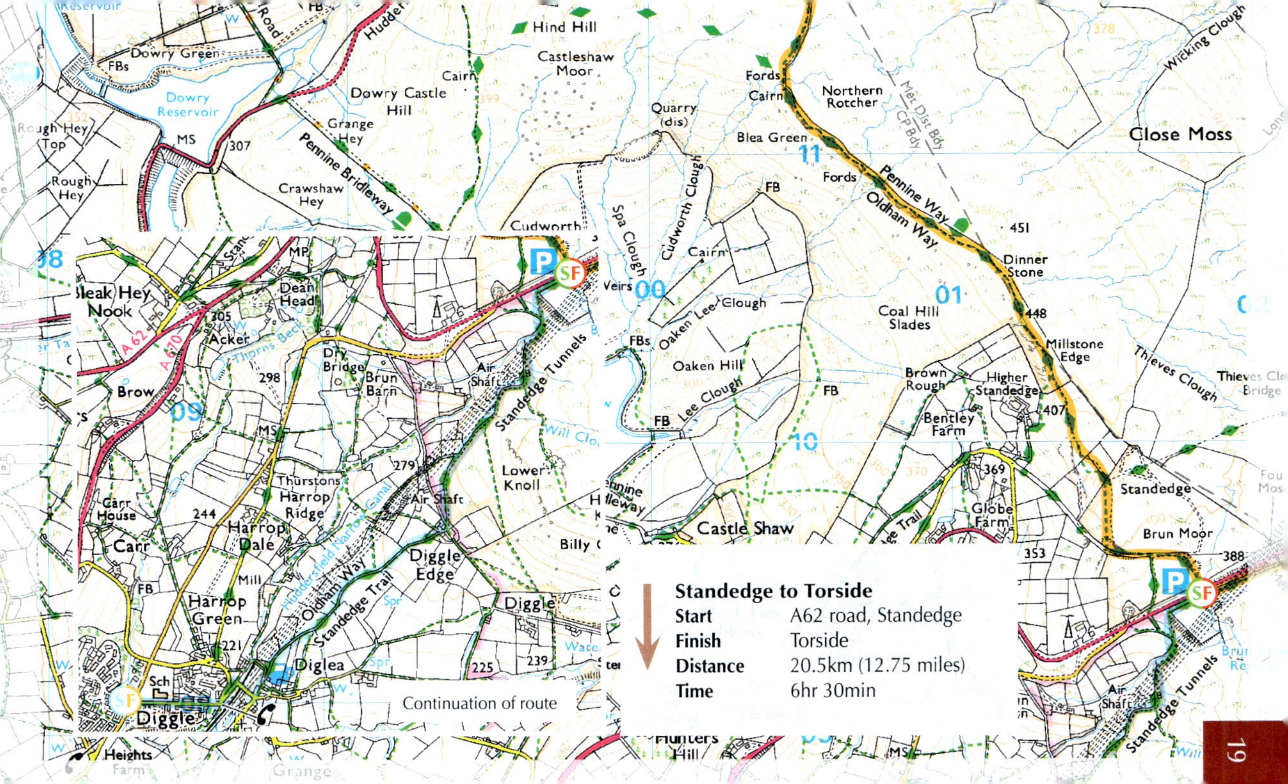
Standedge to Torside
Start A62 road, Standedge
Finish Torside
Distance 20.5km (12.75 miles)
Time 6hr 30min
Continuation of route
Hind Hill
Castleshaw Moor
Dowry Green
FBs
Dowry Reservoir
Dowry Castle Hill
Cairn
Grange Hey
Rough Hey Top
Rough Hey
MS
307
Pennine Bridleway
Crawshaw Hey
Cudworth
Quarry (dis)
Fords
Cairn
Northern Rotcher
Met Dist Bdy
CP Bdy
Close Moss
Wicking Clough
Blea Green
Spa Clough
Cudworth Clough
FB
Fords
Pennine Way
Oldham Way
451
Dinner Stone
448
Millstone Edge
Thieves Clough
Thieves Clough Bridge
Coal Hill Slades
Veirs
Oaken Lee Clough
FBs
Oaken Hill
Lee Clough
FB
Brown Rough
Higher Standedge
407
Bentley Farm
369
Globe Farm
Castle Shaw
Standedge
Brun Moor
388
353
Bleak Hey Nook
A62
A670
305
Acker
Dean Head
MP
Thorns Beck
298
Dry Bridge
Brun Barn
Air Shaft
Standedge Tunnels
Brow
MS
279
Air Shaft
Thurstons Harrop Ridge
Huddersfield Narrow Canal
Lower Knoll
Carr House
244
Harrop Dale
Carr
Mill
Diggle Edge
Diggle
FB
Harrop Green
221
Oldham Way
Standedge Trail
Diglea
225
239
Sch
Diggle
Heights
Hunters Hill
Air Shaft
Standedge Tunnels

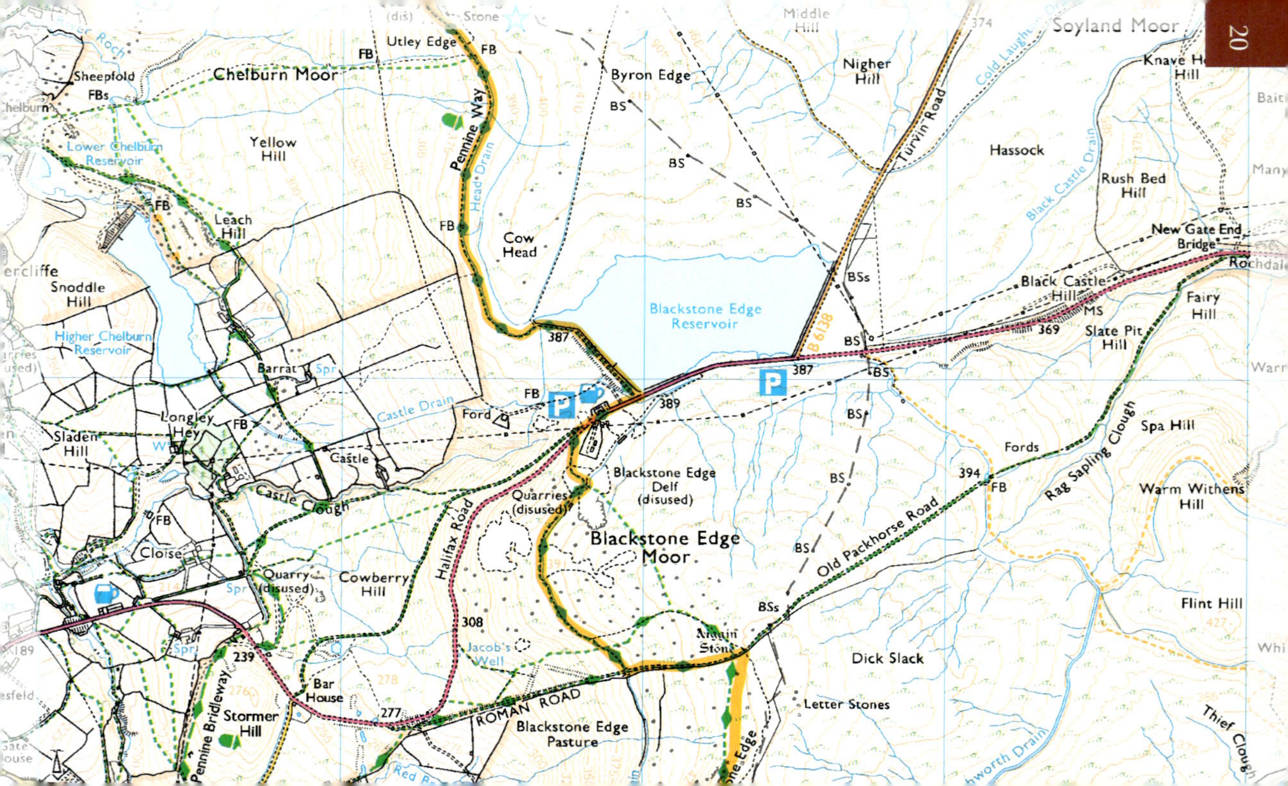

20
Soyland Moor
Sheepfold
FBs
Chelburn Moor
Utley Edge
FB
Byron Edge
Nigher Hill
Middle Hill
Knave Hill
Lower Chelburn Reservoir
Yellow Hill
Pennine Way
Head Drain
Turvin Road
Hassock
Black Castle Drain
Rush Bed Hill
Cold Laughton
Leach Hill
Cow Head
New Gate End Bridge
Rochdale
Snoddle Hill
Blackstone Edge Reservoir
B 6138
Black Castle Hill
MS
Fairy Hill
Slate Pit Hill
Higher Chelburn Reservoir
Barrat
Spr
Castle Drain
Ford
Longley Hey
Sladen Hill
Castle
Castle Clough
Blackstone Edge Delf (disused)
Quarries (disused)
Spa Hill
Fords
Rag Sapling Clough
Warm Withens Hill
Halifax Road
Blackstone Edge Moor
Old Packhorse Road
Cloise
Quarry (disused)
Cowberry Hill
Flint Hill
Jacob's Well
Aiggin Stone
Dick Slack
Bar House
Letter Stones
Stormer Hill
Pennine Bridleway
ROMAN ROAD
Blackstone Edge Pasture
Thief Clough

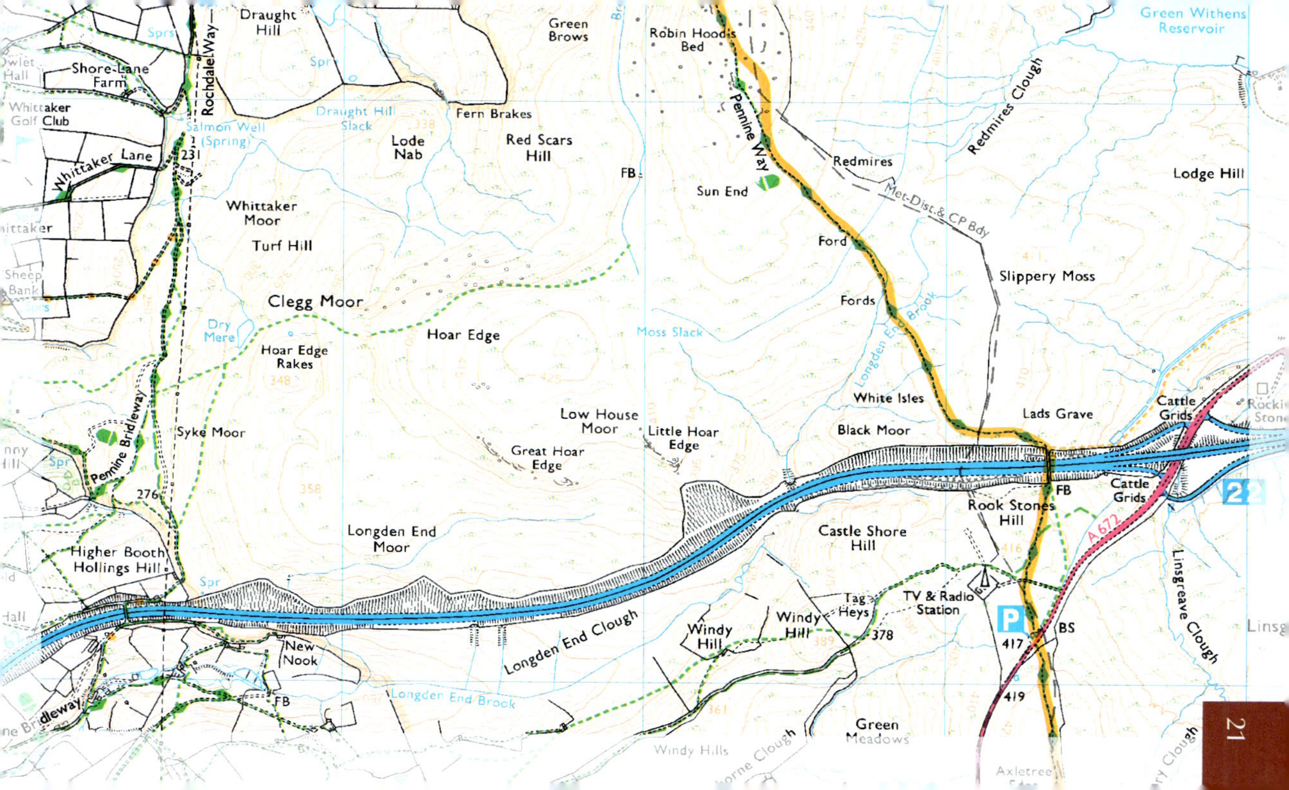
Draught Hill
Green Brows
Robin Hoods Bed
Green Withens Reservoir
Shore-Lane Farm
Rochdale Way
Whittaker Golf Club
Draught Hill Slack
Fern Brakes
Salmon Well (Spring)
231
Lode Nab
Red Scars Hill
Pennine Way
Redmires
Redmires Clough
Lodge Hill
Whittaker Lane
FB
Sun End
Met-Dist.& CP Bdy
Whittaker Moor
Turf Hill
Ford
Slippery Moss
Sheep Bank
Clegg Moor
Fords
Longden End Brook
Dry Mere
Hoar Edge
Moss Slack
Hoar Edge Rakes
348
White Isles
Lads Grave
Cattle Grids
Low House Moor
Little Hoar Edge
Black Moor
Syke Moor
Great Hoar Edge
Pennine Bridleway
FB
Cattle Grids
276
358
Rook Stones Hill
A672
Longden End Moor
Castle Shore Hill
Higher Booth
Hollings Hill
Spr
Tag
Heys
TV & Radio Station
Windy Hill
Windy Hill
378
P
417
BS
Linsgreave Clough
New Nook
Longden End Clough
FB
Longden End Brook
419
Green Meadows
Windy Hills
Axletree
21

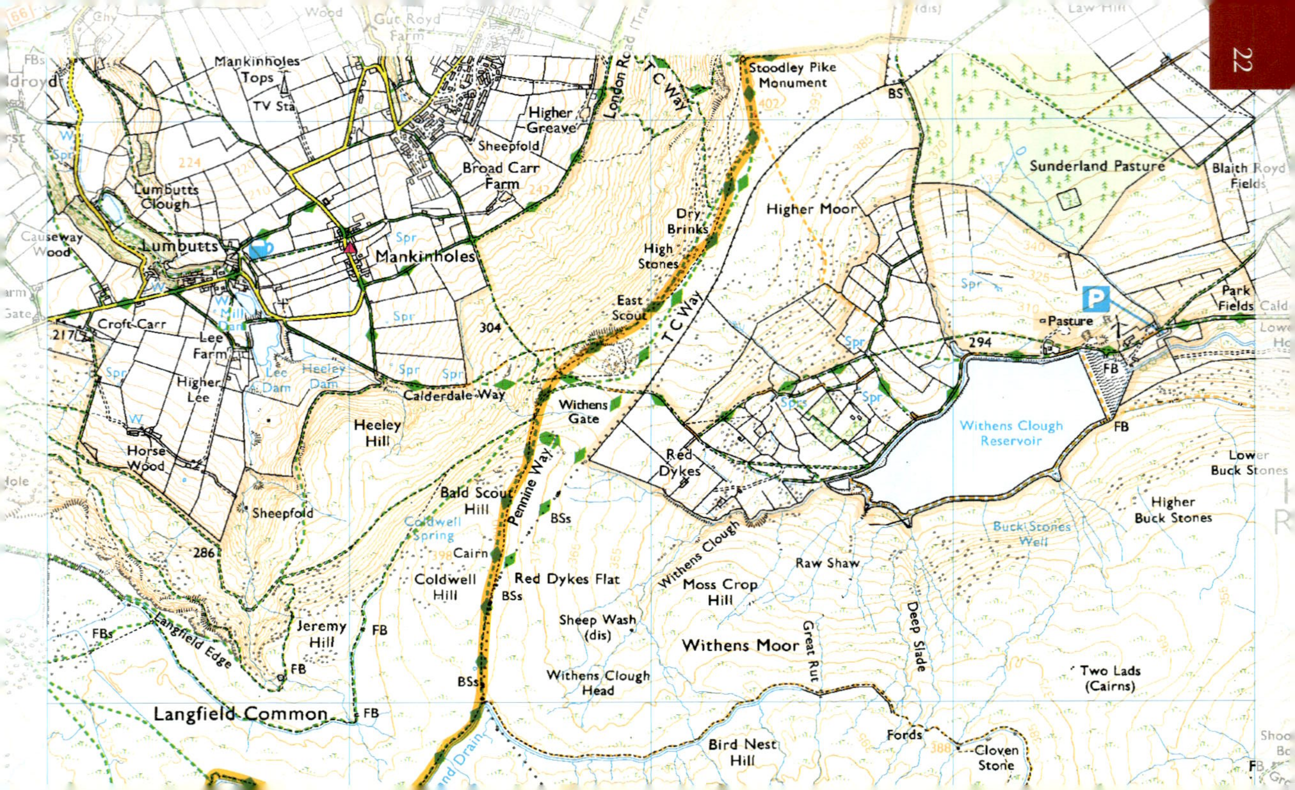
Mankinholes Tops
TV Sta
Higher Greave
Sheepfold
Broad Carr Farm
London Road
T C Way
Stoodley Pike Monument
BS
Sunderland Pasture
Blaith Royd Fields
Higher Moor
Lumbutts Clough
Causeway Wood
Lumbutts
Mankinholes
Spr
Dry Brinks
High Stones
East Scout
T C Way
Park Fields
Pasture
294
304
Croft Carr
Lee Farm
Mill Dam
Lee Dam
Heeley Dam
Higher Lee
Calderdale Way
Withens Gate
Spr
Sprs
FB
Withens Clough Reservoir
FB
Lower Buck Stones
Heeley Hill
Horse Wood
Red Dykes
Higher Buck Stones
Sheepfold
Bald Scout Hill
Pennine Way
BSs
Coldwell Spring
Cairn
Buck Stones Well
286
Coldwell Hill
Red Dykes Flat
BSs
Withens Clough
Raw Shaw
Moss Crop Hill
Sheep Wash (dis)
Jeremy Hill
FB
FBs
Langfield Edge
FB
Withens Moor
Great Rut
Deep Slade
BSs
Withens Clough Head
Two Lads (Cairns)
Langfield Common
FB
Bird Nest Hill
Fords
Cloven Stone

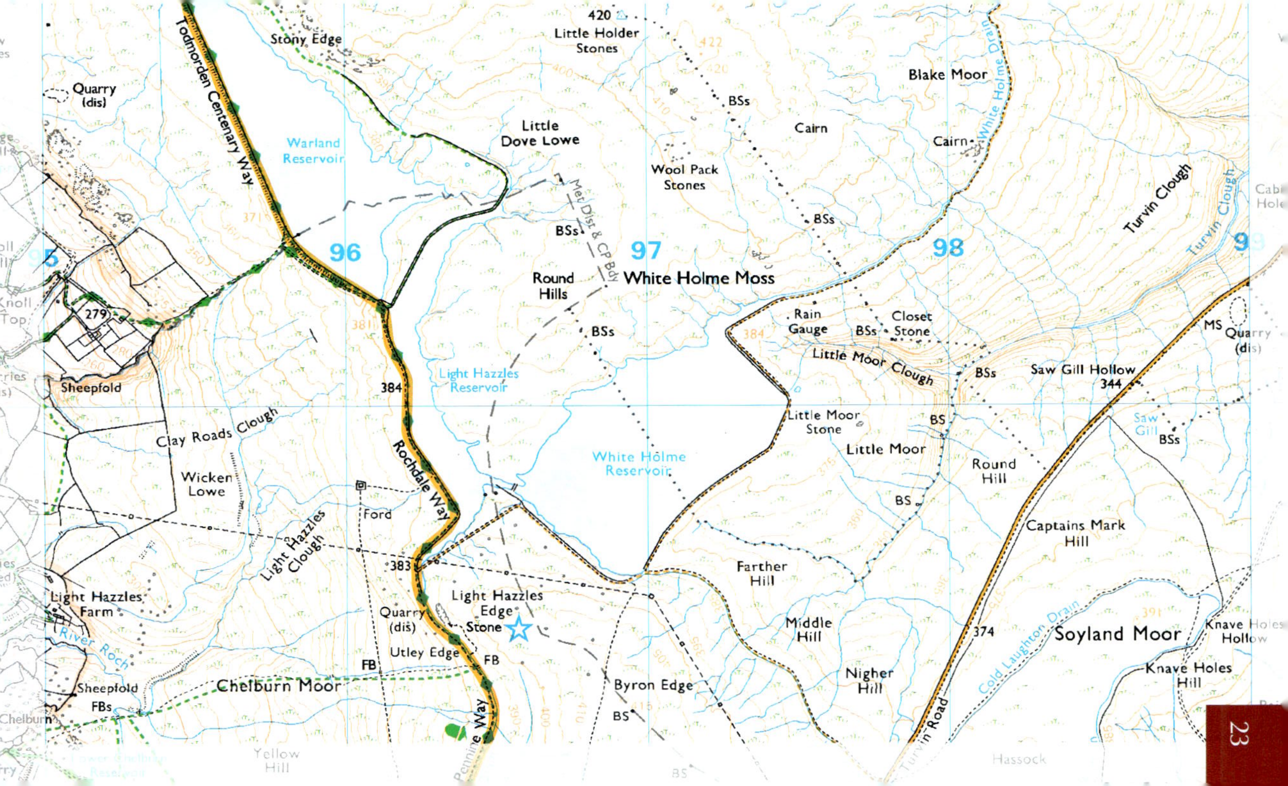
Quarry (dis)
Stony Edge
420
Little Holder Stones
Todmorden Centenary Way
Warland Reservoir
Little Dove Lowe
Wool Pack Stones
BSs
Cairn
Blake Moor
Cairn
White Holme Drain
Turvin Clough
Turvin Clough
Met Dist & CP Bdy
96
97
98
99
279
Round Hills
White Holme Moss
Rain Gauge
BSs
Closet Stone
384
Little Moor Clough
MS
Quarry (dis)
Saw Gill Hollow
344
Light Hazzles Reservoir
384
Sheepfold
Little Moor Stone
BS
Saw Gill
BSs
Little Moor
Round Hill
Clay Roads Clough
Rochdale Way
White Holme Reservoir
Wicken Lowe
Ford
BS
Light Hazzles Clough
Captains Mark Hill
383
Farther Hill
Light Hazzles Farm
Light Hazzles Edge Stone
Quarry (dis)
River Roch
Middle Hill
374
Cold Laughton Drain
Soyland Moor
Knave Holes Hollow
Utley Edge
FB
FB
Knave Holes Hill
Sheepfold
Chelburn Moor
Byron Edge
Nigher Hill
FBs
BS
Turvin Road
Pennine Way
Yellow Hill
Hassock

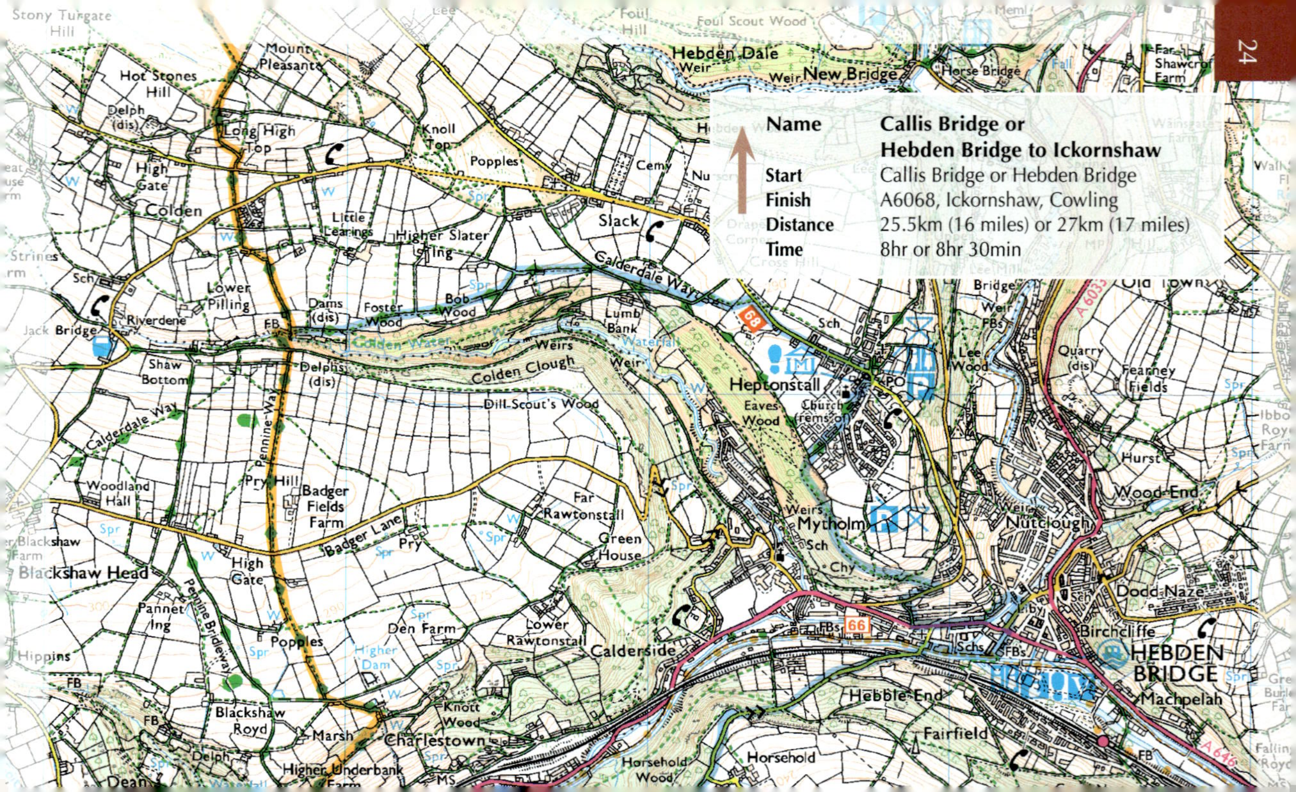

Name	Callis Bridge or Hebden Bridge to Ickornshaw
Start	Callis Bridge or Hebden Bridge
Finish	A6068, Ickornshaw, Cowling
Distance	25.5km (16 miles) or 27km (17 miles)
Time	8hr or 8hr 30min

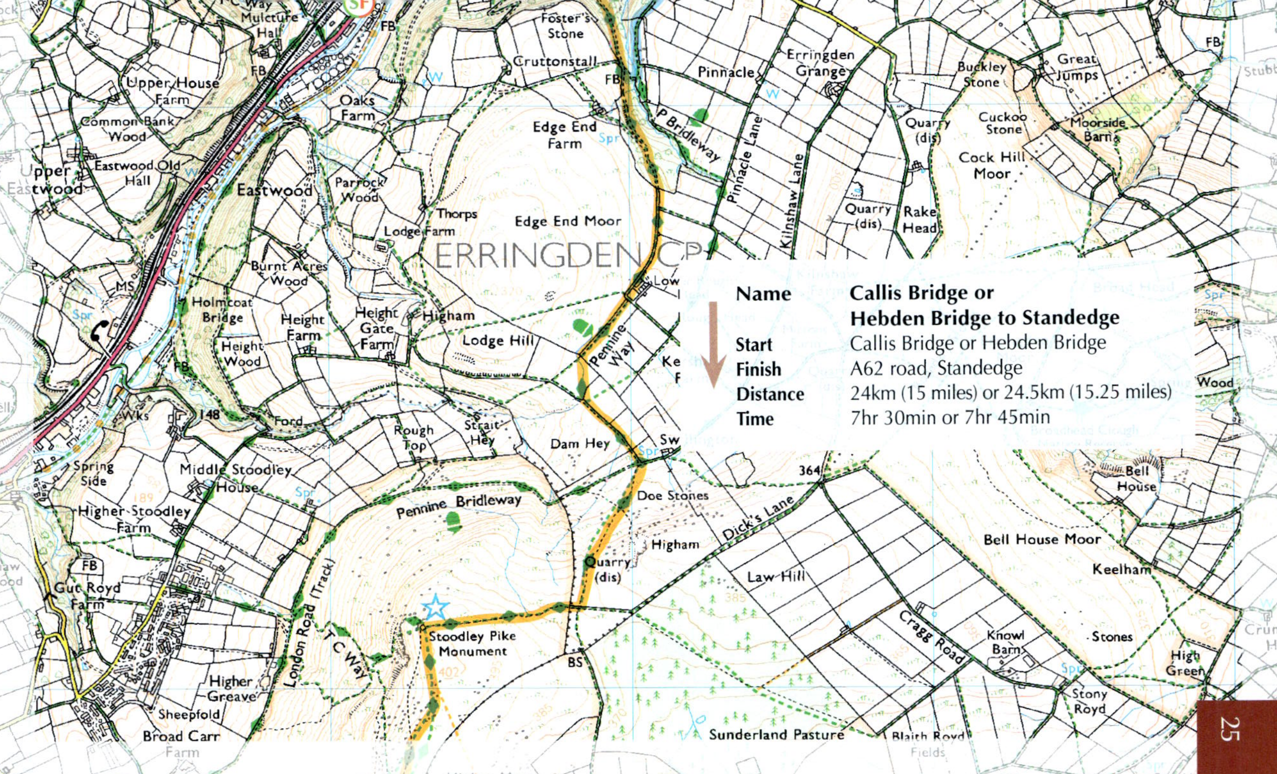
25
Name Callis Bridge or Hebden Bridge to Standedge
Start Callis Bridge or Hebden Bridge
Finish A62 road, Standedge
Distance 24km (15 miles) or 24.5km (15.25 miles)
Time 7hr 30min or 7hr 45min
ERRINGDEN CP
Foster's Stone
Cruttonstall
Edge End Farm
Edge End Moor
Erringden Grange
Pinnacle
Pinnacle Lane
Kilnshaw Lane
P Bridleway
Buckley Stone
Great Jumps
Cuckoo Stone
Moorside Barn
Cock Hill Moor
Quarry (dis)
Rake Head
Mulcture Hall
Upper House Farm
Common Bank Wood
Eastwood Old Hall
Upper Eastwood
Eastwood
Oaks Farm
Parrock Wood
Thorps
Lodge Farm
Burnt Acres Wood
Holmcoat Bridge
Height Farm
Height Wood
Height Gate Farm
Higham
Lodge Hill
Pennine Way
Rough Top
Strait Hey
Dam Hey
Ford
Wks
Spring Side
Middle Stoodley House
Higher Stoodley Farm
Pennine Bridleway
Doe Stones
Dick's Lane
Higham
Quarry (dis)
Law Hill
Bell House
Bell House Moor
Keelham
Cragg Road
Knowl Barn
Stones
High Green
Stony Royd
Stoodley Pike Monument
London Road (Track)
T C Way
BS
Gut Royd Farm
Higher Greave
Sheepfold
Broad Carr Farm
Sunderland Pasture
Blaith Royd Fields
364
148
402

Wadsworth Moor
Walshaw Dean Middle Reservoir
Walshaw Dean Lower Reservoir
Pennine Way
Calder/Aire Link
Pennine Bridleway
Dean Stones Edge
Middle Hill
Pennine Way
361
Lower Fold Hill
331
337
FB
Dam
Grouse Butts
Black Clough
Black Clough Hill
Waterfall
Nouch Brink
Old Dike Hill
Old Dike
Grouse Butts
Shooting Boxes
White Hill
Black Nursery
Lower Edge
Rowshaw
Rowshaw Clough
Hare Edge
High Rakes
Dean Gate
Delf Brink
Jack Allotment
Ford
White Hill
The Grough
Hewer Stones
Grinnel Stones
Lower Stones
Deer Stones
Hoar Nib
New Laithe Farm
New Laithe Moor
Spr
328
Lower Sough
Dam
The Lodge
FB
Fenny Lees
323
Shaw Dike Hill
Round Hill Moor
Shaw Dike
Back Shaw
341
FBs
New Hey
Sheepfold
Weir
Alcomden
Alcomden Water
Holme Ends
Hill Dike
Mere Stones
Greave Height
Greave Pasture
366
344
312
Sutcliffe Rough
292
281
286
Clough Foot
Brown Scout
The Notch
292
FB
Ford
Greave Clough
Sheepfold
Weirs
Sluice
Waterfall
Pisser Rough
Pisser Hill
Pisser Clough
Pig Hole Dike
Little Round Hill
Hudson
The Greave
FB
Waterfall Syke
Grouse Butts
FBs
Great Round Hill
Long Gutter
Quarry (dis)
Slack Stones

Gorple Cottages
Great Rough Hey
Reaps Coppy
King Common Rough
Low Moor
FB
Ox Holes
Pennine Way
King Common
Quarry (dis)
Reaps Level
STALL CP
Reaps Bottom
Reaps Cross (remains of)
Reaps Edge
Standing Stone Hill
Grouse Butts
Ling Hollow
Clough Head Hill
White Mires
Ferny Beds
Coppy
Widdop Gate
High Laithe
High Greenwood House
High Greenwood Farm
Hoar Royd
Pisser Clough
Mould Grain
Boothroyd Farm
Clough House Farm
Clough Head
Green Hill
Black Mires
Pennine Bridleway
Popples Close
Egypt
Rough Hey
Lane Side
Everhill Shaw
Middle Fold
Lower Fold
New Edge
Old Edge
Edge Lane
Park La
Lower Ear Lees
Higher Heath
Moor Lane (Path)
Crabtree Field
Top o'th' Hill
Slade
Rodmer Clough
Greenland
Three Gates End
Greenland Road
Land Farm
School Land
Longtail
Stony Turgate Hill
Hot Stones Hill
Delph (dis)
Long High Top
Mount Pleasant
Knoll Top
Clough Hole Bridge
Bent Head Barn
Greenwood Lee
New Greenwood Lee
Hebden Dale
Hebden Water
Hardcastle Crags
Gibson Mill
Walshaw Wood
Waterfall
Lady Royd Edge
Lady Royd Farm
Lady Royd
Kid Stones
Higher Mansfield House
Mansfield House
Black Scout
Foul Hill
Stony Edge

The Sea
Crumber Hill
Fairy Fold Dike
373
Scotland Hill
Clough Hey Allotment
423
Wolf Stones
Wolf Stones Slack
Great Nick
Fair Well (Spring)
Roger Meadow
399
Bare Hill
Old Bess (Stone)
Old Bess Hill
Stony Edge
356
Millennium Way
Roms Greave Hill
Grouse Butts
Delph (dis)
Burnt Hill
Oakworth Moor
Hob Ing
Boundary Stones
Moss
Great Moss
Bullions
Pennine Way
White Reaps Clough
Flask
Kiln Hill
371
Sheep Shelter
Dean Clough Head
358
Sand Pit Hill
Pine Wood
346
336
Hanging Stone or Water Sheddles Cross
Slippery Stones Farm
Thornton Hill
Sheep Wash
Will Clough
Highfield House
Watersheddles Reservoir
BSs
Moor End
324
Far Two Laws
Two Laws
Crag Top
Sheepfold
Spr
Lodge
343
FB
West End
MS
292
Crag Bottom
Fall
Quarries (dis)
Daisy Mount
Hill Top Farm
Well Head Farm
Moor Lodge Farm
303
Brontë Way
258
Throstles Nest
Dean Clough
Dean Fields
Higher Pitcher Clough
Intake Laithe Farm
River Worth
Burnside Farm
Grey Stones
Little Spring Dike
Silver Hill Farm
234
Dean Field Farm
254
Silver Hill
Old Snap
243
Scar Top
MP
238
Whitestone Clough
Whitestone
Ponden Reservoir
Mill
Hob Lane
Churn Hole
Delph (dis)
Ponden Hall
Rush Isles
Ponden Slack
Ponden Wood
Weir
Lower Slack
Buckley Farm
Grouse Butts
Bracken Hill
Sprs
Cold Knoll

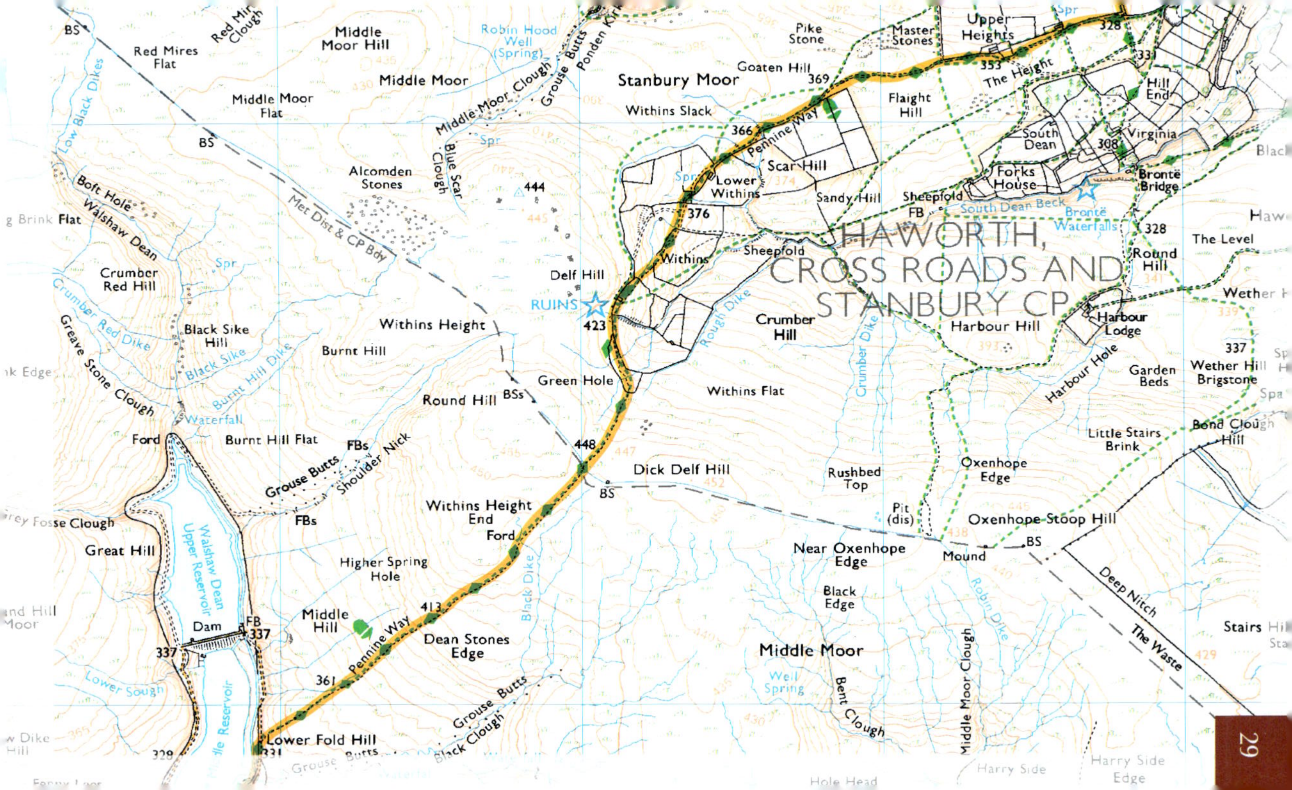
HAWORTH, CROSS ROADS AND STANBURY CP
Red Mires Flat
Red Mires Clough
Middle Moor Hill
Middle Moor
Middle Moor Flat
Robin Hood Well (Spring)
Middle Moor Clough
Grouse Butts
Ponden Kirk
Pike Stone
Master Stones
Upper Heights
Stanbury Moor
Goaten Hill
Withins Slack
The Height
Hill End
Flaight Hill
Virginia
South Dean
Forks House
Brontë Bridge
Sheepfold
FB
South Dean Beck
Brontë Waterfalls
The Level
Round Hill
Wether Hill
Brigstone
Pennine Way
Scar Hill
Lower Withins
Sandy Hill
Withins
Sheepfold
Blue Scar Clough
Alcomden Stones
Met Dist & CP Bdy
Low Black Dikes
Boft Hole
Walshaw Dean
Flat
Crumber Red Hill
Crumber Red Dike
Greave Stone Clough
Black Sike Hill
Black Sike
Burnt Hill Dike
Waterfall
Delf Hill
RUINS
Withins Height
Burnt Hill
Green Hole
Round Hill
BSs
Crumber Hill
Rough Dike
Crumber Dike
Harbour Hill
Harbour Lodge
Harbour Hole
Garden Beds
Withins Flat
Little Stairs Brink
Bond Clough Hill
Ford
Burnt Hill Flat
FBs
Grouse Butts
Shoulder Nick
Dick Delf Hill
BS
Rushbed Top
Oxenhope Edge
Pit (dis)
Oxenhope Stoop Hill
Fosse Clough
Great Hill
Walshaw Dean Upper Reservoir
Withins Height End
Ford
Higher Spring Hole
Black Dike
Near Oxenhope Edge
Mound
Deep Nitch
The Waste
Middle Hill
Dam
Dean Stones Edge
Black Edge
Robin Dike
Stairs
Middle Moor
Well Spring
Bent Clough
Middle Moor Clough
Lower Sough
Reservoir
Lower Fold Hill
Grouse Butts
Black Clough
Harry Side
Harry Side Edge
Hole Head
423
448
413
376
366
369
361
353
337
331
328
308
444
329

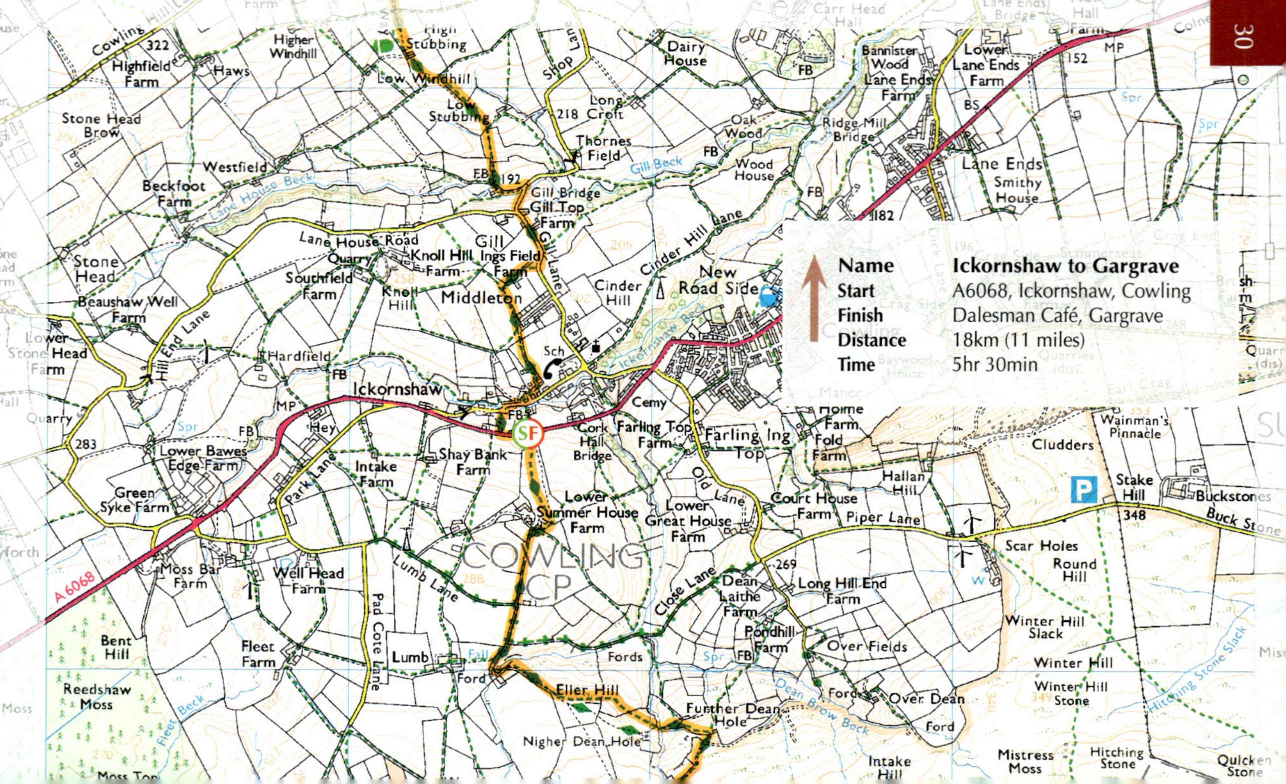

Name	**Ickornshaw to Gargrave**
Start	A6068, Ickornshaw, Cowling
Finish	Dalesman Café, Gargrave
Distance	18km (11 miles)
Time	5hr 30min

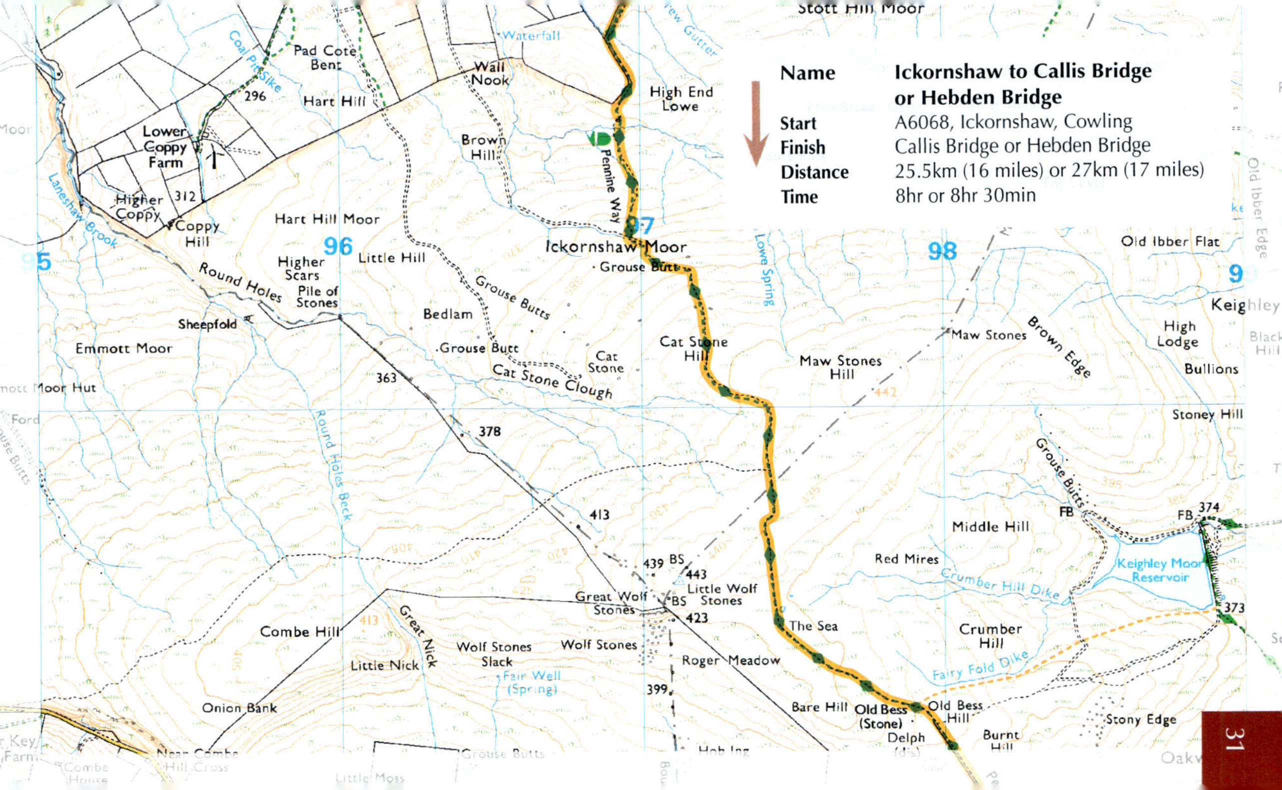
Name Ickornshaw to Callis Bridge or Hebden Bridge
Start A6068, Ickornshaw, Cowling
Finish Callis Bridge or Hebden Bridge
Distance 25.5km (16 miles) or 27km (17 miles)
Time 8hr or 8hr 30min
Stott Hill Moor
Pennine Way
Ickornshaw Moor
Grouse Butt
High End Lowe
Waterfall
Wall Nook
Brown Hill
Pad Cote Bent
Hart Hill
Coal Pit Sike
Lower Coppy Farm
Higher Coppy
Coppy Hill
Laneshaw Brook
Hart Hill Moor
Higher Scars
Little Hill
Round Holes
Pile of Stones
Sheepfold
Emmott Moor
Moor Hut
Bedlam
Grouse Butts
Grouse Butt
Cat Stone
Cat Stone Clough
Cat Stone Hill
Lowe Spring
Round Holes Beck
Maw Stones Hill
Maw Stones
Brown Edge
Old Ibber Flat
Old Ibber Edge
Keighley
High Lodge
Bullions
Stoney Hill
Middle Hill
Red Mires
Crumber Hill Dike
Keighley Moor Reservoir
Crumber Hill
Fairy Fold Dike
The Sea
Little Wolf Stones
Great Wolf Stones
Wolf Stones
Wolf Stones Slack
Fair Well (Spring)
Roger Meadow
Combe Hill
Great Nick
Little Nick
Onion Bank
Bare Hill
Old Bess (Stone)
Old Bess Hill
Delph
Burnt Hill
Stony Edge

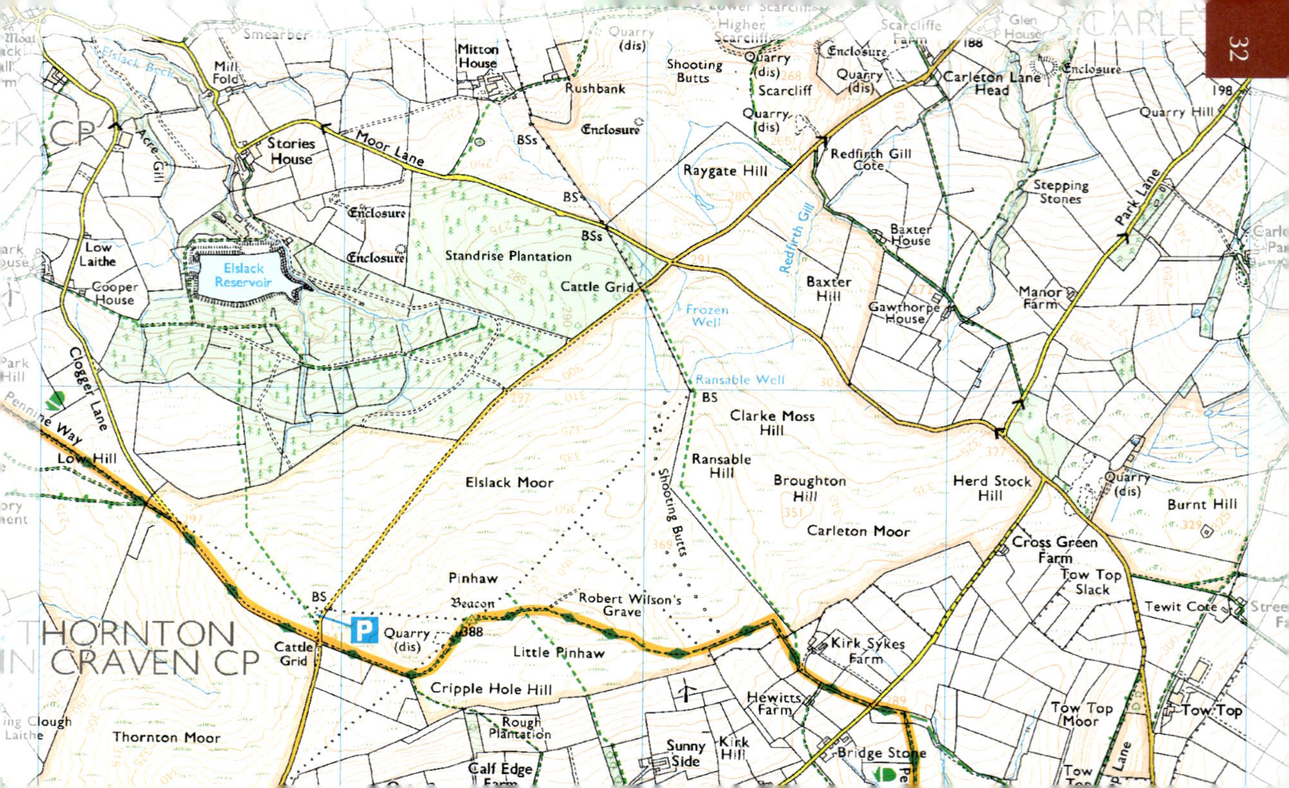
Smearber
Mitton House
Quarry (dis)
Higher Scarcliffe
Scarcliffe Farm
188
Glen House
Mill Fold
Elslack Beck
Rushbank
Shooting Butts
Quarry (dis)
Scarcliff
Enclosure
Quarry (dis)
Carleton Lane Head
Enclosure
198
Quarry Hill
Stories House
Moor Lane
Acre Gill
BSs
Enclosure
Quarry (dis)
Raygate Hill
Redfirth Gill Cote
Stepping Stones
Park Lane
Enclosure
BSs
Baxter House
Low Laithe
Elslack Reservoir
Enclosure
Standrise Plantation
BSs
Redfirth Gill
Cooper House
Cattle Grid
Baxter Hill
Gawthorpe House
Manor Farm
Frozen Well
Clogger Lane
Ransable Well
BS
Clarke Moss Hill
Pennine Way
Low Hill
Ransable Hill
Elslack Moor
Shooting Butts
Broughton Hill
Herd Stock Hill
Quarry (dis)
Burnt Hill
Carleton Moor
Cross Green Farm
Tow Top Slack
Pinhaw
Robert Wilson's Grave
Tewit Cote
BS
Beacon
THORNTON IN CRAVEN CP
Quarry (dis)
388
Kirk Sykes Farm
Cattle Grid
Little Pinhaw
Cripple Hole Hill
Hewitts Farm
Tow Top Moor
Tow Top
Thornton Moor
Rough Plantation
Sunny Side
Kirk Hill
Bridge Stone
Calf Edge Farm
Lane

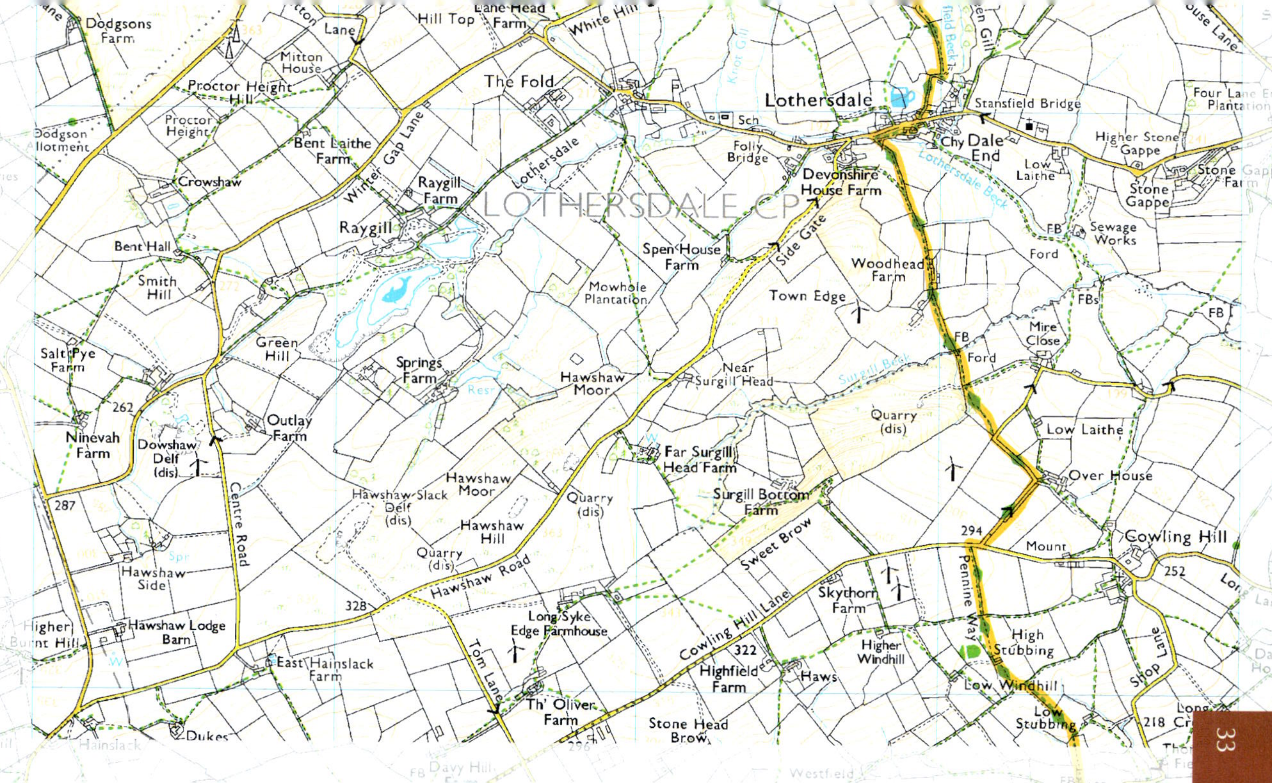
Dodgsons Farm
Lane
Hill Top
Lane Head Farm
White Hill
Mitton House
The Fold
Lothersdale
Proctor Height Hill
Proctor Height
Dodgson Allotment
Bent Laithe Farm
Winter Gap Lane
Lothersdale
Sch
Folly Bridge
Stansfield Bridge
Chy Dale End
Lothersdale Beck
Four Lane Ends Plantation
Higher Stone Gappe
Stone Gappe Farm
Stone Gappe
Low Laithe
Crowshaw
Raygill Farm
Raygill
LOTHERSDALE CP
Devonshire House Farm
Side Gate
Spen House Farm
Woodhead Farm
FB
Sewage Works
Ford
Bent Hall
Smith Hill
Mowhole Plantation
Town Edge
FBs
FB
Mire Close
Ford
Green Hill
Salt Pye Farm
Springs Farm
Hawshaw Moor
Near Surgill Head
Surgill Beck
Resr
262
Outlay Farm
Quarry (dis)
Low Laithe
Ninevah Farm
Dowshaw Delf (dis)
Far Surgill Head Farm
Over House
Centre Road
Hawshaw Moor
Hawshaw Slack Delf (dis)
Quarry (dis)
Surgill Bottom Farm
287
Hawshaw Hill
Sweet Brow
294
Cowling Hill
Quarry (dis)
Mount
Hawshaw Side
Hawshaw Road
Pennine Way
252
328
Skythorn Farm
Higher Burnt Hill
Hawshaw Lodge Barn
Long Syke Edge Farmhouse
Cowling Hill Lane
High Stubbing
Higher Windhill
322
Shop Lane
East Hainslack Farm
Tom Lane
Highfield Farm
Haws
Low Windhill
Th' Oliver Farm
Stone Head Brow
Low Stubbing
218
Dukes

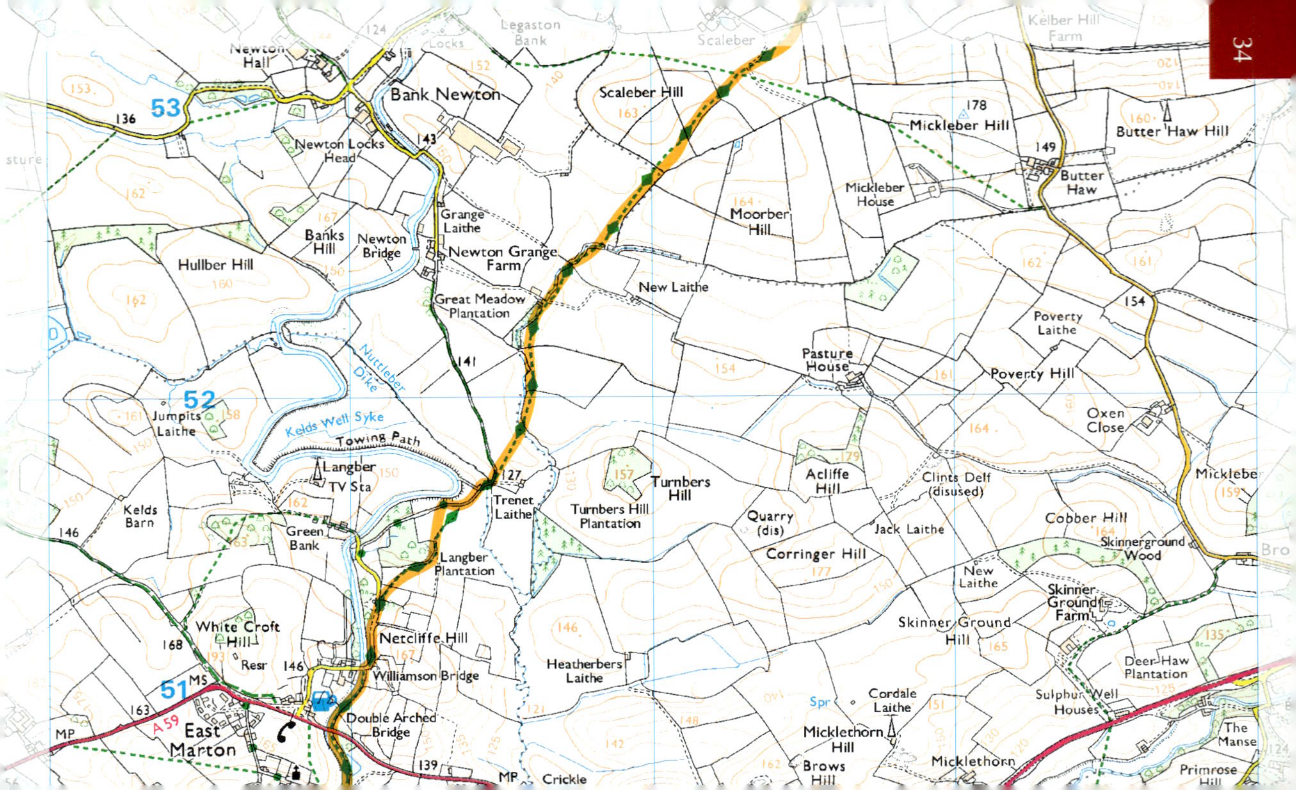
Bank Newton
Newton Hall
Newton Locks Head
Legaston Bank
Locks
Scaleber
Scaleber Hill
Mickleber Hill
Butter Haw Hill
Butter Haw
Kelber Hill Farm
Mickleber House
Moorber Hill
Grange Laithe
Newton Grange Farm
Banks Hill
Newton Bridge
Hullber Hill
New Laithe
Great Meadow Plantation
Poverty Laithe
Poverty Hill
Pasture House
Oxen Close
Mickleber
Nuttleber Dike
Keld Well Syke
Towing Path
Jumpits Laithe
Langber TV Sta
Trenet Laithe
Turnbers Hill
Turnbers Hill Plantation
Acliffe Hill
Clints Delf (disused)
Cobber Hill
Skinnerground Wood
Kelds Barn
Green Bank
Langber Plantation
Quarry (dis)
Jack Laithe
Corringer Hill
New Laithe
Skinner Ground Farm
White Croft Hill
Resr
Netcliffe Hill
Williamson Bridge
Heatherbers Laithe
Skinner Ground Hill
Deer Haw Plantation
Sulphur Well Houses
Cordale Laithe
Spr
Mickléthorn Hill
Brows Hill
Micklethorn
The Manse
Primrose Hill
Double Arched Bridge
East Marton
A59
MS
MP
Crickle
53
52
51

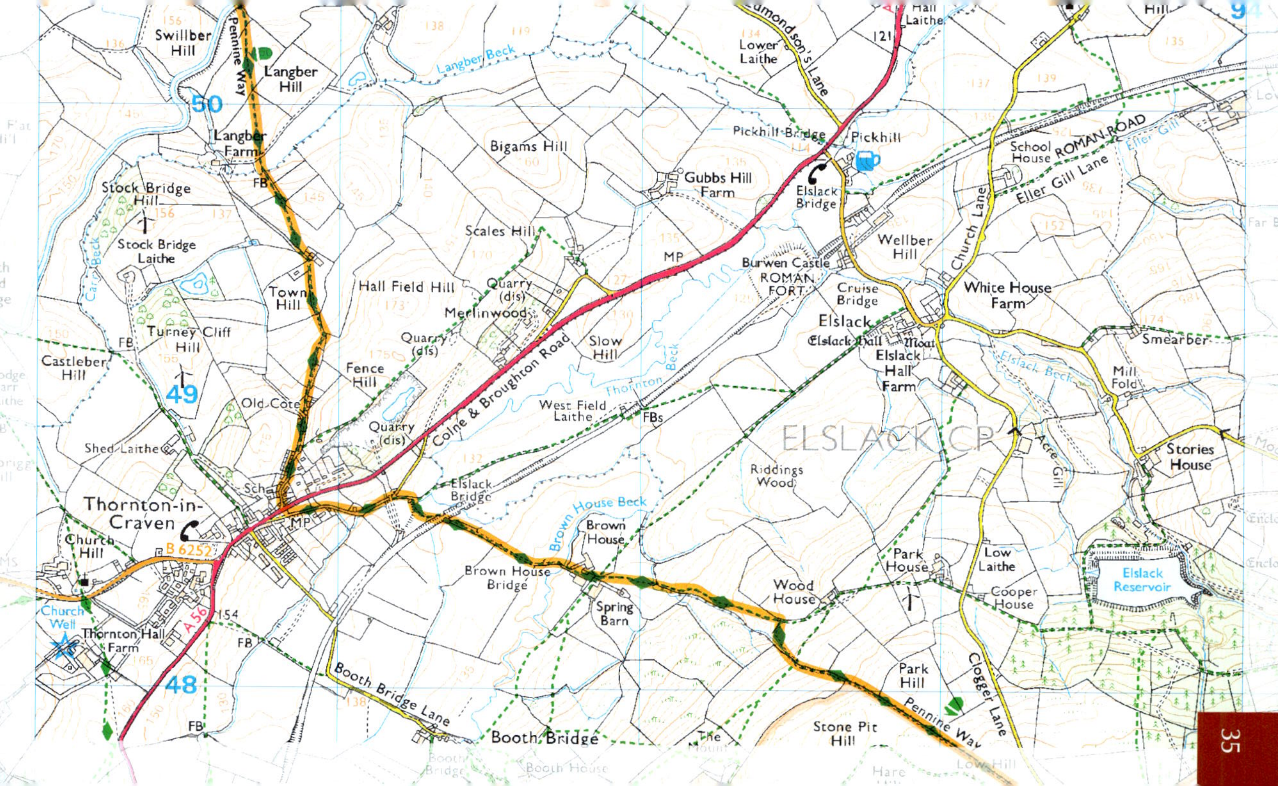
Thornton-in-Craven
Elslack
ELSLACK CP
Elslack Reservoir
Pennine Way
Colne & Broughton Road
Church Lane
Clogger Lane
Booth Bridge Lane
Booth Bridge
Eller Gill Lane
ROMAN ROAD
Burwen Castle ROMAN FORT
Stories House
Smearber
Mill Fold
White House Farm
Acre Gill
Low Laithe
Cooper House
School House
Elslack Beck
Elslack Hall
Moat
Elslack Hall Farm
Park House
Park Hill
Stone Pit Hill
Wellber Hill
Pickhill
Pickhill Bridge
Elslack Bridge
Cruise Bridge
Lower Laithe
Hall Laithe
Gubbs Hill Farm
Riddings Wood
Wood House
Thornton Beck
FBs
Slow Hill
West Field Laithe
Brown House Beck
Brown House
Spring Barn
Brown House Bridge
Bigams Hill
Scales Hill
Quarry (dis)
Merlinwood
Hall Field Hill
Fence Hill
Langber Beck
Langber Hill
Langber Farm
Swillber Hill
Town Hill
Old Cote
Turney Cliff Hill
Stock Bridge Hill
Stock Bridge Laithe
Carr Beck
Castleber Hill
Shed Laithe
Church Hill
Church Well
Thornton Hall Farm
B 6252
A 56
The Mount
MP
FB
48
49
50
121

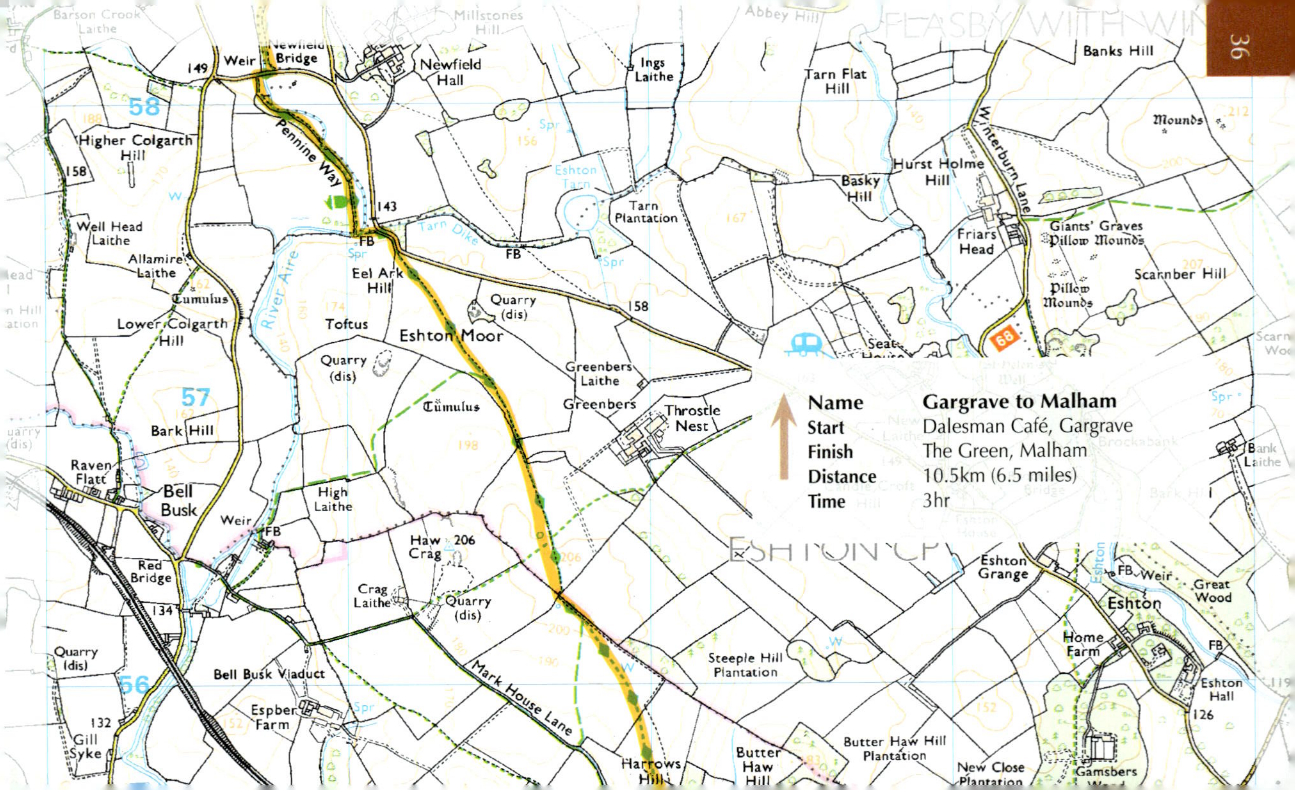

Name	Gargrave to Malham
Start	Dalesman Café, Gargrave
Finish	The Green, Malham
Distance	10.5km (6.5 miles)
Time	3hr

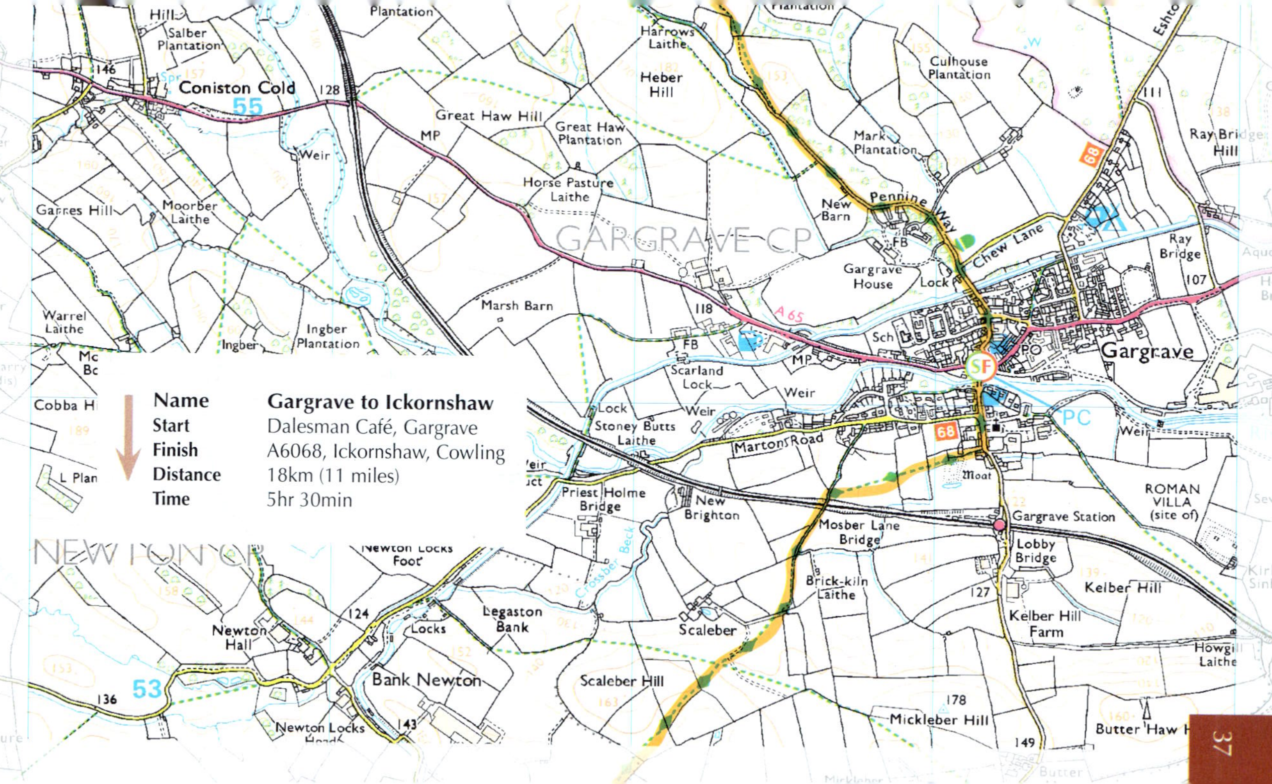

Name	**Gargrave to Ickornshaw**
Start	Dalesman Café, Gargrave
Finish	A6068, Ickornshaw, Cowling
Distance	18km (11 miles)
Time	5hr 30min

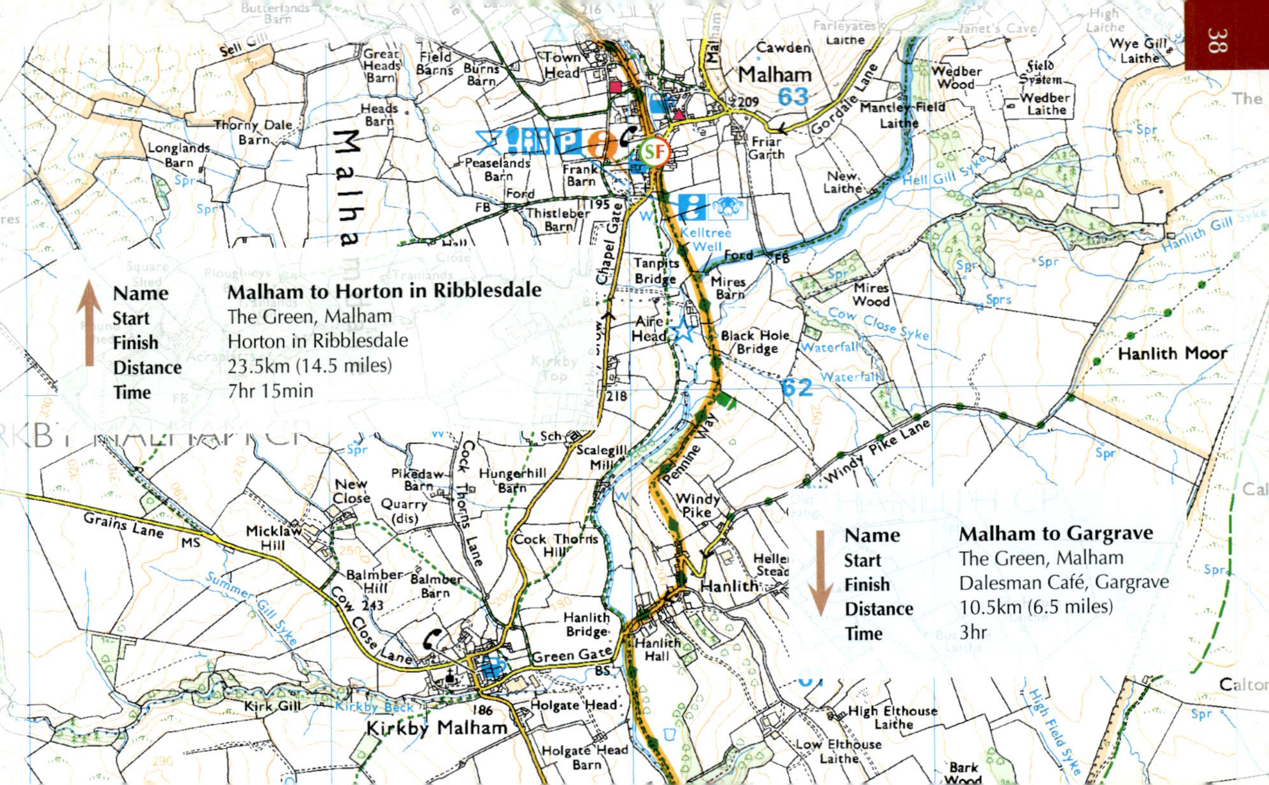
Malham
Kirkby Malham
Hanlith
Hanlith Moor
Pennine Way
Windy Pike Lane
Cow Close Lane
Cock Thorns Lane
Grains Lane
Chapel Gate
Gordale Lane
Green Gate
Hanlith Hall
Hanlith Bridge
Aire Head
Kelltree Well
Tanpits Bridge
Mires Barn
Mires Wood
Black Hole Bridge
Scalegill Mill
Town Head
Friar Garth
Cawden
Malham
63
62
Name
Malham to Horton in Ribblesdale
Start
The Green, Malham
Finish
Horton in Ribblesdale
Distance
23.5km (14.5 miles)
Time
7hr 15min
Name
Malham to Gargrave
Start
The Green, Malham
Finish
Dalesman Café, Gargrave
Distance
10.5km (6.5 miles)
Time
3hr

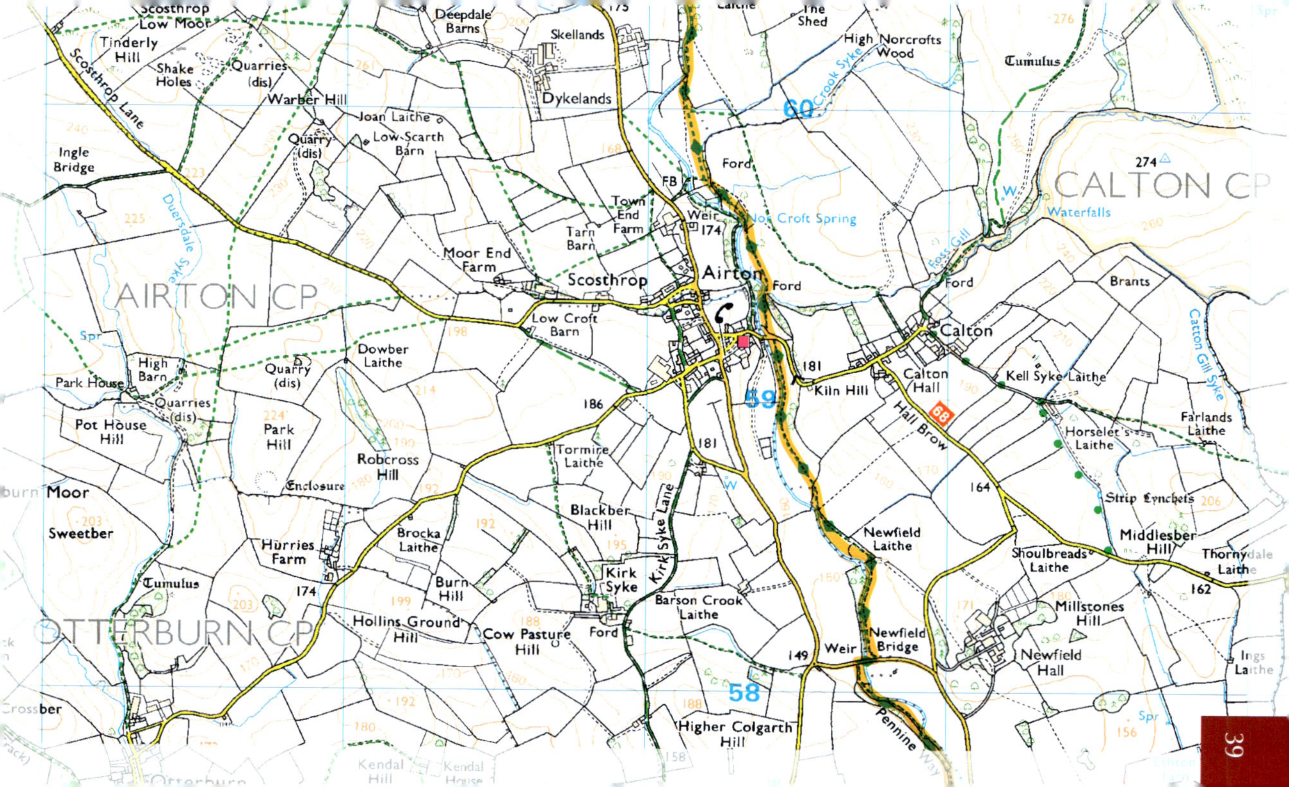
Scosthrop Low Moor
Tinderly Hill
Shake Holes
Quarries (dis)
Deepdale Barns
Skellands
Dykelands
Scosthrop Lane
Warber Hill
Joan Laithe
Low Scarth Barn
Quarry (dis)
Ingle Bridge
Duersdale Syke
AIRTON CP
Spr
High Barn
Park House
Quarries (dis)
Pot House Hill
Quarry (dis)
Dowber Laithe
Park Hill
Robcross Hill
Enclosure
Moor
Sweetber
Hurries Farm
Brocka Laithe
Burn Hill
Tumulus
OTTERBURN CP
Hollins Ground Hill
Cow Pasture Hill
Crossber
Kendal Hill
Kendal House
Moor End Farm
Tarn Barn
Town End Farm
Scosthrop
Low Croft Barn
Tormire Laithe
Blackber Hill
Kirk Syke
Kirk Syke Lane
Barson Crook Laithe
Ford
Higher Colgarth Hill
58
FB
Weir
Airton
Ford
59
Kiln Hill
Weir
Newfield Bridge
Pennine Way
Newfield Laithe
The Shed
High Norcrofts Wood
Crook Syke
60
Ford
Croft Spring
Foss Gill
Ford
Calton
Calton Hall
Hall Brow
68
Tumulus
CALTON CP
Waterfalls
Brants
Kell Syke Laithe
Catton Gill Syke
Farlands Laithe
Horselet's Laithe
Strip Lynchets
Middlesber Hill
Shoulbreads Laithe
Thornydale Laithe
Millstones Hill
Newfield Hall
Ings Laithe
Spr

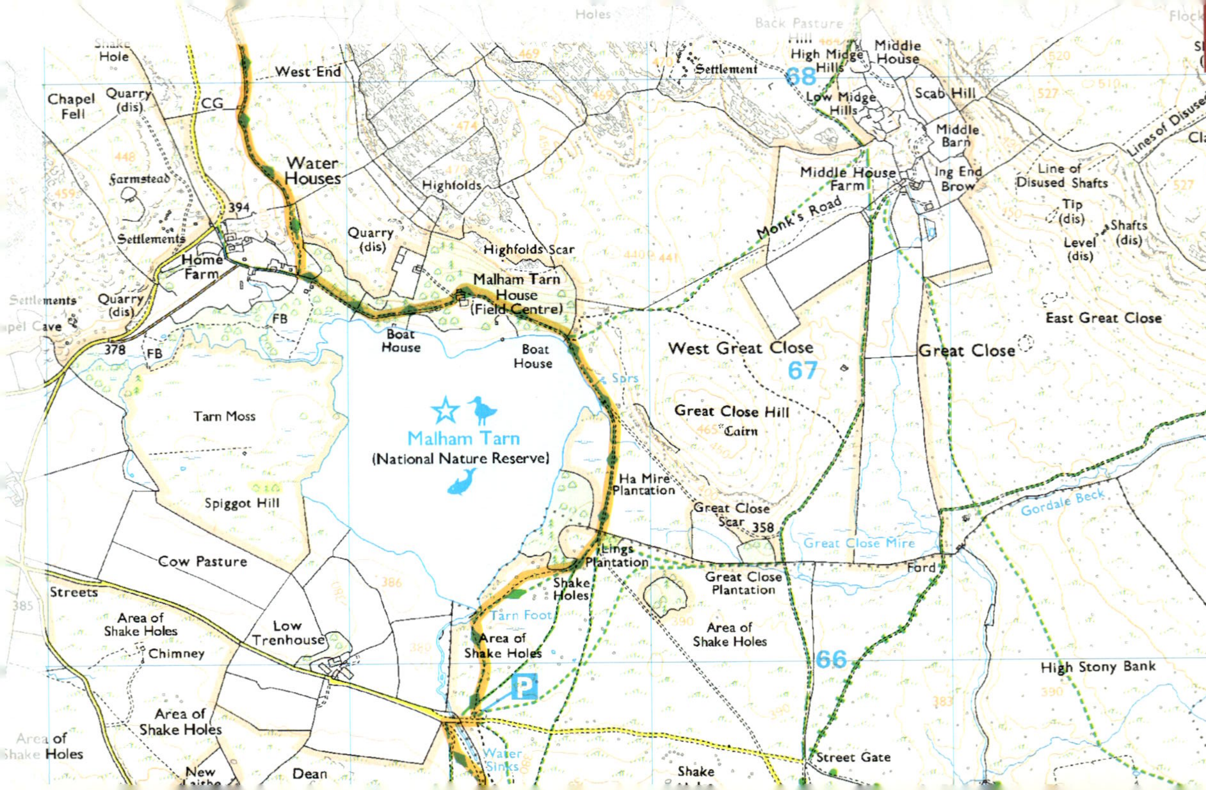
Shake Hole
Chapel Fell
Quarry (dis)
CG
West End
Water Houses
Highfolds
Farmstead
394
Settlements
Home Farm
Quarry (dis)
Highfolds Scar
Malham Tarn House (Field Centre)
Settlement
68
High Midge Hills
Low Midge Hills
Middle House
Scab Hill
Middle Barn
Middle House Farm
Ing End Brow
Lines of Disused Shafts
Clapham High
Line of Disused Shafts
Tip (dis)
Shafts (dis)
Level (dis)
Monk's Road
East Great Close
Settlements
Quarry (dis)
FB
Boat House
Boat House
West Great Close
67
Great Close
378
FB
Spr
Tarn Moss
Malham Tarn
(National Nature Reserve)
Great Close Hill
Cairn
465
Ha Mire Plantation
Spiggot Hill
Great Close Scar
358
Gordale Beck
Great Close Mire
Lings Plantation
Ford
Cow Pasture
Shake Holes
Great Close Plantation
386
Streets
Tarn Foot
Area of Shake Holes
Area of Shake Holes
Low Trenhouse
Chimney
Area of Shake Holes
66
High Stony Bank
P
Area of Shake Holes
Area of Shake Holes
Water Sinks
Street Gate
New Laithe
Dean
Shake
431
390
383

Low Stony Bank
Area of Shake Holes
Shake Hole
Great Cairn
Cross Field Knotts
Settlement & Field System
Hawthorns Lane
Hog House
Wye Gill Syke
Wye Gill Laithe
High Laithe
Gordale Scar
Gordale House
Gordale Beck
Sprs
Waterfalls
New Close Knotts
Gordale Bridge
224
Janet's Foss
Janet's Cave
Field System
Wedber Laithe
Wedber Wood
Mantley Field Laithe
Gordale Lane
New Close
Cattle Grid
376
Settlements
Cairns
Malham Lings
MALHAM CP
65
64
63
Settlements & Field Systems
Dales High Way
Cawden Flats Barn
Farleyates Laithe
New Laithe
Cawden
Malham
Friar Garth
209
Malham Rakes
341
Broad Flats
Shake Holes
Abbot Hills
Broad Scars
Homestead
Sheriff Hill
Shorkley Hill
Shaft (dis)
Cairn
Prior Rakes
Trougate
Malham Beck
216
Town Head
Frank Barn
Malham Cove
FB
Cove Road
High Barn
Peaselands Barn
Ford
Comb Hill
Hut Circle
Watlowes
Ing Scar
Settlement
Raven Scar
Ing Scar Crag
Pennine
Yarnthawe Barn
Long Lane
Burns Barn
Field Barns
336
Great Heads Barn
Heads Barn
Ma
Dean Moor Hill
Dean Scar
Langscar Gate
383
CG
Robin Hill Rigg
Ewe Moor
Settlement & Field System
Waterfall
Butterlands Barn
Sell Gill
Thorny Dale Barn
Langscar
Shafts (dis)
Mined Cave
Spr
Fair Sleets Gate
Jorden Scar
Hoober Edge
Pikedaw Hill
Hanber Side
Longlands Barn
Lang Scar

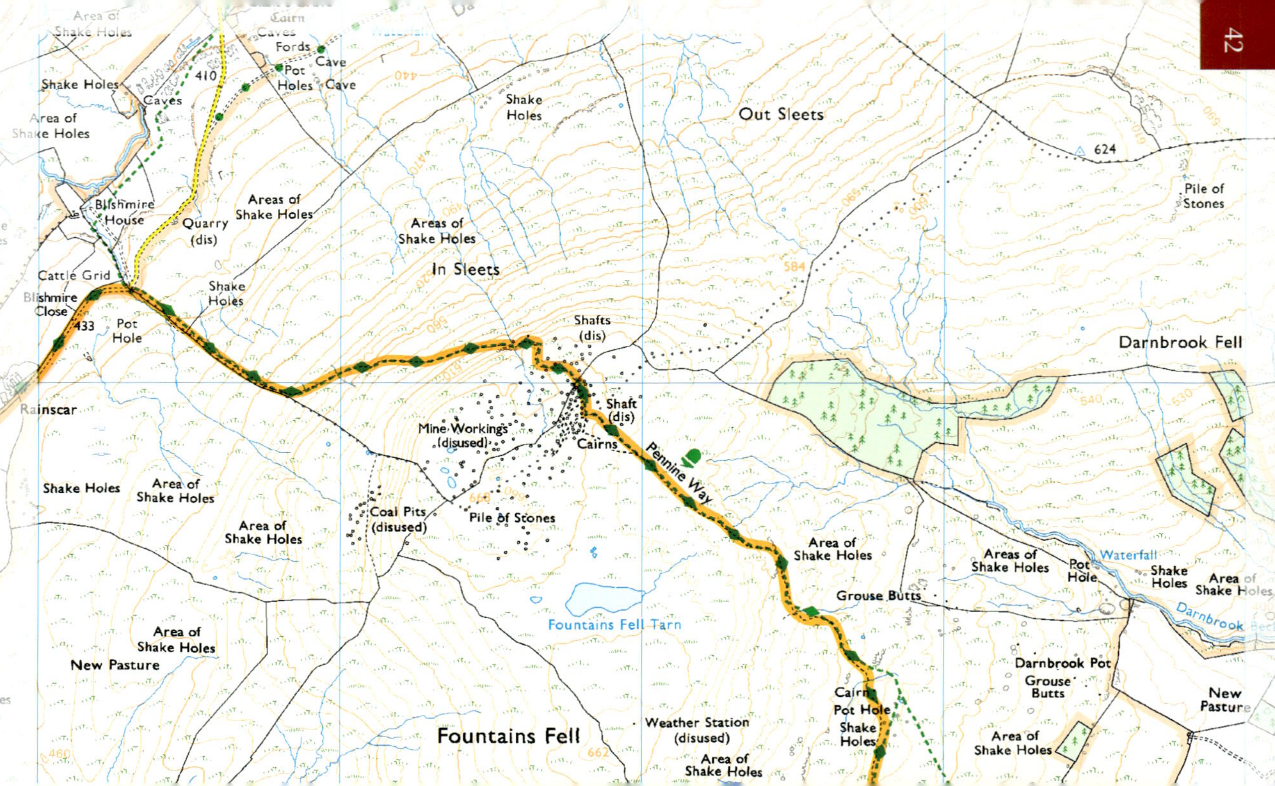
Area of Shake Holes
Caves
Fords
Pot Holes
Cave
Cave
Shake Holes
Caves
Area of Shake Holes
410
Shake Holes
Out Sleets
624
Pile of Stones
Blishmire House
Quarry (dis)
Areas of Shake Holes
Areas of Shake Holes
In Sleets
584
Cattle Grid
Blishmire Close
433
Pot Hole
Shake Holes
Shafts (dis)
Darnbrook Fell
540
530
Rainscar
Shaft (dis)
Mine Workings (disused)
Cairns
Pennine Way
Shake Holes
Area of Shake Holes
Coal Pits (disused)
Pile of Stones
Area of Shake Holes
Area of Shake Holes
Areas of Shake Holes
Pot Hole
Waterfall
Shake Holes
Area of Shake Holes
Grouse Butts
Darnbrook Beck
Fountains Fell Tarn
Area of Shake Holes
New Pasture
Darnbrook Pot
Grouse Butts
Cairn
Pot Hole
Shake Holes
New Pasture
Weather Station (disused)
Fountains Fell
662
Area of Shake Holes
Area of Shake Holes

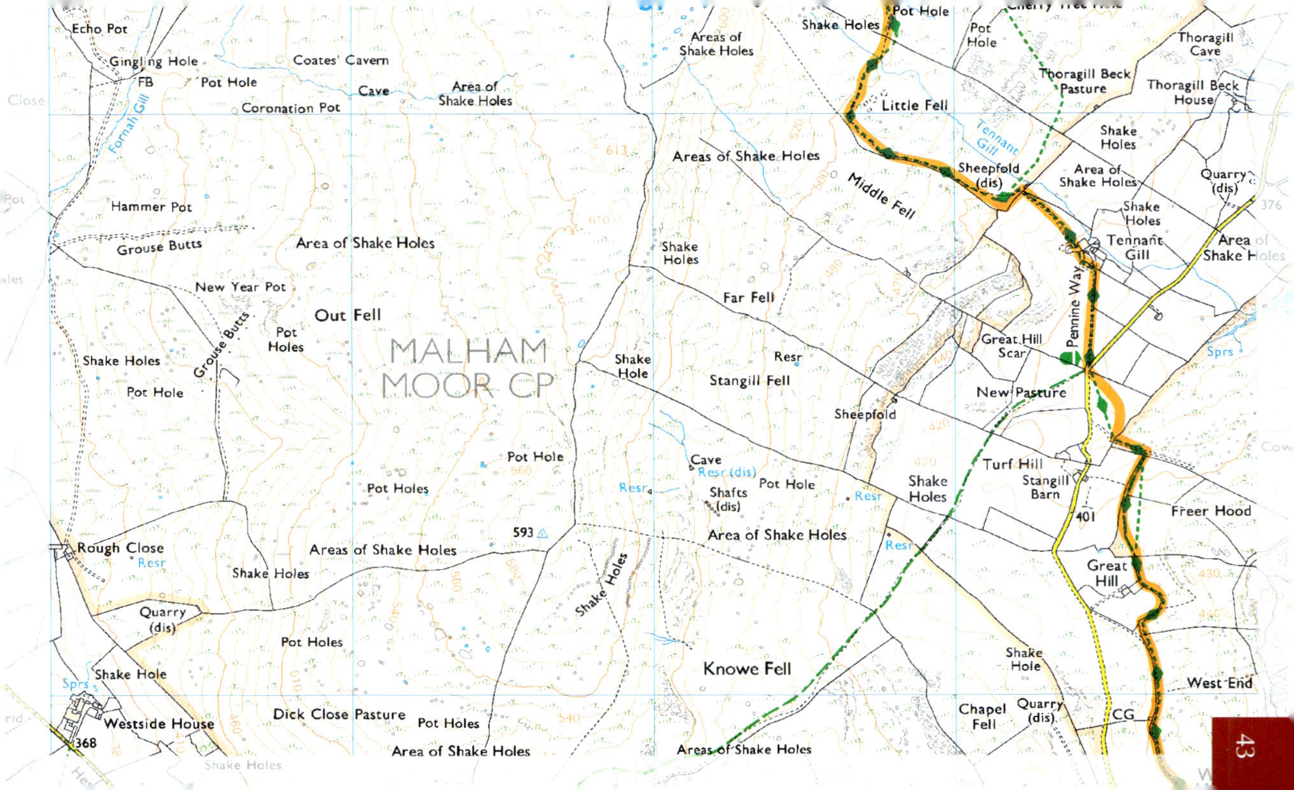
Echo Pot
Gingling Hole
FB
Pot Hole
Coates' Cavern
Cave
Area of Shake Holes
Coronation Pot
Fornah Gill
Hammer Pot
Grouse Butts
Area of Shake Holes
New Year Pot
Out Fell
Pot Holes
Grouse Butts
Shake Holes
Pot Hole
MALHAM MOOR CP
Pot Hole
Pot Holes
593
Rough Close
Resr
Areas of Shake Holes
Shake Holes
Quarry (dis)
Pot Holes
Shake Hole
Sprs
Westside House
368
Dick Close Pasture
Pot Holes
Area of Shake Holes
Areas of Shake Holes
Shake Holes
Little Fell
Pot Hole
Shake Holes
Areas of Shake Holes
Middle Fell
Sheepfold (dis)
Tennant Gill
Pot Hole
Thoragill Beck Pasture
Thoragill Cave
Thoragill Beck House
Shake Holes
Area of Shake Holes
Quarry (dis)
Shake Holes
Tennant Gill
Area of Shake Holes
376
Sprs
Pennine Way
Shake Holes
Far Fell
Great Hill Scar
Resr
Shake Hole
Stangill Fell
New Pasture
Sheepfold
Cave
Resr (dis)
Pot Hole
Shafts (dis)
Resr
Resr
Shake Holes
Turf Hill
Stangill Barn
401
Freer Hood
Area of Shake Holes
Shake Holes
Resr
Great Hill
Knowe Fell
Shake Hole
West End
Chapel Fell
Quarry (dis)
CG
Areas of Shake Holes
613
610
550
520
500
480
470
440
420
430
440
560
580
560
540
510
460
540

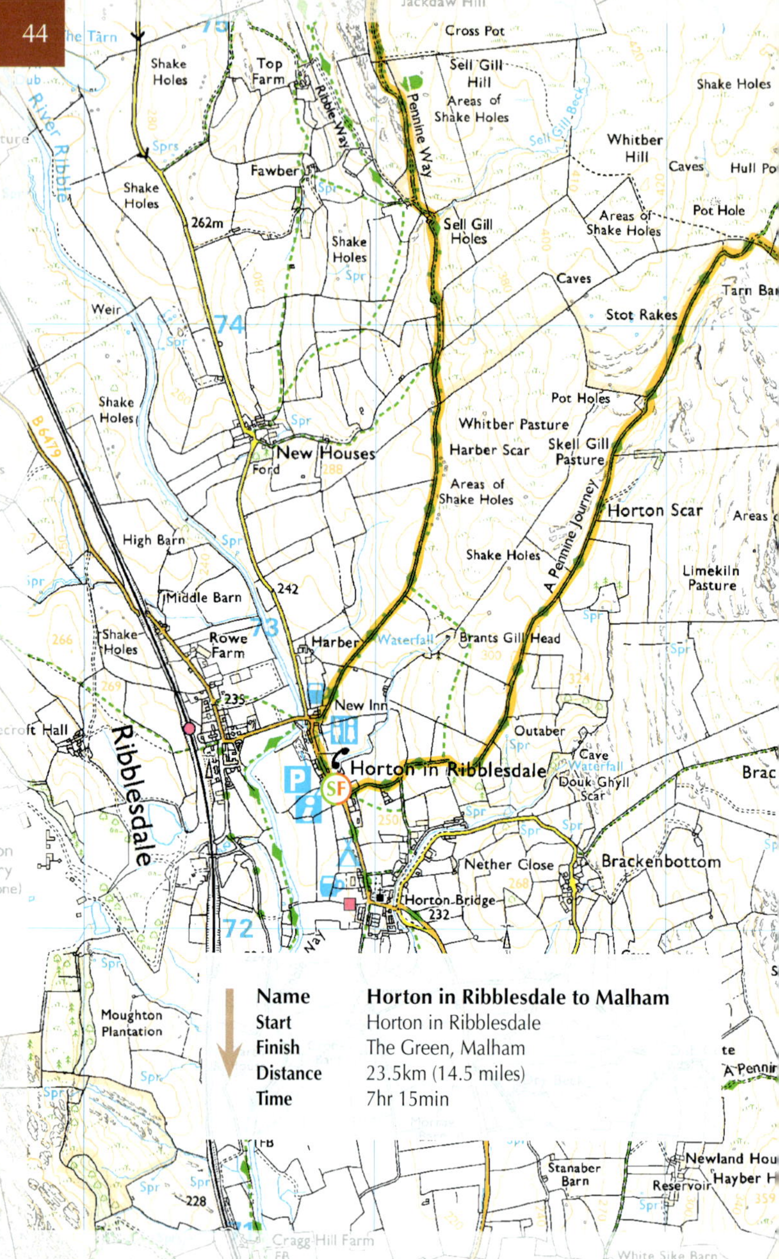

Name	**Horton in Ribblesdale to Malham**
Start	Horton in Ribblesdale
Finish	The Green, Malham
Distance	23.5km (14.5 miles)
Time	7hr 15min

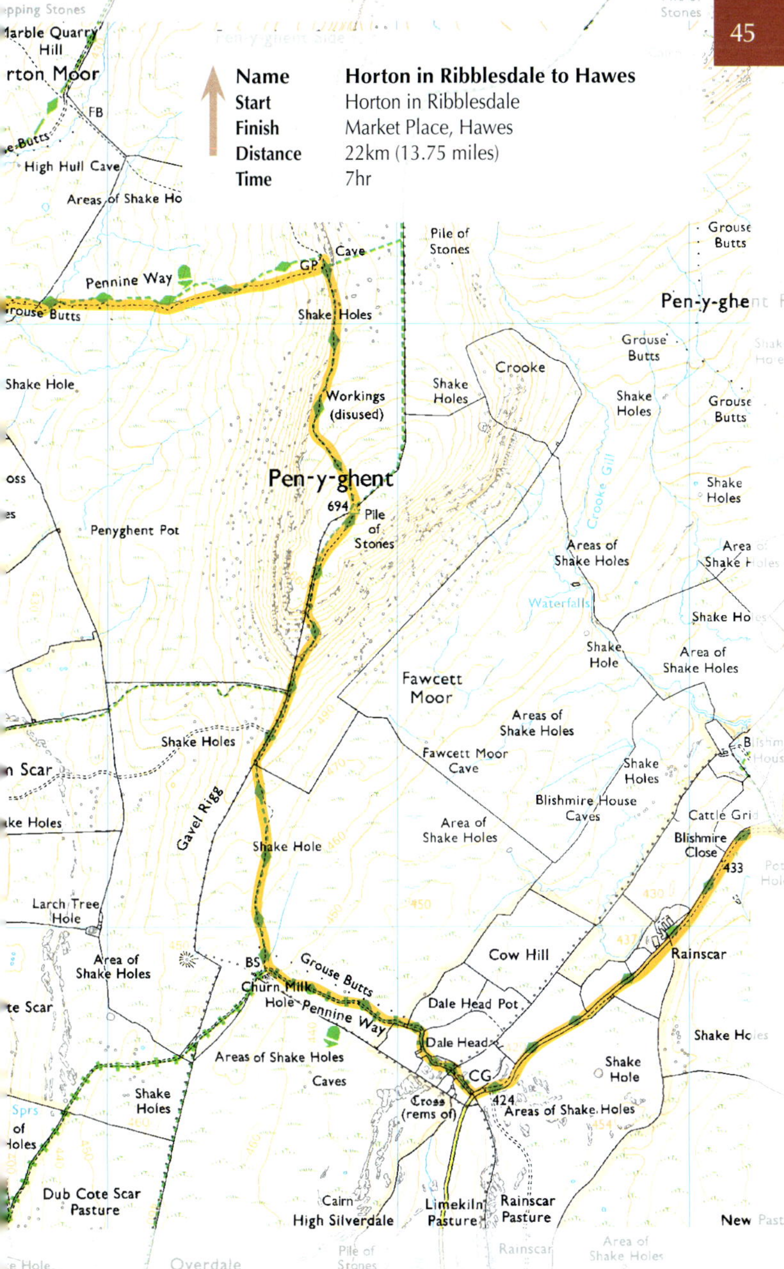
Name Horton in Ribblesdale to Hawes
Start Horton in Ribblesdale
Finish Market Place, Hawes
Distance 22km (13.75 miles)
Time 7hr
Pile of Stones
Hill
rton Moor
FB
High Hull Cave
Areas of Shake Ho
Cave
GP
Pennine Way
Pile of Stones
Grouse Butts
Shake Holes
Pen-y-ghe
Shake Hole
Crooke
Shake Holes
Workings (disused)
Pen-y-ghent
694
Pile of Stones
Penyghent Pot
Crooke Gill
Areas of Shake Holes
Waterfalls
Fawcett Moor
Shake Hole
Area of Shake Holes
Areas of Shake Holes
Fawcett Moor Cave
Blishmire House Caves
Cattle Gri
Blishmire Close
433
Gavel Rigg
Shake Hole
Larch Tree Hole
Area of Shake Holes
BS
Churn Milk Hole
Grouse Butts
Pennine Way
Cow Hill
Rainscar
Dale Head Pot
Dale Head
CG
424
Areas of Shake Holes
Caves
Cross (rems of)
Areas of Shake Holes
Shake Hole
Shake Holes
Dub Cote Scar Pasture
Cairn
High Silverdale
Limekiln Pasture
Rainscar Pasture
New
Overdale

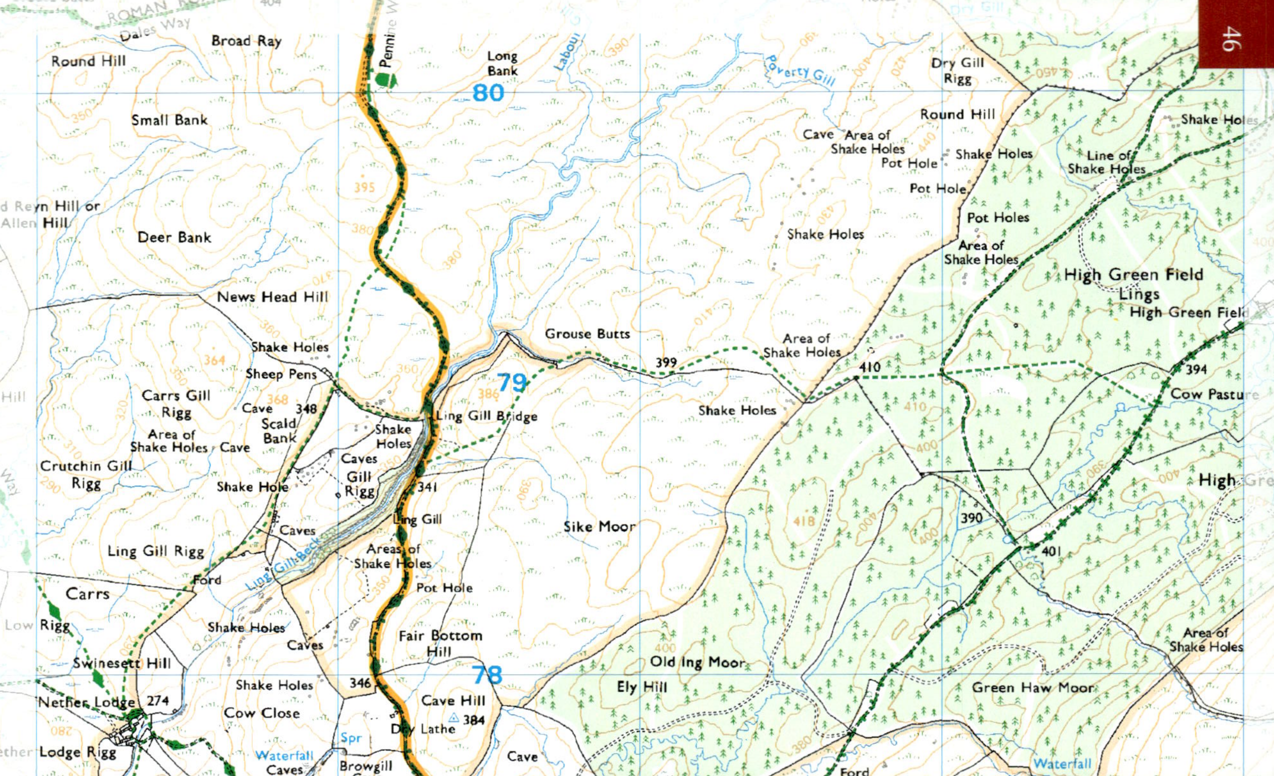
ROMAN
Dales Way
Broad Ray
Round Hill
Pennine Way
Long Bank
80
Poverty Gill
Dry Gill Rigg
Small Bank
Round Hill
Shake Holes
Cave
Area of Shake Holes
Shake Holes
Pot Hole
Line of Shake Holes
395
Pot Hole
Reyn Hill or Allen Hill
Deer Bank
Pot Holes
Shake Holes
Area of Shake Holes
High Green Field
Lings
High Green Field
News Head Hill
Grouse Butts
Shake Holes
Area of Shake Holes
364
399
410
394
Sheep Pens
Cow Pasture
79
Carrs Gill Rigg
Cave
348
Ling Gill Bridge
Shake Holes
Scald Bank
Area of Shake Holes
Cave
Shake Holes
Caves
Crutchin Gill Rigg
Gill Rigg
Shake Hole
341
418
High
390
Ling Gill
Sike Moor
Caves
401
Ling Gill Rigg
Areas of Shake Holes
Ling Gill Beck
Ford
Pot Hole
Carrs
Low Rigg
Shake Holes
Fair Bottom Hill
Area of Shake Holes
Caves
Swinesett Hill
Old Ing Moor
78
Shake Holes
346
Ely Hill
Green Haw Moor
Nether Lodge
274
Cave Hill
Cow Close
384
Spr
Dry Lathe
Lodge Rigg
Waterfall
Caves
Browgill Cave
Cave
Ford
Waterfall

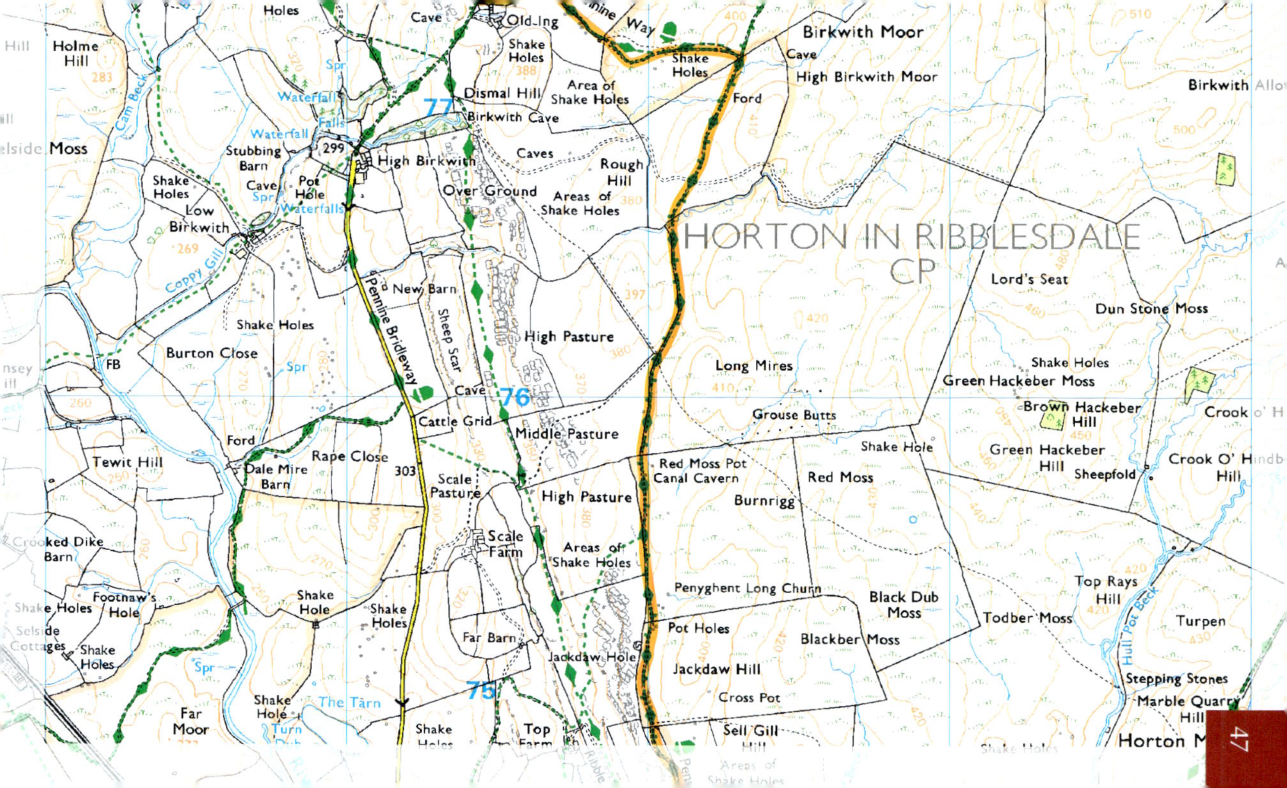
HORTON IN RIBBLESDALE CP
Birkwith Moor
High Birkwith Moor
Birkwith
Cave
Ford
Shake Holes
Pennine Way
Old Ing
Dismal Hill
Area of Shake Holes
Birkwith Cave
Caves
Rough Hill
Areas of Shake Holes
Over Ground
High Birkwith
Waterfall
Falls
Spr
Pot Hole
Waterfalls
Stubbing Barn
Cave
Low Birkwith
Cam Beck
Coppy Gill
Holme Hill
Moss
Burton Close
New Barn
Sheep Scar
Pennine Bridleway
Cattle Grid
Rape Close
Dale Mire Barn
FB
Tewit Hill
High Pasture
Middle Pasture
Long Mires
Grouse Butts
Red Moss Pot
Canal Cavern
Lord's Seat
Dun Stone Moss
Green Hackeber Moss
Brown Hackeber Hill
Green Hackeber Hill
Sheepfold
Crook O' Hindb Hill
Hull Pot Beck
Turpen
Top Rays Hill
Todber Moss
Stepping Stones
Marble Quarry Hill
Horton
Shake Hole
Red Moss
Burnrigg
Black Dub Moss
Blackber Moss
Penyghent Long Churn
Pot Holes
Jackdaw Hill
Cross Pot
Sell Gill Hill
Jackdaw Hole
Scale Farm
Scale Pasture
Far Barn
Top Farm
The Tarn
Far Moor
Footnaw's Hole
Crooked Dike Barn
Selside Cottages
Ribble
75
76
77
299
303

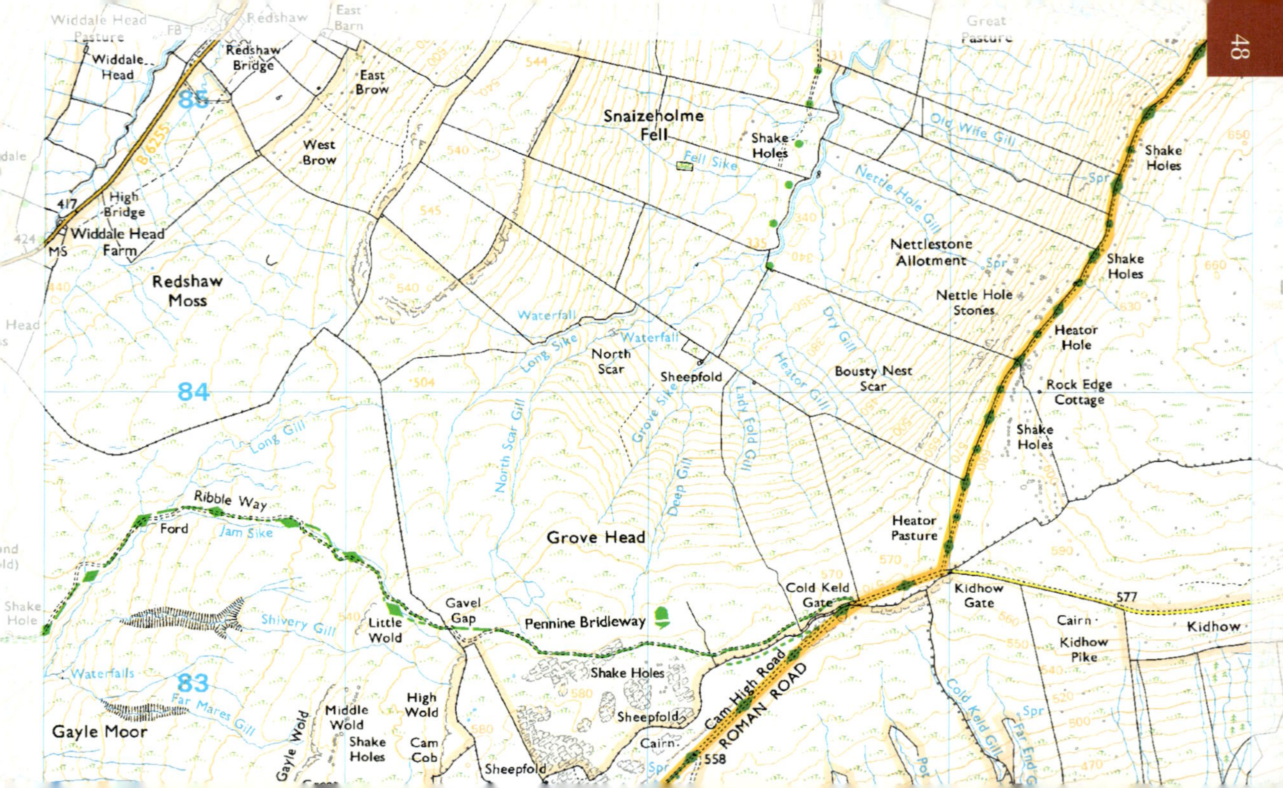

Widdale Head Pasture
FB
Redshaw
East Barn
Great Pasture
Widdale Head
Redshaw Bridge
East Brow
85
Snaizeholme Fell
Shake Holes
Fell Sike
Old Wife Gill
Shake Holes
West Brow
B6255
Nettle Hole Gill
Spr
417
High Bridge
424
Widdale Head Farm
MS
Nettlestone Allotment
Shake Holes
Redshaw Moss
Nettle Hole Stones
Heator Hole
Waterfall
Waterfall
Long Sike
North Scar
Sheepfold
Dry Gill
Heator Gill
Bousty Nest Scar
Rock Edge Cottage
84
Long Gill
North Scar Gill
Grove Sike
Lady Fold Gill
Deep Gill
Shake Holes
Ribble Way
Ford
Jam Sike
Grove Head
Heator Pasture
Cold Keld Gate
Kidhow Gate
577
Gavel Gap
Pennine Bridleway
Little Wold
Shivery Gill
Cairn
Kidhow Pike
Kidhow
Shake Hole
Waterfalls
83
Far Mares Gill
Shake Holes
Cam High Road
ROMAN ROAD
Middle Wold
High Wold
Sheepfold
Cold Keld Gill
Far End G
Gayle Moor
Gayle Wold
Shake Holes
Cam Cob
Cairn
558
Sheepfold

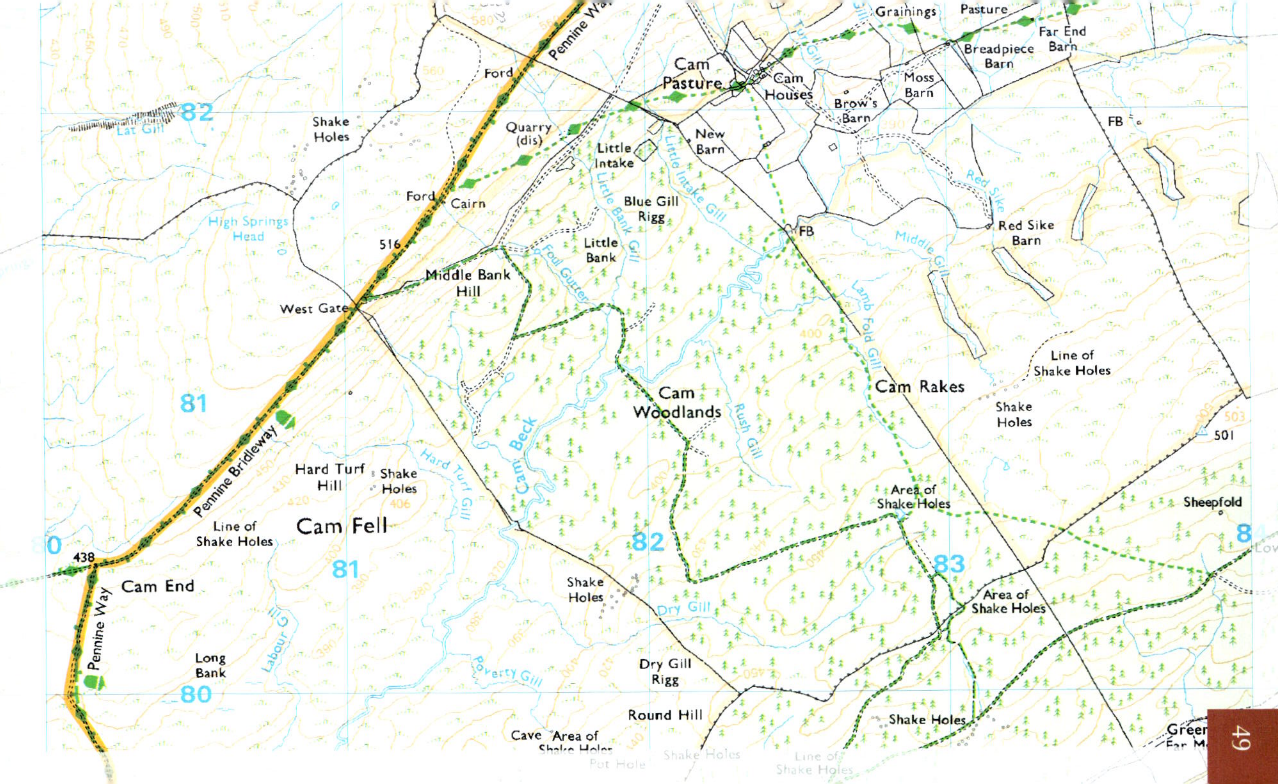

Grainings
Pasture
Far End Barn
Breadpiece Barn
Cam Pasture
Cam Houses
Moss Barn
Brow's Barn
FB
Shake Holes
Quarry (dis)
Little Intake
New Barn
Little Intake Gill
Little Bank Gill
Red Sike
Red Sike Barn
Ford
Cairn
Blue Gill Rigg
High Springs Head
516
Little Bank
Foul Gutter
Middle Gill
Middle Bank Hill
West Gate
Lamb Fold Gill
Line of Shake Holes
Cam Rakes
Cam Woodlands
Rush Gill
Cam Beck
501
Pennine Way
Pennine Bridleway
Hard Turf Hill
Hard Turf Gill
Area of Shake Holes
Sheepfold
Cam Fell
438
Cam End
Labour Gill
Dry Gill
Long Bank
Poverty Gill
Dry Gill Rigg
Round Hill
Cave
82
81
80
83

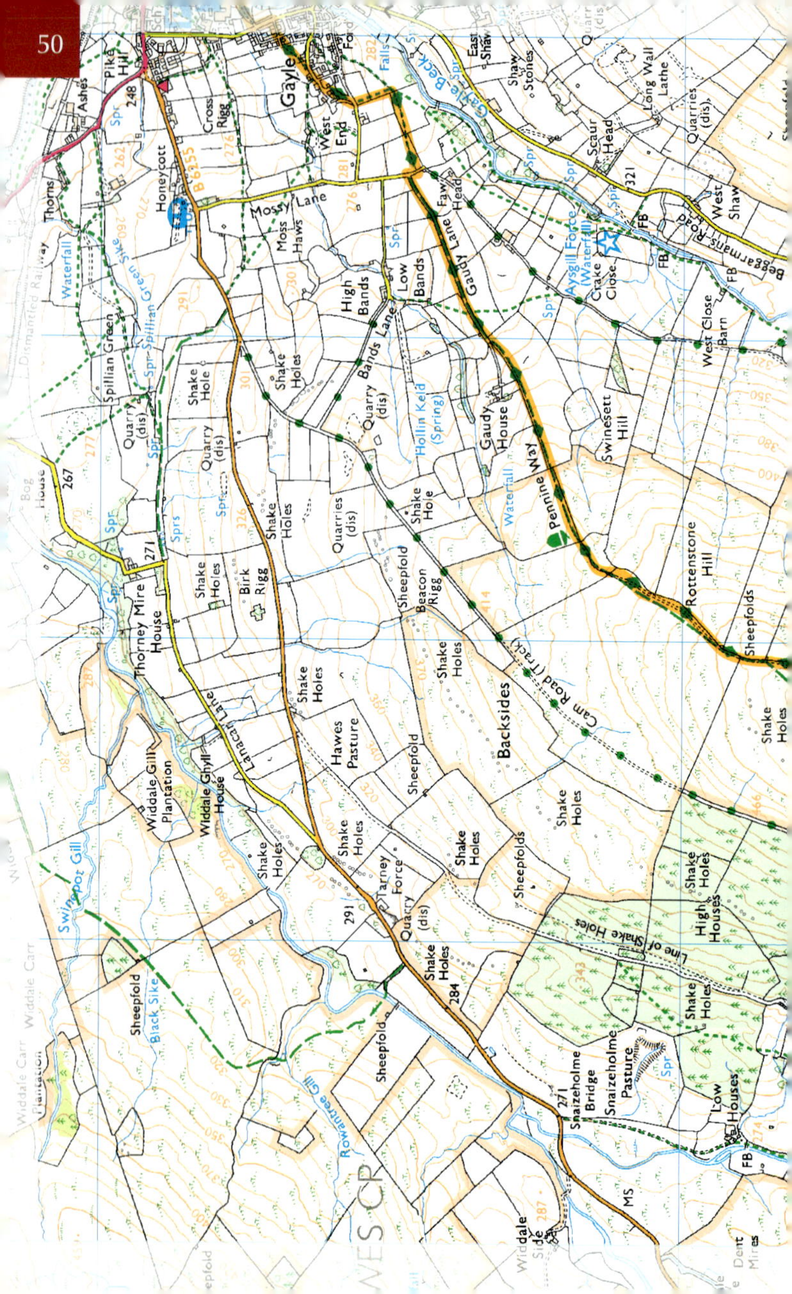
Gayle
West End
Gayle Beck
Falls
Ford
East Shaw
Shaw Stones
Long Wall Lathe
Quarries (dis)
Scaur Head
West Shaw
Beggarmans Road
FB
321
Faw Head
Gaudy Lane
Aysgill Force (Waterfall)
Crake Close
West Close Barn
Swinesett Hill
Rottenstone Hill
Sheepfolds
Pennine Way
Waterfall
Gaudy House
Hollin Keld (Spring)
Low Bands
High Bands
Bands Lane
Quarry (dis)
Mossy Lane
Moss Haws
Cross Rigg
Honeycott
B 6255
Pike Hill
Ashes
Thorns
Dismantled Railway
Waterfall
Spillian Green
Spillian Green Sike
Quarry (dis)
Shake Hole
Shake Holes
Bog House
267
271
Thorney Mire House
Birk Rigg
Quarries (dis)
Sheepfold
Beacon Rigg
Cam Road (Track)
Backsides
Hawes Pasture
Lanacar Lane
Widdale Ghyll House
Widdale Gill Plantation
Swinepot Gill
Black Sike
Tarney Force
Quarry (dis)
Line of Shake Holes
High Houses
Sheepfolds
Snaizeholme Bridge
Snaizeholme Pasture
Low Houses
Rowantree Gill
Widdale Carr
Widdale Side
Dent Mires
MS
284
291
271

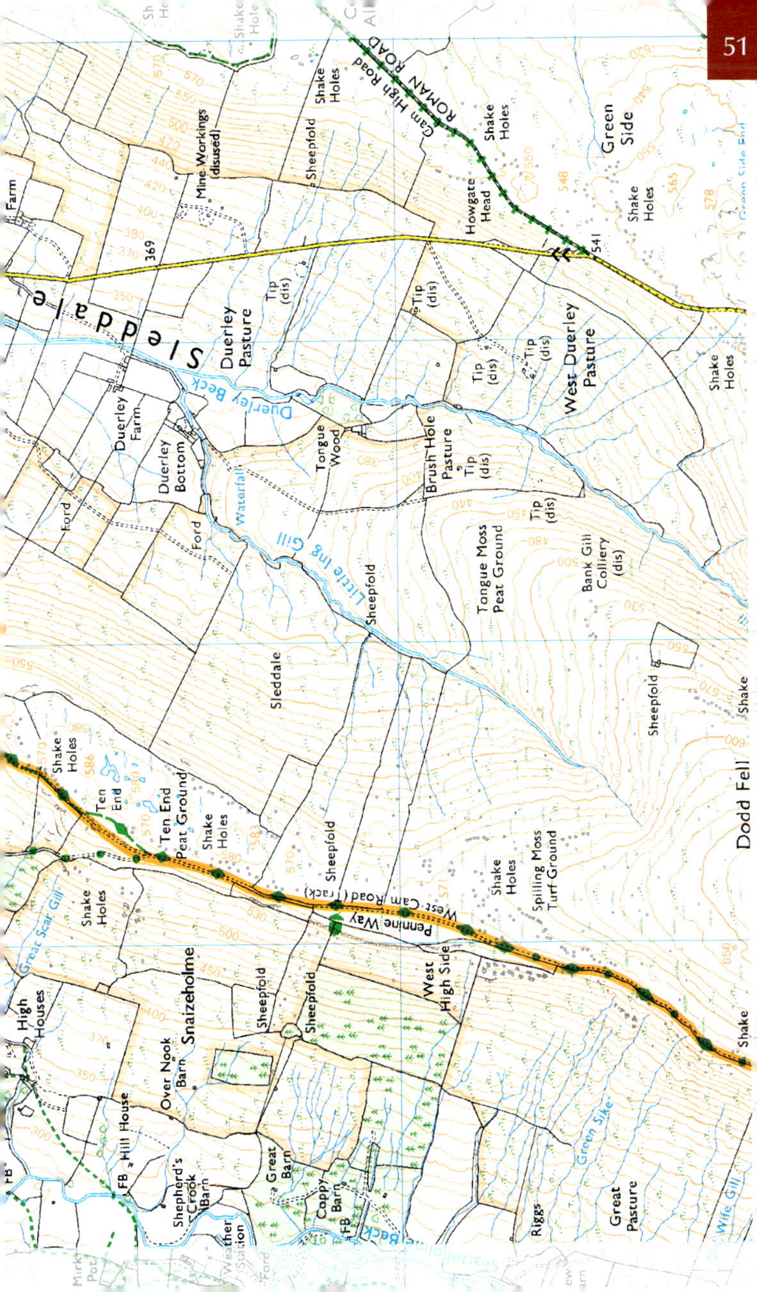

ROMAN ROAD
Cam High Road
Shake Holes
Green Side
Shake Holes
Sheepfold
Shake Holes
Mine Workings (disused)
Farm
369
Howgate Head
541
Shake Holes
548
565
578
Green Side End
Sleddale
Duerley Pasture
Tip (dis)
Tip (dis)
Tip (dis)
Tip (dis)
West Duerley Pasture
Shake Holes
Duerley Beck
Duerley Farm
Duerley Bottom
Tongue Wood
Brush Hole Pasture
Tip (dis)
Tip (dis)
Ford
Ford
Waterfall
Little Ing Gill
Sheepfold
Tongue Moss Peat Ground
Bank Gill Colliery (dis)
Sleddale
Sheepfold
Shake Holes
Shake Holes
586
Ten End
Ten End Peat Ground
Shake Holes
583
Sheepfold
West Cam Road (Track)
Pennine Way
571
Shake Holes
Spilling Moss Turf Ground
Dodd Fell
Great Scar Gill
Shake Holes
High Houses
Snaizeholme
Sheepfold
Sheepfold
West High Side
650
Shake Holes
Over Nook Barn
Hill House
FB
Shepherd's Crook Barn
Great Barn
Coppy Barn
FB
Weather Station
Riggs
Green Sike
Great Pasture
Wife Gill

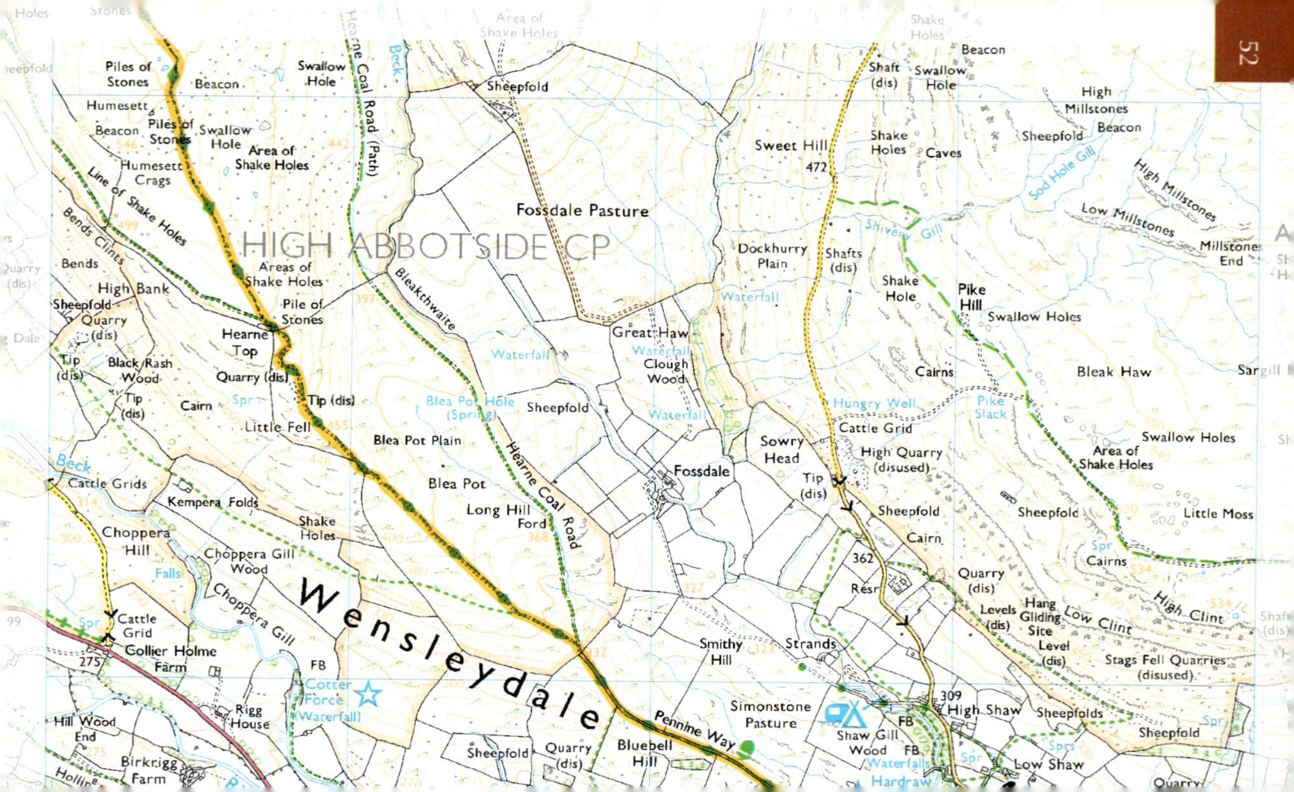

Wensleydale
HIGH ABBOTSIDE CP
Fossdale Pasture
Hearne Coal Road
Hearne Coal Road (Path)
Pennine Way
Bleakchwaite
Blea Pot Plain
Blea Pot
Blea Pot Hole (Spring)
Long Hill Ford
Sheepfold
Fossdale
Clough Wood
Great Haw
Waterfall
Dockhurry Plain
Sweet Hill
472
Shafts (dis)
Shiver Gill
Hungry Well
Cattle Grid
High Quarry (disused)
Sowry Head
Tip (dis)
Shake Hole
Cairns
Pike Hill
Swallow Holes
Pike Slack
Bleak Haw
Area of Shake Holes
Swallow Holes
Little Moss
High Clint
Low Clint
Stags Fell Quarries (disused)
Hang Gliding Site
Levels (dis)
Level (dis)
Quarry (dis)
Cairn
Sheepfolds
High Shaw
Low Shaw
Shaw Gill Wood
Hardraw
Waterfalls
Resr
362
309
Strands
Smithy Hill
Simonstone Pasture
Bluebell Hill
Quarry (dis)
Sheepfold
Cotter Force (Waterfall)
Rigg House
Birkrigg Farm
Hill Wood End
Collier Holme Farm
Cattle Grid
275
Choppera Gill
Choppera Gill Wood
Choppera Hill
Falls
Kempera Folds
Shake Holes
Little Fell
Tip (dis)
Quarry (dis)
Hearne Top
Cairn
Pile of Stones
Areas of Shake Holes
Area of Shake Holes
Swallow Hole
Beacon
Piles of Stones
Humesett Beacon
Humesett Crag
Line of Shake Holes
Bends Clints
Bends
High Bank
Black Rash Wood
Tip (dis)
Cattle Grids
Beck
High Millstones
Low Millstones
Millstones End
Sod Hole Gill
Shake Holes Caves
Shaft (dis)
Swallow Hole
Beacon

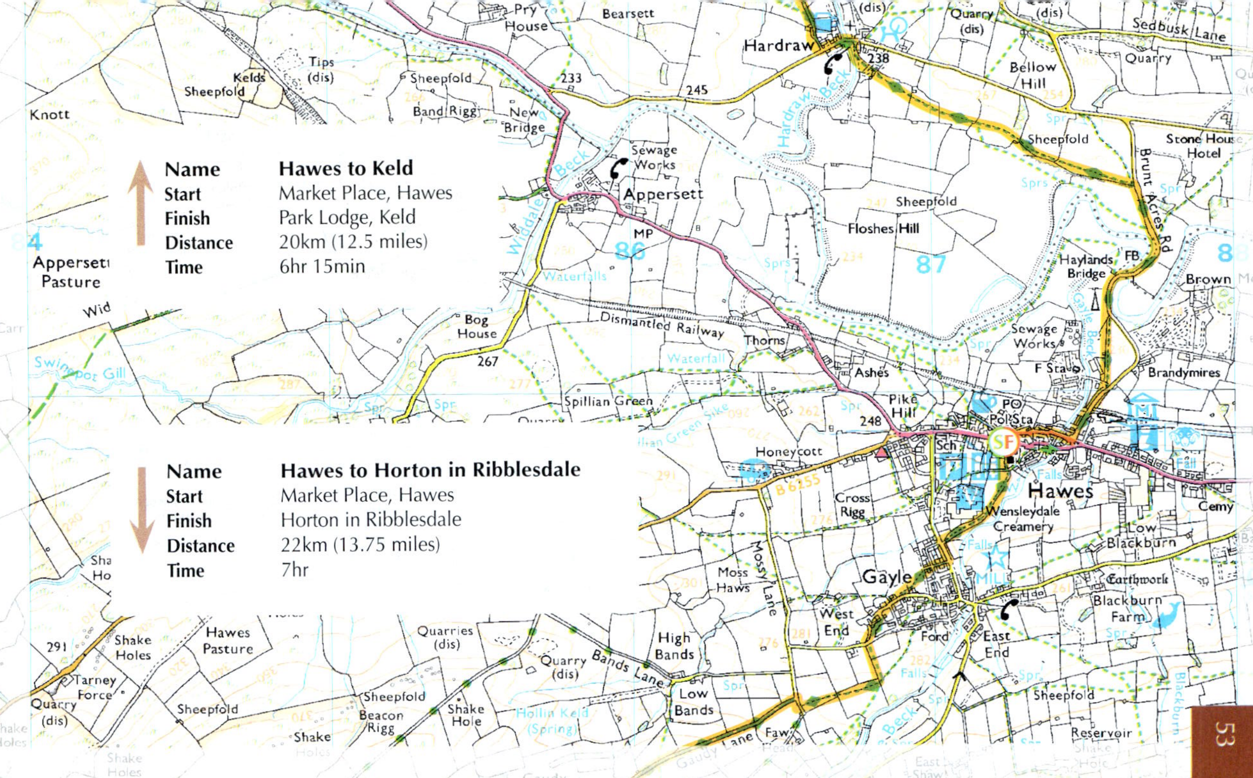

Name: **Hawes to Keld**
Start: Market Place, Hawes
Finish: Park Lodge, Keld
Distance: 20km (12.5 miles)
Time: 6hr 15min

Name: **Hawes to Horton in Ribblesdale**
Start: Market Place, Hawes
Finish: Horton in Ribblesdale
Distance: 22km (13.75 miles)
Time: 7hr

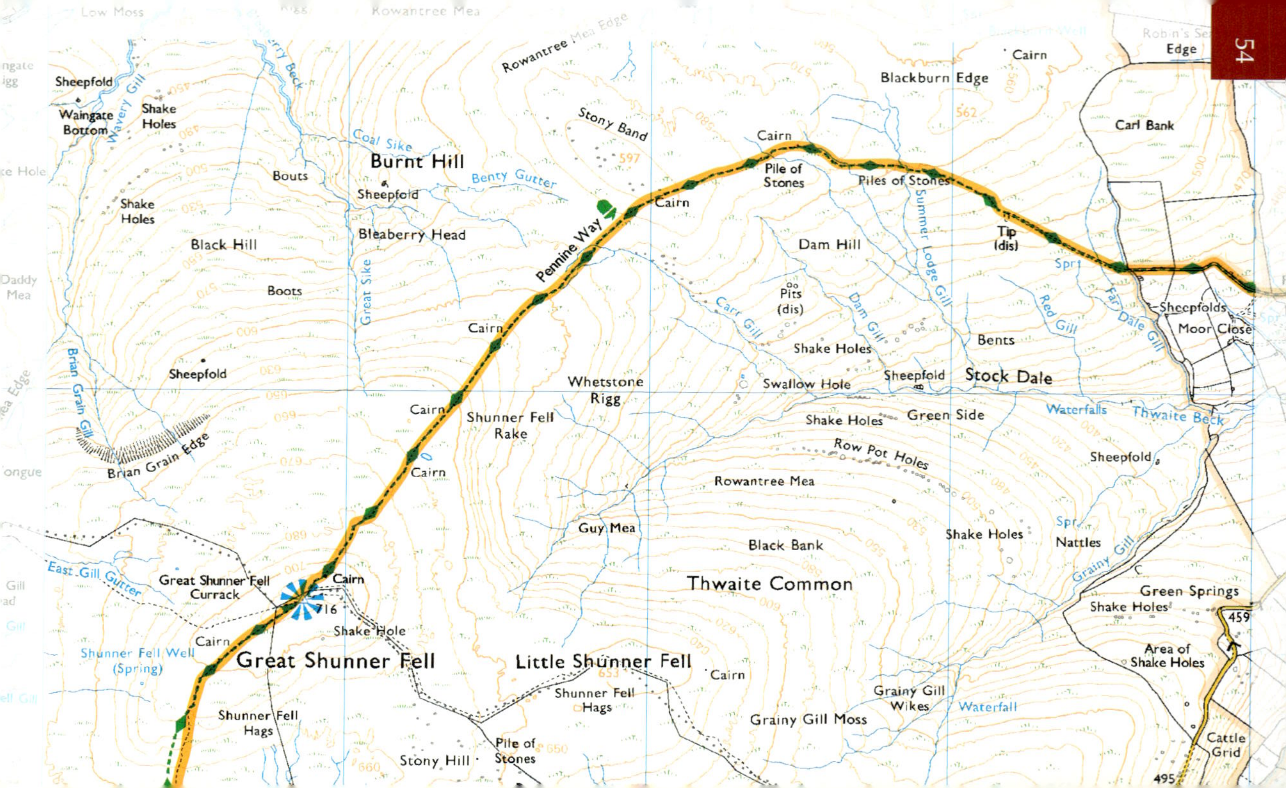

Edge
Carl Bank
Sheepfolds
Moor Close
Far Dale Gill
Thwaite Beck
Green Springs
Shake Holes
Area of Shake Holes
Cattle Grid
459
495
Grainy Gill
Sheepfold
Nattles
Waterfalls
Red Gill
Stock Dale
Tip (dis)
Cairn
Blackburn Edge
562
Bents
Green Side
Shake Holes
Summer Lodge Gill
Piles of Stones
Sheepfold
Dam Gill
Dam Hill
Shake Holes
Row Pot Holes
Waterfall
Grainy Gill Wikes
Grainy Gill Moss
Pile of Stones
Cairn
Pits (dis)
Swallow Hole
Rowantree Mea
Black Bank
Thwaite Common
Carr Gill
Cairn
Stony Band
597
Pennine Way
Whetstone Rigg
Guy Mea
Little Shunner Fell
653
Shunner Fell Hags
Rowantree Mea Edge
Benty Gutter
Shunner Fell Rake
Cairn
650
Pile of Stones
Stony Hill
Burnt Hill
Coal Sike
Sheepfold
Bleaberry Head
Great Sike
Cairn
Great Shunner Fell
Shake Hole
716
660
Bouts
Boots
Black Hill
Sheepfold
Brian Grain Edge
Great Shunner Fell Currack
Cairn
Shunner Fell Hags
Shunner Fell Well (Spring)
Sheepfold
Waingate Bottom
Waverly Gill
Shake Holes
Brian Grain Gill
East Gill Gutter
Rowantree Mea
Low Moss

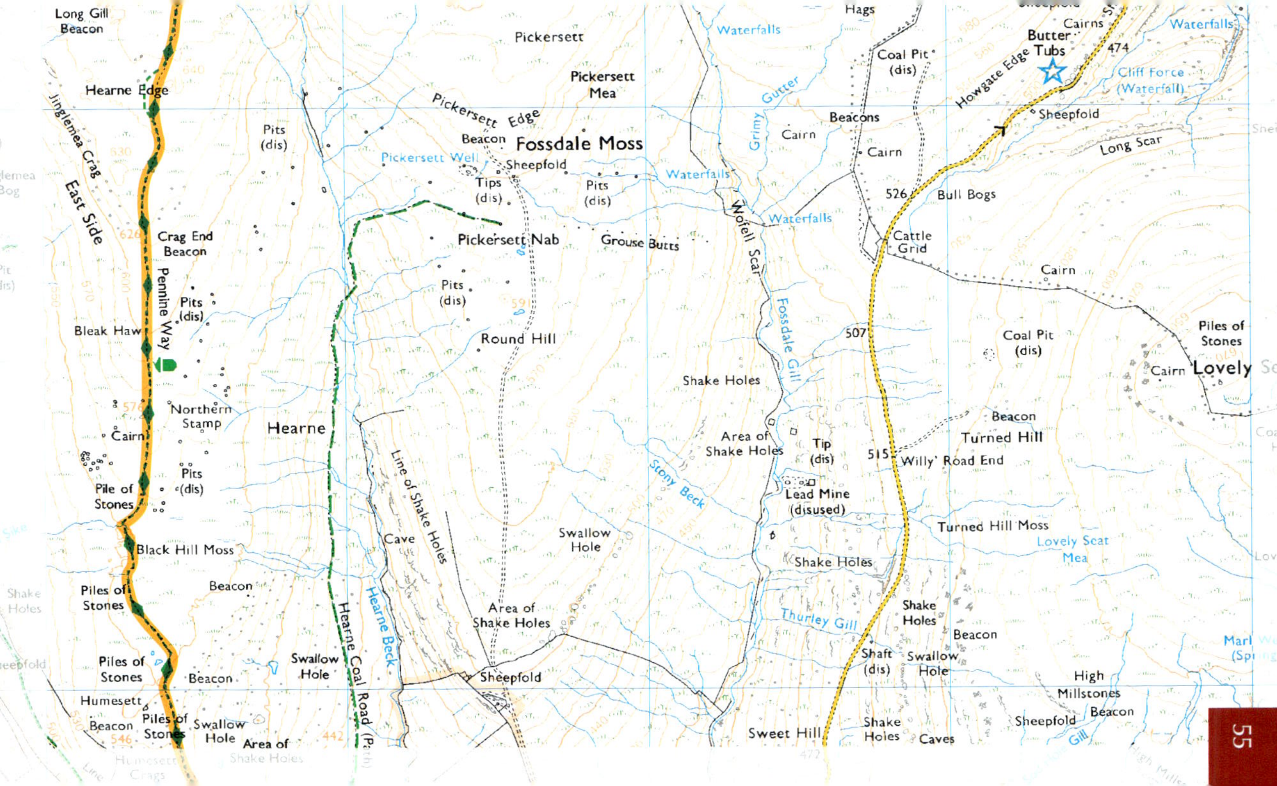

Long Gill Beacon
Hearne Edge
Jinglemea Crag
East Side
Crag End Beacon
Pennine Way
Bleak Haw
Pits (dis)
Northern Stamp
Cairn
Hearne
Pile of Stones
Pits (dis)
Black Hill Moss
Beacon
Piles of Stones
Piles of Stones
Beacon
Humesett
Beacon
Piles of Stones
Swallow Hole
Area of Shake Holes
Swallow Hole
Hearne Coal Road (Path)
Hearne Beck
Line of Shake Holes
Cave
Pits (dis)
Pickersett
Pickersett Mea
Pickersett Edge
Beacon
Fossdale Moss
Pickersett Well
Sheepfold
Tips (dis)
Pits (dis)
Pickersett Nab
Grouse Butts
Pits (dis)
Round Hill
Swallow Hole
Area of Shake Holes
Sheepfold
Waterfalls
Grimy Gutter
Waterfalls
Waterfalls
Wofell Scar
Fossdale Gill
Shake Holes
Area of Shake Holes
Tip (dis)
Stony Beck
Lead Mine (disused)
Shake Holes
Thurley Gill
Sweet Hill
Hags
Coal Pit (dis)
Beacons
Cairn
Cairn
526
Bull Bogs
Cattle Grid
Cairn
507
515
'Willy' Road End
Coal Pit (dis)
Beacon
Turned Hill
Turned Hill Moss
Lovely Seat Mea
Shake Holes
Beacon
Shaft (dis)
Swallow Hole
Shake Holes
Caves
High Millstones
Beacon
Sheepfold
Gill
Cairns
Butter Tubs
474
Howgate Edge
Cliff Force (Waterfall)
Waterfalls
Sheepfold
Long Scar
Piles of Stones
Cairn
Lovely

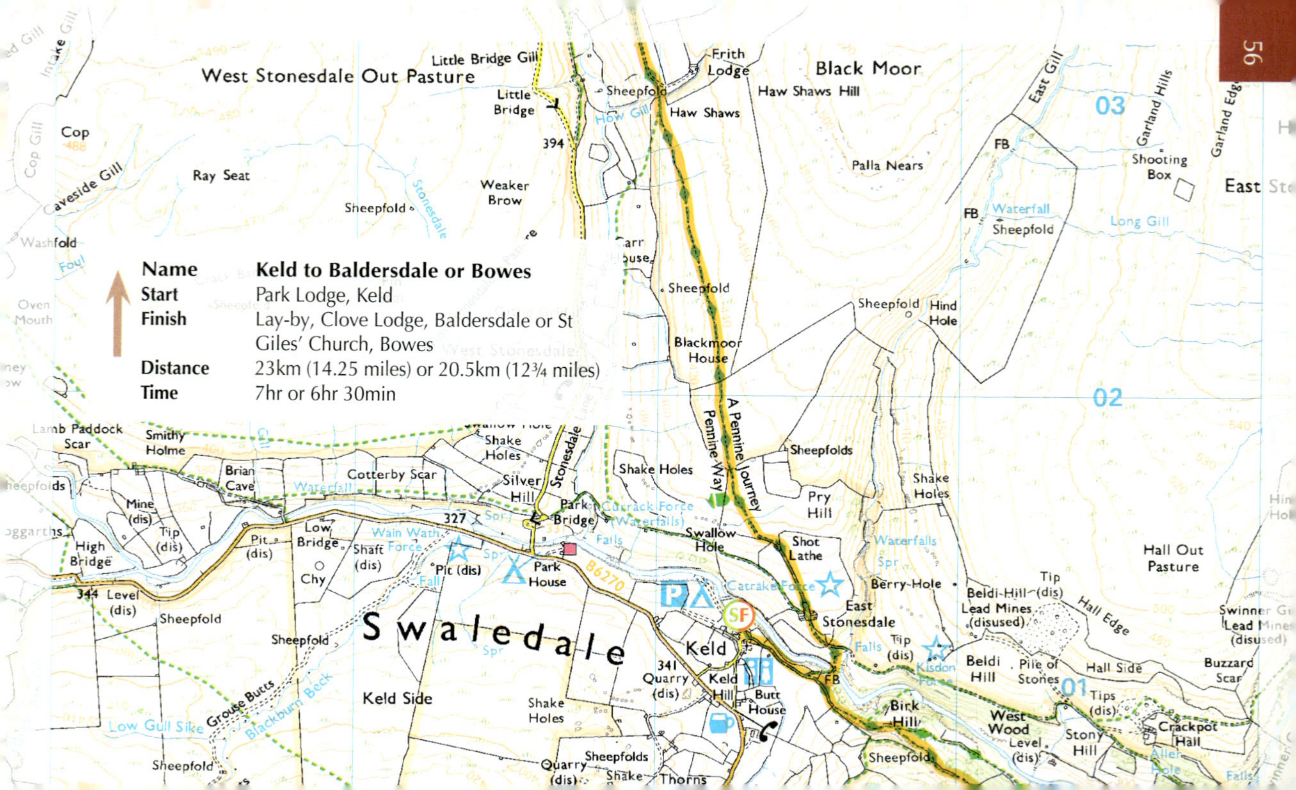

Name	**Keld to Baldersdale or Bowes**
Start	Park Lodge, Keld
Finish	Lay-by, Clove Lodge, Baldersdale or St Giles' Church, Bowes
Distance	23km (14.25 miles) or 20.5km (12¾ miles)
Time	7hr or 6hr 30min

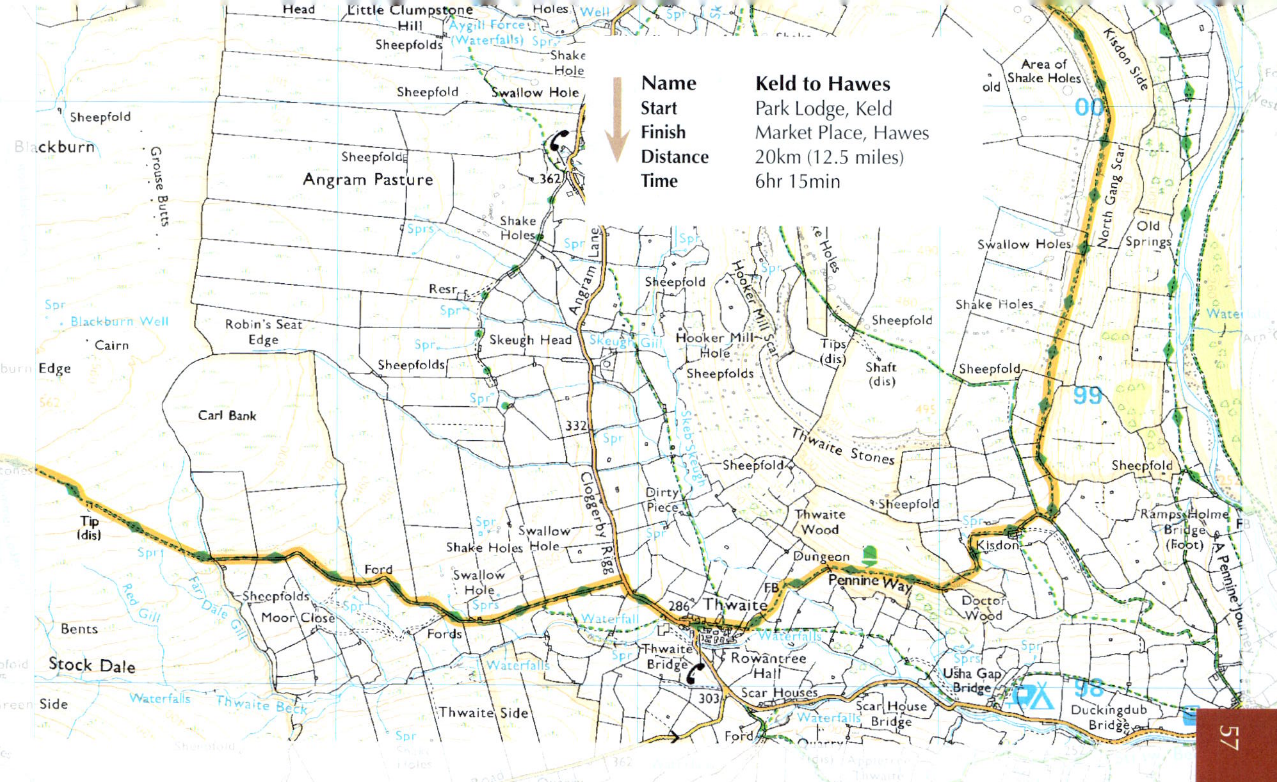
Name Keld to Hawes
Start Park Lodge, Keld
Finish Market Place, Hawes
Distance 20km (12.5 miles)
Time 6hr 15min
Kisdon Side
North Gang Scar
Old Springs
Area of Shake Holes
Swallow Holes
Shake Holes
Sheepfold
Ramps Holme Bridge (Foot)
A Pennine Journey
Kisdon
Doctor Wood
Usha Gap Bridge
Duckingdub Bridge
Scar House Bridge
Pennine Way
Thwaite Stones
Thwaite Wood
Dungeon
Shaft (dis)
Tips (dis)
Hooker Mill Scar
Hooker Mill Hole
Sheepfolds
Skeb Skeugh
Dirty Piece
Thwaite
Rowantree Hall
Scar Houses
Thwaite Bridge
Waterfalls
Ford
Angram Lane
Cloggerby Rigg
Skeugh Head
Skeugh Gill
Swallow Hole
Resr
Fords
Thwaite Side
Little Clumpstone Hill
Aygill Force (Waterfalls)
Angram Pasture
Robin's Seat Edge
Carl Bank
Moor Close
Far Dale Gill
Red Gill
Thwaite Beck
Grouse Butts
Blackburn Well
Cairn
Blackburn
Edge
Tip (dis)
Bents
Stock Dale
Side

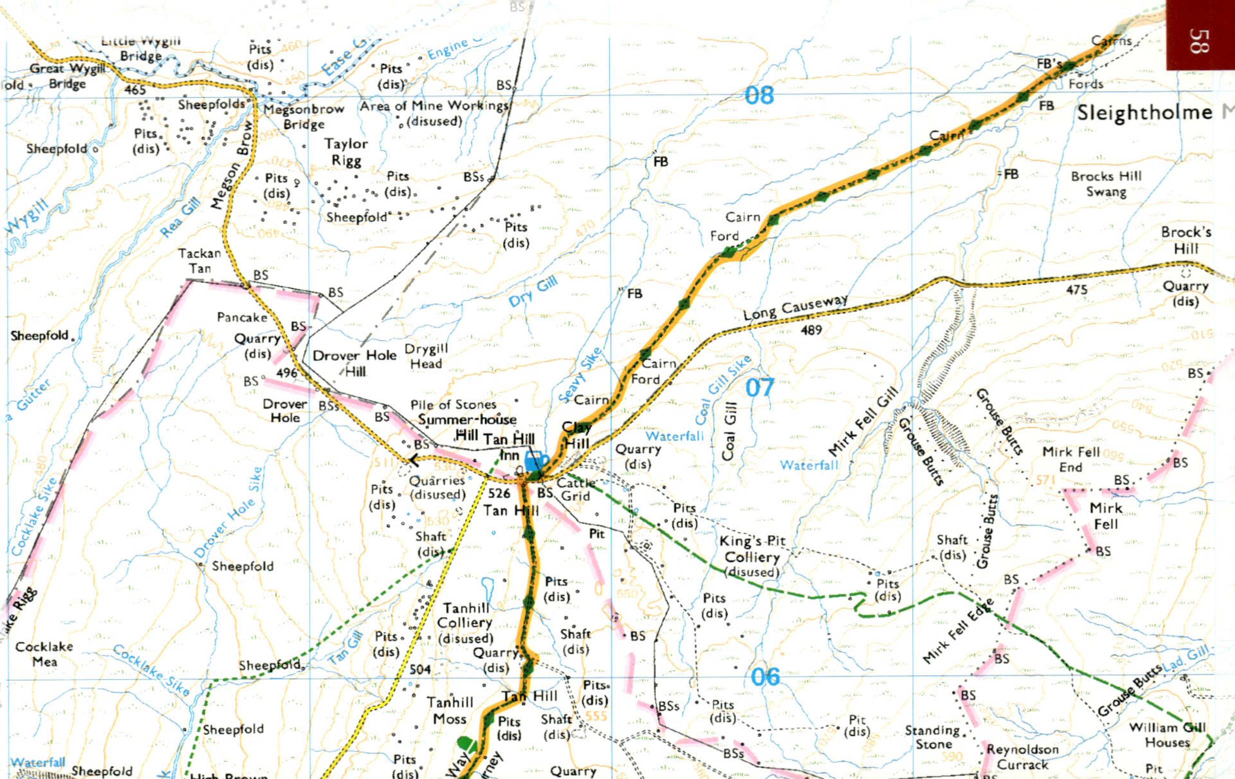
Sleightholme
Brock's Hill
Quarry (dis)
Brocks Hill Swang
Cairns
Fords
FB's
FB
Cairn
Cairn Ford
475
489
Long Causeway
Grouse Butts
Mirk Fell End
Mirk Fell
Mirk Fell Gill
Mirk Fell Edge
Lad Gill
William Gill Houses
Reynoldson Currack
Standing Stone
Shaft (dis)
Pits (dis)
Pit (dis)
Waterfall
07
08
06
Coal Gill
Coal Gill Sike
King's Pit Colliery (disused)
Seavy Sike
Clay Hill
Cattle Grid
Inn
Tan Hill
526
Summer-house Hill
Pile of Stones
Dry Gill
Drygill Head
Drover Hole Hill
Drover Hole
Drover Hole Sike
Quarries (disused)
Tanhill Colliery (disused)
Tanhill Moss
504
Tan Gill
Way
Area of Mine Workings (disused)
Taylor Rigg
Sheepfold
Engine Gutter
Ease Gill
Megsonbrow Bridge
Megson Brow
Rea Gill
Tackan Tan
Pancake
496
Sheepfolds
465
Little Wygill Bridge
Great Wygill Bridge
Wygill
Cocklake Sike
Cocklake Rigg
Cocklake Mea
BS
BSs

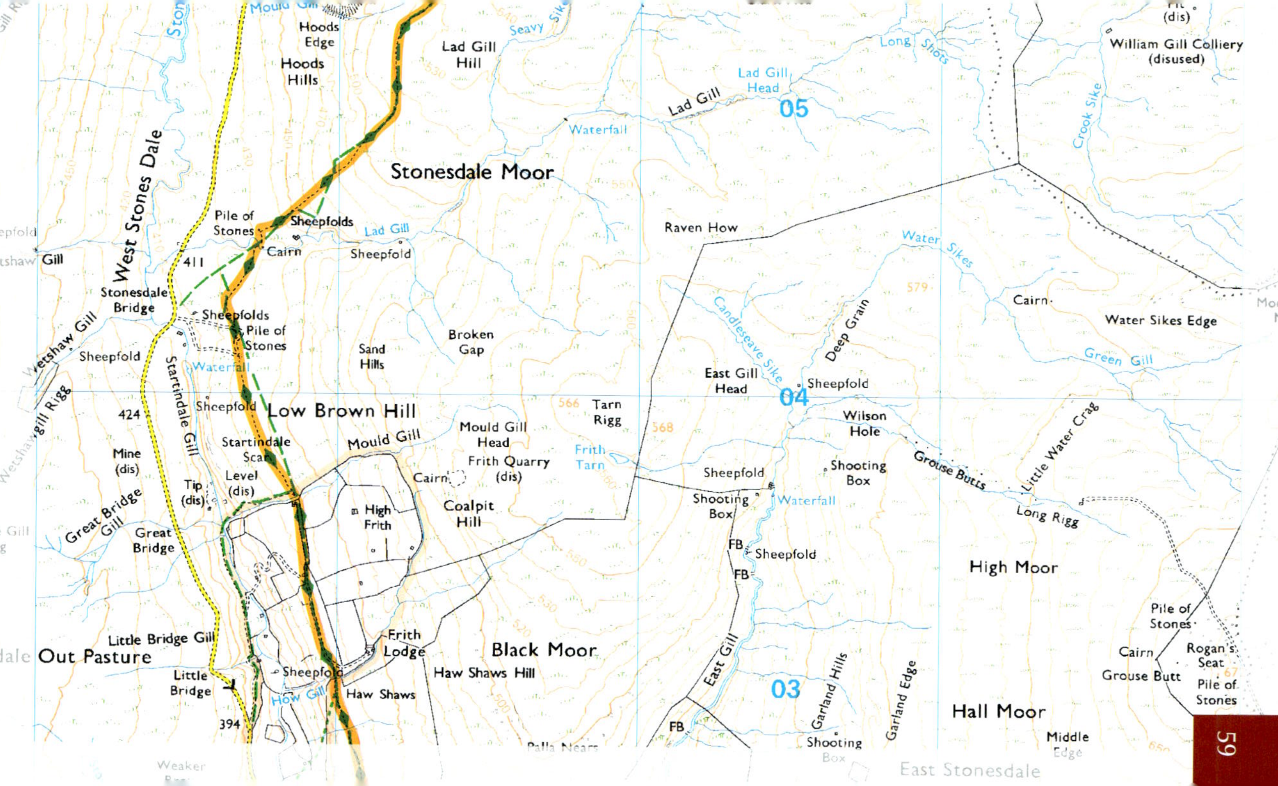

Hoods Edge
Hoods Hills
Lad Gill Hill
Seavy Sike
Long Shots
William Gill Colliery (disused)
Lad Gill Head
Lad Gill
05
Waterfall
Crook Sike
West Stones Dale
Stonesdale Moor
Pile of Stones
Sheepfolds
Lad Gill
Raven How
Cairn
Sheepfold
411
Gill
Water Sikes
Stonesdale Bridge
579
Cairn
Water Sikes Edge
Sheepfolds
Pile of Stones
Broken Gap
Sand Hills
Deep Grain
Candleseave Sike
Green Gill
Wetshaw Gill
Sheepfold
Waterfall
East Gill Head
Sheepfold
04
Startindale Gill
Sheepfold
Low Brown Hill
566
Tarn Rigg
424
Wetshawgill Rigg
Wilson Hole
Mould Gill Head
Mould Gill
568
Little Water Crag
Startindale Scar
Frith Quarry (dis)
Frith Tarn
Mine (dis)
Cairn
Sheepfold
Shooting Box
Grouse Butts
Level (dis)
Tip (dis)
High Frith
Coalpit Hill
Shooting Box
Waterfall
Long Rigg
Great Bridge Gill
Great Bridge
FB
Sheepfold
High Moor
FB
Pile of Stones
Little Bridge Gill
Frith Lodge
Black Moor
Out Pasture
Cairn
Rogan's Seat
Little Bridge
Sheepfold
Haw Shaws Hill
East Gill
Grouse Butt
Pile of Stones
How Gill
Haw Shaws
03
Garland Hills
Garland Edge
Hall Moor
394
FB
Shooting Box
Middle Edge
East Stonesdale

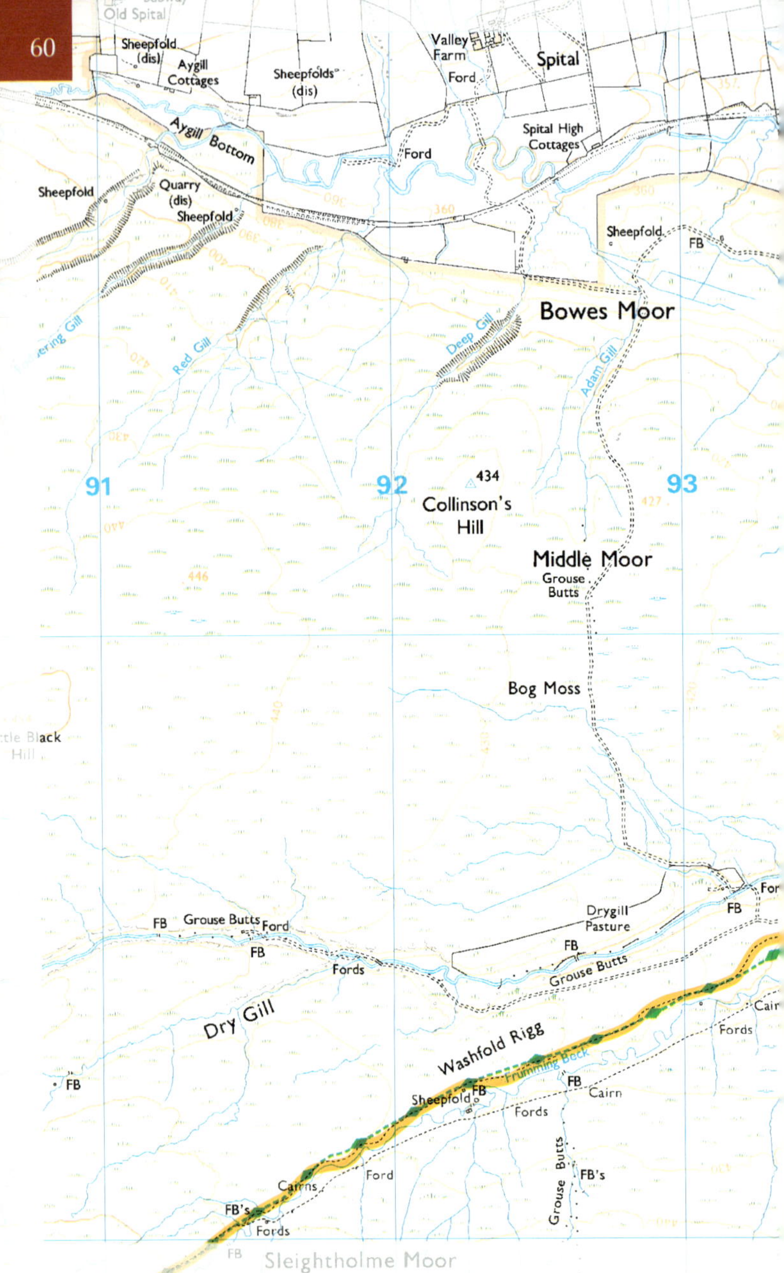
Subway
Old Spital
Sheepfold (dis)
Aygill Cottages
Sheepfolds (dis)
Valley Farm
Spital
Ford
Aygill Bottom
Spital High Cottages
Ford
Sheepfold
Quarry (dis)
Sheepfold
Sheepfold
FB
Bowes Moor
Red Gill
Deep Gill
Adam Gill
91
92
93
434
Collinson's Hill
Middle Moor
Grouse Butts
Bog Moss
ttle Black Hill
Drygill Pasture
For
FB
FB
Grouse Butts
Ford
FB
Fords
FB
Grouse Butts
Dry Gill
Washfold Rigg
Frumming Beck
Cair
Fords
FB
FB
Sheepfold
FB
Cairn
Fords
Grouse Butts
FB's
Ford
Cairns
FB's
Fords
FB
Sleightholme Moor

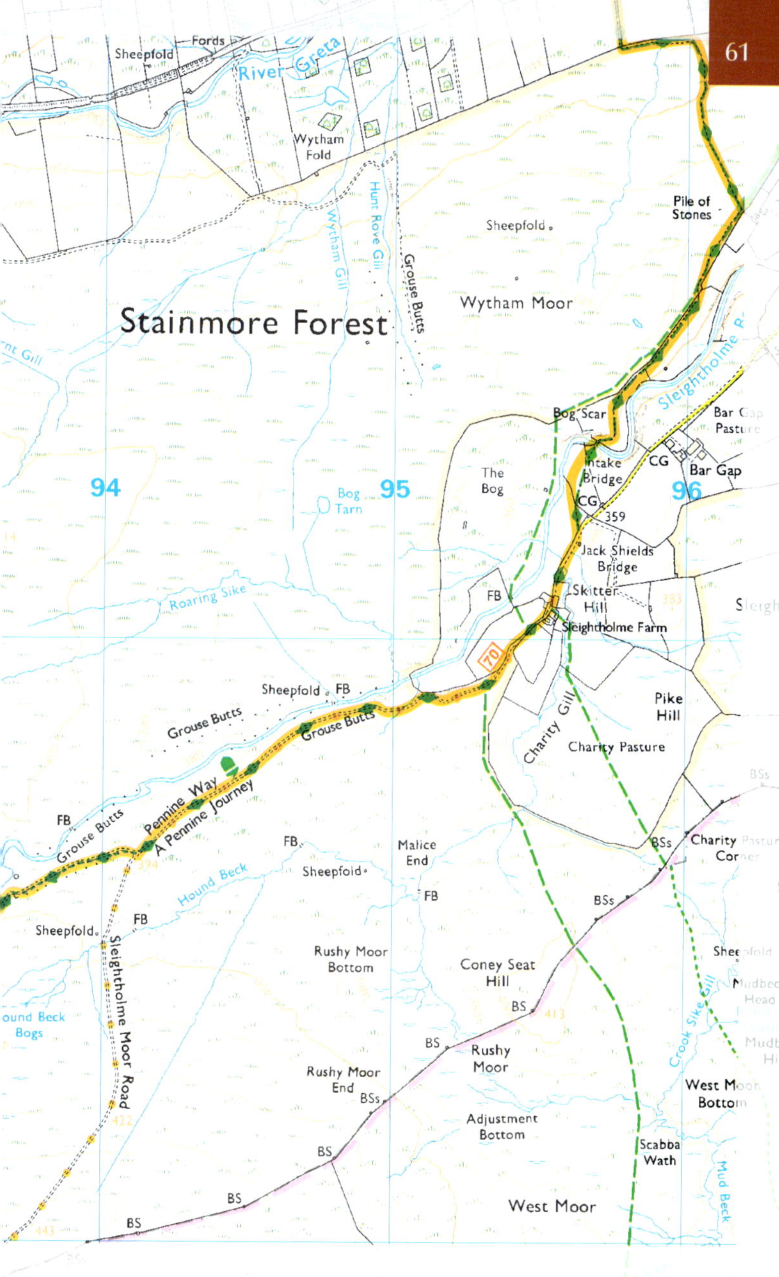

Sheepfold
Fords
River Greta
Wytham Fold
Hunt Rove Gill
Wytham Gill
Grouse Butts
Pile of Stones
Sheepfold
Wytham Moor
Stainmore Forest
Sleightholme Beck
Bog Scar
Bar Gap Pasture
The Bog
Intake Bridge
CG
Bar Gap
94
95
96
Bog Tarn
CG
359
Jack Shields Bridge
Roaring Sike
FB
Skitter Hill
Sleightholme Farm
70
Sheepfold
FB
Grouse Butts
Grouse Butts
Pike Hill
Charity Gill
Charity Pasture
Pennine Way
A Pennine Journey
FB
Grouse Butts
BSs
Charity Pasture Corner
FB
Malice End
Sheepfold
Hound Beck
394
FB
BSs
FB
Sheepfold
Sleightholme Moor Road
Rushy Moor Bottom
Coney Seat Hill
Sheepfold
Mudbeck Head
BS
413
Hound Beck Bogs
BS
Rushy Moor
Crook Sike Gill
Rushy Moor End
BSs
West Moor Bottom
Adjustment Bottom
422
BS
Scabba Wath
Mud Beck
BS
West Moor
BS
443

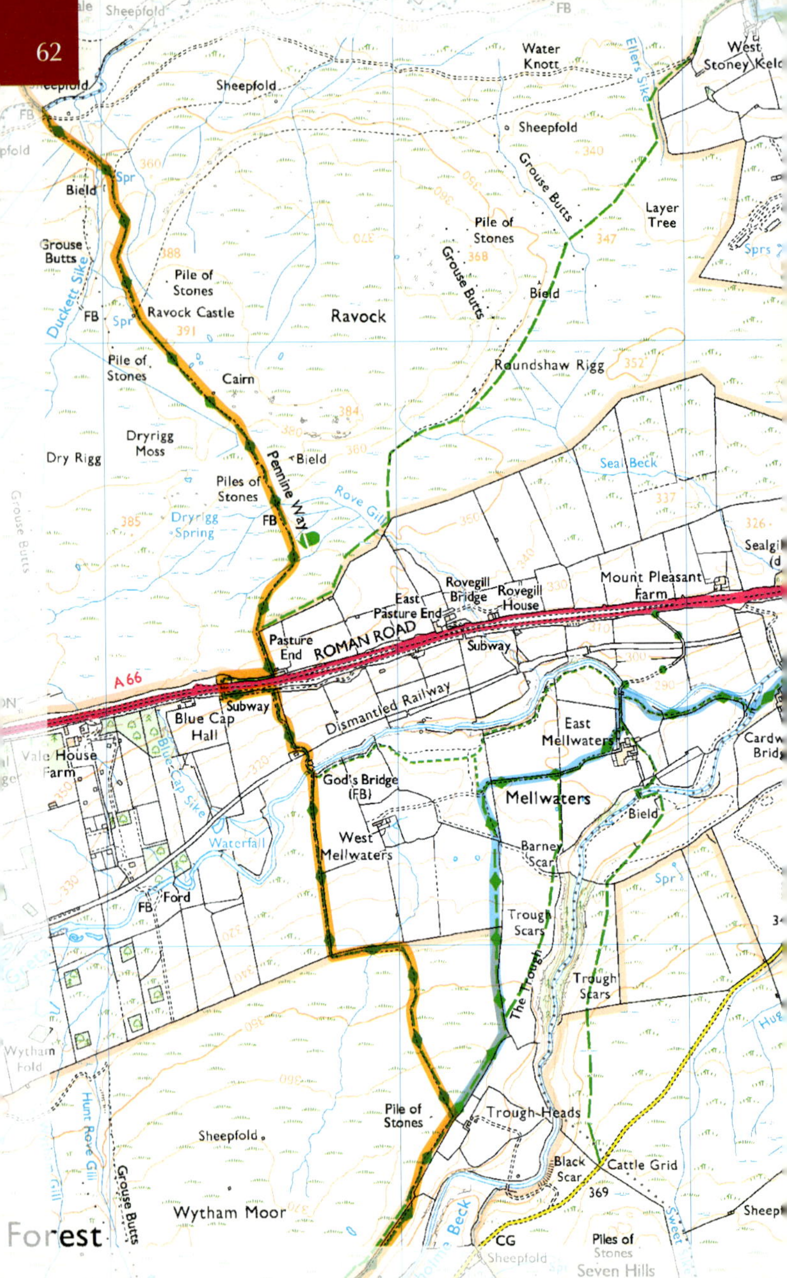
Sheepfold
Water Knott
West Stoney Keld
Sheepfold
Sheepfold
Bield
Grouse Butts
Duckett Sike
Pile of Stones
Ravock Castle
Ravock
Pile of Stones
Grouse Butts
Layer Tree
Bield
Pile of Stones
Cairn
Roundshaw Rigg
Dryrigg Moss
Dry Rigg
Pennine Way
Bield
Piles of Stones
Dryrigg Spring
Rove Gill
Seal Beck
Mount Pleasant Farm
Rovegill Bridge
Rovegill House
East Pasture End
Pasture End
ROMAN ROAD
Subway
A 66
Subway
Blue Cap Hall
Vale House Farm
Blue Cap Sike
Dismantled Railway
East Mellwaters
God's Bridge (FB)
Mellwaters
Bield
West Mellwaters
Waterfall
Barney Scar
Ford
Trough Scars
The Trough
Trough Scars
Wytham Fold
Pile of Stones
Trough Heads
Sheepfold
Hunt Rove Gill
Grouse Butts
Black Scar
Cattle Grid
Wytham Moor
Forest
CG
Sheepfold
Piles of Stones
Seven Hills

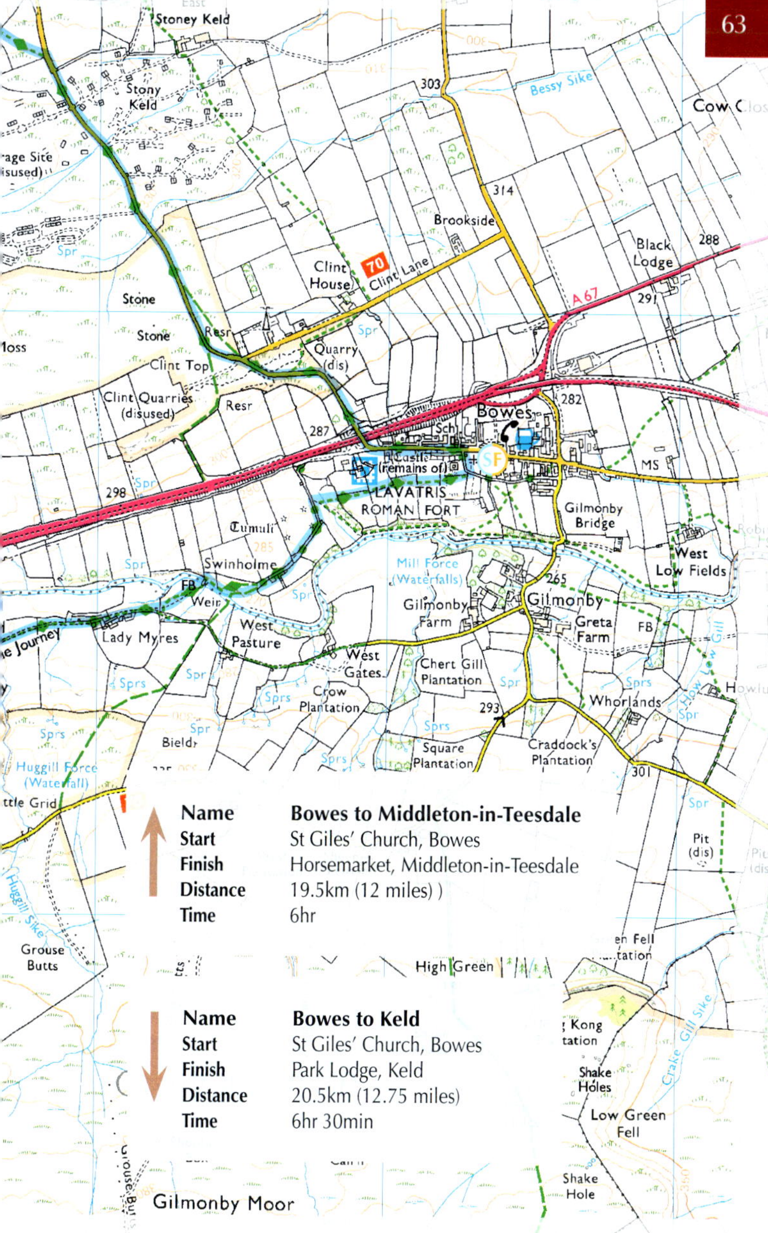

↑	**Name**	**Bowes to Middleton-in-Teesdale**
	Start	St Giles' Church, Bowes
	Finish	Horsemarket, Middleton-in-Teesdale
	Distance	19.5km (12 miles))
	Time	6hr

↓	**Name**	**Bowes to Keld**
	Start	St Giles' Church, Bowes
	Finish	Park Lodge, Keld
	Distance	20.5km (12.75 miles)
	Time	6hr 30min

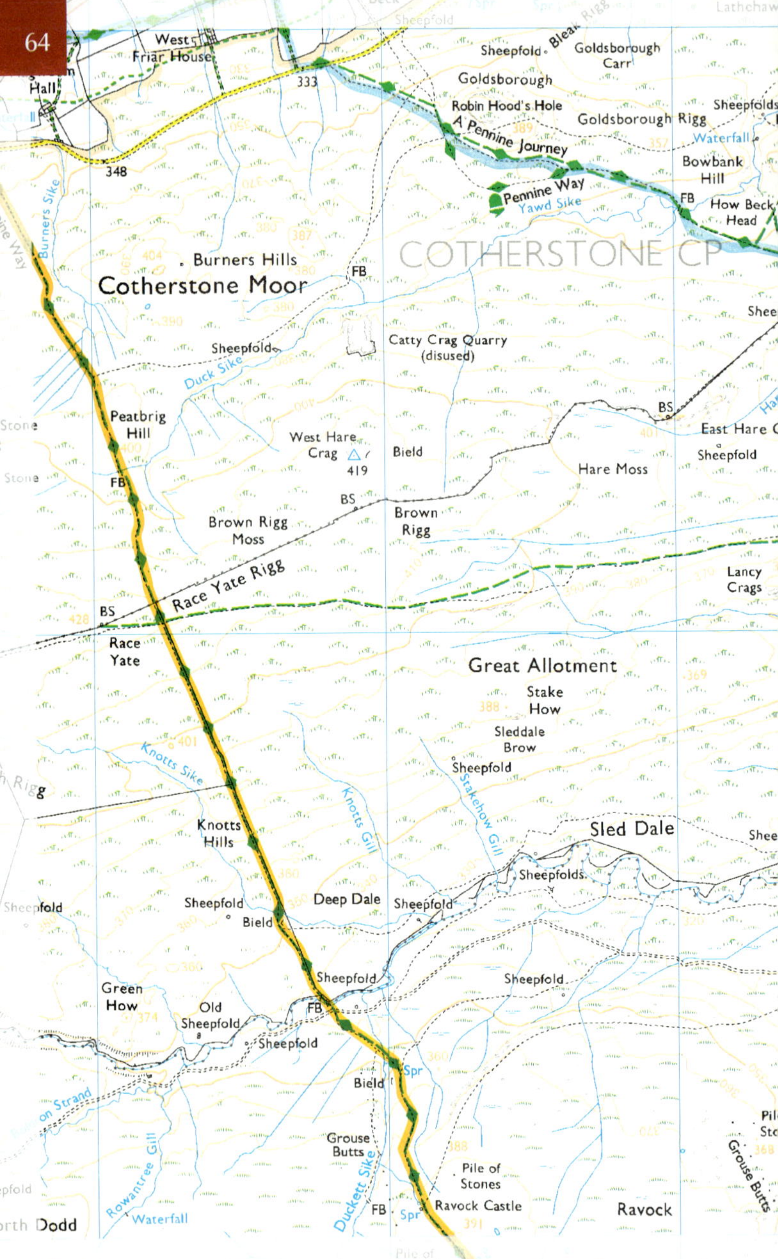

West Friar House
Hall
333
348
Sheepfold
Bleak Rigg
Goldsborough Carr
Goldsborough
Robin Hood's Hole
A Pennine Journey
Goldsborough Rigg
Sheepfolds
Waterfall
Bowbank Hill
Pennine Way
Yawd Sike
FB
How Beck Head
Burners Sike
Burners Hills
Cotherstone Moor
COTHERSTONE CP
FB
Catty Crag Quarry (disused)
Sheepfold
Duck Sike
Peatbrig Hill
FB
West Hare Crag
419
Bield
BS
East Hare
Sheepfold
Hare Moss
BS
Brown Rigg Moss
Brown Rigg
Race Yate Rigg
Lancy Crags
BS
Race Yate
Great Allotment
Stake How
Sleddale Brow
Sheepfold
Knotts Sike
Stakehow Gill
Knotts Gill
Knotts Hills
Sled Dale
Sheepfolds
Sheepfold
Bield
Deep Dale
Sheepfold
Sheepfold
Sheepfold
Green How
Old Sheepfold
FB
Sheepfold
Sheepfold
Bield
Spr
Grouse Butts
Duckett Sike
Pile of Stones
Ravock Castle
FB
Spr
Ravock
Grouse Butts
Rowantree Gill
Waterfall

Loup's Crag
Tinklers Quarry (disused)
Spr
East Loups's
FB
Spr
Butts
Loup's's Hill
Sunny Brow
Ford
Scur Beck
by Well (Spring)
Long Rigg
Grouse Butts
Ravock Plantation
Sheepfold
DANGER AREA
West Loups's
Sprs
Ford
Ravock Rigg
Whitstone Rigg
FB
Gill Feet
Gill Beck
Kearton Rigg
Loup's Plantation
Stonefold Rigg
Battle Hill
Stable Sike
Kirkstreveland Rigg
ld Rigg
Spr
Scotty Rigg
adyfold Crags
Hazelgill Beck
LARTINGTON CP
Nova Scotia
Hazelgill Rigg
Windbreak
Hazelgill
W
Spr
Deepdale Beck
Ford
FB
Levy Pool
Strand Foot
Crag Bridge
Sheepfold
Spr
Stoney Keld
Stonykeld Spring
Spr
East Stoney Keld
Ellers Sike
West Stoney Keld
Tute Hill
Stony Keld
303
Storage Site (disused)
Layer Tree
Spr
Sprs
Philip Hill
Spr
Clint House
70
Clint Lane
Stone

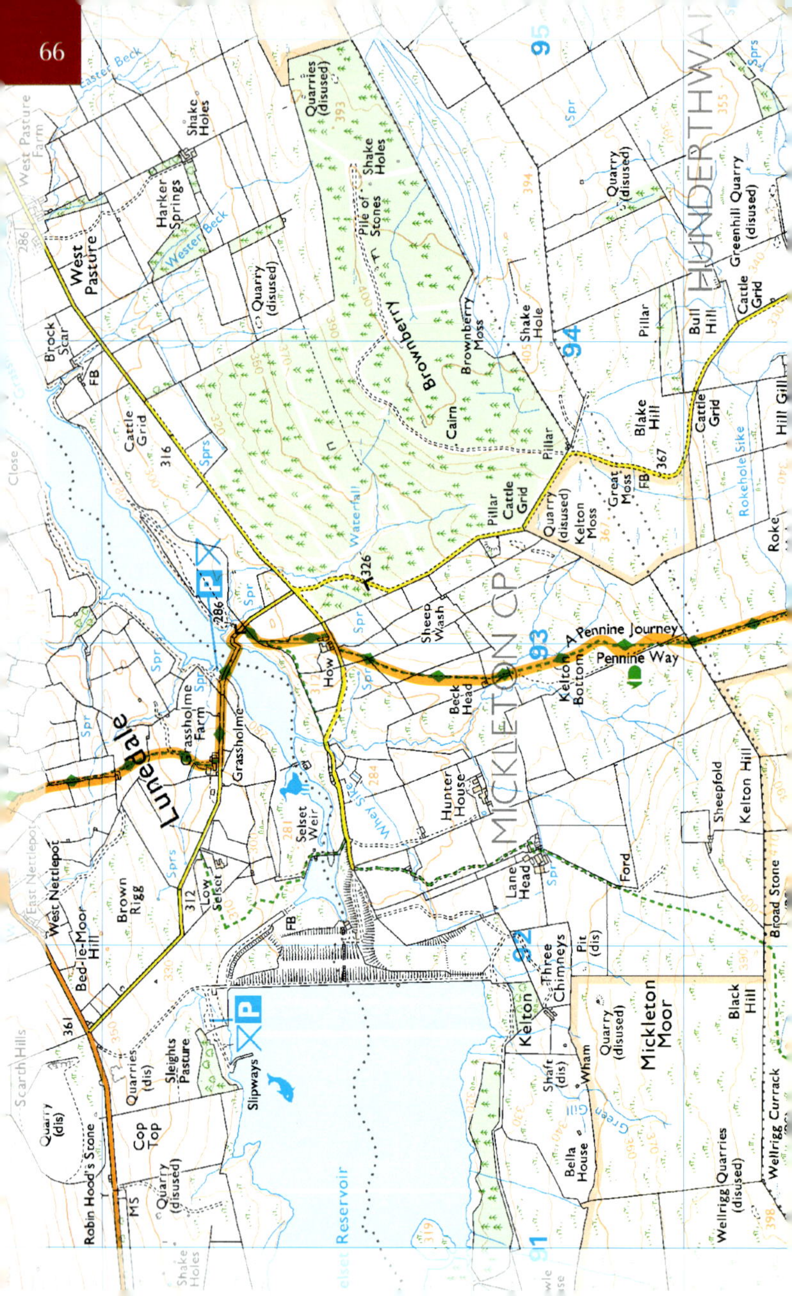

Lunedale
Mickleton CP
Hunderthwaite
Mickleton Moor
Brownberry
Selset Reservoir
Selset Weir
Grassholme
Grassholme Farm
West Pasture
West Pasture Farm
Harker Springs
Wester Beck
Easter Beck
Brock Scar
Shake Holes
Quarries (disused)
Quarry (disused)
Pile of Stones
Brownberry Moss
Shake Hole
Cairn
Pillar
Cattle Grid
Waterfall
Kelton Moss
Great Moss
Blake Hill
Bull Hill
Greenhill Quarry (disused)
Rokehole Sike
Hill Gill
Roke
Sheep Wash
How
Beck Head
Kelton Bottom
Pennine Way
A Pennine Journey
Hunter House
Whey Sike
Lane Head
Ford
Sheepfold
Kelton Hill
Broad Stone
Black Hill
Three Chimneys
Kelton
Pit (dis)
Quarry (disused)
Shaft (dis)
Wham
Green Gill
Bella House
Wellrigg Quarries (disused)
Wellrigg Currack
Low Selset
Brown Rigg
West Nettlepot
East Nettlepot
Bed-le-Moor Hill
Scarth Hills
Quarries (dis)
Sleights Pasture
Slipways
Cop Top
Robin Hood's Stone
Quarry (disused)
MS
Shake Holes
Close
Reservoir

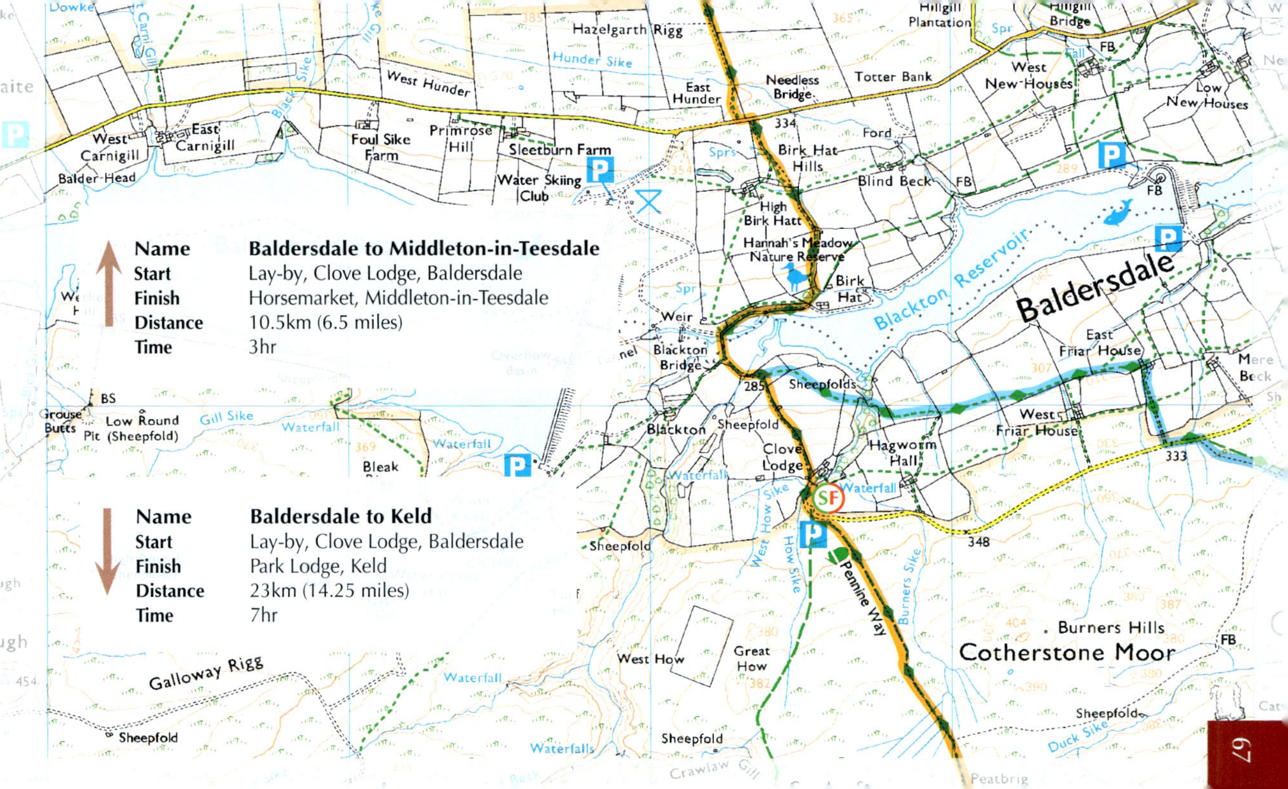

Name	**Baldersdale to Middleton-in-Teesdale**
Start	Lay-by, Clove Lodge, Baldersdale
Finish	Horsemarket, Middleton-in-Teesdale
Distance	10.5km (6.5 miles)
Time	3hr

Name	**Baldersdale to Keld**
Start	Lay-by, Clove Lodge, Baldersdale
Finish	Park Lodge, Keld
Distance	23km (14.25 miles)
Time	7hr

Name	**Middleton-in-Teesdale to Langdon Beck**
Start	Horsemarket, Middleton-in-Teesdale
Finish	Langdon Beck Hotel
Distance	14km (8.75 miles)
Time	4hr 15min

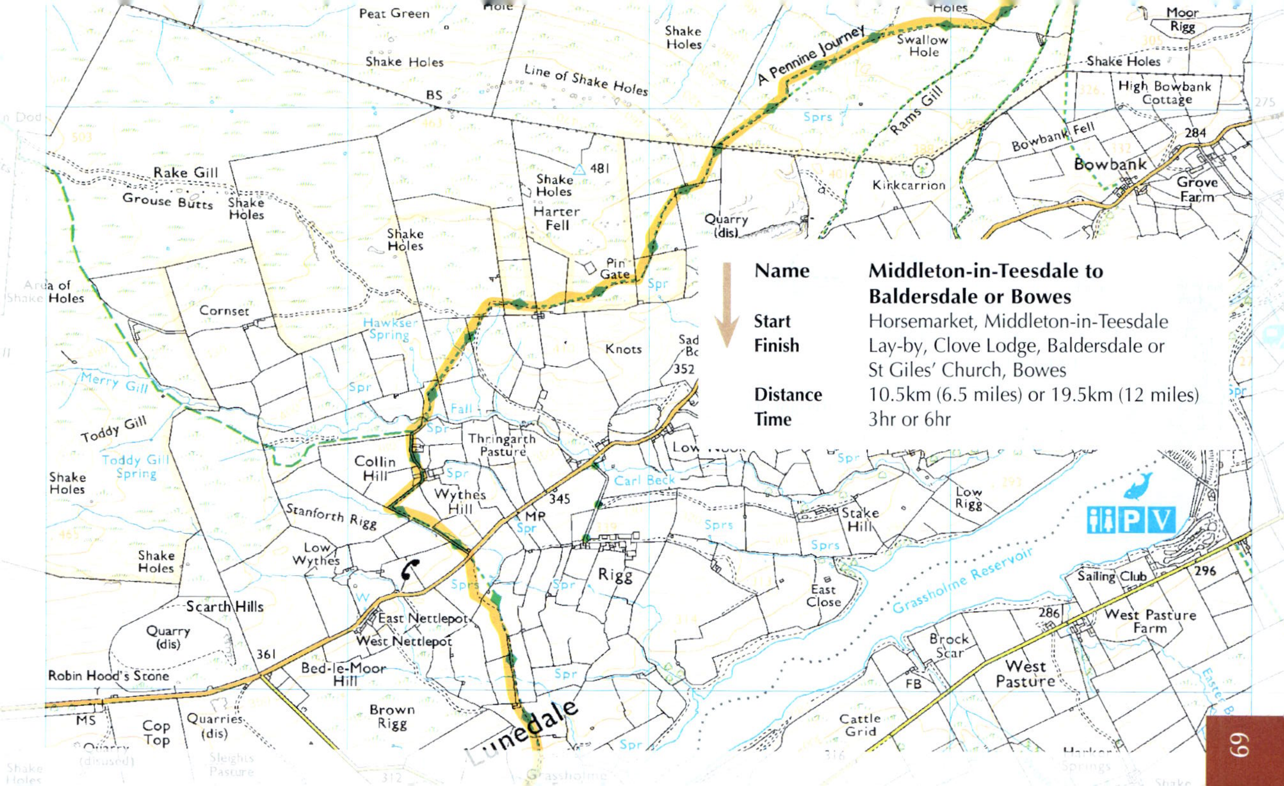
Name
Middleton-in-Teesdale to Baldersdale or Bowes
Start
Horsemarket, Middleton-in-Teesdale
Finish
Lay-by, Clove Lodge, Baldersdale or St Giles' Church, Bowes
Distance
10.5km (6.5 miles) or 19.5km (12 miles)
Time
3hr or 6hr
A Pennine Journey
Peat Green
Shake Holes
Line of Shake Holes
Swallow Hole
Rams Gill
Kirkcarrion
High Bowbank Cottage
Bowbank Fell
Bowbank
Grove Farm
Moor Rigg
Rake Gill
Grouse Butts
Harter Fell
Pin Gate
Quarry (dis)
Knots
Cornset
Hawkser Spring
Merry Gill
Toddy Gill
Toddy Gill Spring
Collin Hill
Thringarth Pasture
Wythes Hill
Stanforth Rigg
Low Wythes
Carl Beck
Rigg
Stake Hill
Low Rigg
East Close
Grassholme Reservoir
Sailing Club
West Pasture Farm
West Pasture
Brock Scar
Cattle Grid
Scarth Hills
East Nettlepot
West Nettlepot
Bed-le-Moor Hill
Robin Hood's Stone
Brown Rigg
Cop Top
Quarries (dis)
Lunedale

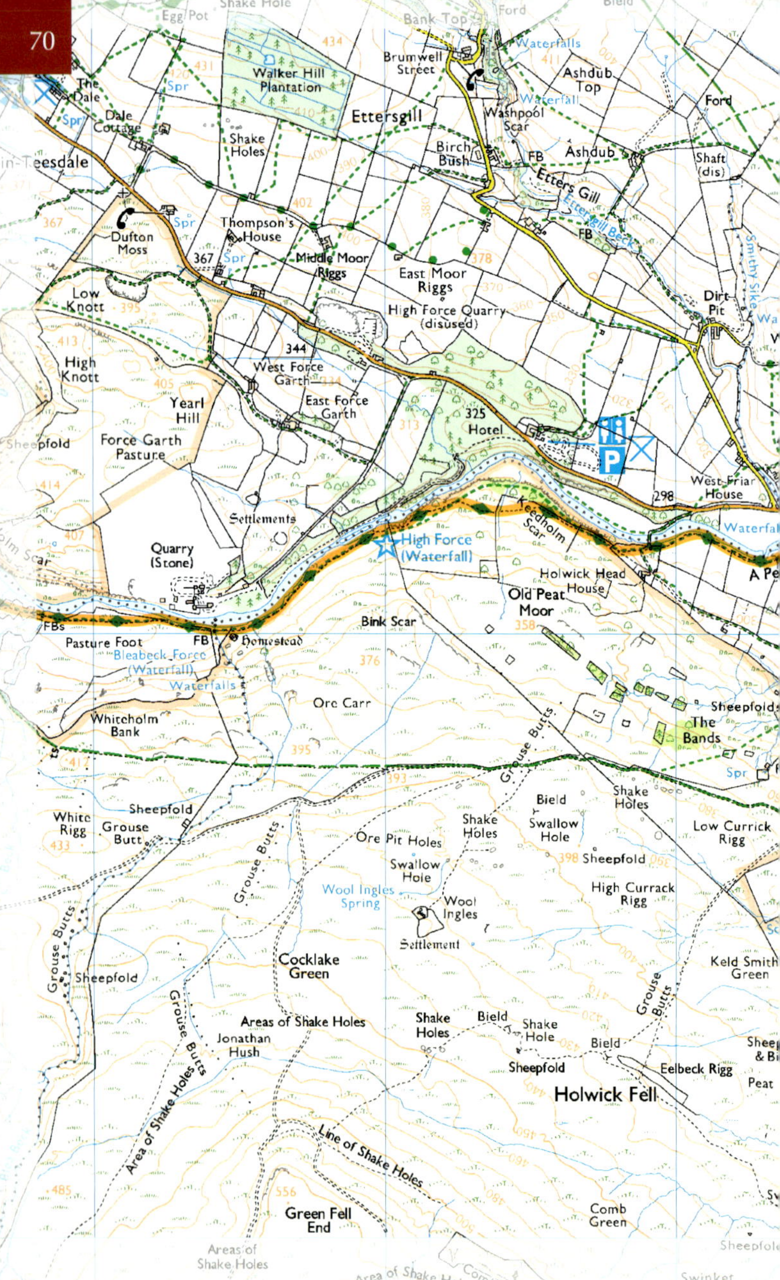

Shake Hole
Egg Pot
Bank Top
Ford
Bield
Walker Hill Plantation
Brumwell Street
Waterfalls
Ashdub Top
Ford
The Dale
Spr
Dale Cottage
Ettersgill
Waterfall
Washpool Scar
Shake Holes
Birch Bush
FB
Ashdub
Shaft (dis)
-in-Teesdale
Etters Gill
Ettersgill Beck
Thompson's House
Dufton Moss
Middle Moor Riggs
East Moor Riggs
Smithy Sike
Low Knott
High Force Quarry (disused)
Dirt Pit
High Knott
West Force Garth
East Force Garth
Yearl Hill
Hotel
Sheepfold
Force Garth Pasture
West Friar House
Settlements
Keedholm Scar
Quarry (Stone)
High Force (Waterfall)
Holwick Head House
Old Peat Moor
Holm Scar
Bink Scar
FBs
Pasture Foot
FB
Homestead
Bleabeck Force (Waterfall)
Waterfalls
Ore Carr
Sheepfolds
The Bands
Whitcholm Bank
Grouse Butts
Spr
Bield
Shake Holes
White Rigg
Sheepfold
Grouse Butt
Ore Pit Holes
Swallow Hole
Low Currick Rigg
Sheepfold
Wool Ingles Spring
Wool Ingles
High Currack Rigg
Settlement
Cocklake Green
Keld Smith Green
Sheepfold
Areas of Shake Holes
Shake Holes
Bield
Shake Hole
Jonathan Hush
Bield
Sheepfold
Eelbeck Rigg
Holwick Fell
Peat
Area of Shake Holes
Line of Shake Holes
Comb Green
Green Fell End
Areas of Shake Holes
Swinket

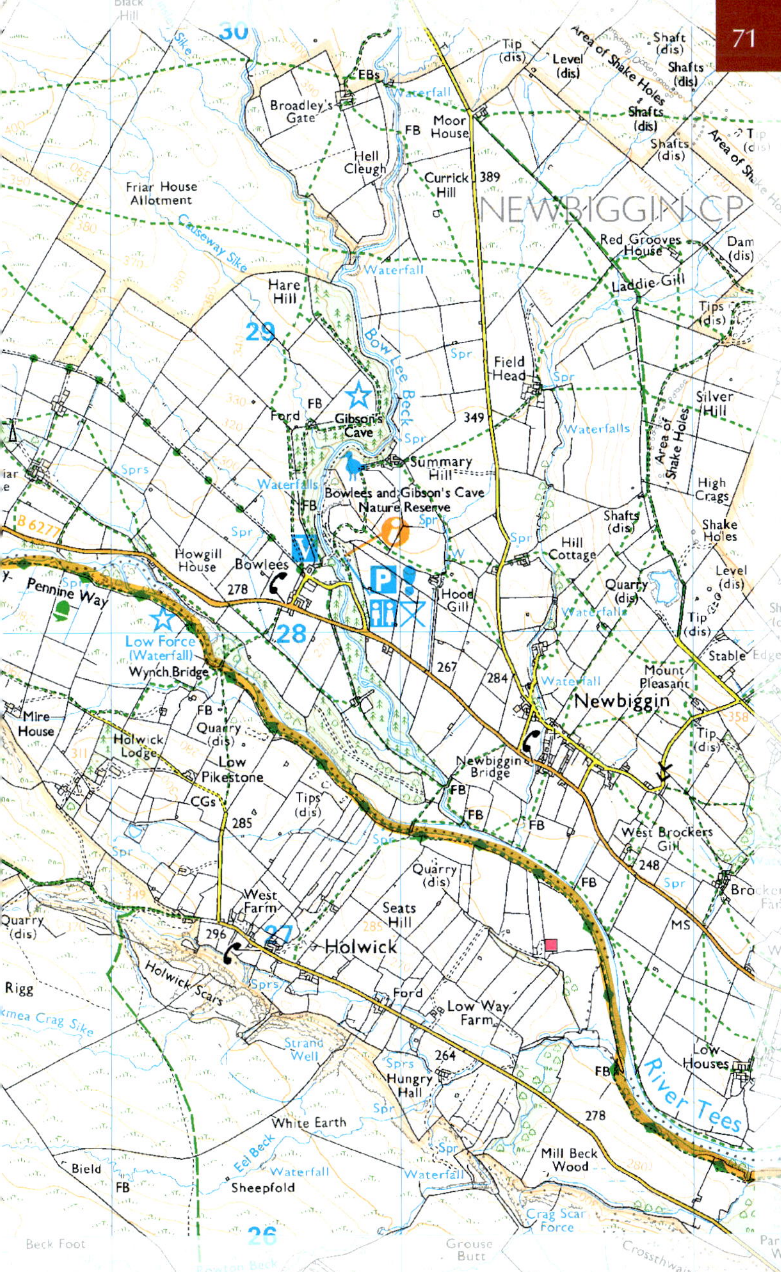
Black Hill
Broadley's Gate
Moor House
Hell Cleugh
Currick Hill
389
Friar House Allotment
Causeway Sike
NEWBIGGIN CP
Area of Shake Holes
Shafts (dis)
Level (dis)
Tip (dis)
Red Grooves House
Laddie Gill
Hare Hill
Waterfall
Bow Lee Beck
Field Head
Silver Hill
Ford
Gibson's Cave
349
Summary Hill
Waterfalls
Bowlees and Gibson's Cave Nature Reserve
High Crags
Shake Holes
Hill Cottage
Howgill House
Bowlees
278
Pennine Way
Hood Gill
Quarry (dis)
Low Force (Waterfall)
Wynch Bridge
B 6277
267
284
Stable Edge
Mount Pleasant
Newbiggin
Mire House
Holwick Lodge
Quarry (dis)
Low Pikestone
Newbiggin Bridge
Tips (dis)
CGs
285
West Brockers Gill
248
Quarry (dis)
Seats Hill
West Farm
296
Holwick
Holwick Scars
Ford
Low Way Farm
Rigg
Strand Well
264
Hungry Hall
Low Houses
River Tees
278
White Earth
Eel Beck
Waterfall
Sheepfold
Bield
Mill Beck Wood
Crag Scar Force
Beck Foot
Grouse Butt

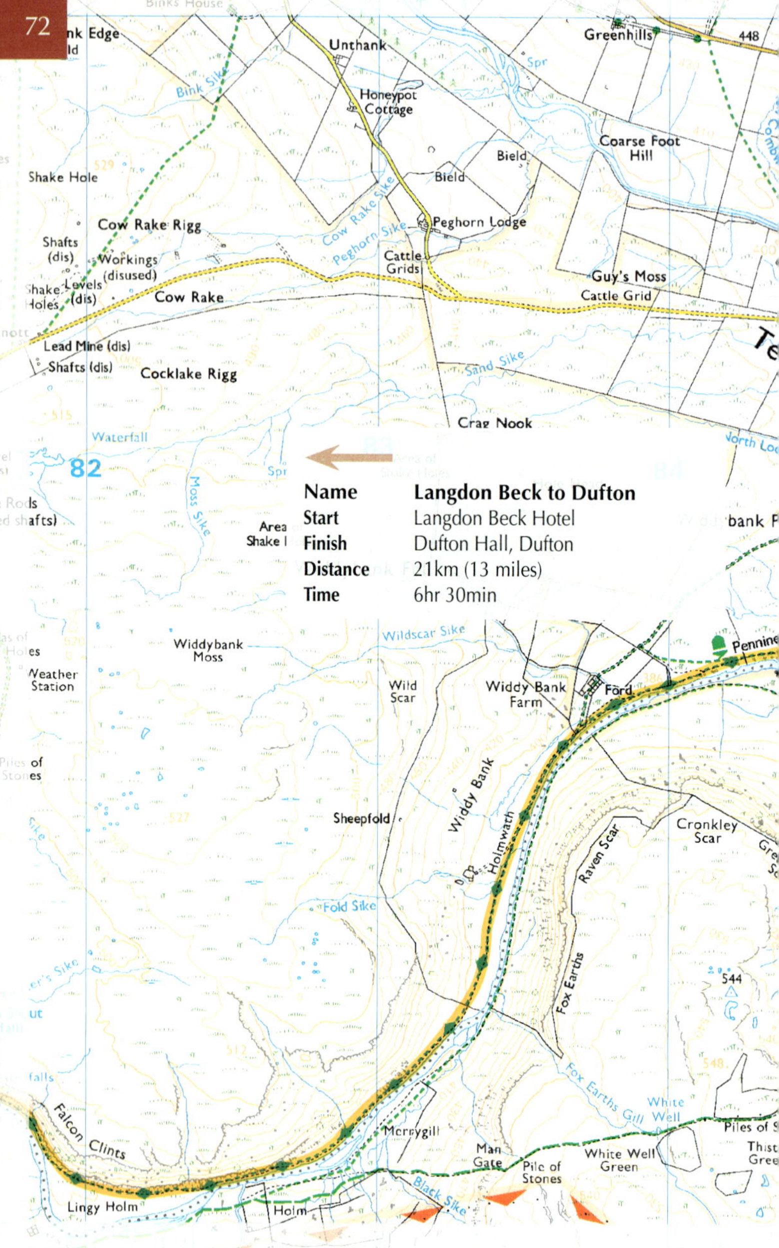

Name	Langdon Beck to Dufton
Start	Langdon Beck Hotel
Finish	Dufton Hall, Dufton
Distance	21km (13 miles)
Time	6hr 30min

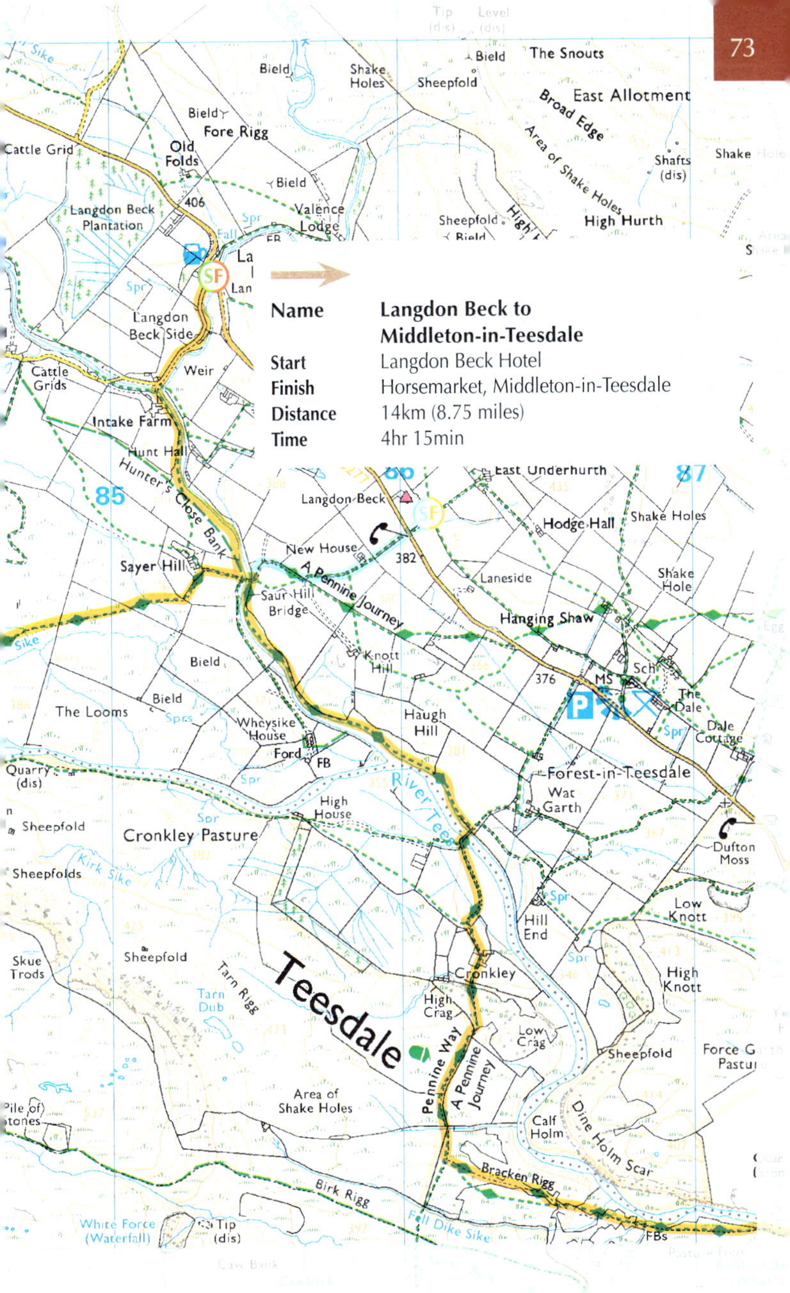

Name	**Langdon Beck to Middleton-in-Teesdale**
Start	Langdon Beck Hotel
Finish	Horsemarket, Middleton-in-Teesdale
Distance	14km (8.75 miles)
Time	4hr 15min

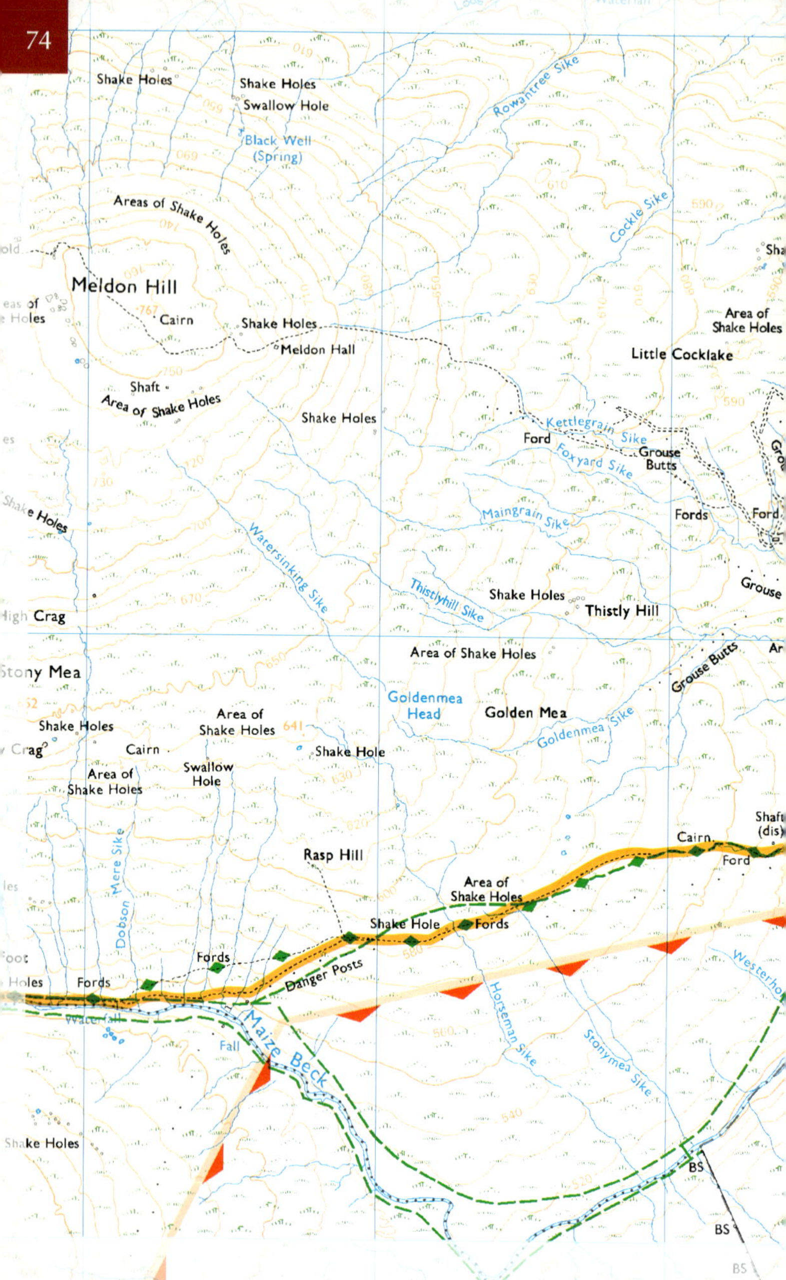

Shake Holes
Shake Holes
Swallow Hole
Black Well (Spring)
Rowantree Sike
Areas of Shake Holes
Cockle Sike
Meldon Hill
Cairn
Shake Holes
Meldon Hall
Area of Shake Holes
Little Cocklake
Shaft
Area of Shake Holes
Shake Holes
Kettlegrain Sike
Ford
Foxyard Sike
Grouse Butts
Fords
Ford
Maingrain Sike
Shake Holes
Watersinking Sike
Thistlyhill Sike
Shake Holes
Thistly Hill
Grouse
High Crag
Area of Shake Holes
Stony Mea
Grouse Butts
Goldenmea Head
Golden Mea
Goldenmea Sike
Shake Holes
Area of Shake Holes
Crag
Cairn
Shake Hole
Area of Shake Holes
Swallow Hole
Dobson Mere Sike
Rasp Hill
Cairn
Ford
Area of Shake Holes
Shake Hole
Fords
Fords
Danger Posts
Fords
Holes
Waterfall
Maize Beck
Fall
Horseman Sike
Stonymea Sike
Westerhop
Shake Holes
BS
BS
BS

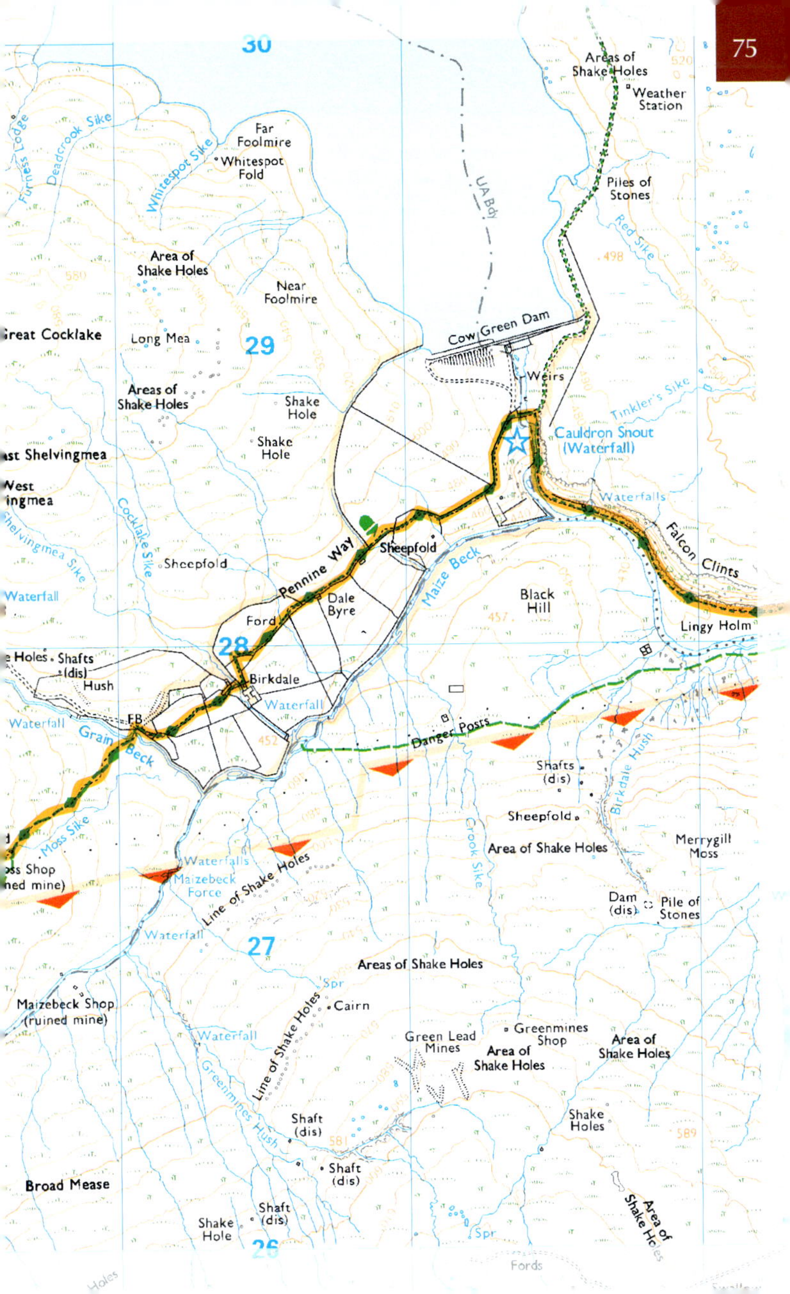

30
Areas of Shake Holes
Weather Station
Furness Lodge
Deadcrook Sike
Far Foolmire
Whitespot Sike
Whitespot Fold
UA Bdy
Piles of Stones
Red Sike
Area of Shake Holes
Near Foolmire
Great Cocklake
Long Mea
29
Cow Green Dam
Weirs
Areas of Shake Holes
Shake Hole
Tinkler's Sike
Cauldron Snout (Waterfall)
Shake Hole
East Shelvingmea
West Shelvingmea
Waterfalls
Falcon Clints
Cocklake Sike
Shelvingmea Sike
Sheepfold
Pennine Way
Sheepfold
Maize Beck
Black Hill
Waterfall
Dale Byre
Ford
Lingy Holm
28
Shake Holes
Shafts (dis)
Hush
Birkdale
Waterfall
Waterfall
FB
Grain Beck
Danger Posts
Shafts (dis)
Birkdale Hush
Moss Sike
Sheepfold
Crook Sike
Area of Shake Holes
Merrygill Moss
Moss Shop (ruined mine)
Waterfalls
Maizebeck Force
Line of Shake Holes
Dam (dis)
Pile of Stones
Waterfall
27
Areas of Shake Holes
Spr
Cairn
Maizebeck Shop (ruined mine)
Line of Shake Holes
Waterfall
Green Lead Mines
Greenmines Shop
Area of Shake Holes
Area of Shake Holes
Greenmines Hush
Shaft (dis)
Shake Holes
Shaft (dis)
Broad Mease
Shaft (dis)
Shake Hole
Area of Shake Holes
Spr
26
Fords

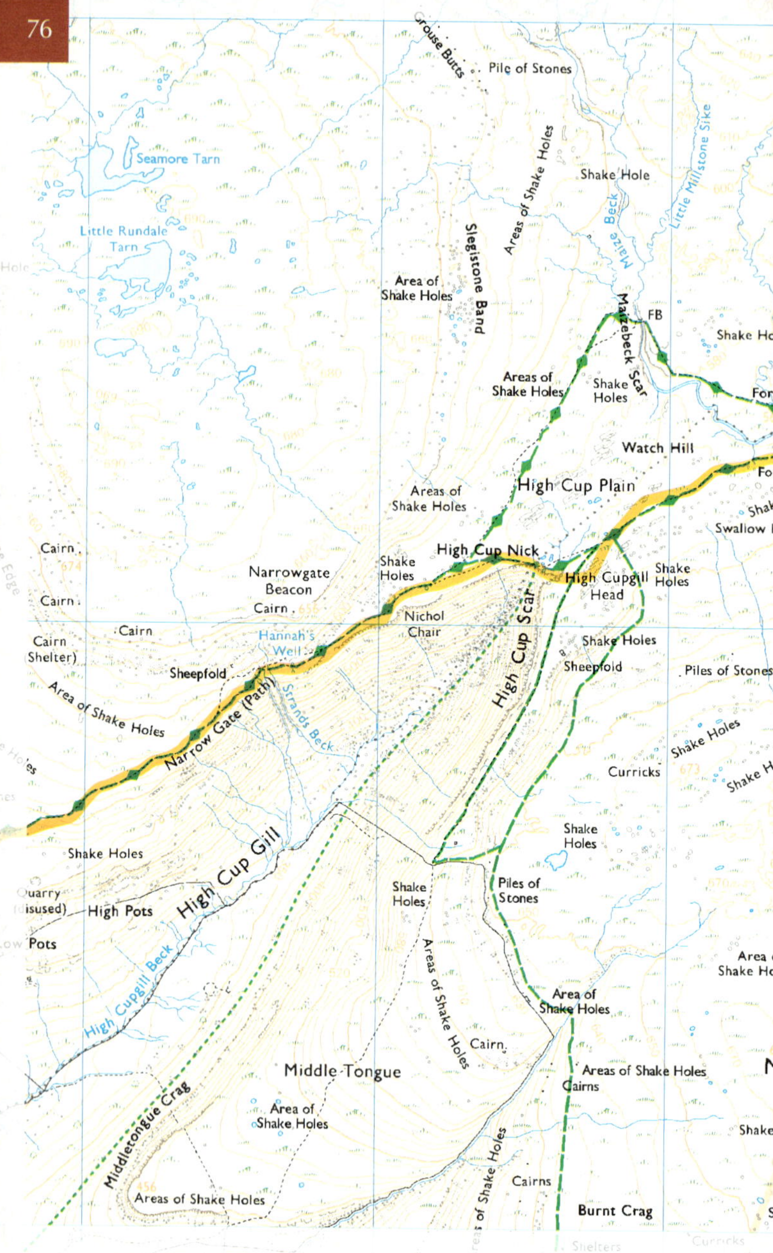

Grouse Butts
Pile of Stones
Seamore Tarn
Little Rundale Tarn
Areas of Shake Holes
Shake Hole
Maize Beck
Little Millstone Sike
Slegistone Band
Area of Shake Holes
Maizebeck Scar
FB
Shake Holes
Areas of Shake Holes
Shake Holes
Watch Hill
High Cup Plain
Areas of Shake Holes
Swallow H
Cairn
Cairn
High Cup Nick
Narrowgate Beacon
Shake Holes
High Cupgill Head
Shake Holes
Cairn
Nichol Chair
Cairn
Cairn (Shelter)
Hannah's Well
Shake Holes
Sheepfold
Sheepfold
Piles of Stones
High Cup Scar
Area of Shake Holes
Narrow Gate (Path)
Strands Beck
Shake Holes
Curricks
Shake Holes
Shake Holes
High Cup Gill
Shake Holes
Quarry (disused)
High Pots
Low Pots
Piles of Stones
High Cupgill Beck
Areas of Shake Holes
Area of Shake Holes
Cairn
Middle Tongue
Areas of Shake Holes
Cairns
Middletongue Crag
Area of Shake Holes
Areas of Shake Holes
Areas of Shake Holes
Cairns
Burnt Crag

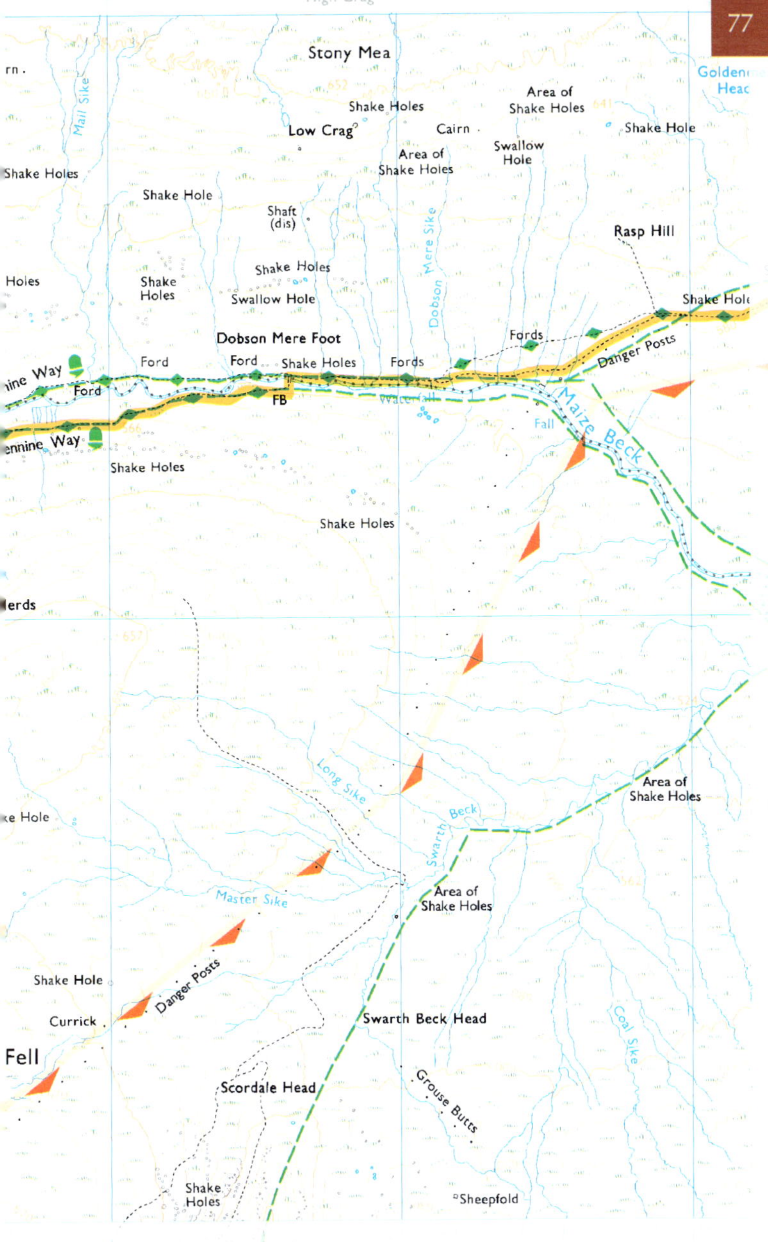
High Crag
Stony Mea
Low Crag
Shake Holes
Area of
Shake Holes
Cairn
Swallow
Hole
Shake Hole
Goldenq
Head
Shake Holes
Shake Hole
Shaft
(dis)
Rasp Hill
Shake Holes
Swallow Hole
Dobson Mere Sike
Holes
Shake
Holes
Dobson Mere Foot
Fords
Shake Hole
Danger Posts
Ford
Ford
Shake Holes
Fords
Pennine Way
Ford
FB
Waterfall
Fall
Maize Beck
Pennine Way
Shake Holes
Shake Holes
Herds
Long Sike
Area of
Shake Holes
Swarth Beck
Shake Hole
Master Sike
Area of
Shake Holes
Shake Hole
Danger Posts
Currick
Swarth Beck Head
Coal Sike
Fell
Scordale Head
Grouse Butts
Shake
Holes
Sheepfold
Mail Sike

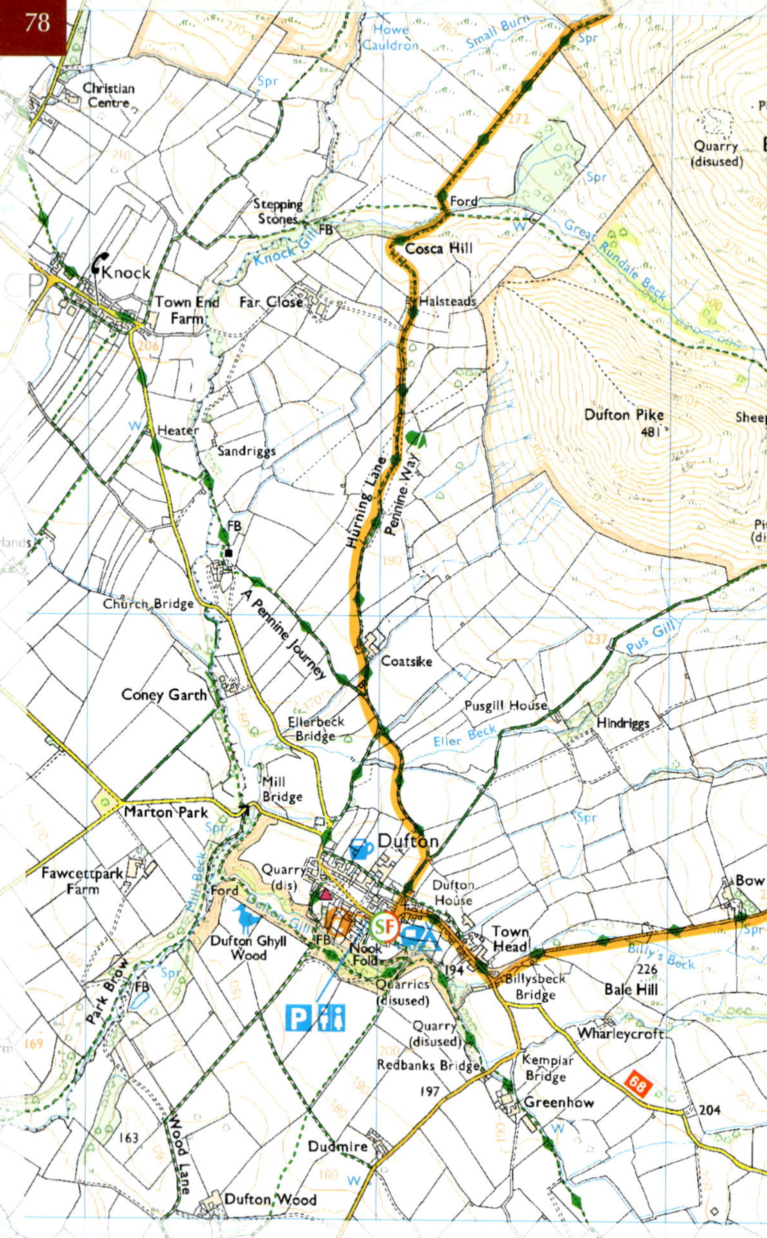
Howe Cauldron
Small Burn
Spr
Christian Centre
272
Quarry (disused)
Stepping Stones
FB
Ford
Knock Gill
Cosca Hill
Great Rundale Beck
Knock
Town End Farm
Far Close
Halsteads
206
Dufton Pike
481
Heater
Sandriggs
Hurning Lane
Pennine Way
FB
190
Church Bridge
A Pennine Journey
237
Pus Gill
Coatsike
Coney Garth
Pusgill House
Hindriggs
Ellerbeck Bridge
Eller Beck
Mill Bridge
Marton Park
Dufton
Fawcettpark Farm
Quarry (dis)
Dufton House
Bow
Ford
Dufton Gill
Mill Beck
Dufton Ghyll Wood
FB
Nook Fold
SF
Town Head
Billy's Beck
194
Billysbeck Bridge
226
Bale Hill
Park Brow
FB
Quarries (disused)
Quarry (disused)
Wharleycroft
169
Redbanks Bridge
Kemplar Bridge
68
197
Greenhow
204
163
Wood Lane
Dudmire
Dufton Wood

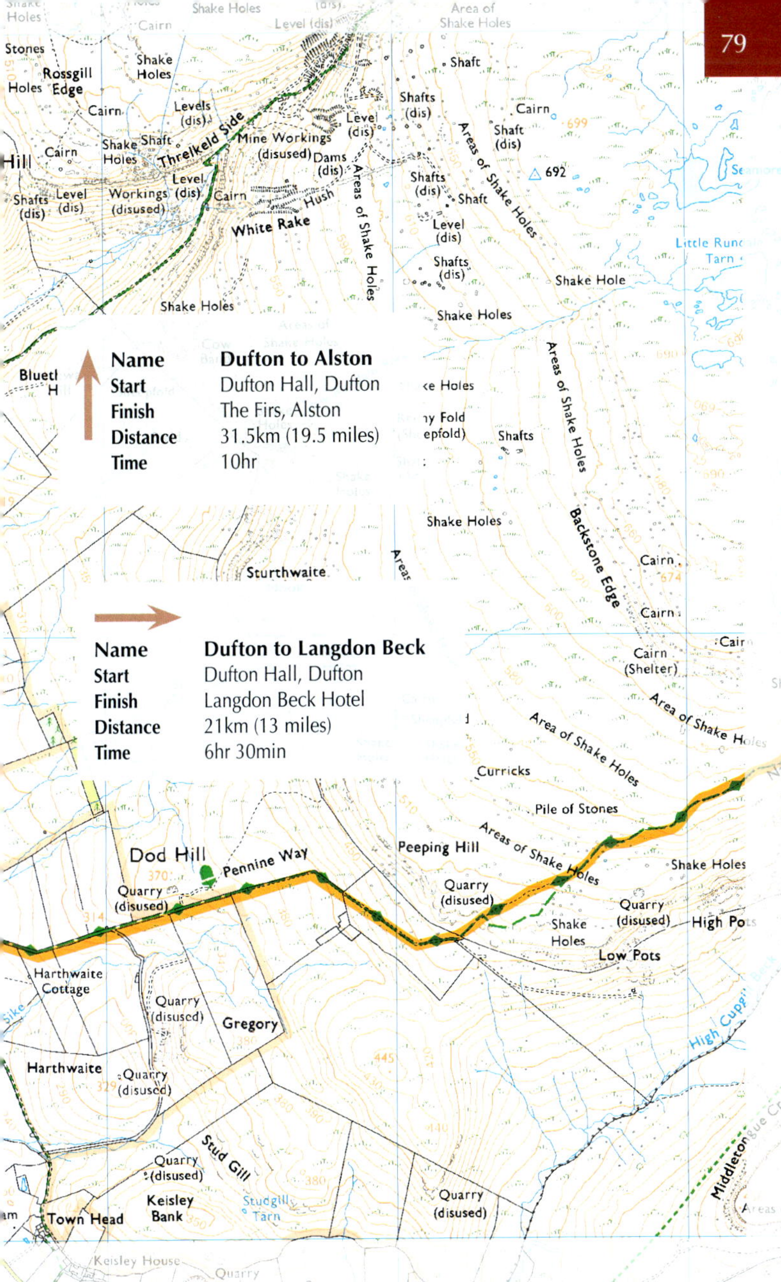

Name	**Dufton to Alston**
Start	Dufton Hall, Dufton
Finish	The Firs, Alston
Distance	31.5km (19.5 miles)
Time	10hr

Name	**Dufton to Langdon Beck**
Start	Dufton Hall, Dufton
Finish	Langdon Beck Hotel
Distance	21km (13 miles)
Time	6hr 30min

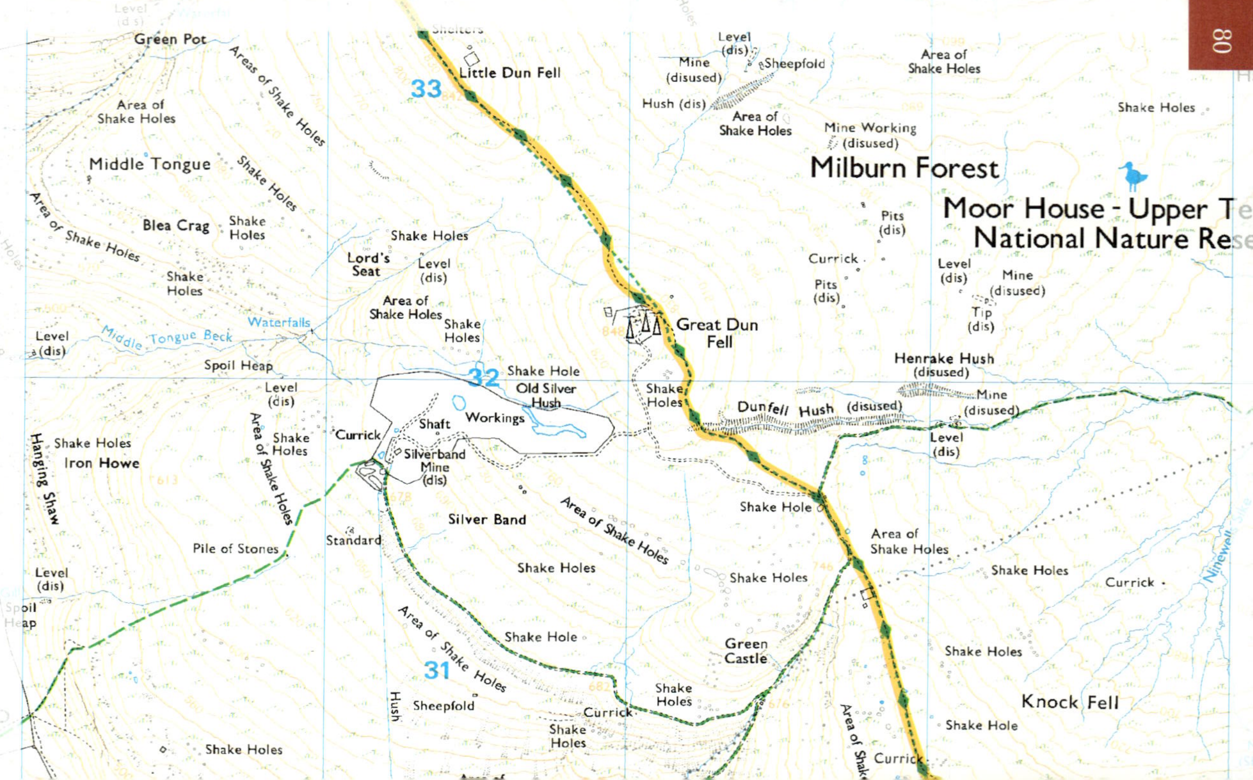
Green Pot
Areas of Shake Holes
Area of Shake Holes
Middle Tongue
Shake Holes
Blea Crag
Shake Holes
Area of Shake Holes
Shake Holes
Level (dis)
Middle Tongue Beck
Waterfalls
Spoil Heap
Lord's Seat
Shake Holes
Level (dis)
Area of Shake Holes
Shake Holes
33
Little Dun Fell
Mine (disused)
Level (dis)
Sheepfold
Hush (dis)
Area of Shake Holes
Mine Working (disused)
Area of Shake Holes
Shake Holes
Milburn Forest
Moor House - Upper Tees
National Nature Reser
Pits (dis)
Currick
Pits (dis)
Level (dis)
Mine (disused)
Tip (dis)
Great Dun Fell
Henrake Hush (disused)
32
Shake Hole
Old Silver Hush
Workings
Shaft
Shake Holes
Dunfell Hush (disused)
Mine (disused)
Level (dis)
Level (dis)
Shake Holes
Area of Shake Holes
Currick
Silverband Mine (dis)
Hanging Shaw
Shake Holes
Iron Howe
Silver Band
Area of Shake Holes
Shake Hole
Area of Shake Holes
Standard
Pile of Stones
Shake Holes
Shake Holes
Shake Holes
Currick
Nineveh Sike
Level (dis)
Spoil Heap
Shake Hole
Green Castle
Shake Holes
31
Area of Shake Holes
Hush
Sheepfold
Currick
Shake Holes
Shake Holes
Area of Shake Holes
Knock Fell
Shake Hole
Currick
Shake Holes

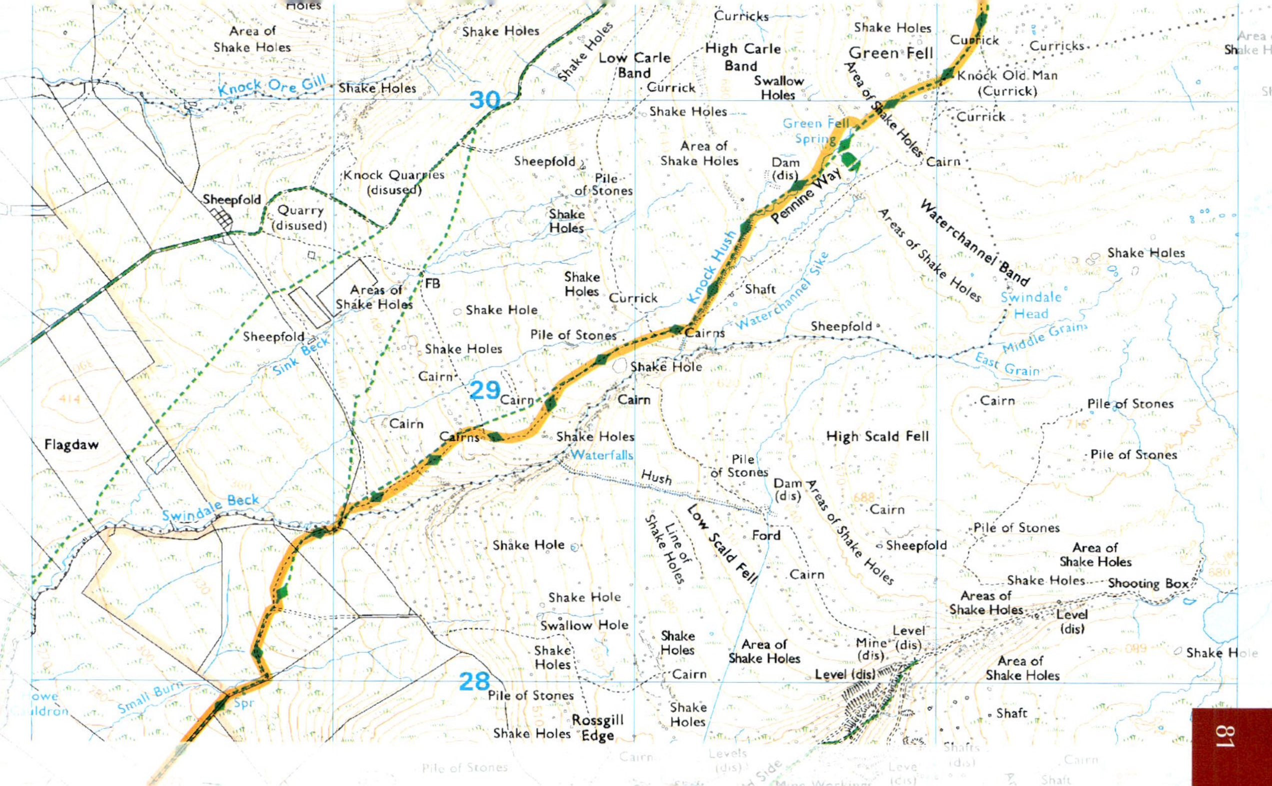
Area of Shake Holes
Shake Holes
Knock Ore Gill
Low Carle Band
Currick
Curricks
High Carle Band
Swallow Holes
Green Fell
Knock Old Man (Currick)
Area of Shake Holes
Green Fell Spring
Dam (dis)
Pennine Way
Cairn
Waterchannel Band
Areas of Shake Holes
Swindale Head
Middle Grain
East Grain
Sheepfold
Pile of Stones
Knock Quarries (disused)
Quarry (disused)
Knock Hush
Shaft
Waterchannel Sike
Cairns
Areas of Shake Holes
FB
Shake Hole
Sink Beck
29
30
28
Flagdaw
Waterfalls
Hush
High Scald Fell
Low Scald Fell
Line of Shake Holes
Ford
Swindale Beck
Swallow Hole
Shooting Box
Level (dis)
Mine (dis)
Rossgill Edge
Small Burn
Spr
Shaft

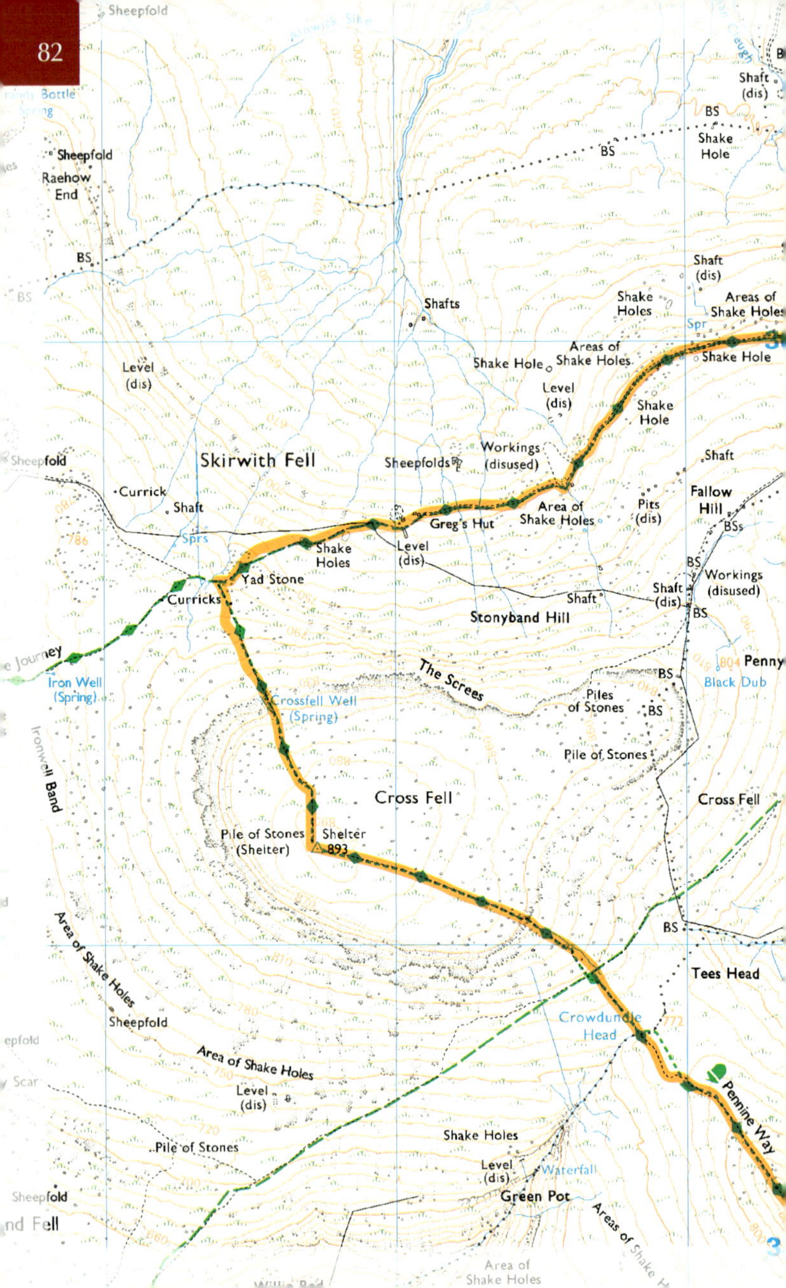
Sheepfold
Alnwick Sike
Shaft (dis)
BS
Shake Hole
Sheepfold
Raehow End
BS
Shaft (dis)
Shafts
Shake Holes
Areas of Shake Holes
Spr
Level (dis)
Shake Hole
Areas of Shake Holes
Shake Hole
Level (dis)
Shake Hole
Sheepfold
Skirwith Fell
Sheepfolds
Workings (disused)
Shaft
Currick
Shaft
Area of Shake Holes
Pits (dis)
Fallow Hill
BSs
786
Sprs
Greg's Hut
Shake Holes
Level (dis)
Yad Stone
Curricks
BS
Workings (disused)
Shaft
Shaft (dis)
BS
Stonyband Hill
Journey
The Screes
BS
804
Penny
Iron Well (Spring)
Crossfell Well (Spring)
Piles of Stones
BS
Black Dub
Ironwell Band
Pile of Stones
Cross Fell
Cross Fell
Pile of Stones (Shelter)
Shelter 893
BS
Tees Head
Area of Shake Holes
Sheepfold
Crowdundle Head
772
Area of Shake Holes
Pennine Way
Level (dis)
Shake Holes
Pile of Stones
Level (dis)
Waterfall
Sheepfold
Green Pot
Areas of Shake Holes
Area of Shake Holes

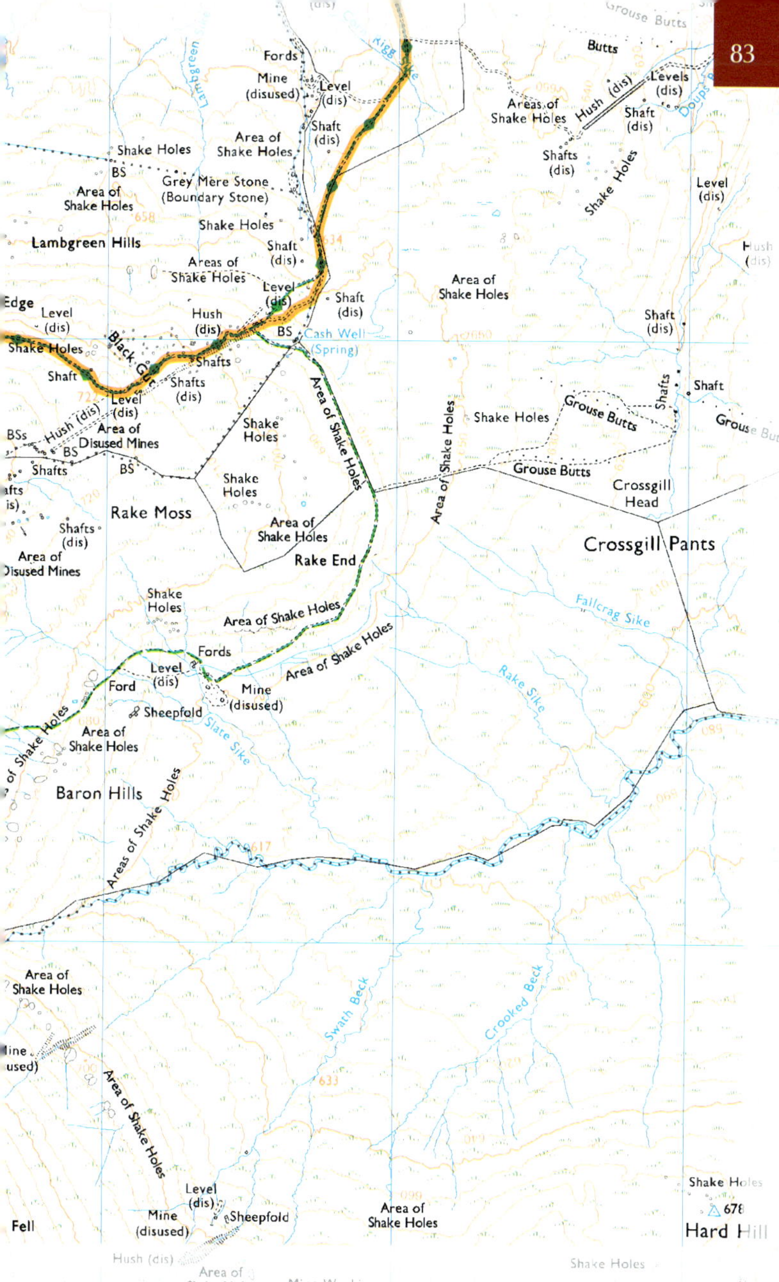
Fords
Mine (disused)
Level (dis)
Shaft (dis)
Area of Shake Holes
Shake Holes
BS
Grey Mere Stone (Boundary Stone)
Area of Shake Holes
Shake Holes
Lambgreen Hills
Shaft (dis)
Areas of Shake Holes
Level (dis)
Shaft (dis)
Edge
Level (dis)
Hush (dis)
BS
Cash Well (Spring)
Shake Holes
Black Gutter
Shafts
Shaft
Shafts (dis)
Level (dis)
Hush (dis)
Area of Disused Mines
BSs
BS
Shafts
BS
Shake Holes
Shake Holes
Area of Shake Holes
Rake Moss
Shafts (dis)
Area of Disused Mines
Area of Shake Holes
Rake End
Shake Holes
Area of Shake Holes
Fords
Level (dis)
Ford
Mine (disused)
Area of Shake Holes
Sheepfold
Slate Sike
Area of Shake Holes
Baron Hills
Areas of Shake Holes
Butts
Levels (dis)
Areas of Shake Holes
Hush (dis)
Shaft (dis)
Shafts (dis)
Shake Holes
Level (dis)
Hush (dis)
Area of Shake Holes
Shaft (dis)
Shafts
Shaft
Shake Holes
Grouse Butts
Area of Shake Holes
Grouse Butts
Crossgill Head
Crossgill Pants
Fallcrag Sike
Rake Sike
Area of Shake Holes
Shake Holes
Area of Shake Holes
Swath Beck
Crooked Beck
Area of Shake Holes
Level (dis)
Mine (disused)
Sheepfold
Fell
Area of Shake Holes
Shake Holes
678
Hard Hill
Hush (dis)
Shake Holes

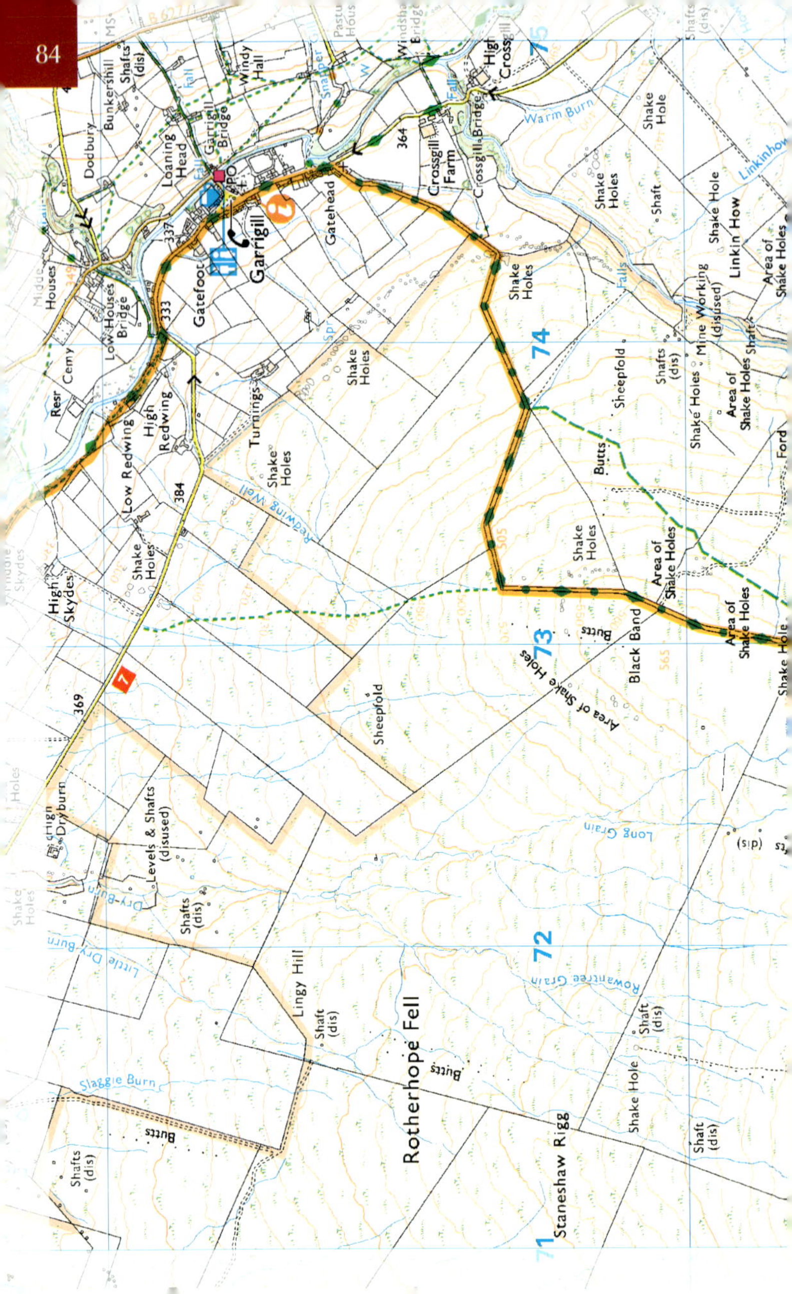

Garrigill
Gatefoot
Gatehead
Loaning Head
Garrigill Bridge
PO
Windy Hall
Dodbury
Bunkershill
Shafts (dis)
Middle Houses
Low Houses Bridge
Cemy
Resr
Low Redwing
High Redwing
Turnings
Crossgill Farm
Crossgill Bridge
High Crossgill
Warm Burn
Redwing Well
High Skydes
High Dryburn
Dry Burn
Little Dry Burn
Slaggie Burn
Levels & Shafts (disused)
Lingy Hill
Rotherhope Fell
Staneshaw Rigg
Rowantree Grain
Long Grain
Sheepfold
Area of Shake Holes
Black Band
Butts
Shake Holes
Mine Working (disused)
Linkin How
Ford
369
384
333
337
364
505
565
71
72
73
74
75

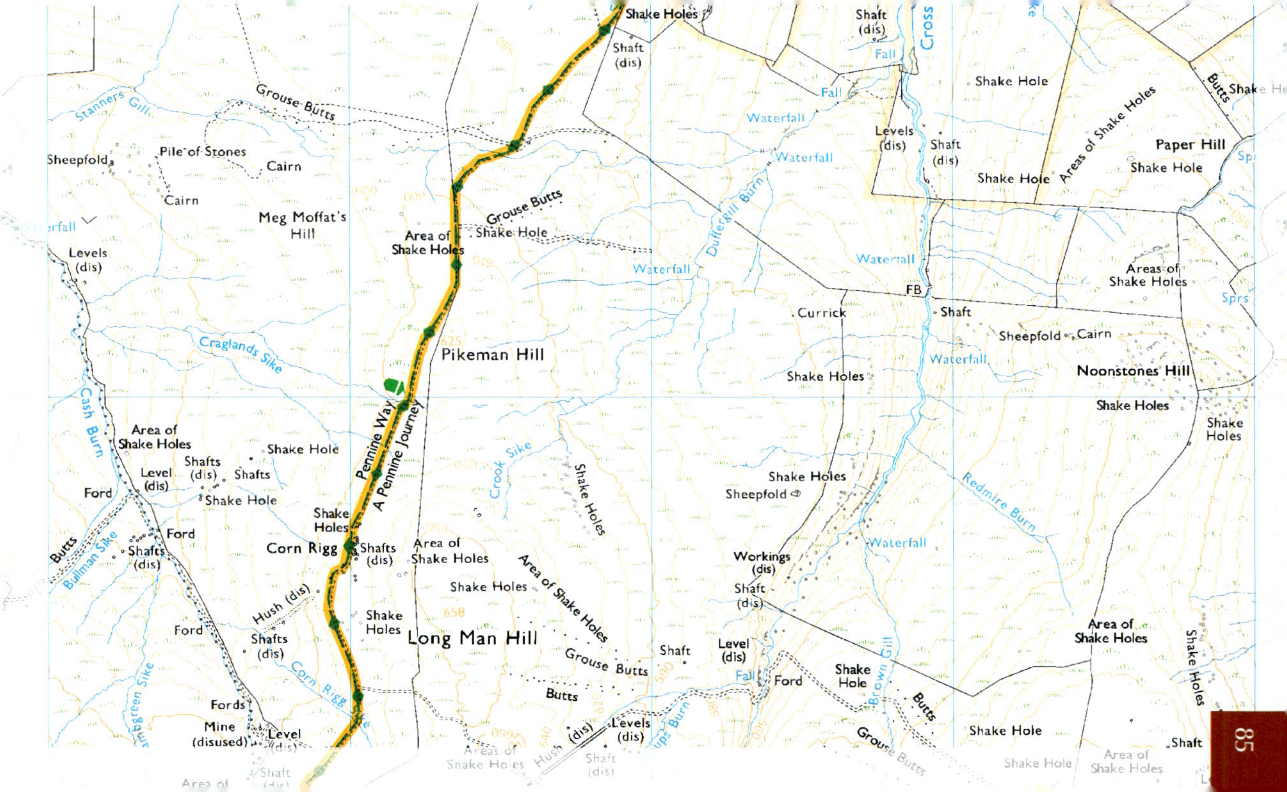
Pennine Way
A Pennine Journey
Pikeman Hill
Long Man Hill
Corn Rigg
Meg Moffat's Hill
Noonstones Hill
Paper Hill
Stanners Gill
Craglands Sike
Cash Burn
Bullman Sike
Crook Sike
Corn Rigg Sike
Duffergill Burn
Redmire Burn
Brown Gill
Cross
Pile of Stones
Cairn
Sheepfold
Grouse Butts
Butts
Area of Shake Holes
Areas of Shake Holes
Shake Holes
Shake Hole
Shafts (dis)
Shaft (dis)
Shaft
Levels (dis)
Level (dis)
Hush (dis)
Mine (disused)
Ford
Fords
Workings (dis)
Waterfall
Fall
FB
Currick
Sprs
625
658

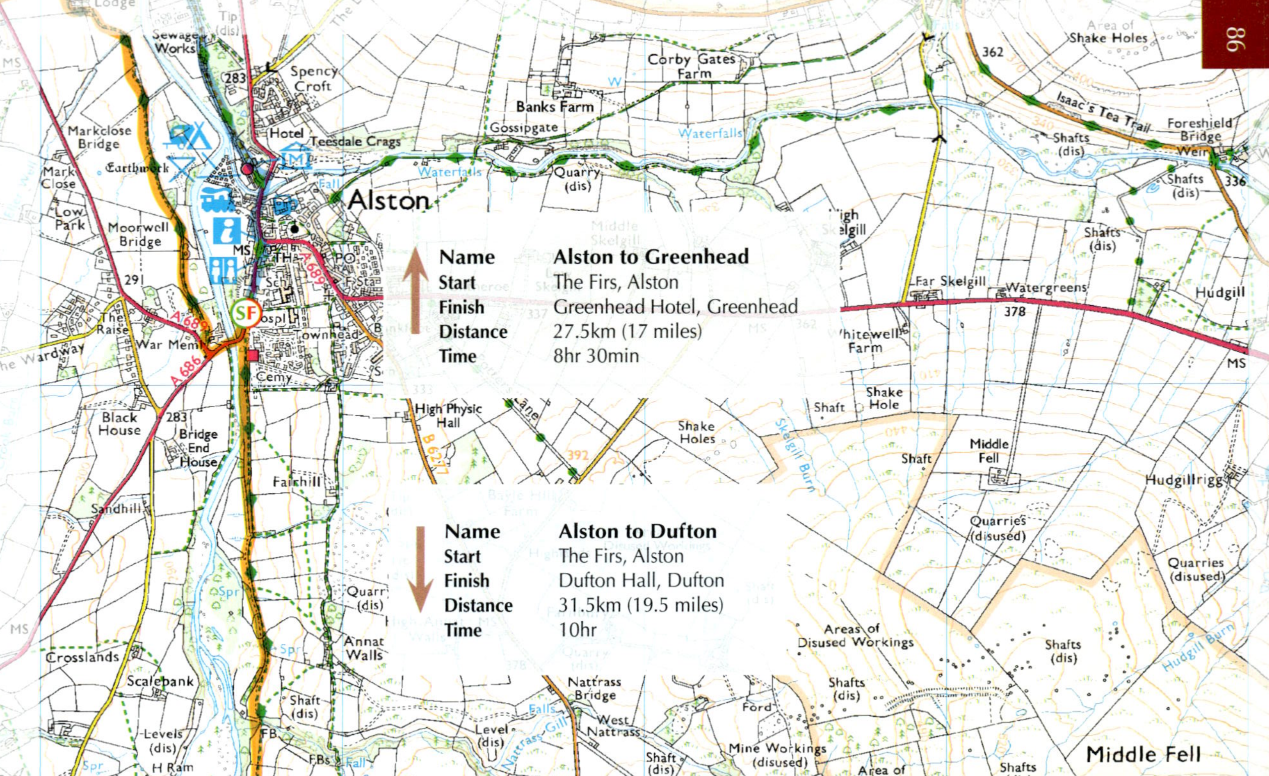
Alston
Name Alston to Greenhead
Start The Firs, Alston
Finish Greenhead Hotel, Greenhead
Distance 27.5km (17 miles)
Time 8hr 30min
Name Alston to Dufton
Start The Firs, Alston
Finish Dufton Hall, Dufton
Distance 31.5km (19.5 miles)
Time 10hr
Isaac's Tea Trail
Middle Fell
Corby Gates Farm
Banks Farm
Gossipgate
Teesdale Crags
Spency Croft
Sewage Works
Markclose Bridge
Mark Close
Low Park
Moorwell Bridge
The Raise
War Mem
The Wardway
Black House
Bridge End House
Sandhill
Crosslands
Scalebank
Fairhill
Annat Walls
High Physic Hall
Far Skelgill
Watergreens
Hudgill
Foreshield Bridge
Hudgillrigg
Middle Fell
Nattrass Bridge
West Nattrass
Skelgill Burn
Hudgill Burn
Nattrass Gill

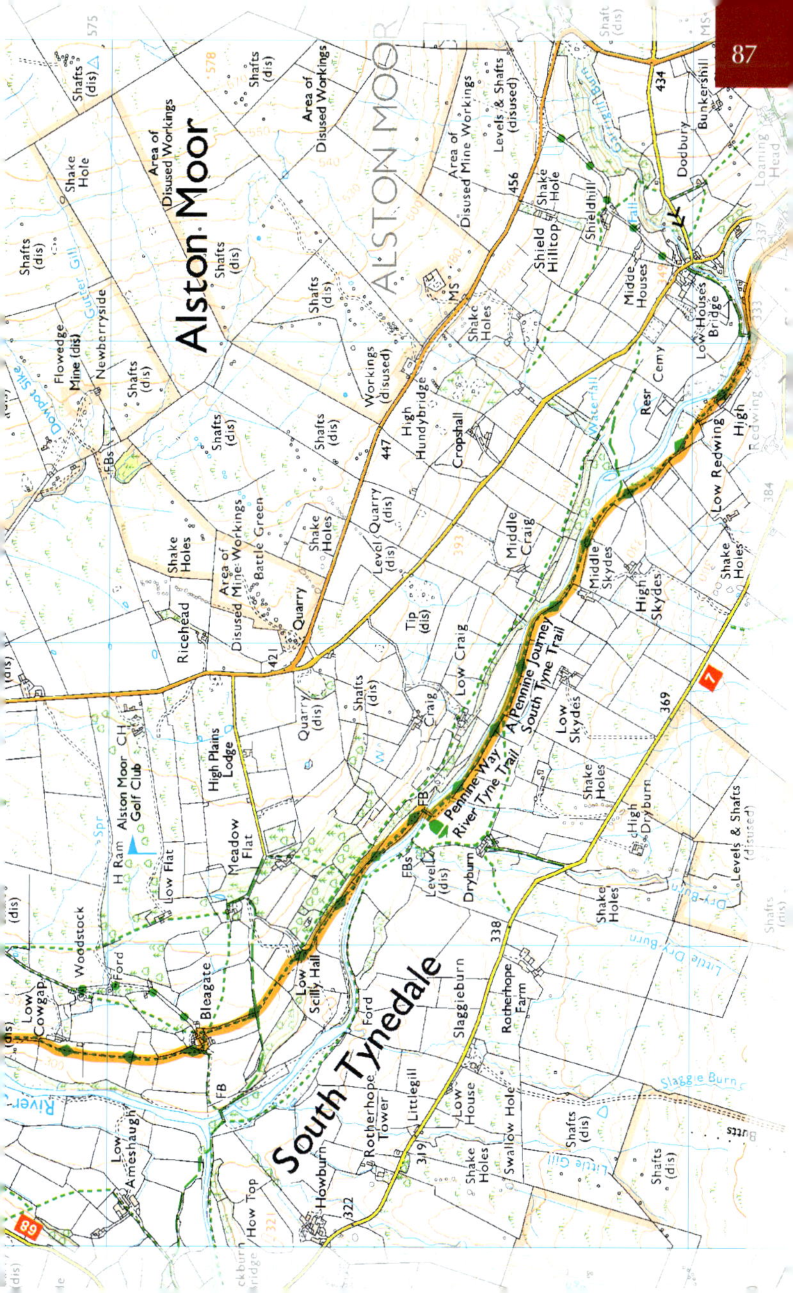

Alston Moor
ALSTON MOOR
South Tynedale
Pennine Way
River Tyne Trail
A Pennine Journey
South Tyne Trail
Low Cowgap
Woodstock
Ford
Low Ameshaugh
River
Spr
H Ram
Alston Moor Golf Club
CH
Low Flat
Bleagate
FB
How Top
Meadow Flat
High Plains Lodge
Ricehead
Shake Holes
Area of Disused Mine Workings
Battle Green
Quarry
Quarry (dis)
Low Scilly Hall
Howburn
Rotherhope Tower
Littlegill
Low House
Shake Holes
Swallow Hole
Slaggieburn
Rotherhope Farm
Dryburn
Level (dis)
FBs
FB
Craig
Low Craig
Shafts (dis)
Tip (dis)
Level (dis)
Quarry (dis)
Middle Craig
Low Skydes
Middle Skydes
High Skydes
High Dryburn
Little Gill
Little Dry Burn
Dry Burn
Slaggie Burn
Butts
Levels & Shafts (disused)
Low Redwing
High Redwing
Resr
Cemy
Waterfall
Fall
Garrigill Burn
Low Houses Bridge
Midde Houses
Shieldhill
Shield Hilltop
Shake Hole
Dodbury
Bunkershill
Loaning Head
Levels & Shafts (disused)
Area of Disused Mine Workings
MS
High Hundybridge
Cropshall
Workings (disused)
Area of Disused Workings
Shafts (dis)
Flowedge Mine (dis)
Newberryside
Dowpot Sike
Gutter Gill
FBs
Shake Hole
322 319 338 369 421 447 393 456 434 333 337 384 578 575 321
68
7

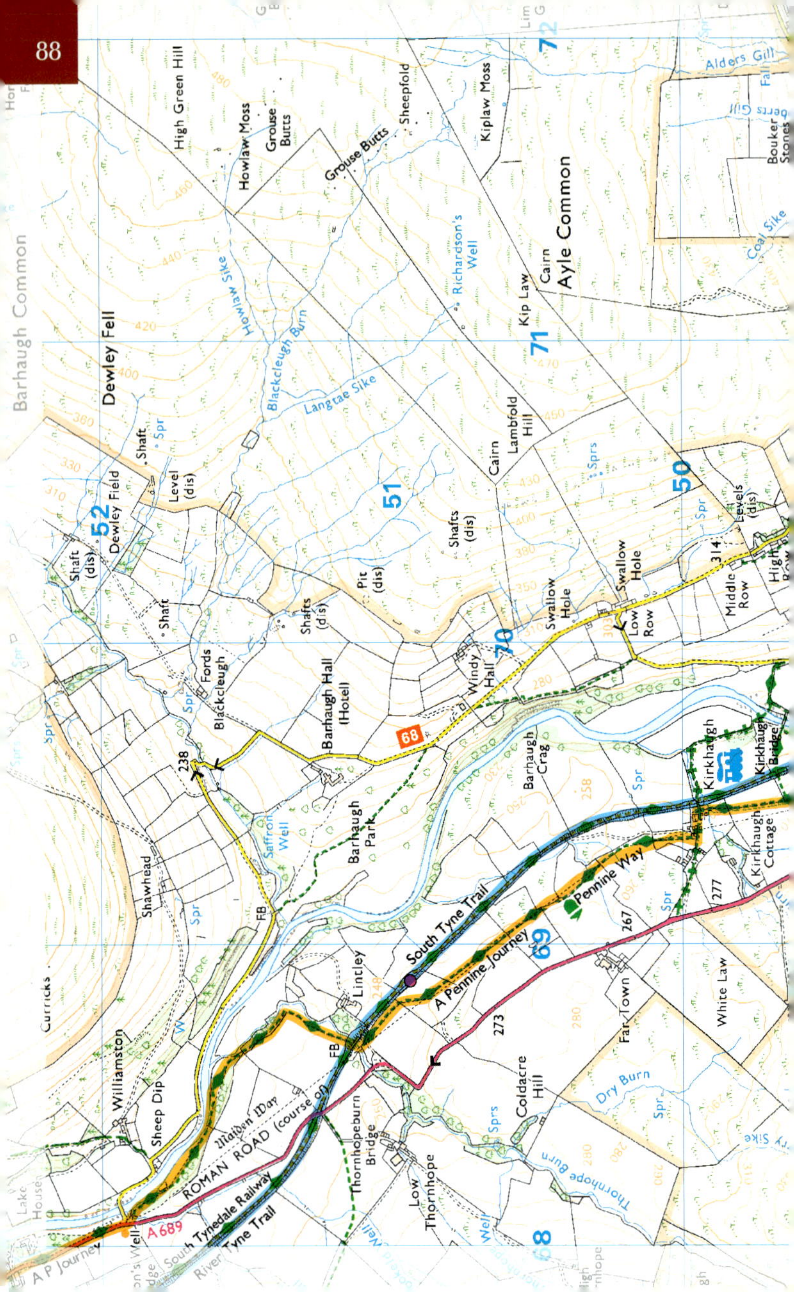

Barhaugh Common
Dewley Fell
High Green Hill
Howlaw Moss
Grouse Butts
Grouse Butts
Sheepfold
Kiplaw Moss
Alders Gill
Bouker Stones
Ayle Common
Cairn
Kip Law
Richardson's Well
Howlaw Sike
Blackcleugh Burn
Langtae Sike
Lambfold Hill
Cairn
Coal Sike
Spr
Shaft
Level (dis)
Dewley Field
Dewley
Shaft (dis)
Shaft
Fords
Blackcleugh
Shafts (dis)
Pit (dis)
Shafts (dis)
Sprs
Levels (dis)
Swallow Hole
Swallow Hole
Low Row
Middle Row
High Row
Windy Hall
Barhaugh Hall (Hotel)
Barhaugh Park
Saffron Well
Barhaugh Crag
Kirkhaugh
Kirkhaugh Bridge
Kirkhaugh Cottage
Shawhead
FB
Lintley
South Tyne Trail
Pennine Way
A Pennine Journey
White Law
Far Town
Currick
Williamston
Sheep Dip
Maiden Way
ROMAN ROAD (course of)
Thornhopeburn Bridge
Low Thornhope
Coldacre Hill
Dry Burn
Thornhope Burn
South Tynedale Railway
South Tyne Trail
River
A 689
Lake House
Well
A P Journey
Sprs
FB

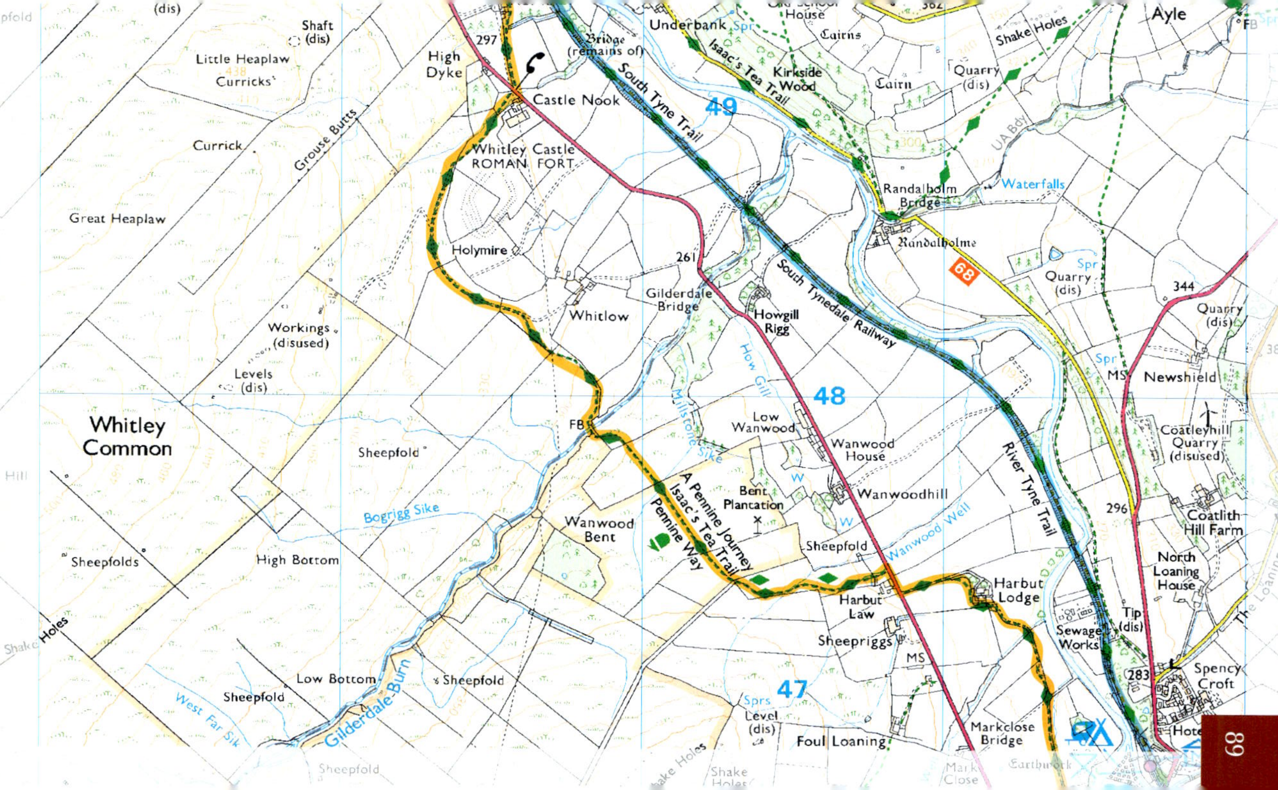
Ayle
Shake Holes
Quarry (dis)
Waterfalls
UA Bdy
Randalholm Bridge
Randalholme
68
Cairn
Cairns
Kirkside Wood
Isaac's Tea Trail
Underbank
Spr
49
South Tyne Trail
Bridge (remains of)
Castle Nook
Whitley Castle ROMAN FORT
297
High Dyke
Holymire
Whitlow
Gilderdale Bridge
261
South Tynedale Railway
Howgill Rigg
How Gill
48
Low Wanwood
Wanwood House
Wanwoodhill
Wanwood Well
River Tyne Trail
Harbut Lodge
Harbut Law
Sheepriggs
Sheepfold
Bent Plantation
Millstone Sike
A Pennine Journey
Isaac's Tea Trail
Pennine Way
FB
Wanwood Bent
47
Level (dis)
Foul Loaning
Markclose Bridge
Sewage Works
Tip (dis)
283
Spency Croft
North Loaning House
Coatlith Hill Farm
Coatleyhill Quarry (disused)
Newshield
Quarry (dis)
344
MS
296
The Loaning
Hotel
Shake Holes
Earthwork
Gilderdale Burn
Bogrigg Sike
Sheepfold
Low Bottom
High Bottom
West Far Sike
Whitley Common
Sheepfolds
Levels (dis)
Workings (disused)
Grouse Butts
Shaft (dis)
Little Heaplaw
438
Curricks
Currick
Great Heaplaw

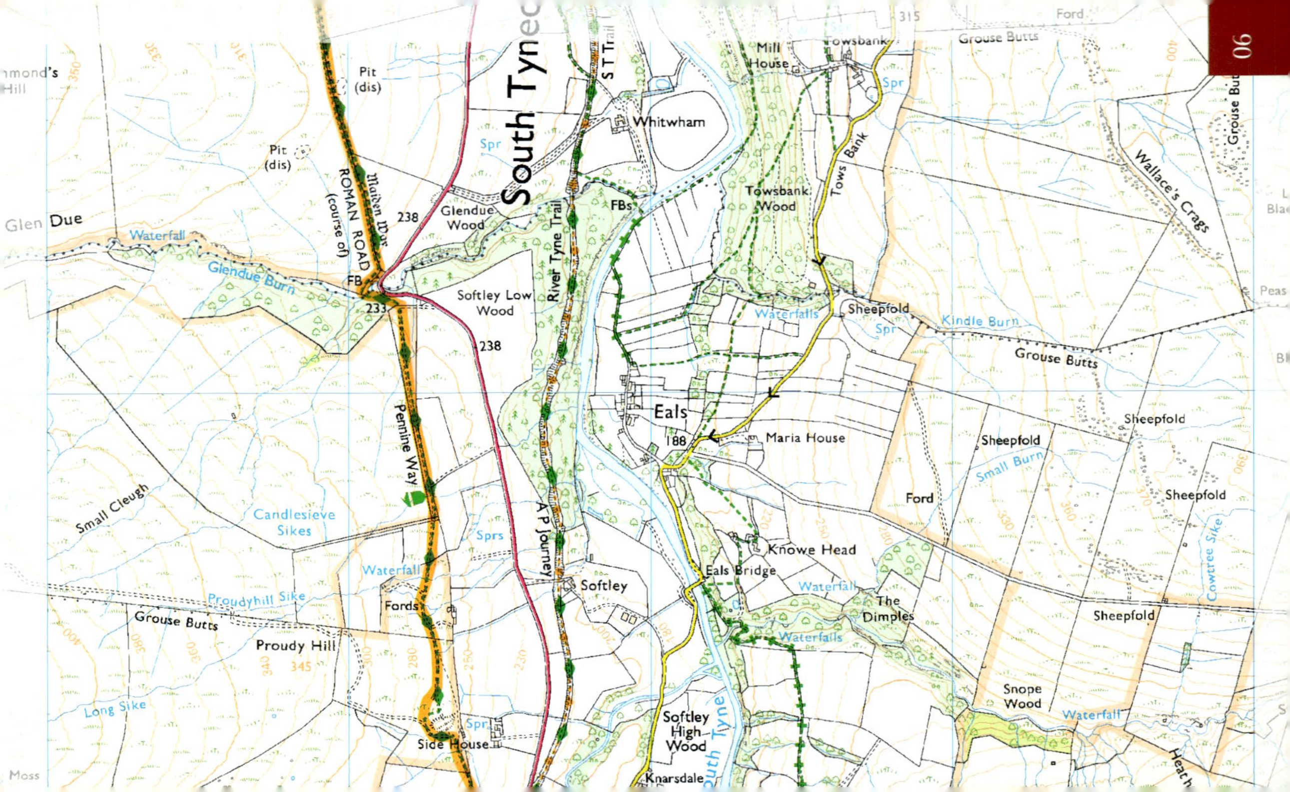

Glen Due
Waterfall
Glendue Burn
Pit (dis)
Maiden Way
ROMAN ROAD
(course of)
FB
Glendue Wood
South Tyne
Spr
S T Trail
Whitwham
FBs
River Tyne Trail
Softley Low Wood
Mill House
Towsbank
Towsbank Wood
Tows Bank
Wallace's Crags
Grouse Butts
Ford
Waterfalls
Sheepfold
Kindle Burn
Eals
Maria House
Small Burn
Pennine Way
Small Cleugh
Candlesieve Sikes
Sprs
A P Journey
Softley
Knowe Head
Eals Bridge
Waterfall
The Dimples
Cowtree Sike
Proudyhill Sike
Fords
Grouse Butts
Proudy Hill
Long Sike
Side House
Softley High Wood
Knarsdale
Snope Wood
Heath
Moss

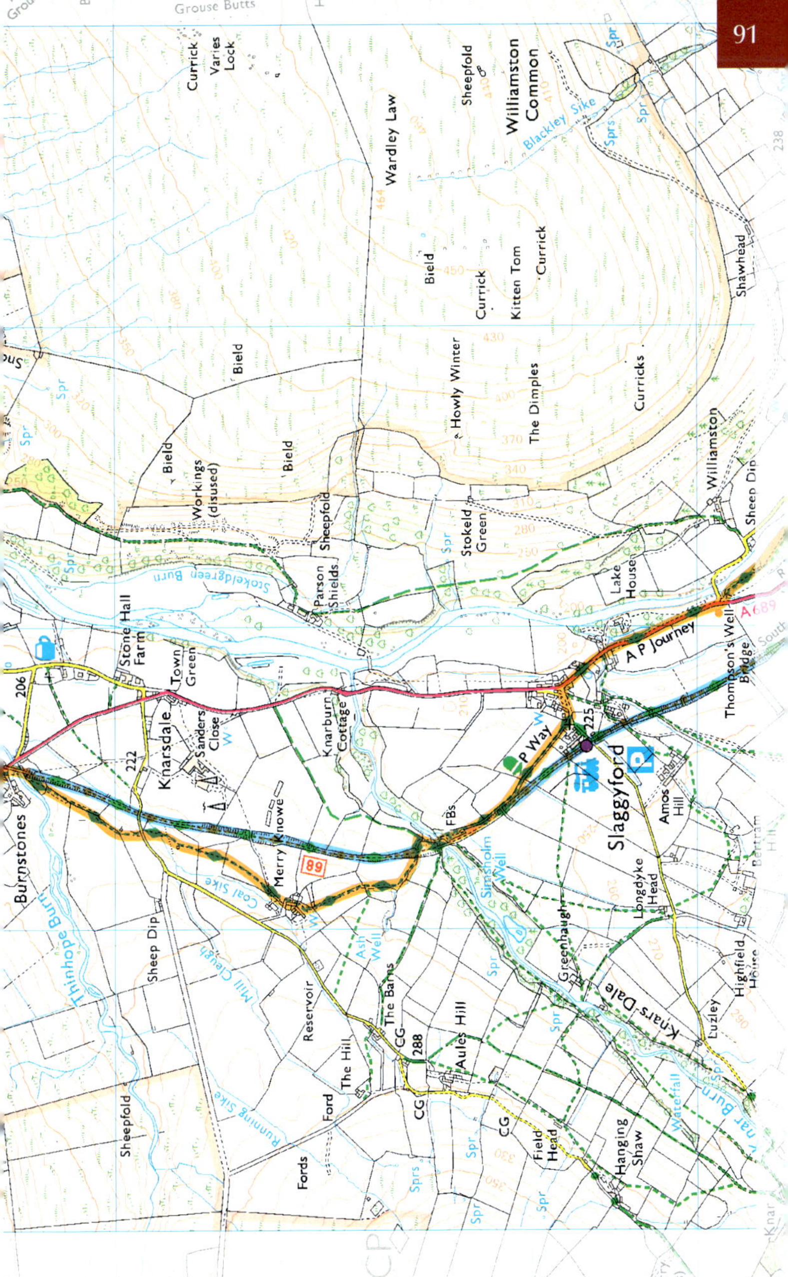

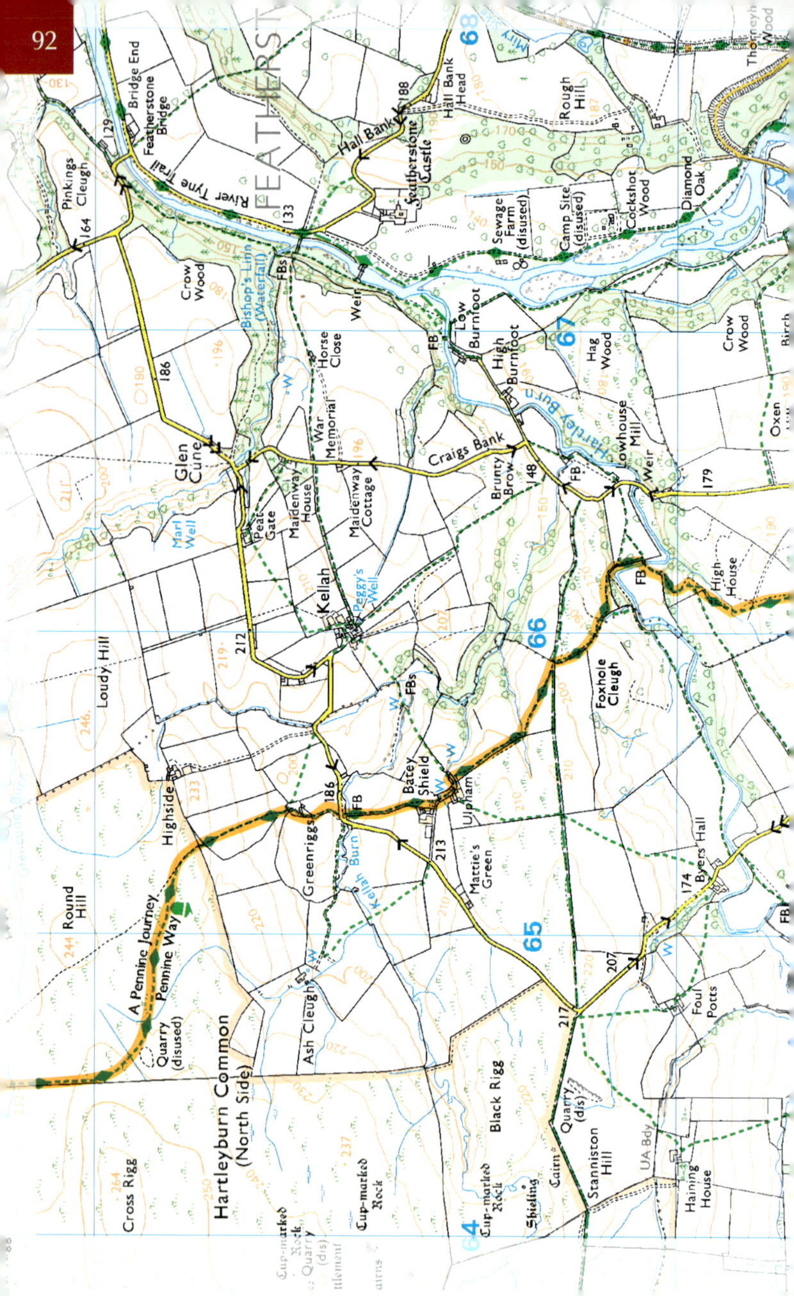

FEATHERSTONE
Bridge End
Featherstone Bridge
Pinkings Cleugh
River Tyne Trail
Hall Bank
Hall Bank Head
Featherstone Castle
Rough Hill
Sewage Farm (disused)
Camp Site (disused)
Cockshot Wood
Diamond Oak
Thorneyhope Wood
Miry Sike
Crow Wood
Bishop's Linn (Waterfall)
Weir
Low Burnfoot
High Burnfoot
Horse Close
Hag Wood
War Memorial
Hartley Burn
Lowhouse Mill
Craigs Bank
Glen Cune
Brunty Brow
Maidenway House
Maidenway Cottage
Peat Gate
Marl Well
Kellah
Peggy's Well
High House
Foxhole Cleugh
Loudy Hill
Highside
Batey Shield
Upham
Greenriggs
Kellah Burn
Mattie's Green
Byers Hall
Round Hill
A Pennine Journey
Pennine Way
Quarry (disused)
Ash Cleugh
Foul Potts
Hartleyburn Common (North Side)
Black Rigg
Quarry (dis)
Stanniston Hill
UA Bdy
Haining House
Cross Rigg
Cup-marked Rock
Shieling
Cairn
Crow Wood
Oxen
Birch

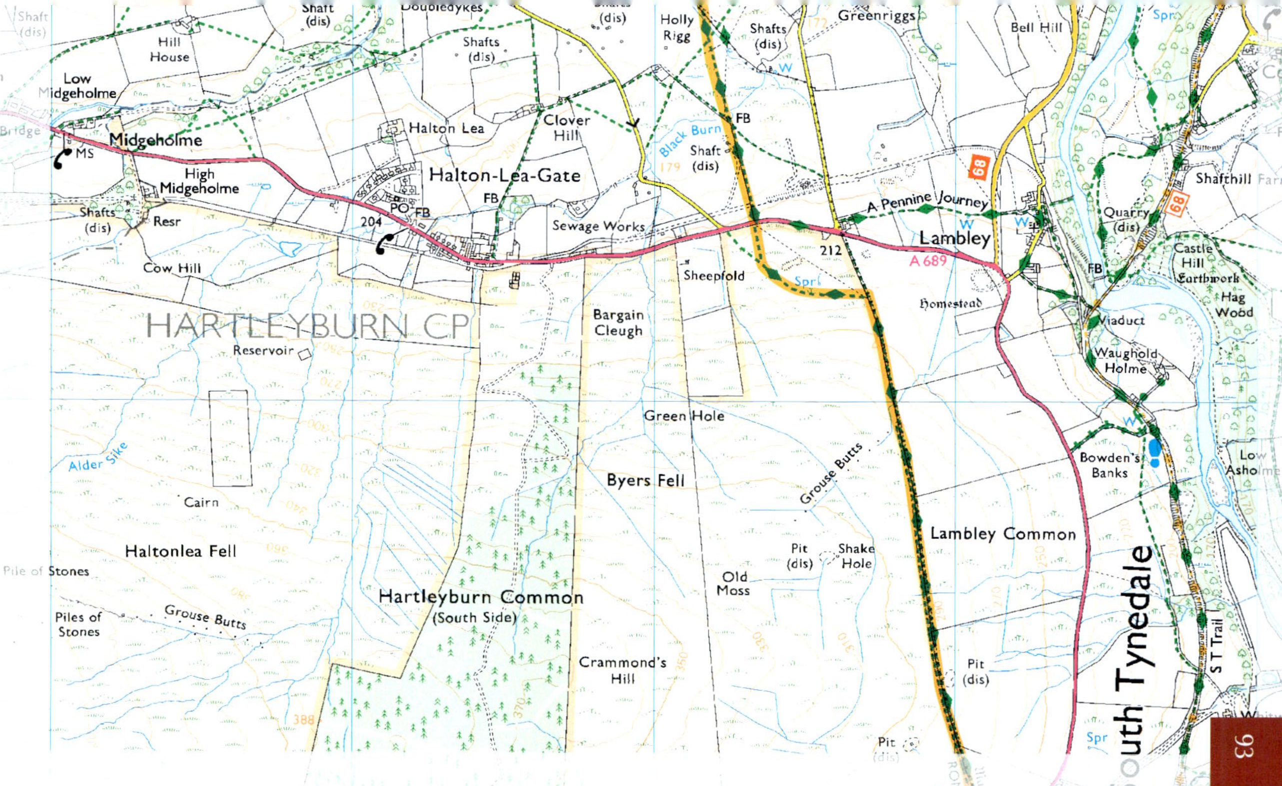
Hill House
Low Midgeholme
Bridge
Midgeholme
MS
High Midgeholme
Shafts (dis)
Resr
Cow Hill
Halton Lea
Halton-Lea-Gate
PO
FB
204
Clover Hill
Shafts (dis)
Sewage Works
Holly Rigg
Black Burn
Shaft (dis)
179
Greenriggs
Bell Hill
Shafthill Farm
A Pennine Journey
Lambley
A 689
212
Sheepfold
Spr
Quarry (dis)
Castle Hill Earthwork
Hag Wood
Viaduct
Waughold Holme
Homestead
HARTLEYBURN CP
Reservoir
Bargain Cleugh
Green Hole
Byers Fell
Grouse Butts
Bowden's Banks
Low Asholme
Alder Sike
Cairn
Haltonlea Fell
Pile of Stones
Piles of Stones
Grouse Butts
Hartleyburn Common (South Side)
Crammond's Hill
Old Moss
Pit (dis)
Shake Hole
Lambley Common
Pit (dis)
South Tynedale
S T Trail
388

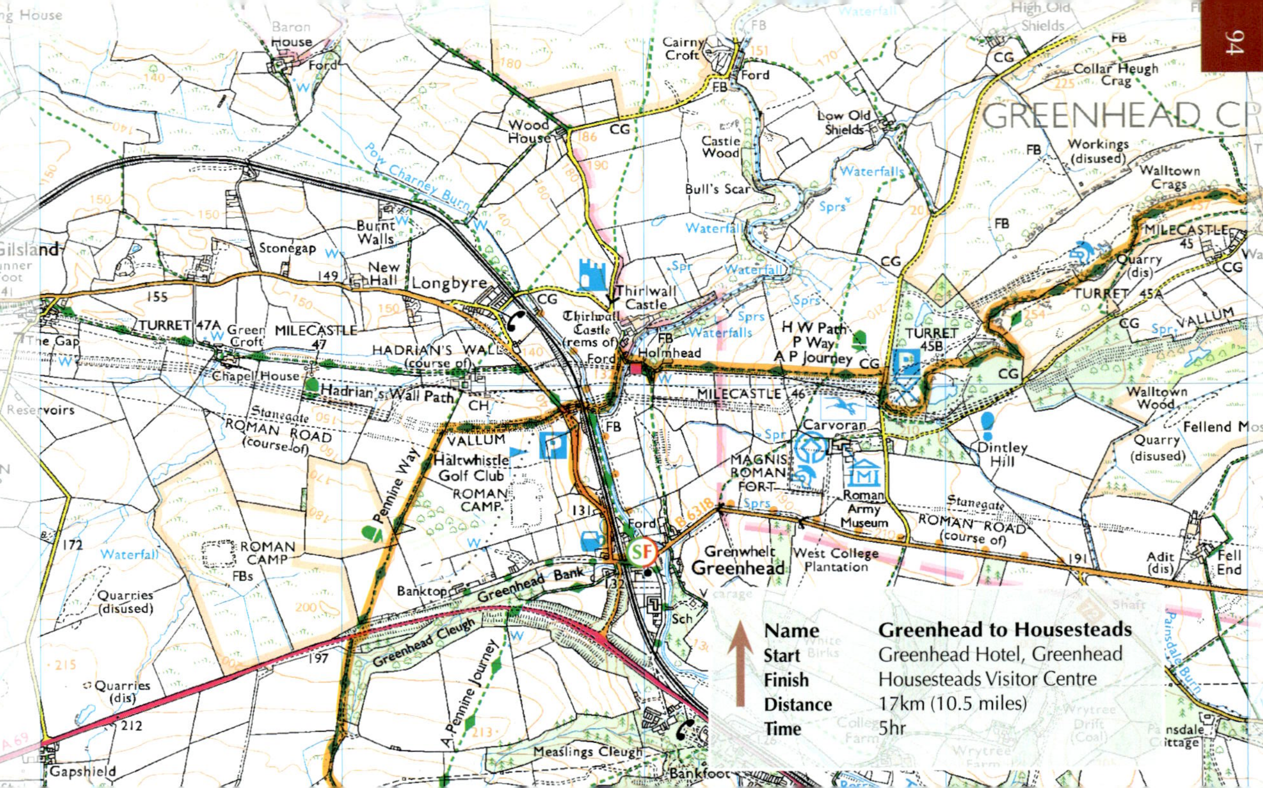

Name Greenhead to Housesteads
Start Greenhead Hotel, Greenhead
Finish Housesteads Visitor Centre
Distance 17km (10.5 miles)
Time 5hr
GREENHEAD CP
Greenhead
Gilsland
Longbyre
Thirlwall Castle
Walltown Crags
Carvoran
Roman Army Museum
MAGNIS ROMAN FORT
HADRIAN'S WALL (course of)
Hadrian's Wall Path
Pennine Way
A Pennine Journey
VALLUM
Haltwhistle Golf Club
Stanegate ROMAN ROAD (course of)
Pow Charney Burn
Painsdale Burn
Greenhead Cleugh

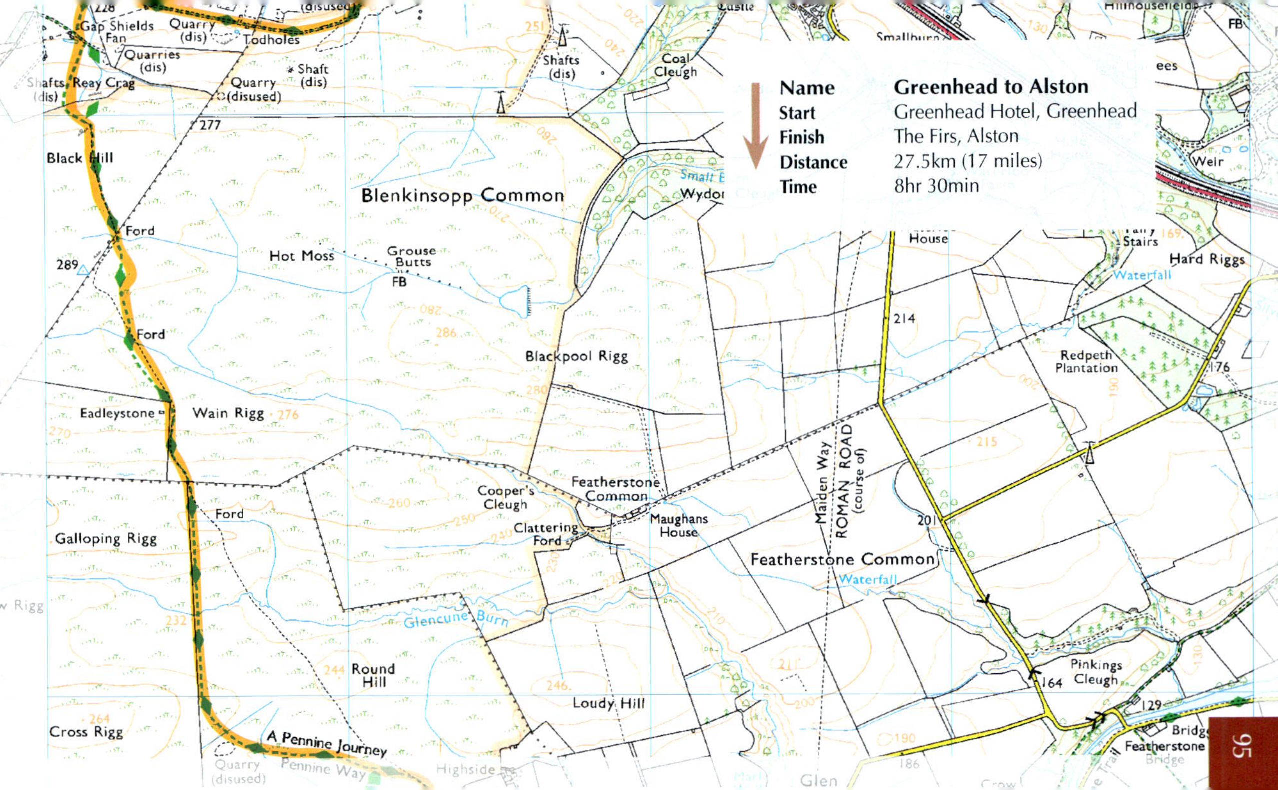

Name Greenhead to Alston
Start Greenhead Hotel, Greenhead
Finish The Firs, Alston
Distance 27.5km (17 miles)
Time 8hr 30min
Gap Shields Fan
Quarry (dis)
Todholes
Quarries (dis)
Shaft (dis)
Shafts (dis)
Reay Crag
Quarry (disused)
277
Shafts (dis)
Coal Cleugh
Black Hill
Blenkinsopp Common
Ford
289
Hot Moss
Grouse Butts
FB
Ford
Blackpool Rigg
Eadleystone
Wain Rigg
276
Ford
Galloping Rigg
Cooper's Cleugh
Featherstone Common
Clattering Ford
Maughans House
Maiden Way
ROMAN ROAD (course of)
Featherstone Common
Waterfall
Glencune Burn
232
244
Round Hill
Loudy Hill
264
Cross Rigg
A Pennine Journey
Pennine Way
Quarry (disused)
Highside
Glen
House
214
215
201
164
Pinkings Cleugh
129
Bridge
Featherstone Bridge
Redpeth Plantation
176
Hard Riggs
Stairs
Waterfall
Weir
Smallburn
FB

FBs
Inner Dodd
Brown Rigg
Moss Peteral
Calfclose Sike
Tipalt Burn
Farglow
Croft Sike
Bield
Cat Cleugh
Ford
Low Tipalt
Waterfall
Dowy Scar
Hangingshields Rigg
High Old Shields
North Plantation
Collar Heugh Crag
Allolee Rigg
HADRIAN'S WALL
GREENHEAD CP
TURRET 44A
MILECASTLE 44
TURRET 44B
ROMAN MILITARY WAY (course of)
Workings (disused)
Walltown Crags
Alloa Lea
King Arthur's Well
MILECASTLE 45
Quarry (dis)
Walltown
Lowtown
VALLUM (course of)
TURRET 45A
VALLUM
Blake Law
TURRET 45B
Peat Steel
Walltown Wood
HALTWH
Fellend Moss
Quarry (disused)
Dintley Hill
Haltwhistle Common
Peatsteel Crags
Stanegate
ROMAN ROAD (course of)
Shaft (dis)
ROMAN CAMP
Greenwood
Adit (dis)
Fell End
Shaft
Painsdale Burn
Hardriggs
Wrytree

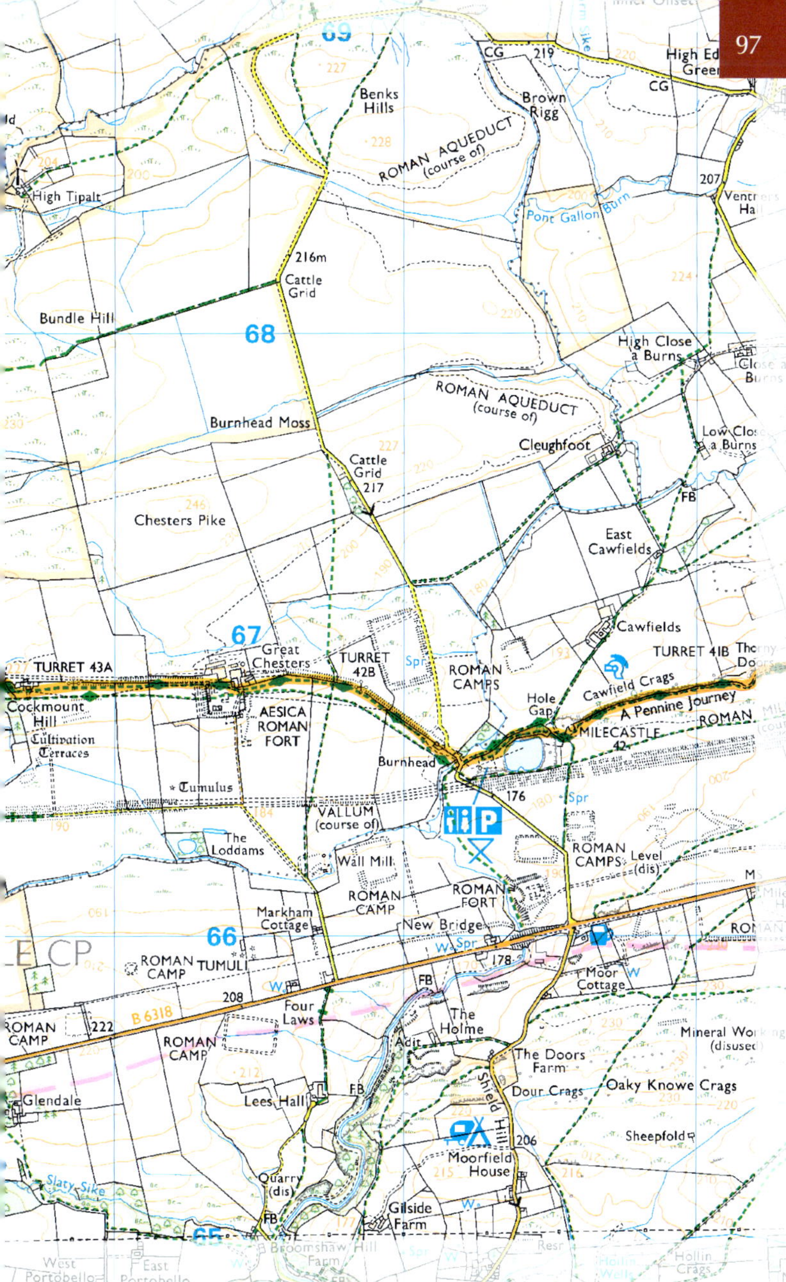

High Edges Green
CG
Edges Green
Wealside
Swallow Crags
FB
Ford
Fond Tom Pool
ROMAN AQUEDUCT (course of)
Spr
207
Ventners Hall
Bullyhouse Rigg
Longsyke
FB
Ford
Saughy Rigg
Caw Burn
Waterfall
Cowburn Rigg
Cawburn Shield
H Ram
Black Hill
Well House
263
High Close a Burns
Close a Burns
Bridge End
W
Sook Hill
Melkridge Common
Hexagon Plantation
Low Close a Burns
FB
Winshield Crags
345
TURRET 40A
MELKRIDGE CP
DITCH
East wfields
Sheepfold
Lodhams Slack
P Way
H W Path
TURRET 40B
MILECASTLE 41
Cawfields
TURRET 41B
Thorny Doors
TURRET 41A
Caw Gap
Bogle Hole
239
Crags
Pennine Journey
ROMAN MILITARY WAY (course of)
VALLUM
Winshie
ECASTLE 42
Resr
Shield on the Wall
Waterh
MS
Mare & Foal
Level (dis)
MS
215
236
Stanegate ROMAN ROAD (course of)
Milestone House
ROMAN CAMP
W
Hill Top
Hallpeat Moss
Melkridge Tilery
Mineral Workings (disused)
Oaky Knowe Crags
254
266
High Plantation
Sheepfold
Bayldon
Hollin Crags
Common House
Shaft (dis)
Middle

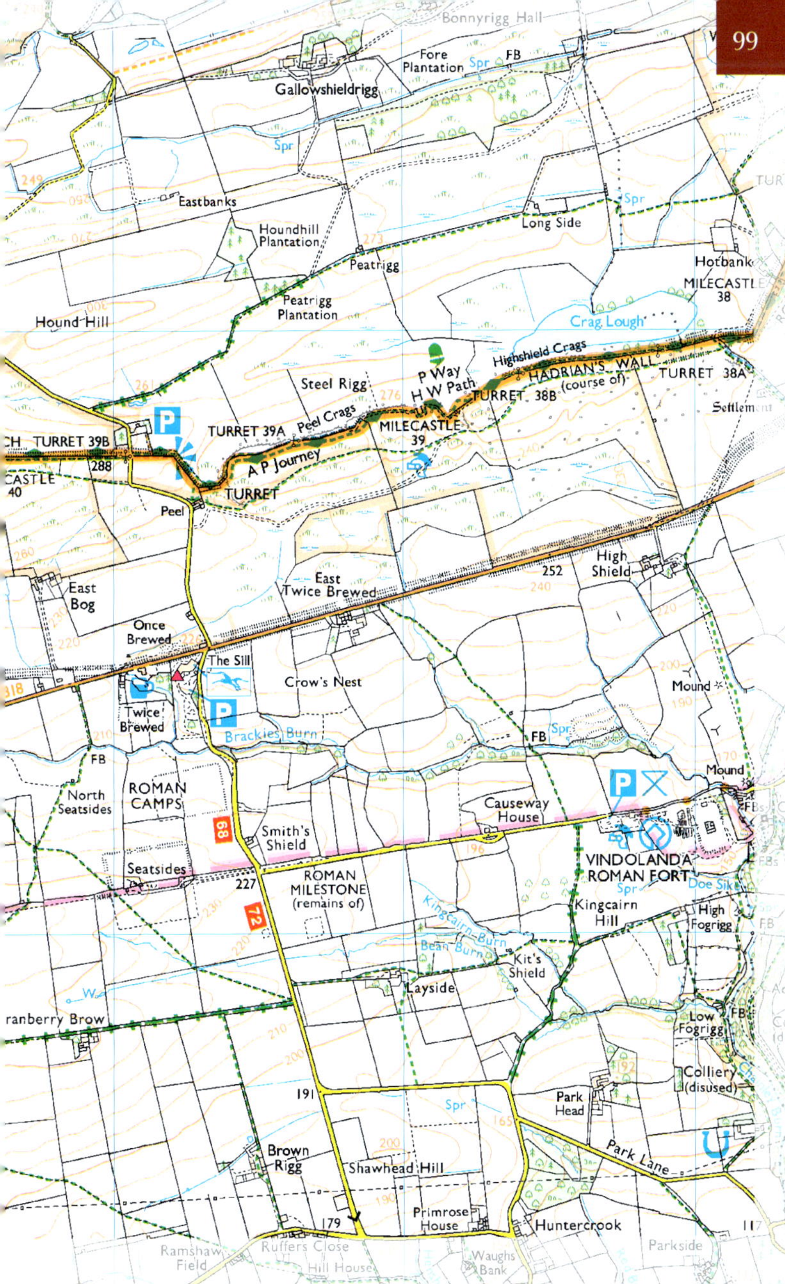
Bonnyrigg Hall
Fore Plantation
Spr
FB
Gallowshieldrigg
Spr
249
Eastbanks
Houndhill Plantation
273
Peatrigg
Long Side
Spr
Hotbank
MILECASTLE 38
Peatrigg Plantation
Hound Hill
Crag Lough
Highshield Crags
HADRIAN'S WALL (course of)
TURRET 38A
P Way
H W Path
Steel Rigg
276
TURRET 38B
Settlement
261
Peel Crags
TURRET 39A
MILECASTLE 39
TURRET 39B
288
A P Journey
CASTLE 40
TURRET
Peel
260
East Twice Brewed
252
High Shield
240
East Bog
Once Brewed
The Sill
Crow's Nest
Mound
Twice Brewed
Brackies Burn
FB
Spr
FB
North Seatsides
ROMAN CAMPS
Mound
Causeway House
68
Smith's Shield
196
VINDOLANDA ROMAN FORT
Seatsides
227
ROMAN MILESTONE (remains of)
Spr
Doe Sike
Kingcairn Hill
High Fogrigg
72
Kingcairn Burn
Bean Burn
Kit's Shield
Layside
ranberry Brow
Low Fogrigg
FB
192
Colliery (disused)
191
Park Head
Spr
165
Park Lane
Brown Rigg
200
Shawhead Hill
Primrose House
179
Huntercrook
Ramshaw Field
Ruffers Close
Hill House
Waughs Bank
Parkside

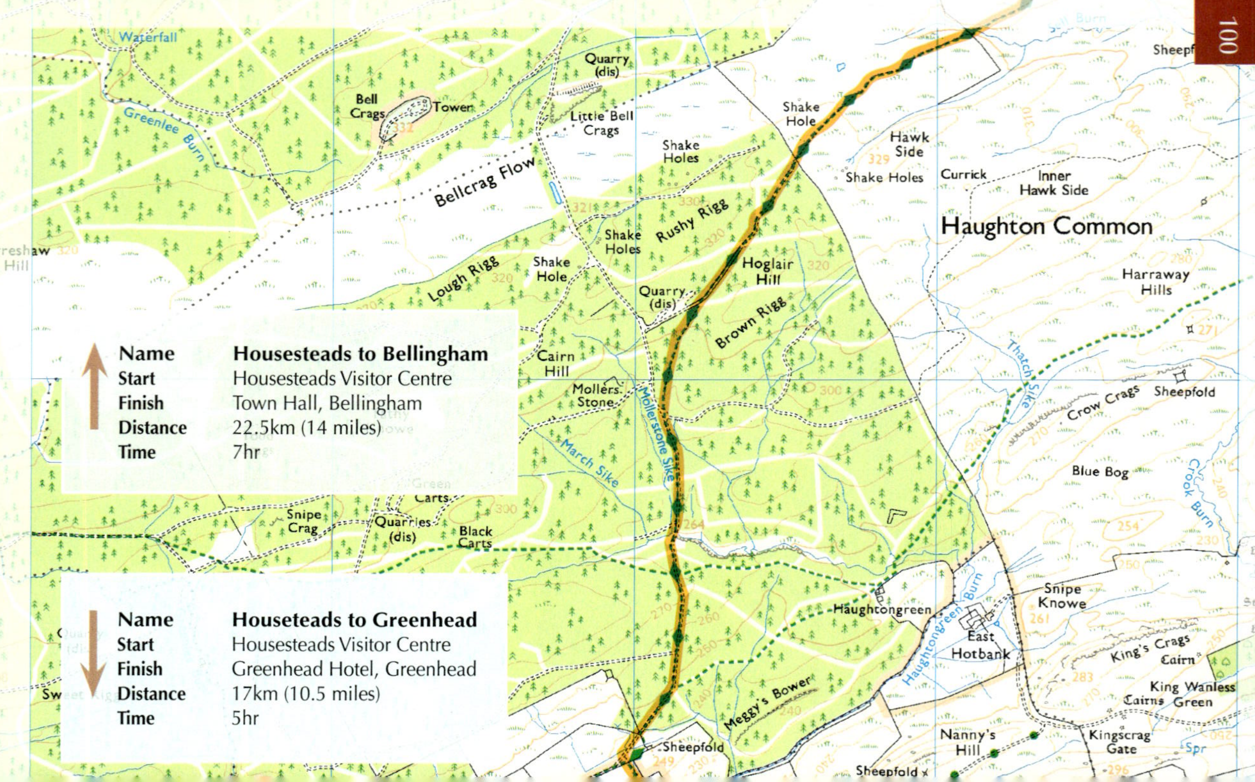

Name	**Housesteads to Bellingham**
Start	Housesteads Visitor Centre
Finish	Town Hall, Bellingham
Distance	22.5km (14 miles)
Time	7hr

Name	**Houseteads to Greenhead**
Start	Housesteads Visitor Centre
Finish	Greenhead Hotel, Greenhead
Distance	17km (10.5 miles)
Time	5hr

Ford
FB
Bield
Sheepfold
West Stonefolds
Ford
Jingling Well
Spr
Sewingshields Crags
Cragend
Boat House
Stone Circle
Enclosure
Greenlee Lough
(National Nature Reserve)
Broomlee Lough
TURRET 35B
Dove Crag
A Pennine Journey
HADRIAN'S WALL (course of)
ROMAN CAMP
Jenkins Burn
Waterfall
FB
Sheepfold
Ridley Common
Enclosure
King's Wicket
FB
Hadrian's Wall Path
MILECASTLE 36
Sheepfold
Kennel Crags
Clew Hill
King's Hill
TURRET 36A
West Hotbank
Bonnyrigg Hall
Caw Lough
White Bank
Housesteads
VERCOVICIVM ROMAN FORT
ROMAN WELL
VALLUM
Fore Plantation
FB
Pennine Way
Cuddy's Crags
Housesteads Crags
Knag Burn
TURRET 37A
MILECASTLE 37
Hotbank Crags
HADRIAN'S WALL
TURRET 37B
CULTIVATION TERRACES
ROMAN WELL
Chapel Hill
New Beggarbog
Beggar Bog
Long Side
MILITARY WAY
Tumulus
Hotbank
MILECASTLE 38
ROMAN MILITARY WAY (course of)
VALLUM (course of)
Deafley Rigg
Mound
Crag Lough
Bradley
Highshield Crags
HADRIAN'S WALL (course of)
TURRET 38A
P Way
H W Path
248m
Little Shield
Knag Burn

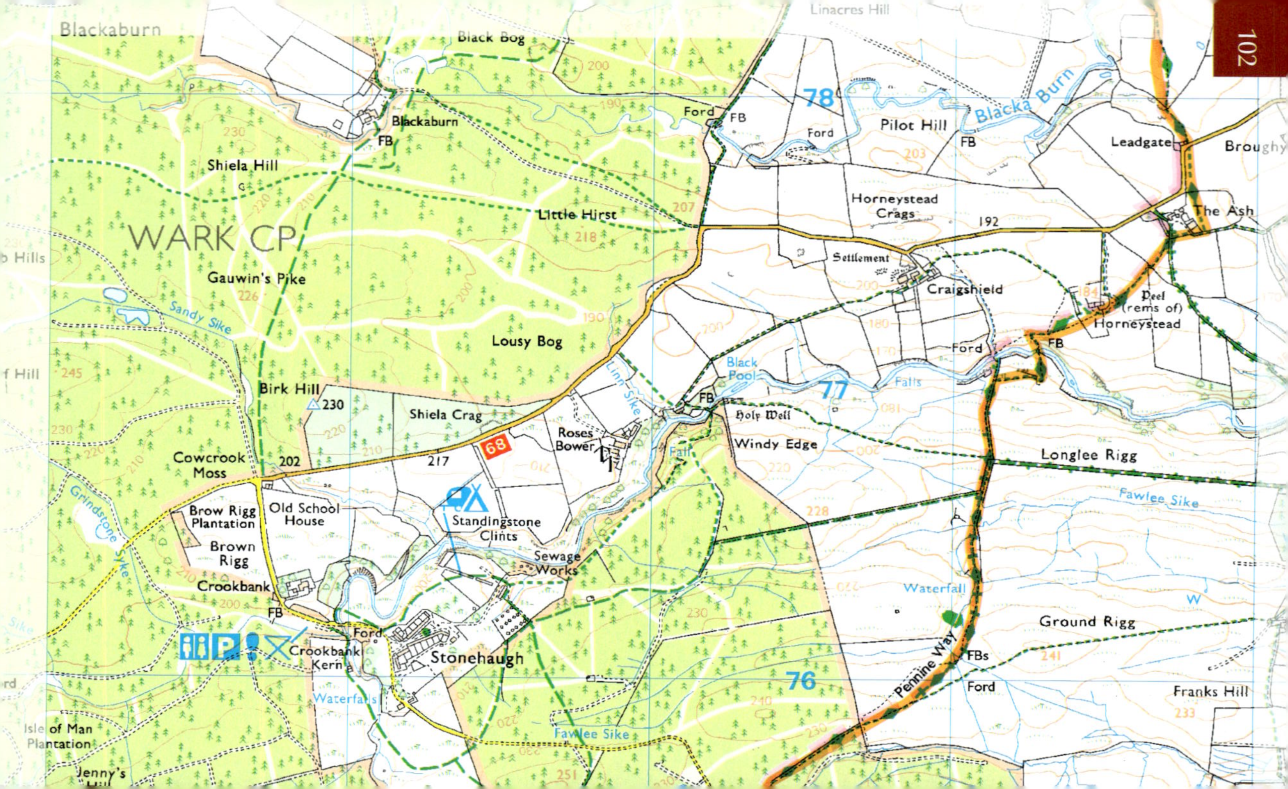
Blackaburn
Black Bog
Linacres Hill
Blackaburn
FB
Shiela Hill
Ford
FB
Ford
78
Pilot Hill
Blacka Burn
FB
Leadgate
Broughy
WARK CP
Little Hirst
Horneystead Crags
192
The Ash
Settlement
Craigshield
Peel (rems of)
Horneystead
Gauwin's Pike
Sandy Sike
Lousy Bog
Ford
FB
Black Pool
77
Falls
Birk Hill
230
Shiela Crag
FB
Holy Well
Windy Edge
Linn Sike
Roses Bower
68
217
Longlee Rigg
Cowcrook Moss
202
Fall
Fawlee Sike
Brow Rigg Plantation
Old School House
Standingstone Clints
Grindstone Syke
Brown Rigg
Sewage Works
Crookbank
Waterfall
FB
Ford
Crookbank Kern
Stonehaugh
Ground Rigg
76
Pennine Way
FBs
Ford
Franks Hill
Waterfalls
Fawlee Sike
Isle of Man Plantation
Jenny's

Broadpool Common
Fords
Standard
Waterfall
247
Sheepfold
241
226
Middleburn
Ladyhill
BS
75
Crozier's Hill
Sheepfold
FB
Coalcleugh
Deer Stand
South Plantation
Waterfall
Pennine Way
FB
Broadpool
FB
Sheepfold
Burn
Greystone Cleugh
Brown Hill
Spr
Waterfalls
Cleugh
Haggyshaw Plantation
Coston Burn
Level (dis)
Whitelee
Waterfall
74
FB
Black Law
Coal Cleugh
Cross (remains of)
Level (dis)
Shake Hole
Currick
Sell Burn
Sheepfold
Sheepfold
Ford
Townshield Bank
Standingstone Rigg
Sell Burn
73
FBs
FBs
The Lumps
Curricks
Harvest Green
Shake Hole
Hawk Side
Shake Holes

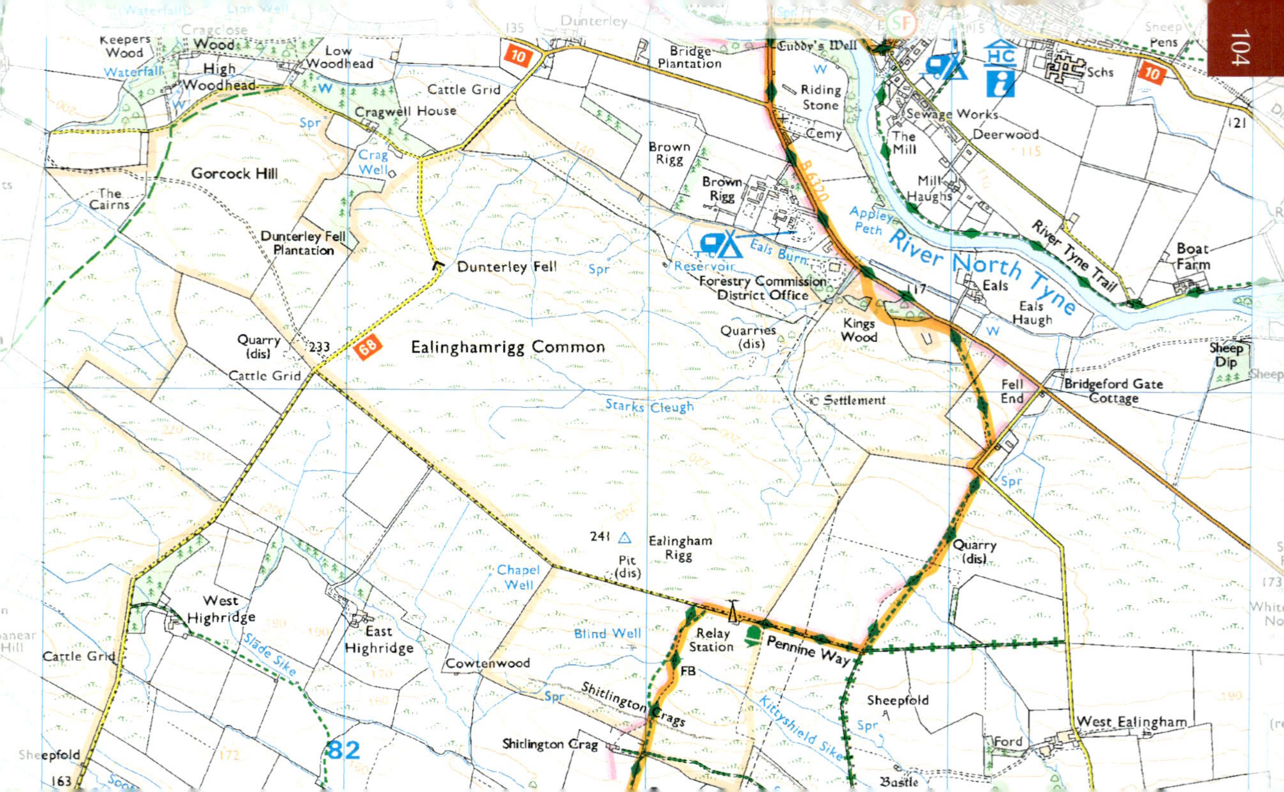
River North Tyne
River Tyne Trail
Pennine Way
B 6320
Boat Farm
Sheep Dip
Bridgeford Gate Cottage
Schs
Deerwood
Sewage Works
The Mill
Mill Haughs
Eals
Eals Haugh
Fell End
Quarry (dis)
Appley Peth
Kings Wood
Settlement
Cuddy's Well
Riding Stone
Cemy
Eals Burn
Forestry Commission District Office
Quarries (dis)
Brown Rigg
Reservoir
Bridge Plantation
Ealingham Rigg
Relay Station
FB
Starks Cleugh
Pit (dis)
Blind Well
Shitlington Crags
Shitlington Crag
West Ealingham
Ford
Sheepfold
Bastle
Kittyshield Sike
Dunterley
Dunterley Fell
Ealinghamrigg Common
Chapel Well
Cowtenwood
Cattle Grid
Cragwell House
Crag Well
Low Woodhead
High Woodhead
Dunterley Fell Plantation
Gorcock Hill
Quarry (dis)
East Highridge
West Highridge
Slade Sike
Keepers Wood
Waterfall
The Cairns
Cragclose Wood
Sheepfold
10
68
82
233
241

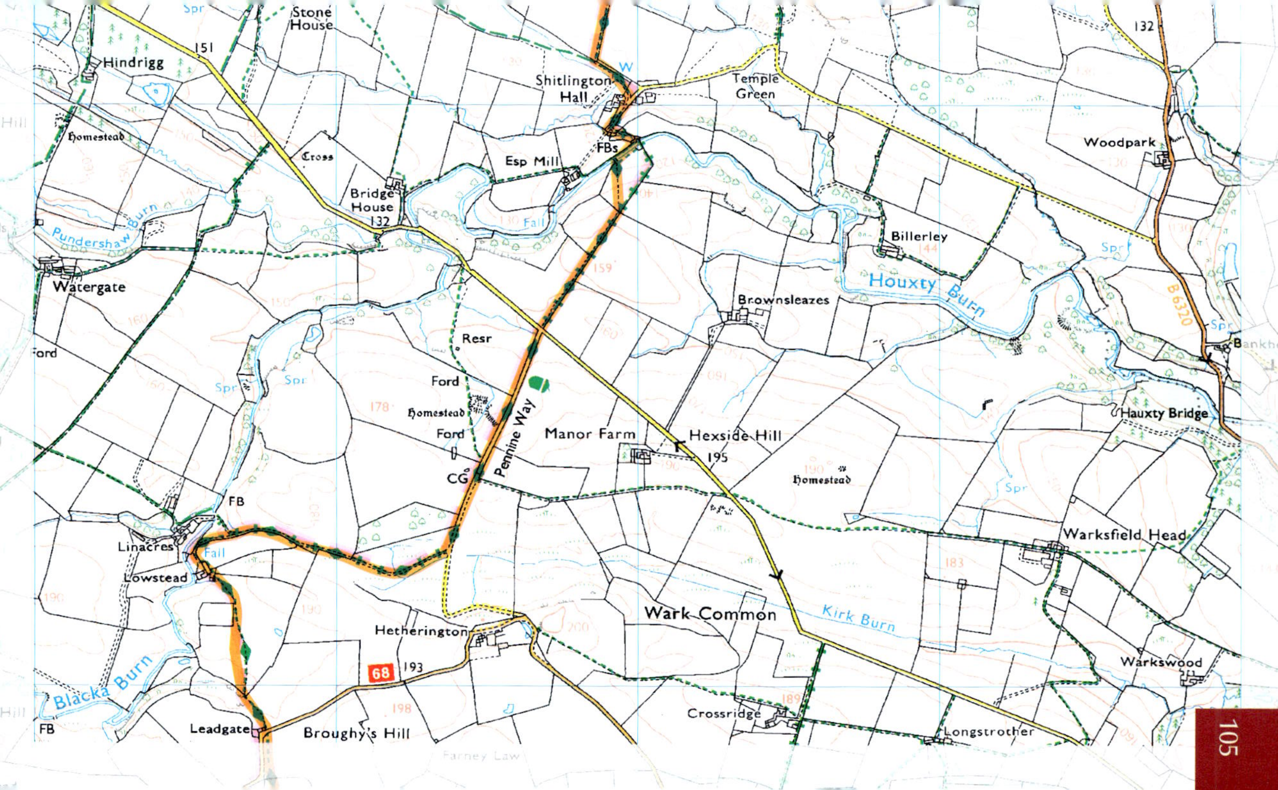
Stone House
Hindrigg
151
Shitlington Hall
W
Temple Green
132
Homestead
Cross
Esp Mill
FBs
Woodpark
Bridge House
132
Fall
Billerley
144
Pundershaw Burn
Watergate
159
Houxty Burn
Brownsleazes
B 6320
Resr
Ford
Ford
Homestead
178
Ford
Pennine Way
Manor Farm
Hexside Hill
195
Hauxty Bridge
CG
Homestead
FB
Linacres
Fall
Lowstead
Warksfield Head
183
Wark Common
Kirk Burn
Hetherington
68
193
198
Blacka Burn
FB
Leadgate
Broughy's Hill
Crossridge
189
Longstrother
Warkswood
Spr

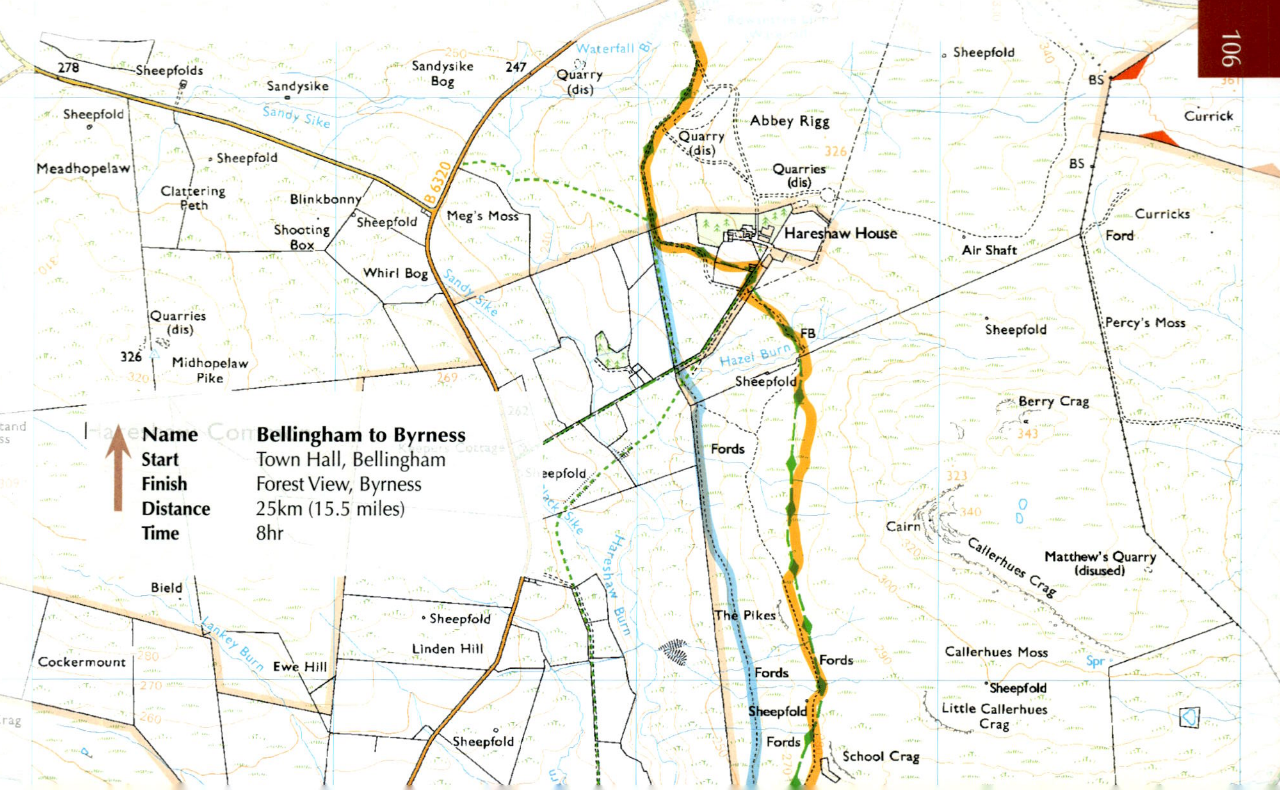
Name Bellingham to Byrness
Start Town Hall, Bellingham
Finish Forest View, Byrness
Distance 25km (15.5 miles)
Time 8hr
Sheepfolds
Sandysike
Sheepfold
Meadhopelaw
Sheepfold
Clattering Peth
Blinkbonny
Shooting Box
Sheepfold
Sandysike Bog
Quarry (dis)
Waterfall
B 6320
Meg's Moss
Whirl Bog
Sandy Sike
Quarries (dis)
Midhopelaw Pike
Abbey Rigg
Quarry (dis)
Quarries (dis)
Hareshaw House
Air Shaft
Sheepfold
Currick
Curricks
Ford
Percy's Moss
BS
Hazel Burn
FB
Sheepfold
Fords
Berry Crag
Cairn
Callerhues Crag
Matthew's Quarry (disused)
Hareshaw Burn
The Pikes
Fords
Fords
Sheepfold
Fords
Callerhues Moss
Spr
Sheepfold
Little Callerhues Crag
School Crag
Bield
Lankey Burn
Ewe Hill
Cockermount
Sheepfold
Linden Hill
Sheepfold

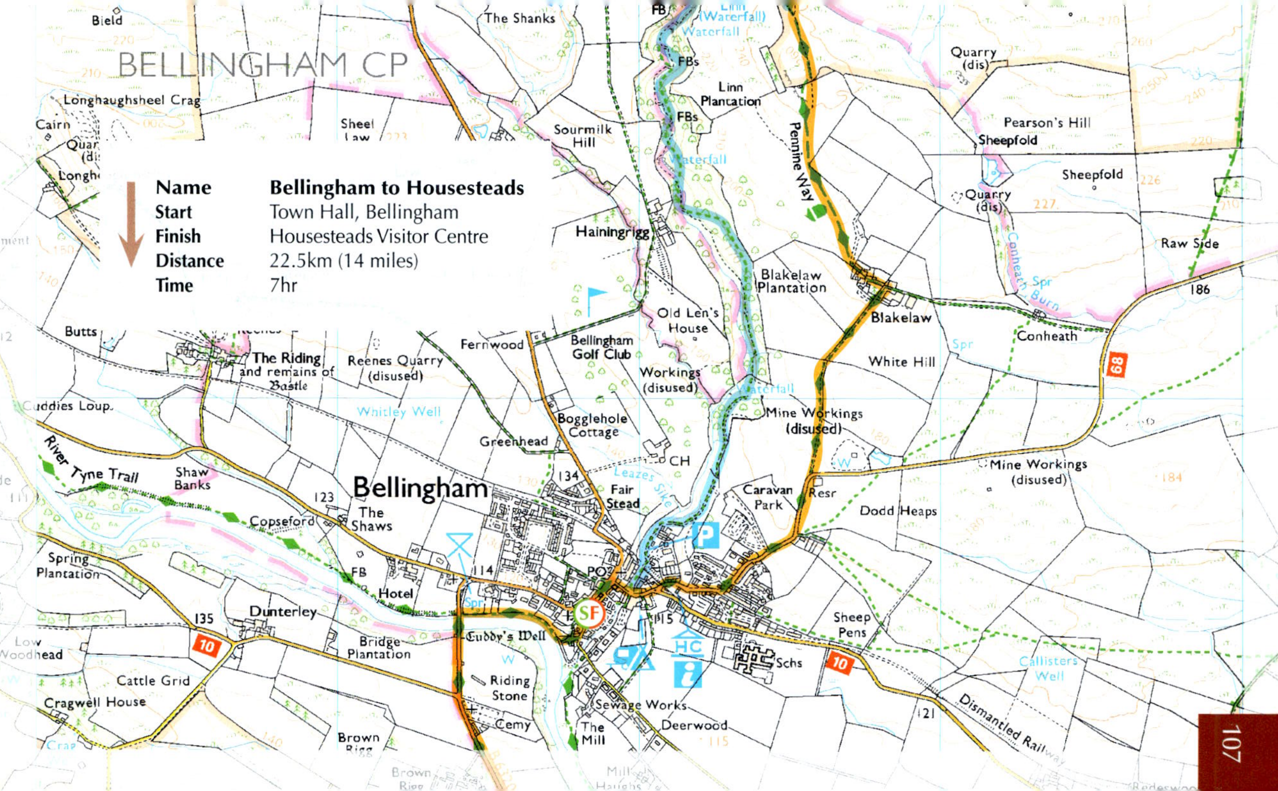

BELLINGHAM CP
Name Bellingham to Housesteads
Start Town Hall, Bellingham
Finish Housesteads Visitor Centre
Distance 22.5km (14 miles)
Time 7hr
Bellingham
Pennine Way
River Tyne Trail
Bield
Longhaughsheel Crag
Cairn
The Shanks
Sheel Law
Sourmilk Hill
Haininggrigg
Linn Plantation
FBs
Waterfall
Blakelaw Plantation
Blakelaw
White Hill
Conheath
Conheath Burn
Pearson's Hill
Sheepfold
Quarry (dis)
Raw Side
Butts
The Riding and remains of Bastle
Reenes Quarry (disused)
Fernwood
Bellingham Golf Club
Old Len's House
Workings (disused)
Mine Workings (disused)
Cuddies Loup
Whitley Well
Greenhead
Bogglehole Cottage
CH
Leazes Sike
Fair Stead
Caravan Park
Resr
Dodd Heaps
Shaw Banks
Copseford
The Shaws
FB
Hotel
Spring Plantation
Dunterley
Bridge Plantation
Cuddy's Well
Riding Stone
Cemy
Low Woodhead
Cattle Grid
Cragwell House
Brown Rigg
Sewage Works
Deerwood
The Mill
Mill Haughs
Sheep Pens
Schs
Callisters Well
Dismantled Railway
PO
SF
HC
Spr

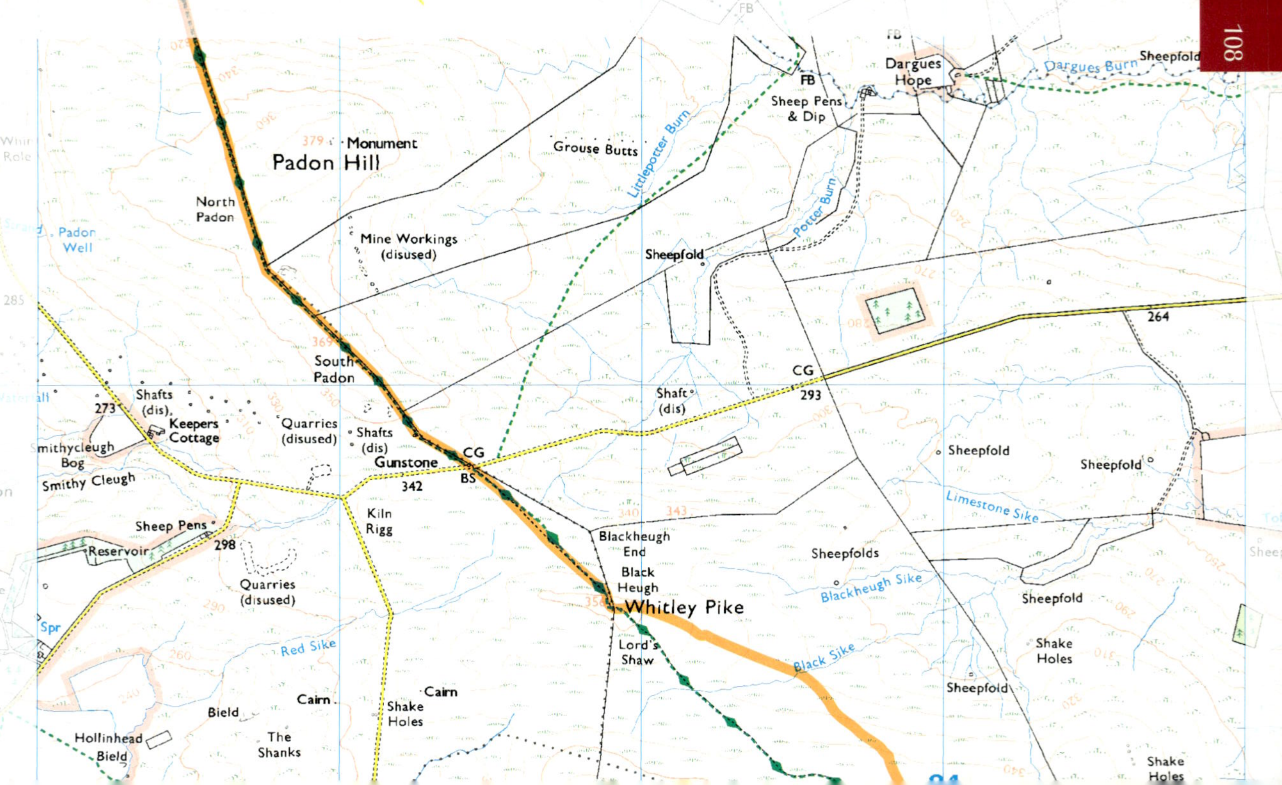

Padon Hill
379
Monument
Grouse Butts
Littlepotter Burn
FB
Sheep Pens & Dip
FB
Dargues Hope
Dargues Burn
Sheepfold
North Padon
Padon Well
Mine Workings (disused)
Sheepfold
Potter Burn
264
South Padon
369
CG
293
Shafts (dis)
273
Keepers Cottage
Quarries (disused)
Shafts (dis)
Shaft (dis)
Smithycleugh Bog
Smithy Cleugh
Gunstone
CG
BS
342
Sheepfold
Sheepfold
Kiln Rigg
Limestone Sike
Sheep Pens
298
Reservoir
Quarries (disused)
Blackheugh End
Black Heugh
Whitley Pike
Sheepfolds
Blackheugh Sike
Sheepfold
Spr
Red Sike
Lord's Shaw
Black Sike
Shake Holes
Sheepfold
Cairn
Cairn
Shake Holes
Bield
Hollinhead Bield
The Shanks
Shake Holes

Shafts (dis)
Black Crag
Cairn
Cairn
Shake Holes
Gray Stone
Blackmoor Skirt
364
365
Millstone Edge
BS
Grouse Butts
Cairn
BS
Pin Hole
Grouse Butts
336
Blackcrag Wood
Shake Hole
Shake Hole
Sundaysight Cleugh
Waterfalls
Spr
Cairn
Ninewell Eyes
W
BS
Lough Shaw
Grouse Butts
BS
295
North Sundaysight
Sheepfold
302
Sundaysight
BS
262
W
John Side
Johnside Sike
Pennine Way
Trough
Wr Twr
Catcleugh Crags
Sheepfold
Sandysike Rigg
299
Harper's Sike
Sheepfold
Saughy Sike
Brockley Burn
Rowantree Linn (Waterfall)
310
Waterfall
278
Sheepfolds
Sandysike
Sandysike Bog
247
Quarry (dis)
Sheepfold
Sandy Sike
Abbey Rigg
Quarry (dis)
281
Quarry (dis)
Sheepfold
326
Meadhopelaw
Clattering
Quarries (dis)

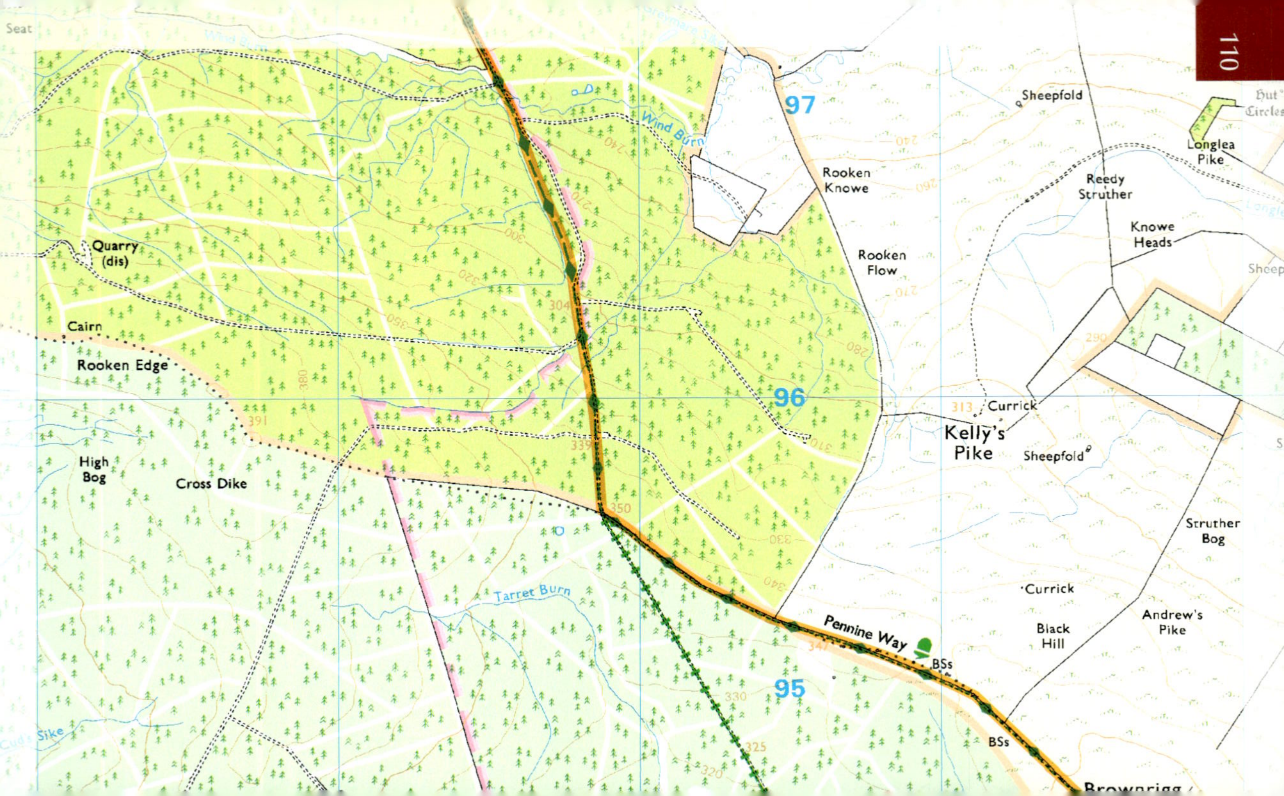
Seat
Wind Burn
Sheepfold
Hut Circles
Longlea Pike
97
Rooken Knowe
Reedy Struther
Knowe Heads
Quarry (dis)
Rooken Flow
304
Cairn
Rooken Edge
96
313
Currick
Kelly's Pike
Sheepfold
339
391
High Bog
Cross Dike
350
Struther Bog
Currick
Tarret Burn
Andrew's Pike
Black Hill
Pennine Way
347
BSs
95
Cud's Sike
BSs

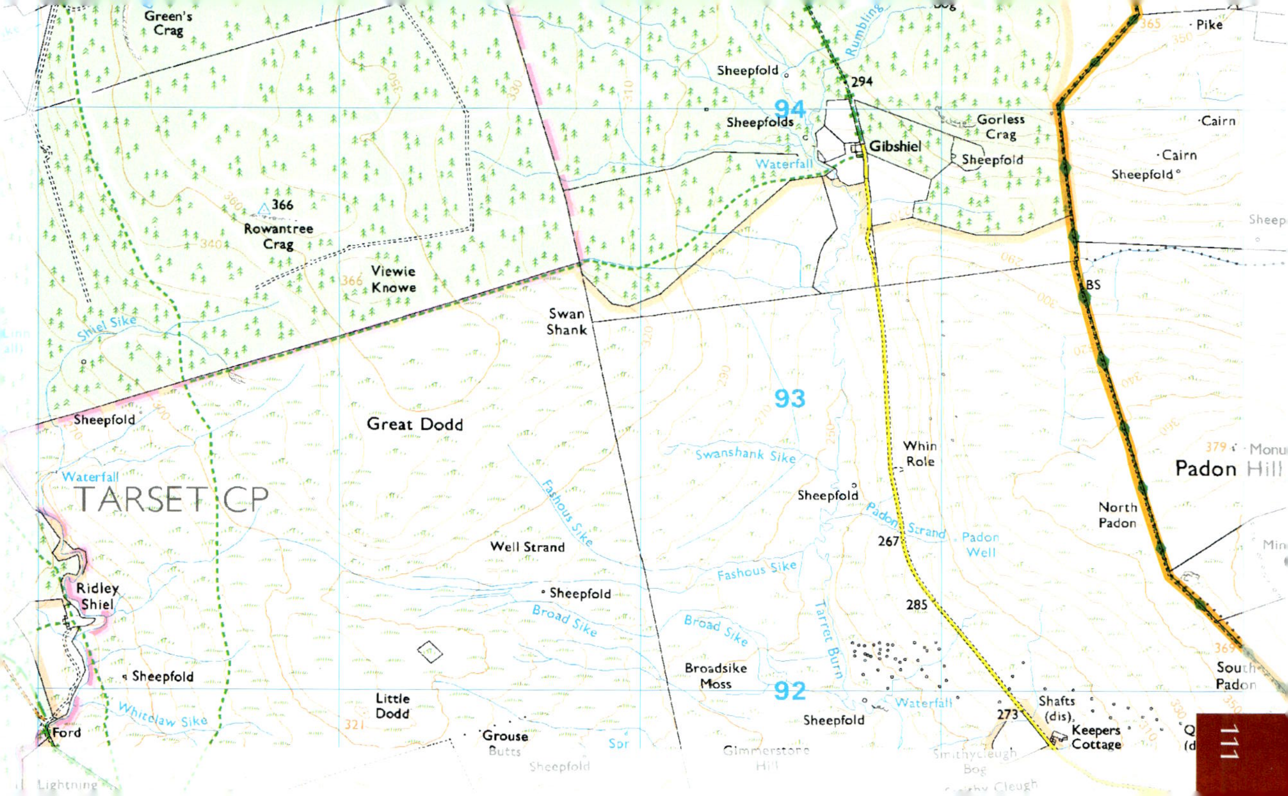

Green's Crag
Sheepfold
294
Rumbling
94
Sheepfolds
Gibshiel
Gorless Crag
Sheepfold
Cairn
Cairn
Sheepfold
Pike
Waterfall
366
Rowantree Crag
Viewie Knowe
366
BS
Sheep
Shiel Sike
Swan Shank
93
Sheepfold
Great Dodd
Whin Role
379
Monu
Padon Hill
Swanshank Sike
Waterfall
TARSET CP
Sheepfold
Fashous Sike
North Padon
Padon Strand
Padon Well
267
Well Strand
Fashous Sike
Ridley Shiel
Sheepfold
Broad Sike
Broad Sike
Tarret Burn
285
Sheepfold
Broadsike Moss
92
South Padon
Little Dodd
321
Whitelaw Sike
Waterfall
273
Shafts (dis)
Keepers Cottage
Ford
Grouse Butts
Sheepfold
Gimmerstone Hill
Smithycleugh Bog
Sheepfold
Lightning

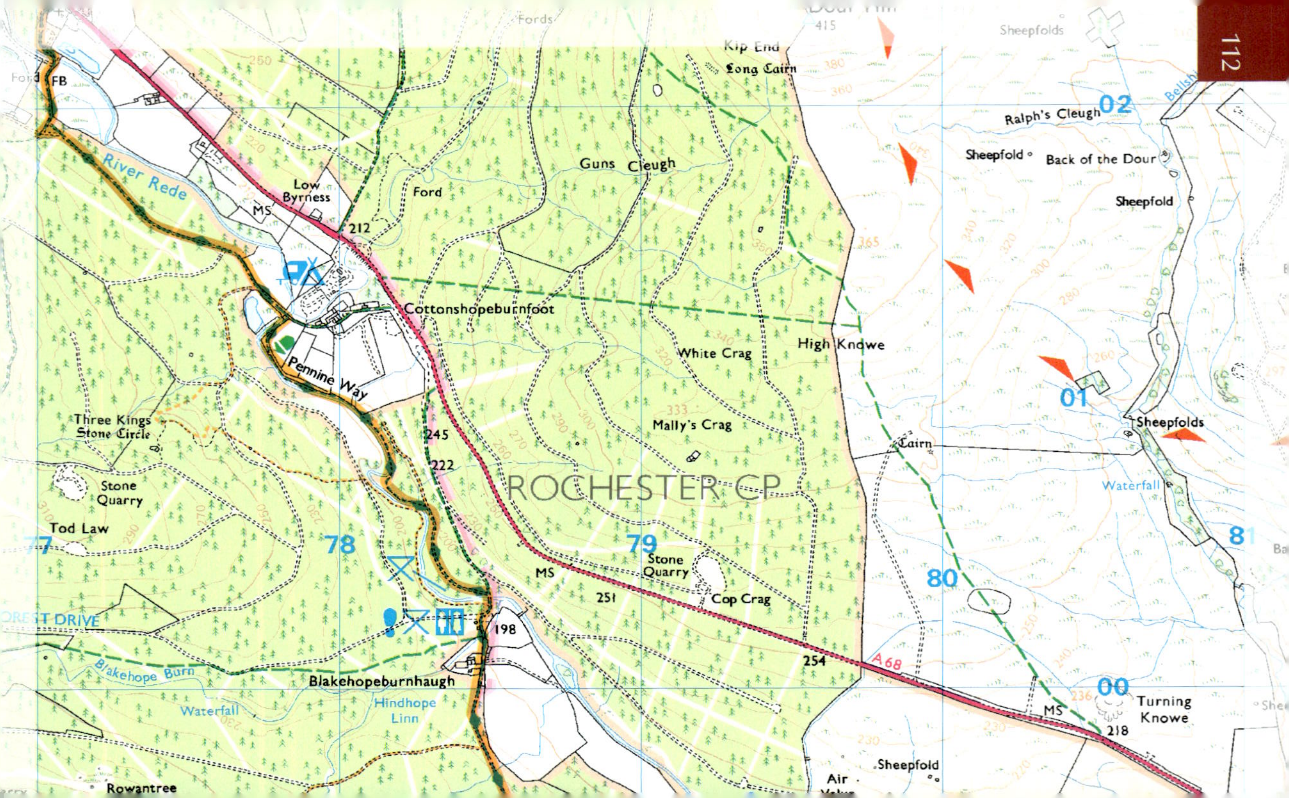

Fords
415
Sheepfolds
Kip End
Long Cairn
Ford
FB
02
Ralph's Cleugh
Sheepfold
Back of the Dour
Sheepfold
River Rede
Guns Cleugh
Low Byrness
Ford
MS
212
365
Cottonshopeburnfoot
High Knowe
White Crag
Pennine Way
01
Sheepfolds
Three Kings Stone Circle
245
Mally's Crag
Cairn
222
ROCHESTER CP
Waterfall
Stone Quarry
Tod Law
77
78
79
Stone Quarry
81
MS
80
251
Cop Crag
FOREST DRIVE
198
254
A68
Blakehope Burn
Blakehopeburnhaugh
00
Turning Knowe
Waterfall
Hindhope Linn
MS
218
Sheepfold
Air
Rowantree

Tod Sike
Hindhope Crag
Clotty Sike
Deadwood Cleugh
Dead Wood
99
Quarry (dis)
Bessy's Sike
Hindhope Burn
Peg's Height
Waterfalls
Hanging Crag
Settle
241
Sheepfold
Quarry (dis)
266
Rowantree Sike
Currick
Blackwool Law
98
Quarry (dis)
Greymare Sike
Pennine Way
Waterfa
The Seat
Wind Burn
Greymare Sike
97
Wind Burn
Rooken Knowe

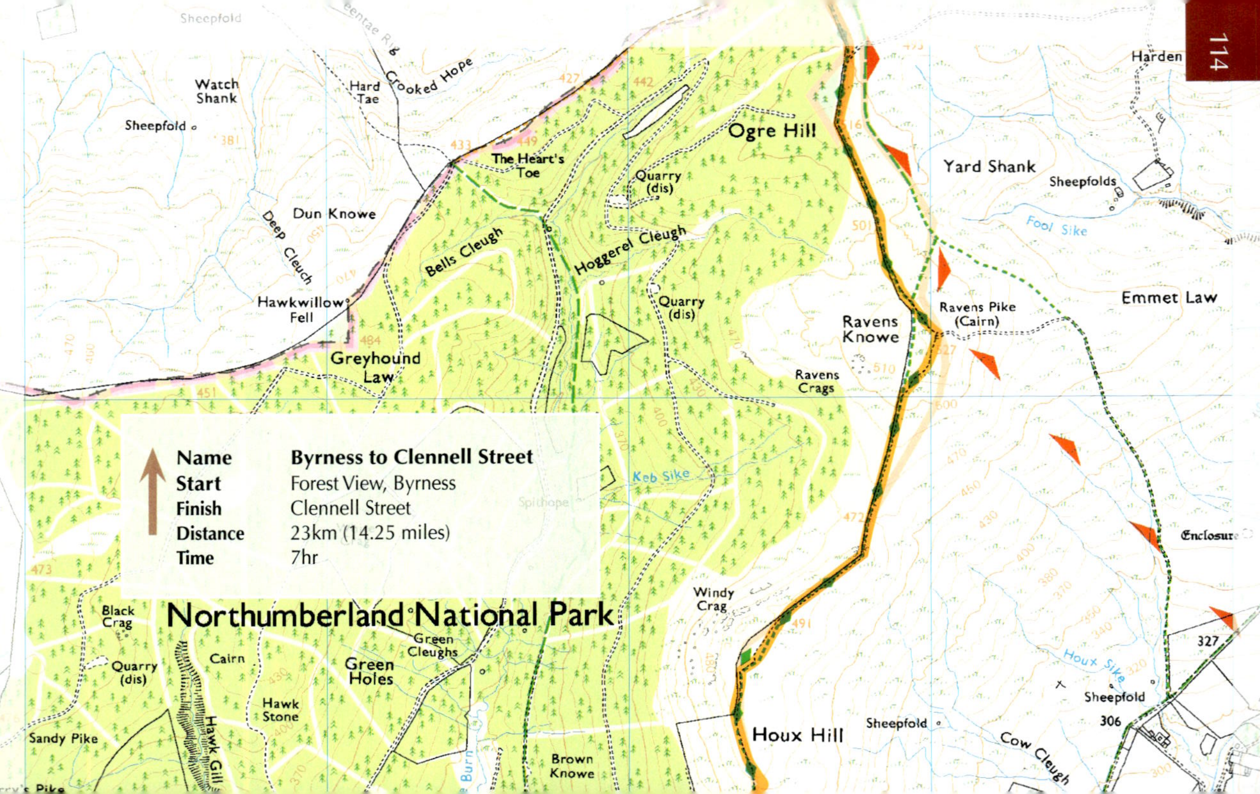
Name Byrness to Clennell Street
Start Forest View, Byrness
Finish Clennell Street
Distance 23km (14.25 miles)
Time 7hr
Northumberland National Park
Ogre Hill
Yard Shank
Emmet Law
Harden
Sheepfolds
Fool Sike
Ravens Pike (Cairn)
Ravens Knowe
Ravens Crags
Windy Crag
Houx Hill
Houx Sike
Sheepfold
Cow Cleugh
Enclosure
Watch Shank
Hard Tae
Crooked Hope
Dun Knowe
Deep Cleuch
Hawkwillow Fell
Greyhound Law
The Heart's Toe
Quarry (dis)
Bells Cleugh
Hoggerel Cleugh
Keb Sike
Black Crag
Cairn
Green Cleughs
Green Holes
Hawk Stone
Hawk Gill
Sandy Pike
Brown Knowe

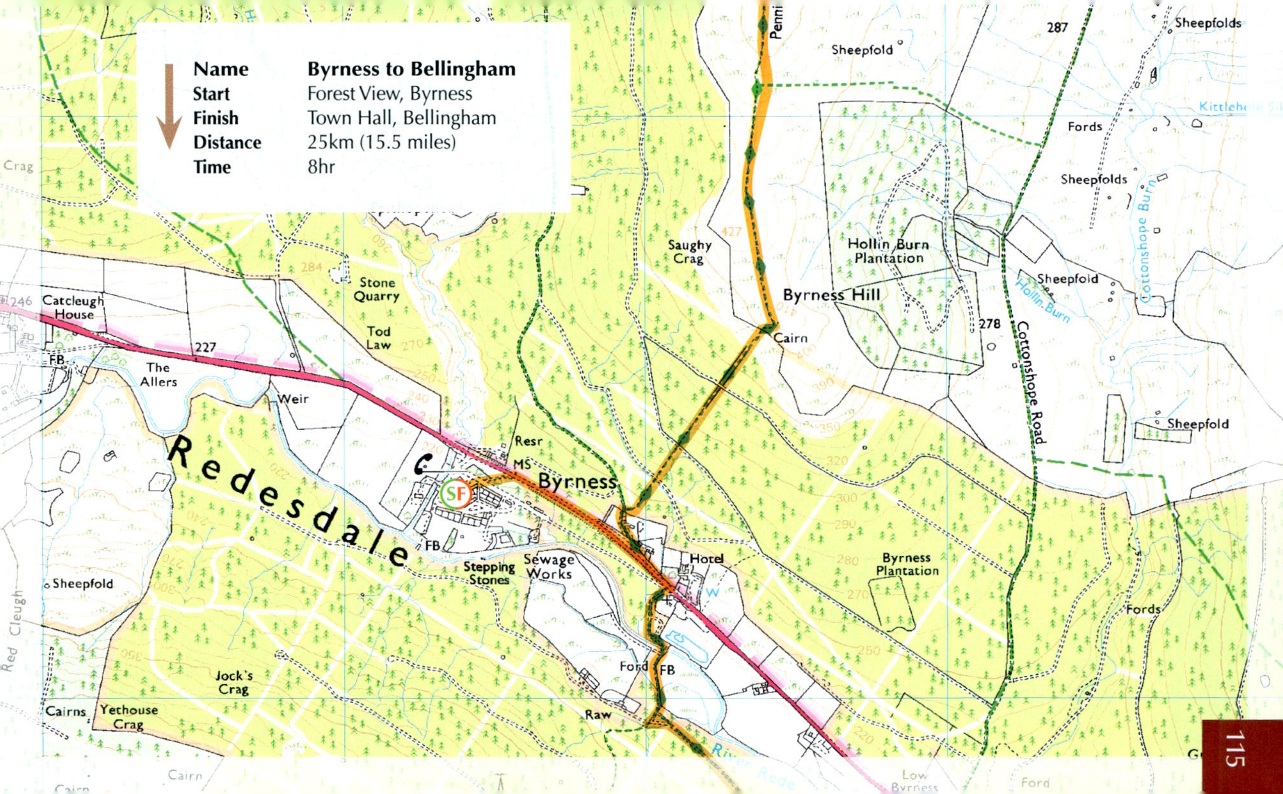

Name
Byrness to Bellingham
Start
Forest View, Byrness
Finish
Town Hall, Bellingham
Distance
25km (15.5 miles)
Time
8hr
Redesdale
Byrness
Byrness Hill
Byrness Plantation
Hollin Burn Plantation
Cottonshope Road
Cottonshope Burn
Hollin Burn
Saughy Crag
Cairn
Stone Quarry
Tod Law
Catcleugh House
The Allers
Weir
Resr
MS
Hotel
Sewage Works
Stepping Stones
Ford
FB
Raw
Jock's Crag
Yethouse Crag
Cairns
Sheepfold
Sheepfolds
Fords
Red Cleugh
Crag
Low Byrness
River Rede
Penni

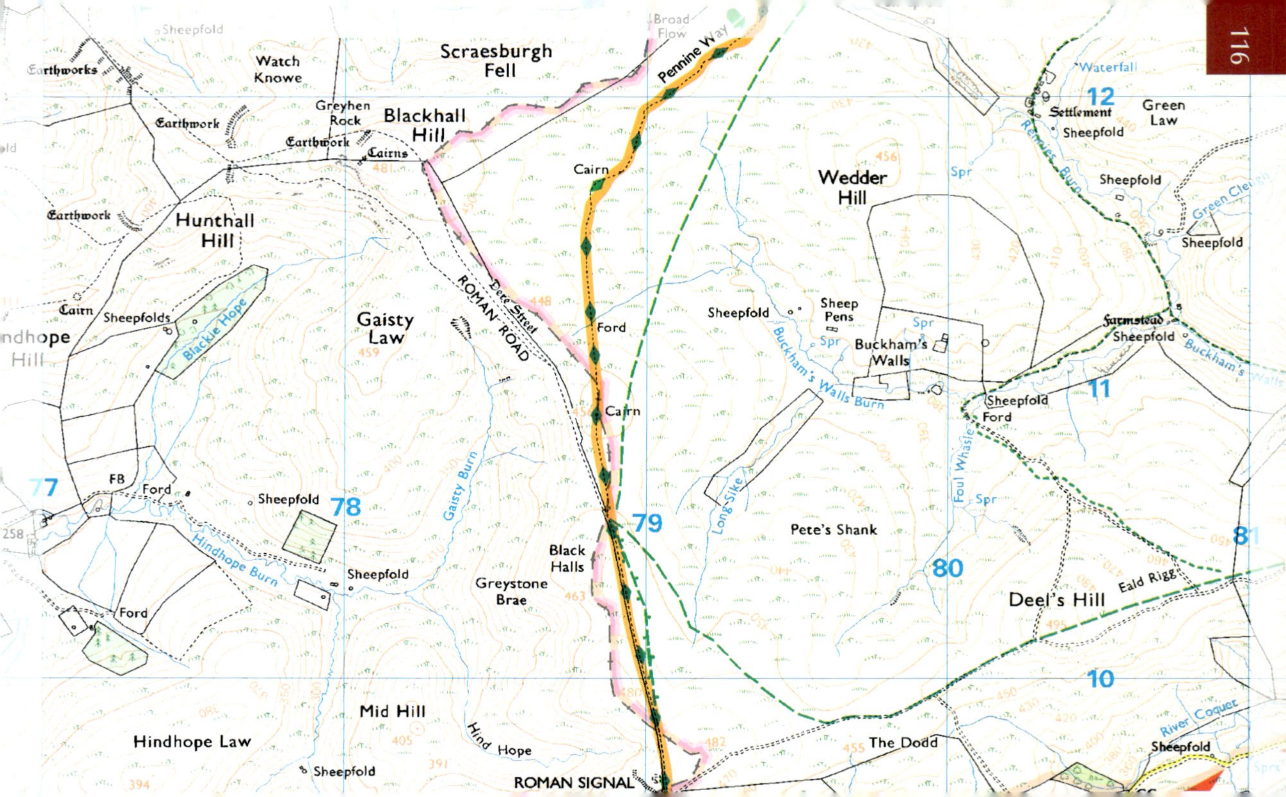
Sheepfold
Earthworks
Watch Knowe
Scraesburgh Fell
Broad Flow
Pennine Way
Earthwork
Greyhen Rock
Blackhall Hill
Earthwork
Cairns
Cairn
Earthwork
Hunthall Hill
Cairn
Sheepfolds
Blackie Hope
ndhope Hill
Gaisty Law
Dere Street
ROMAN ROAD
Ford
Cairn
FB
Ford
Sheepfold
Gaisty Burn
Hindhope Burn
Sheepfold
Ford
Black Halls
Greystone Brae
Mid Hill
Hindhope Law
Hind Hope
Sheepfold
ROMAN SIGNAL
Wedder Hill
Sheepfold
Sheep Pens
Spr
Buckham's Walls
Buckham's Walls Burn
Long Sike
Pete's Shank
Foul Whasle
Sheepfold
Ford
Farmstead
Sheepfold
Buckham's Walls
Waterfall
Settlement
Sheepfold
Green Law
Remnies Burn
Sheepfold
Green Cleugh
Sheepfold
Deel's Hill
Eald Rigg
The Dodd
River Coquet
Sheepfold

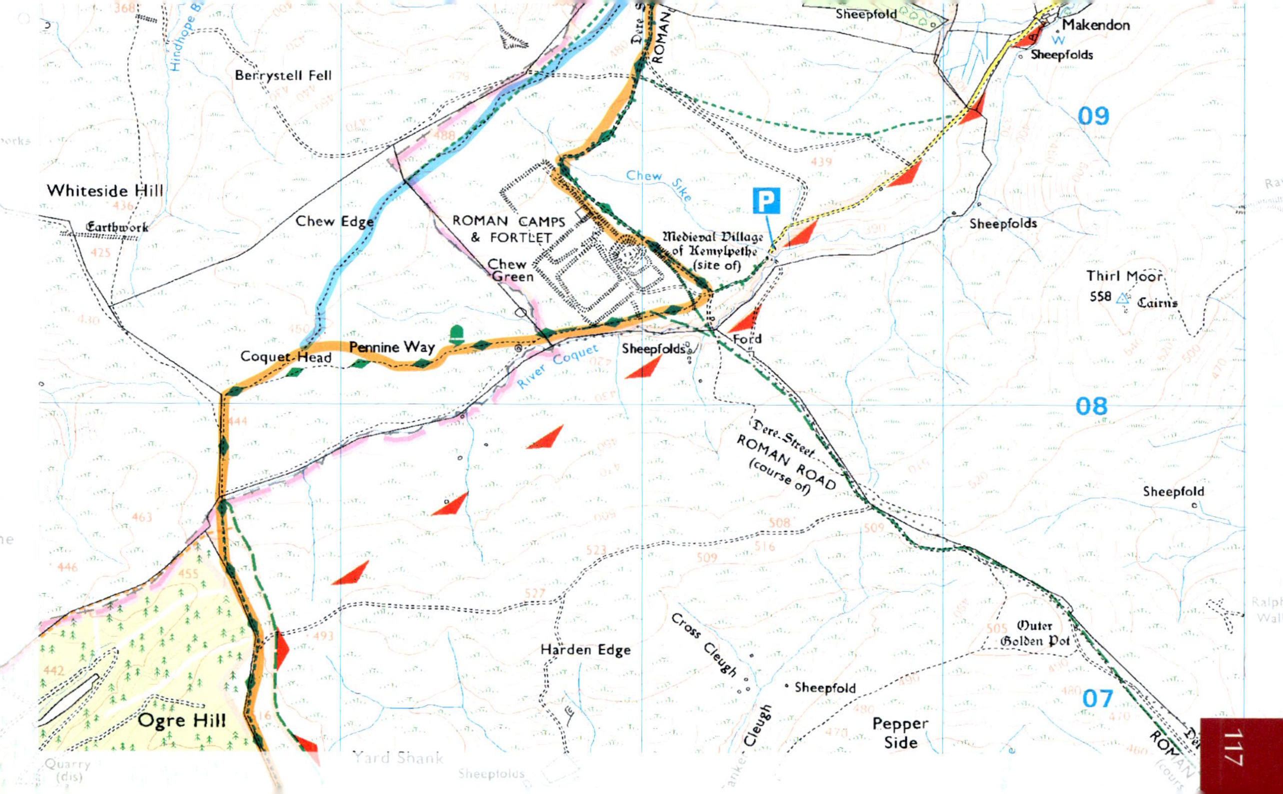
Berrystell Fell
Sheepfold
Makendon
Sheepfolds
09
Whiteside Hill
Earthwork
Chew Edge
ROMAN CAMPS & FORTLET
Chew Green
Chew Sike
Medieval Village of Kemylpethe (site of)
Sheepfolds
Thirl Moor
558
Cairns
Coquet Head
Pennine Way
River Coquet
Sheepfolds
Ford
08
Dere Street ROMAN ROAD (course of)
Sheepfold
Harden Edge
Cross Cleugh
Sheepfold
Outer Golden Pot
Ogre Hill
Pepper Side
07
Yard Shank

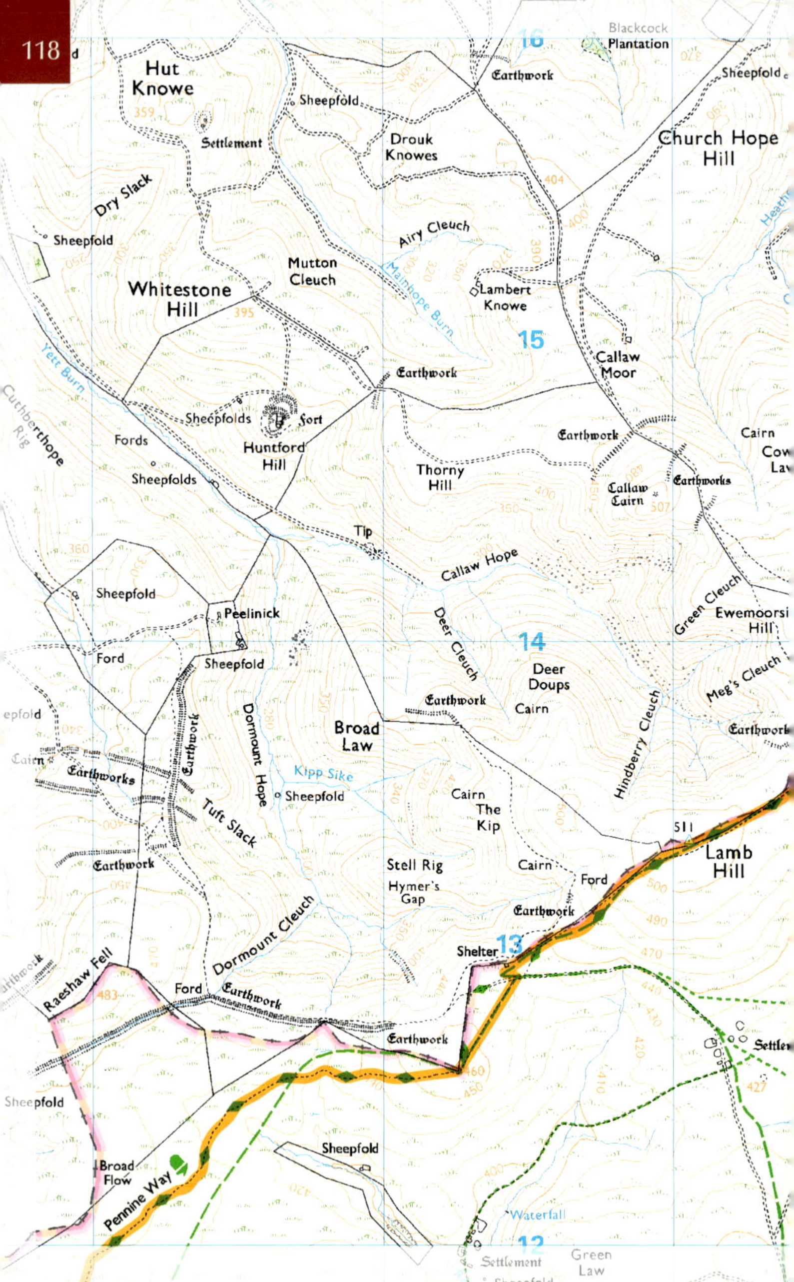
Hut Knowe
359
Settlement
Sheepfold
Drouk Knowes
Earthwork
16
Blackcock Plantation
Sheepfold
Church Hope Hill
404
400
Dry Slack
Sheepfold
Airy Cleuch
Mutton Cleuch
Mainhope Burn
Lambert Knowe
Whitestone Hill
395
15
Callaw Moor
Yett Burn
Cuthberthope Rig
Earthwork
Sheepfolds
Fort
Huntford Hill
Fords
Sheepfolds
Earthwork
Cairn
Thorny Hill
Earthworks
Callaw Cairn
507
Tip
Callaw Hope
Sheepfold
Peelinick
Deer Cleuch
Green Cleuch
Ewemoorside Hill
14
Ford
Sheepfold
Deer Doups
Cairn
Meg's Cleuch
Earthwork
Dormount Hope
Broad Law
Hindberry Cleuch
Earthwork
Cairn
Earthworks
Earthwork
Kipp Sike
Sheepfold
Tuft Slack
Cairn
The Kip
511
Lamb Hill
Earthwork
Stell Rig
Hymer's Gap
Cairn
Ford
Earthwork
Dormount Cleuch
Shelter
13
Raeshaw Fell
483
Ford
Earthwork
Earthwork
Settlement
427
Sheepfold
Broad Flow
Sheepfold
Pennine Way
Waterfall
12
Settlement
Green Law

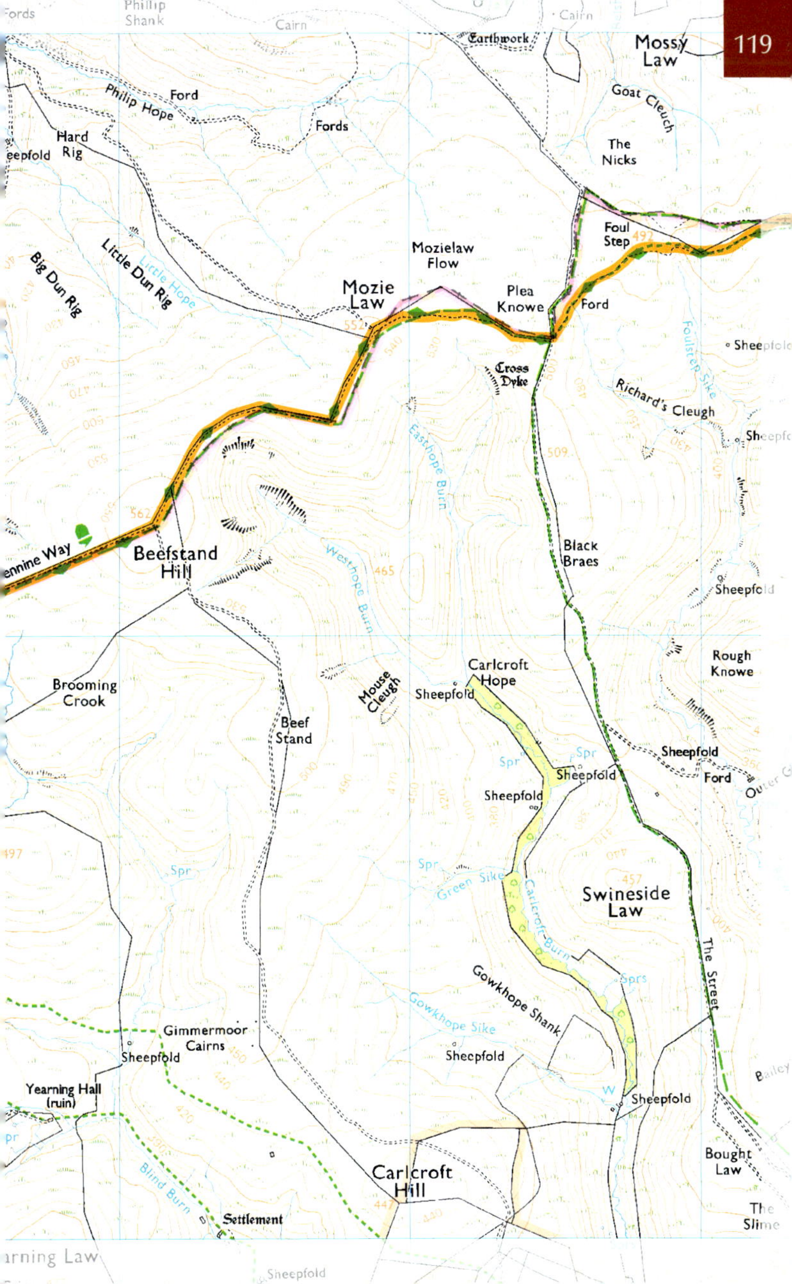

Mossy Law
Goat Cleuch
The Nicks
Earthwork
Cairn
Phillip Shank
Fords
Philip Hope
Ford
Hard Rig
Foul Step
492
Mozielaw Flow
Mozie Law
552
Plea Knowe
Ford
Little Dun Rig
Little Hope
Big Dun Rig
Cross Dyke
Richard's Cleugh
Foulstep Sike
Sheepfold
509
Eastshope Burn
562
Beefstand Hill
Pennine Way
Black Braes
Westhope Burn
465
Carlcroft Hope
Rough Knowe
Brooming Crook
Mouse Cleugh
Sheepfold
Beef Stand
Spr
Ford
Swineside Law
457
Green Sike
Carlcroft Burn
Gowkhope Shank
Gowkhope Sike
The Street
Sprs
Gimmermoor Cairns
Yearning Hall (ruin)
Blind Burn
Settlement
Carlcroft Hill
447
Bought Law
The Slime
Yearning Law
Bailey

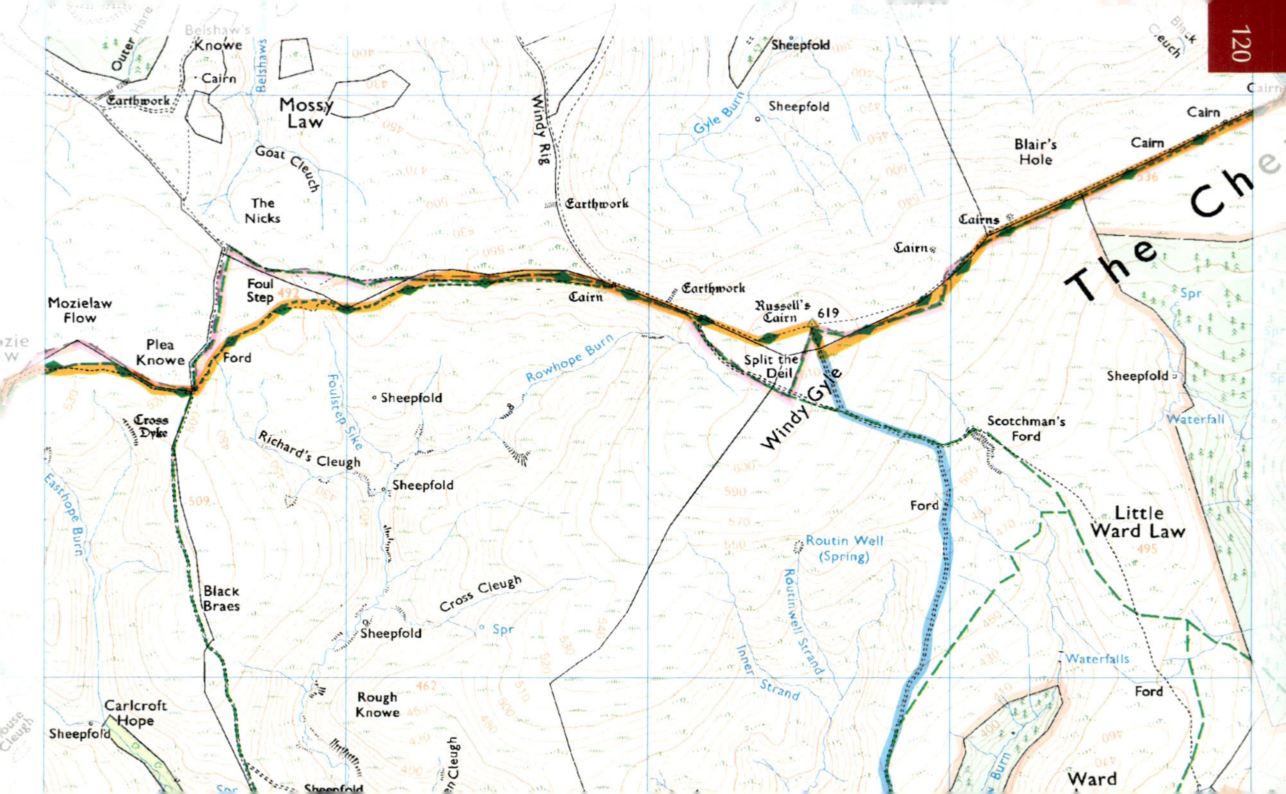

Outer Hare
Belshaw's Knowe
Cairn
Earthwork
Belshaws Burn
Mossy Law
Goat Cleuch
The Nicks
Windy Rig
Earthwork
Sheepfold
Gyle Burn
Sheepfold
Black Cleuch
Cairn
Cairn
Blair's Hole
Cairns
Cairn
The Ch
Spr
Earthwork
Cairn
Foul Step
492
Mozielaw Flow
Plea Knowe
Ford
Russell's Cairn
619
Split the Deil
Windy Gyle
Sheepfold
Waterfall
Scotchman's Ford
Rowhope Burn
Foulstep Sike
Sheepfold
Cross Dyke
Richard's Cleugh
Sheepfold
Easthope Burn
509
Ford
Little Ward Law
495
Routin Well (Spring)
Routinwell Strand
Inner Strand
Black Braes
Cross Cleugh
Spr
Sheepfold
Waterfalls
Ford
Carlcroft Hope
Sheepfold
Rough Knowe
462
Ward

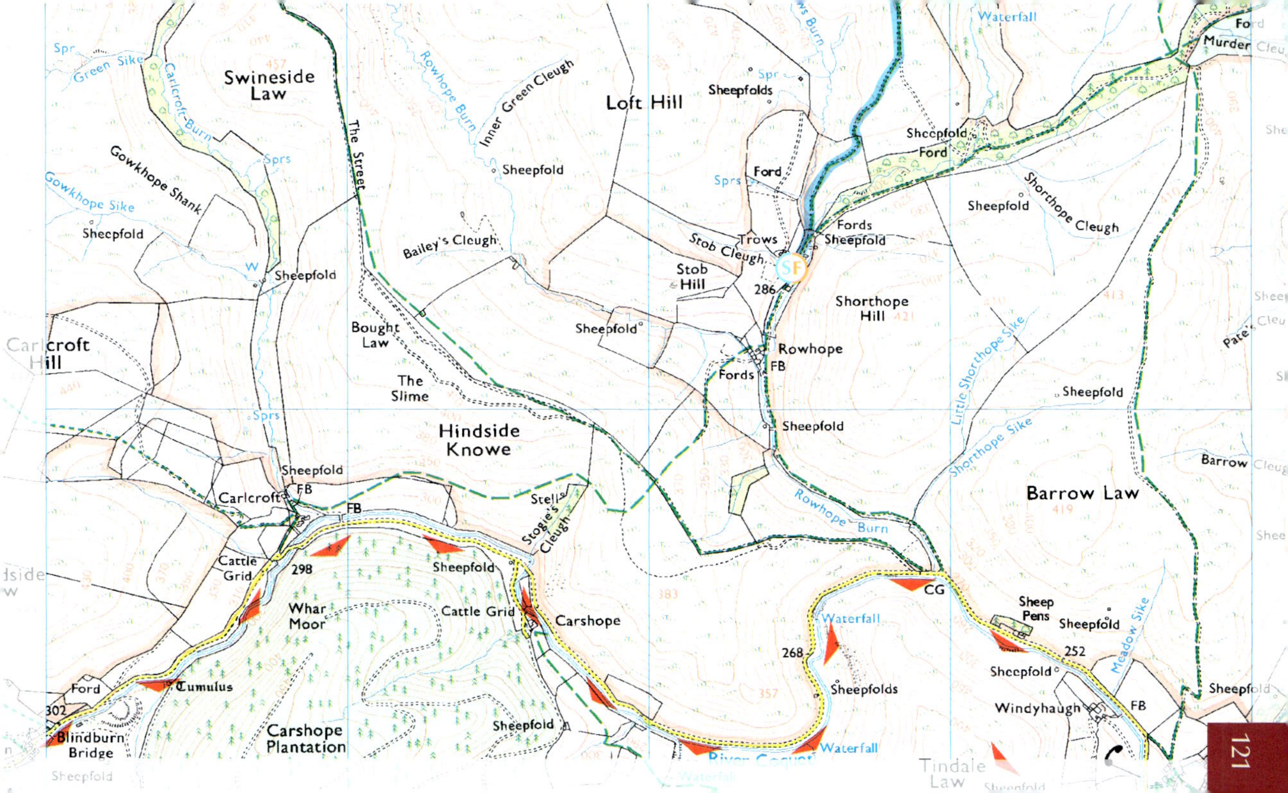
Swineside Law
Loft Hill
Sheepfolds
Green Sike
Carlcroft Burn
Gowkhope Shank
Gowkhope Sike
The Street
Rowhope Burn
Inner Green Cleugh
Bailey's Cleugh
Stob Cleugh
Stob Hill
Trows
Fords
Sheepfold
Shorthope Hill
Shorthope Cleugh
Rowhope
FB
Murder Cleugh
Ford
Waterfall
Pate's Cleugh
Little Shorthope Sike
Shorthope Sike
Barrow Cleugh
Barrow Law
Carlcroft Hill
Bought Law
The Slime
Hindside Knowe
Carlcroft
Stell
Stogie's Cleugh
Cattle Grid
298
Whar Moor
Carshope
CG
268
Sheepfolds
Sheep Pens
252
Meadow Sike
Windyhaugh
Cumulus
302
Blindburn Bridge
Carshope Plantation
River Coquet
Tindale Law
Sprs
Spr
286

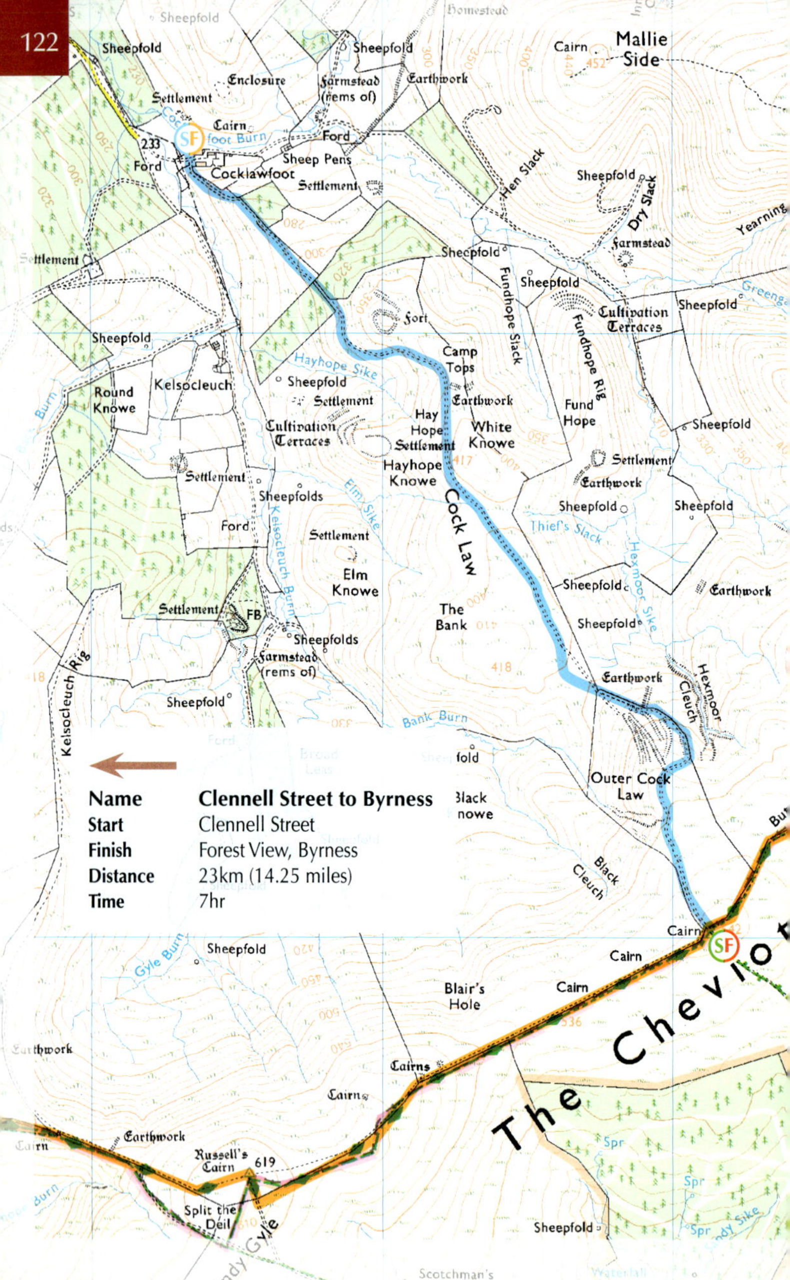

Name	**Clennell Street to Byrness**
Start	Clennell Street
Finish	Forest View, Byrness
Distance	23km (14.25 miles)
Time	7hr

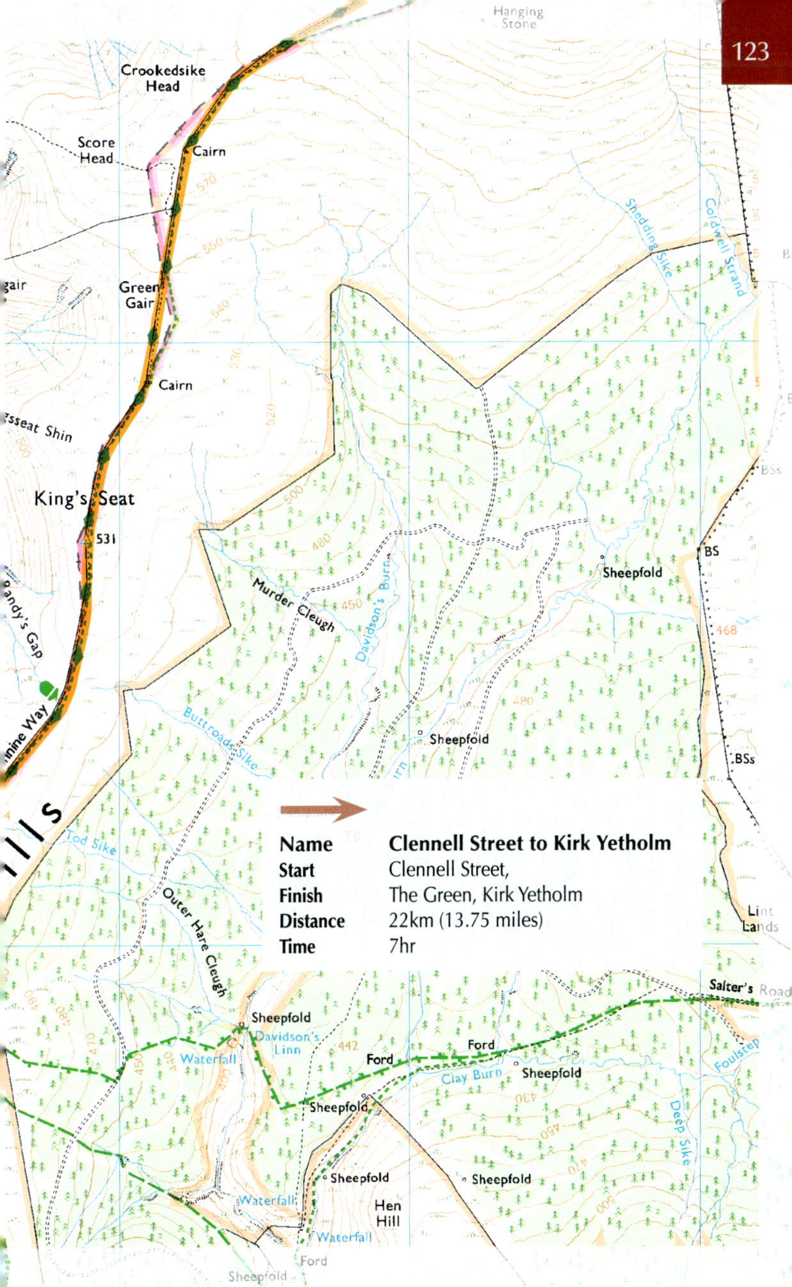

Name	**Clennell Street to Kirk Yetholm**
Start	Clennell Street,
Finish	The Green, Kirk Yetholm
Distance	22km (13.75 miles)
Time	7hr

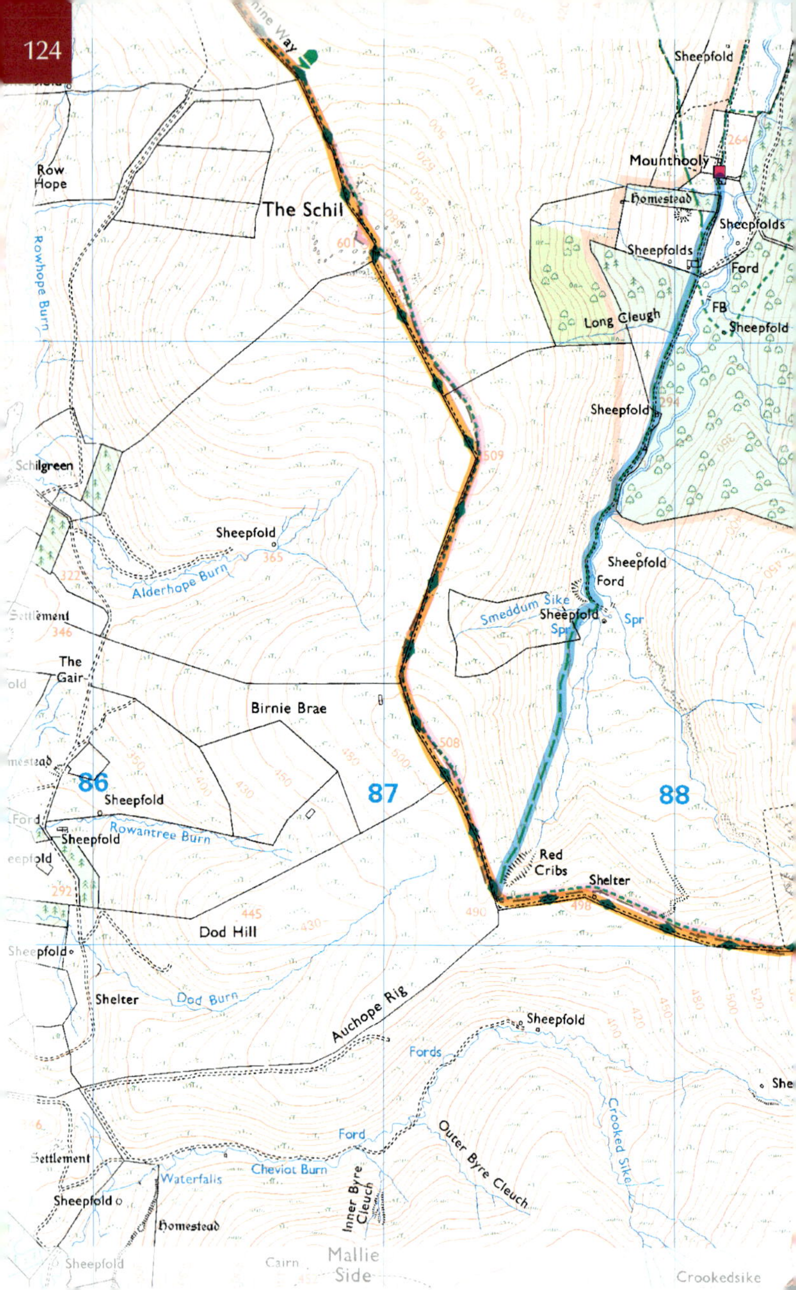

Pennine Way
Sheepfold
Mounthooly
Row Hope
The Schil
Homestead
Sheepfolds
Sheepfolds
Ford
Rowhope Burn
FB
Long Cleugh
Sheepfold
Sheepfold
Schilgreen
Sheepfold
Sheepfold
Ford
Alderhope Burn
Smeddum Sike
Sheepfold
Spr
Spr
Settlement
The Gair
Birnie Brae
86
87
88
Sheepfold
Rowantree Burn
Sheepfold
Red Cribs
Shelter
Dod Hill
Sheepfold
Shelter
Dod Burn
Auchope Rig
Sheepfold
Fords
Outer Byre Cleuch
Crooked Sike
Ford
Settlement
Waterfalls
Cheviot Burn
Inner Byre Cleuch
Sheepfold
Homestead
Sheepfold
Cairn
Mallie Side
Crookedsike

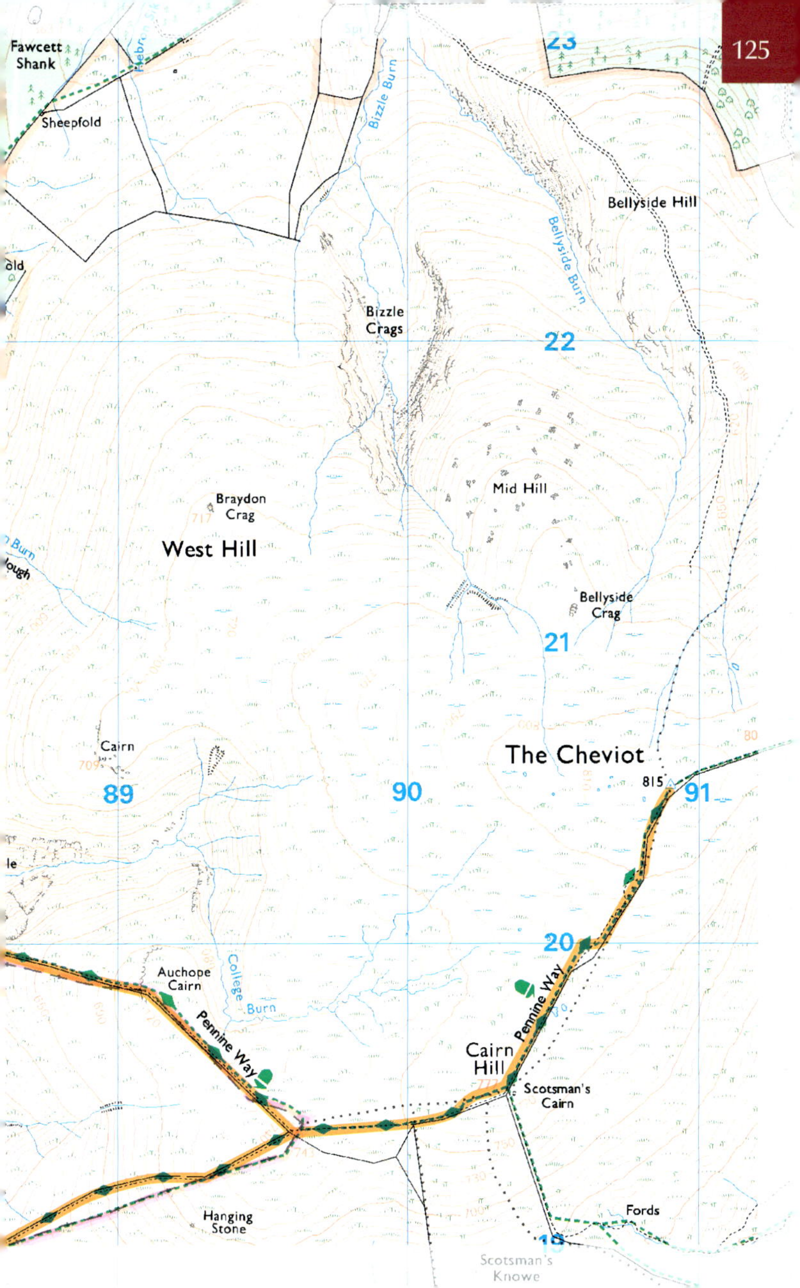

Fawcett Shank
Sheepfold
Bizzle Burn
23
Bellyside Hill
Bellyside Burn
Bizzle Crags
22
Mid Hill
Braydon Crag
717
West Hill
Bellyside Crag
21
Cairn
709
The Cheviot
815
89
90
91
20
Auchope Cairn
College Burn
Pennine Way
Pennine Way
Cairn Hill
Scotsman's Cairn
Hanging Stone
Fords
19
Scotsman's Knowe

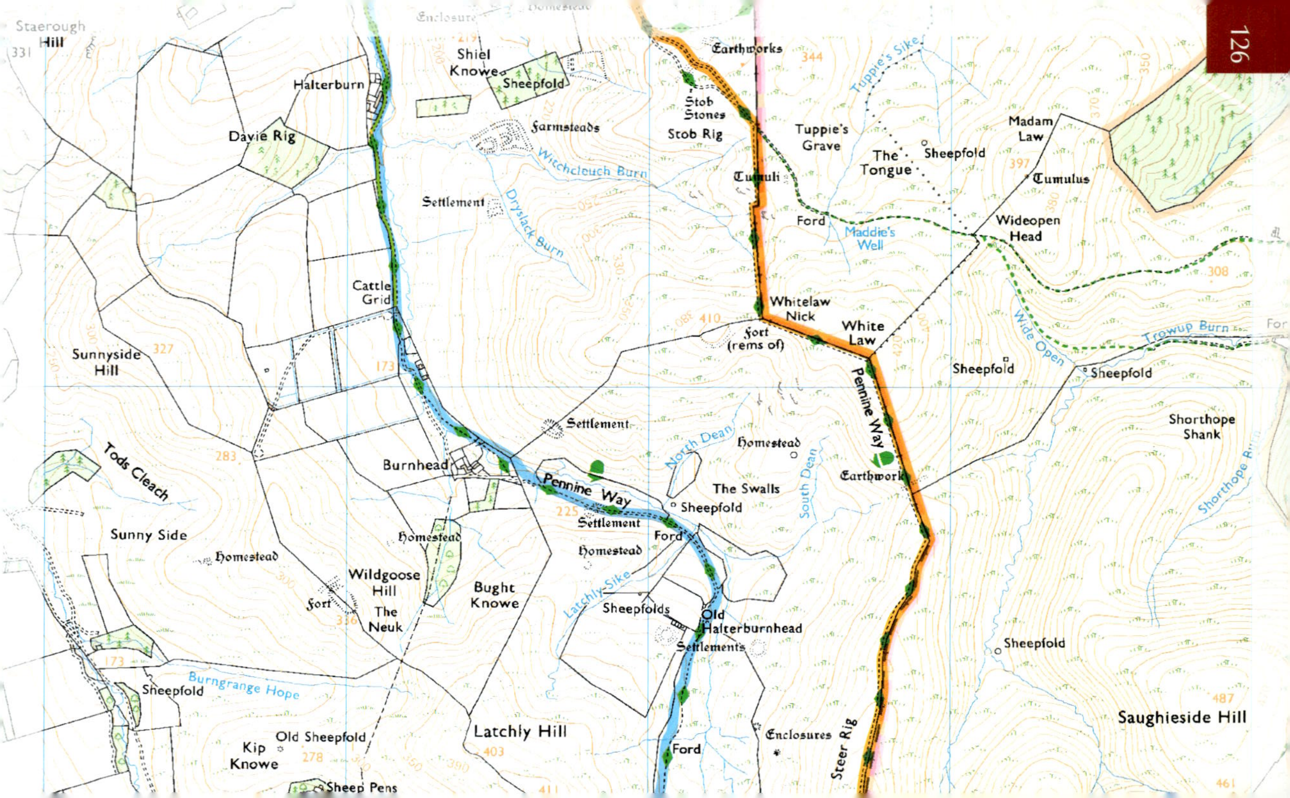
Pennine Way
Pennine Way
Trowup Burn
Shorthope Burn
Shorthope Shank
Saughieside Hill
Sheepfold
Wide Open
Madam Law
Tumulus
Wideopen Head
Sheepfold
The Tongue
Tuppie's Sike
Tuppie's Grave
Maddie's Well
Ford
White Law
Whitelaw Nick
Earthwork
Steer Rig
South Dean
Earthworks
Tumuli
Fort (rems of)
Homestead
The Swalls
Enclosures
Old Halterburnhead
Settlements
Stob Stones
Stob Rig
North Dean
Sheepfold
Ford
Sheepfolds
Ford
Settlement
Settlement
Homestead
Latchly Sike
Witchcleuch Burn
Drysklack Burn
Farmsteads
Sheepfold
Sheepfold
Shiel Knowe
Settlement
Latchly Hill
Bught Knowe
Burnhead
Homestead
Wildgoose Hill
The Neuk
Cattle Grid
Halterburn
Davie Rig
Fort
Homestead
Old Sheepfold
Sheep Pens
Kip Knowe
Burngrange Hope
Sheepfold
Sunny Side
Tods Cleach
Sunnyside Hill
Staerough Hill
Enclosure

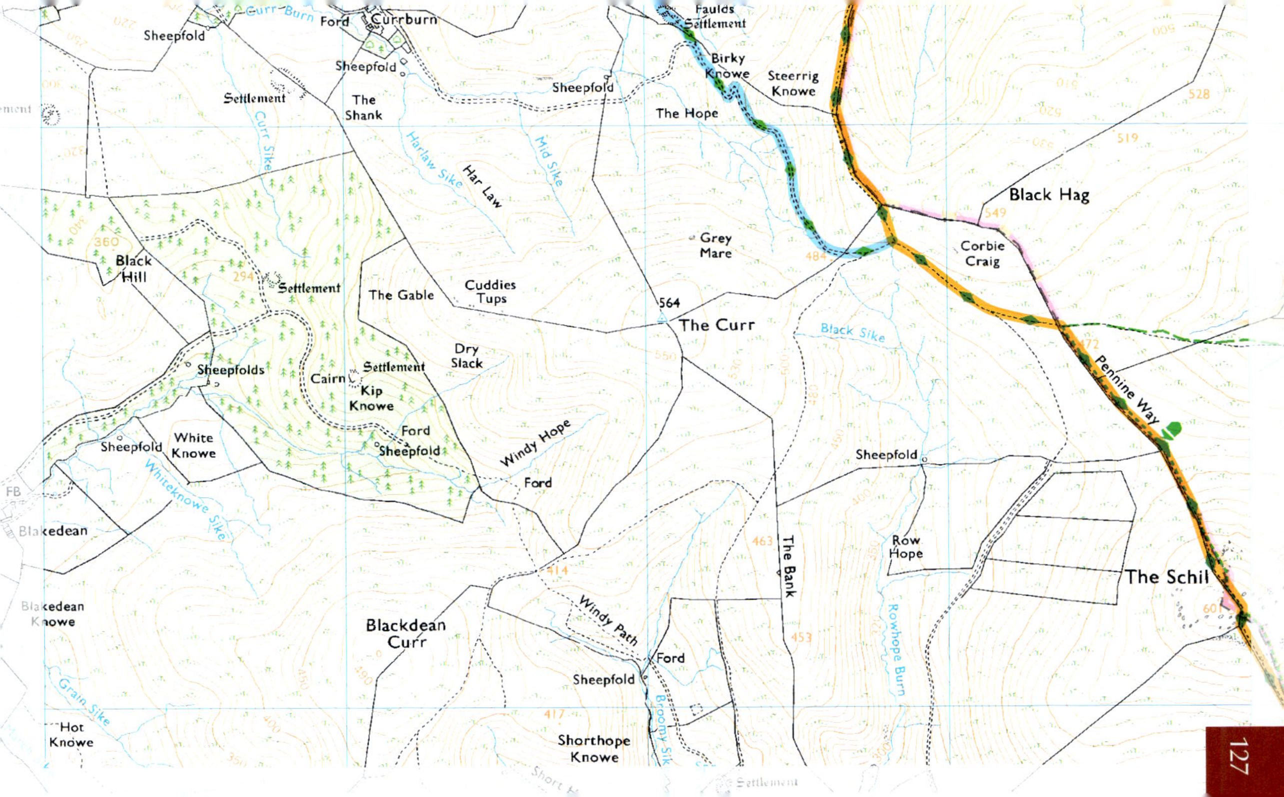

Curr Burn
Ford
Currburn
Faulds Settlement
Sheepfold
Birky Knowe
Steerrig Knowe
528
Settlement
The Shank
The Hope
519
Curr Sike
Harlaw Sike
Har Law
Mid Sike
Black Hag
549
360
Black Hill
294
Grey Mare
484
Corbie Craig
Cuddies Tups
The Gable
564
The Curr
Black Sike
Pennine Way
Dry Slack
Sheepfolds
Cairn
Kip Knowe
Ford
Sheepfold
White Knowe
Windy Hope
Whiteknowe Sike
FB
Blakedean
463
The Bank
Row Hope
The Schil
601
414
Windy Path
Blakedean Knowe
Blackdean Curr
453
Rowhope Burn
Grain Sike
417
Broomy Sike
Hot Knowe
Shorthope Knowe

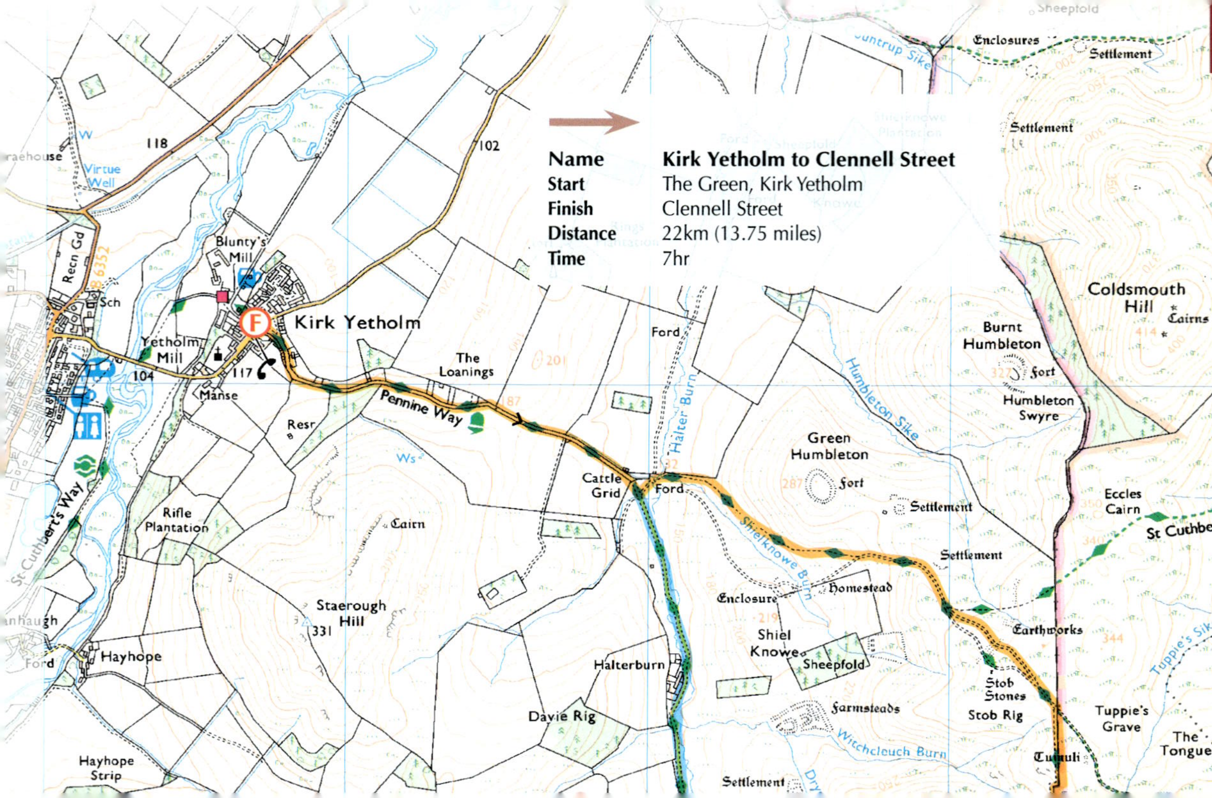

Name	**Kirk Yetholm to Clennell Street**
Start	The Green, Kirk Yetholm
Finish	Clennell Street
Distance	22km (13.75 miles)
Time	7hr

LEGEND OF SYMBOLS USED ON ORDNANCE SURVEY 1:25,000 (EXPLORER) MAPPING

ROADS AND PATHS

Not necessarily rights of way

M1 or A6(M) Motorway
S Service Area
7 Junction Number
A 35 Dual carriageway
S Service Area
T1 Toll road junction
A30 Main road
B 3074 Secondary road
Narrow road with passing places
Road under construction
Road generally more than 4 m wide
Road generally less than 4 m wide
Other road, drive or track, fenced and unfenced
Gradient: steeper than 20% (1 in 5); 14% (1 in 7) to 20% (1 in 5)
Ferry Ferry; Ferry P – passenger only
Path

RAILWAYS

Multiple track } standard
Single track } gauge
Narrow gauge or Light rapid transit system (LRTS) and station
Road over; road under; level crossing
Cutting; tunnel; embankment
Station, open to passengers; siding

PUBLIC RIGHTS OF WAY

Footpath
Bridleway
Byway open to all traffic
Restricted byway

The representation on this map of any other road, track or path is no evidence of the existence of a right of way

ARCHAEOLOGICAL AND HISTORICAL INFORMATION

Site of antiquity
VILLA Roman
Visible earthwork
1066 Site of battle (with date)
Castle Non-Roman

Information provided by English Heritage for England and the Royal Commissions on the Ancient and Historical Monuments for Scotland and Wales

OTHER PUBLIC ACCESS

• • •	Other routes with public access	The exact nature of the rights on these routes and the existence of any restrictions may be checked with the local highway authority. Alignments are based on the best information available
◆ ◆ ◆	Recreational route	
◆ ◆ ◆	National Trail	Long Distance Route
- - - - - -	Permissive footpath	Footpaths and bridleways along which landowners have permitted public use but which are not rights of way. The agreement may be withdrawn
— — — —	Permissive bridleway	
• • •	Traffic-free cycle route	
1 1	National cycle network	route number – traffic free; on road

ACCESS LAND

Firing and test ranges in the area. Danger! Observe warning notices

Access permitted within managed controls, for example, local byelaws. Visit **www.access.mod.uk** for information

England and Wales

Access land boundary and tint

Access land in wooded area

Access information point

Portrayal of access land on this map is intended as a guide to land which is normally available for access on foot, for example access land created under the Countryside and Rights of Way Act 2000, and land managed by the National Trust, Forestry Commission and Woodland Trust. Access for other activities may also exist. Some restrictions will apply; some land will be excluded from open access rights. The depiction of rights of access does not imply or express any warranty as to its accuracy or completeness. Observe local signs and follow the Countryside Code. Visit **www.countrysideaccess.gov.uk** for up-to-date information

BOUNDARIES

- National
- County (England)
- Unitary Authority (UA), Metropolitan District (Met Dist), London Borough (LB) or District (Scotland & Wales are solely Unitary Authorities)
- Civil Parish (CP) (England) or Community (C) (Wales)
- National Park boundary

VEGETATION

Limits of vegetation are defined by positioning of symbols

- Coniferous trees
- Non-coniferous trees
- Coppice
- Orchard
- Scrub
- Bracken, heath or rough grassland
- Marsh, reeds or saltings

HEIGHTS AND NATURAL FEATURES

52 ·	Ground survey height	Surface heights are to the nearest metre above mean sea level. Where two heights are shown, the first height is to the base of the triangulation pillar and the second (in brackets) to the highest natural point of the hill
284 ·	Air survey height	

HEIGHTS AND NATURAL FEATURES (continued)

Vertical face/cliff

75
60
50

Loose rock | Boulders | Outcrop | Scree

Contours are at 5 or 10 metre vertical intervals

Water

Mud

Sand; sand and shingle

SELECTED TOURIST AND LEISURE INFORMATION

- Building of historic interest
- Cadw
- HC Heritage centre
- Camp site
- Caravan site
- Camping and caravan site
- Castle / fort
- Cathedral / Abbey
- Craft centre
- Country park
- Cycle trail
- Mountain bike trail
- Cycle hire
- English Heritage
- Fishing
- Forestry Commission Visitor centre
- Garden / arboretum
- Golf course or links
- Historic Scotland
- Information centre, all year
- Information centre, seasonal
- Horse riding
- Museum
- National Park Visitor Centre (park logo) e.g. Yorkshire Dales
- Nature reserve
- National Trust
- Other tourist feature
- P Parking
- P&R Park and ride, all year
- P&R Park and ride, seasonal
- Picnic site
- Preserved railway
- PC Public Convenience
- Public house/s
- Recreation / leisure / sports centre
- Roman site (Hadrian's Wall only)
- Slipway
- Telephone, emergency
- Telephone, public
- Telephone, roadside assistance
- Theme / pleasure park
- Viewpoint
- V Visitor centre
- Walks / trails
- World Heritage site / area
- Water activites
- Boat trips
- Boat hire

(For complete legend and symbols, see any OS Explorer map)

NOTES

NOTES

The 'Hebden Bridge Loop' leads off-route into Hebden Bridge

OTHER CICERONE TRAIL GUIDES

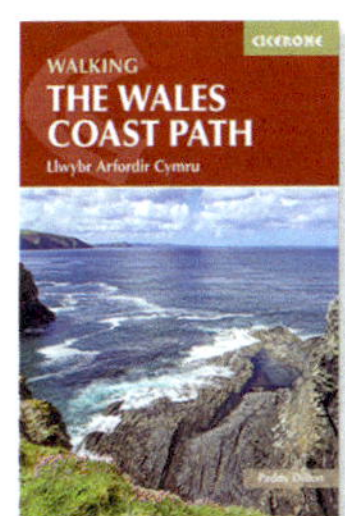

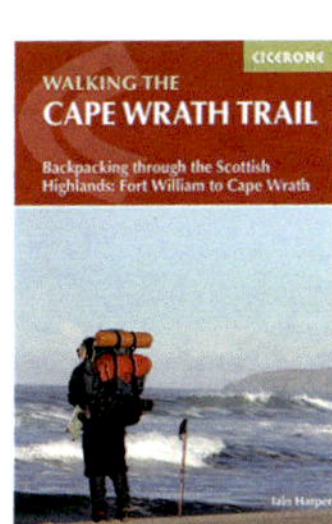

Cicerone National Trails Guides

The South West Coast Path
The South Downs Way
The North Downs Way
The Ridgeway National Trail
The Thames Path
The Cotswold Way
The Peddars Way and
  Norfolk Coast Path
The Cleveland Way and
  the Yorkshire Wolds Way
Cycling the Pennine Bridleway
Hadrian's Wall Path
The Pembrokeshire Coast Path
Offa's Dyke Path
Glyndŵr's Way
The Southern Upland Way
The Speyside Way
The West Highland Way
The Great Glen Way

Visit our website for a full list of Cicerone Trail Guides
www.cicerone.co.uk

CICERONE

Trust Cicerone to guide your next adventure, wherever it may be around the world...

Discover guides for hiking, mountain walking, backpacking, trekking, trail running, cycling and mountain biking, ski touring, climbing and scrambling in Britain, Europe and worldwide.

Connect with Cicerone online and find inspiration.

- buy books and ebooks
- articles, advice and trip reports
- GPX files and updates
- regular newsletter

cicerone.co.uk